I0753008

Captured

How neoliberalism transformed the Australian state

PUBLIC AND SOCIAL POLICY SERIES

Gaby Ramia, Series Editor

The Public and Social Policy series publishes books that pose challenging questions about policy from national, comparative and international perspectives. The series explores policy design, implementation and evaluation; the politics of policy making; and analyses of particular areas of public and social policy.

At a turning point: work, care and family policies in Australia
Ed. Marian Baird, Elizabeth Hill and Sydney Colussi

Australian social attitudes IV: the age of insecurity
Ed. Shaun Wilson and Markus Hadler

Australian universities: a conversation about public good
Ed. Julia Horne and Matthew A.M. Thomas

Buying and selling the poor: inside Australia's privatised welfare-to-work market
Siobhan O'Sullivan, Michael McGann and Mark Considine

Captured: How neoliberalism transformed the Australian state
Ed. Phillip Toner and Michael Rafferty

Engaging China: How Australia can lead the way again
Ed. Jamie Reilly and Jingdong Yuan

Globalisation, the state and regional Australia
Amanda Walsh

Markets, rights and power in Australian social policy
Ed. Gabrielle Meagher and Susan Goodwin

One planet, one health
Ed. Merrilyn Walton

Quit smoking weapons of mass distraction
Simon Chapman

Risking together: how finance is dominating everyday life in Australia
Dick Bryan and Mike Rafferty

Wind turbine syndrome: a communicated disease
Simon Chapman and Fiona Crichton

Captured

How neoliberalism transformed the Australian state

Edited by Phillip Toner
and Michael Rafferty

SYDNEY UNIVERSITY PRESS

First published by Sydney University Press

Sydney University Press
Gadigal Country
Fisher Library F03
University of Sydney NSW 2006
Australia
sup.info@sydney.edu.au
sydneyuniversitypress.com.au

A catalogue record for this book is available from the National Library of Australia.

ISBN 9781761540325 hardback
ISBN 9781743329825 epub
ISBN 9781743329818 pdf

Cover design by Naomi van Groll

We acknowledge the traditional owners of the lands on which Sydney University Press is located, the Gadigal people of the Eora Nation, and we pay our respects to the knowledge embedded forever within the Aboriginal Custodianship of Country.

Contents

Introduction

Four decades ago, faced with a series of economic, political and social crises, business and government elites in Australia, along with those in many other nations, were convinced by a well-organised ideological insurgency of the need for a radical change in economic policy (Stedman Jones 2012). What at first was presented as a series of technical changes in economic policy (monetarism, privatisation, fiscal restraint), rather quickly became a sweeping project to carry out a radical reordering of class relations and the social-democratic state (see Balogh 1978 for the changes in Britain and McFarlane 1977 for Australia). This ideological project, which Philip Mirowski (2013) has termed a "neoliberal thought collective", convinced economic and political elites to use state power to create and extend markets (Gray 1998), remake economic and social policy and dramatically alter the relation of workers to capital and citizens to government (Pusey 1991, Brown 2015). The promise, initially at least, was that these technical adjustments might require some temporary sacrifice but would restore stability and lead to a surge of competition, productivity and common prosperity by unleashing the animal spirits of market capitalism.

Forty years later it is clear that for the wealthy few this has indeed been a historically unprecedented time of acquisition and capital accumulation, but for most the promises have gone largely unfulfilled. Indeed, we are living through an age of great instability, disillusionment and despair (Case and Deaton 2020; Foa et al. 2020; Collier et al. 2021; Jones 2021; Center for Disease Control and Prevention 2023; Reid 2023). Inequality of income and wealth has been rising (see OECD 2014 for the adverse effects of rising income and wealth inequality; OECD 2023a for developed nations and an outline of some transmission mechanisms from inequality to low growth); most workers have experienced long-term declining relative living standards (Stanford 2018; Chapter 6 in this volume); and corporate political and market power has reached historic levels. Crouch (2016) has referred to the normalisation of private oligopolies as "corporate neoliberalism", which he describes as "an economy in which key industries are dominated by small numbers of large corporations which, because of their size and the importance of their sectors, have a political salience incompatible with the assumptions of neoclassical theory", while the significant political role of corporations in the state has been referred to, borrowing from recent Russian oligarchies, as "state capture" (Innes 2016; see also Edwards 2019; Innes 2021; Maher 2021; Tran 2021; West 2023). Younger generations are increasingly giving up on attaining the living standards of their parents. The status of prevailing neoliberal ideas and policy has taken multiple shocks and its credibility is in increasing disarray. But without a proper understanding of the ideas and interests driving neoliberalism, or a coherent alternative, many people have turned to incoherent populism for an explanation and salvation and, failing that, even to forms of nihilism (Coombs 2022). Disillusion and anxiety also constitute the dominant mood among the economic and policy elites, within Australia and internationally.

Given these ongoing crises, many observers have concluded that we are living through the last phase in the uncontested dominance of neoliberal social and economic policy and culture, but just how threatening the current crises are to the neoliberal order is a matter of some controversy and debate. *Captured* is a contribution to that important debate, by providing new research findings on what neoliberalism is in both its ideological and public policy dimensions in Australia.

Internationally, a neoliberal *ideological* project can be traced back to at least the 1950s, especially associated with the Mont Pelerin Society (Stedman Jones 2012; Mirowski 2013). But the rise of neoliberalism as the dominant mode of public and private governance only emerged in the 1970s from a crisis in the social-democratic state caused by rising global economic and financial instability, stagflation and conflict over income distribution (crises of accumulation and legitimacy). The crucial move came, as MacWilliam (2023) has noted, when neoliberal ideology was able to be attached to state power. While neoliberal public policy did not restore stability or reduce conflict, it did succeed in its own terms in restoring or extending what Mattei (2022) has termed the "capital order", broadly speaking where social relations are subordinated to the disciplines and requirements of the "market" (a proxy for capital accumulation). But it has achieved this at significant cost, and it is these costs that are now threatening the current legitimacy of neoliberalism. The research presented in *Captured* attests to the socially destructive nature of neoliberal practice and the challenge it has posed to the economic and social security of most citizens.

It might be thought that the (multiple) failures to re-establish capitalism on the terms of the postwar boom (broadly framed in terms of shared prosperity – "a rising tide lifting all boats") would have proven fatal to the strength and durability of neoliberalism. But as Peck and Tickell noted three decades ago:

> The apparent strength of neoliberalism has come about *not* because it provides a potential "regulatory fix" [for the breakdown in Keynesianism] ... but on the contrary because it represents the politics of the unresolved crisis. Neoliberalism ... should be seen as a symptom of ... the after-Fordism crisis (1994, 319, emphasis in original).

Peck and Tickell suggested that one way to understand this paradox is by conceptualising neoliberalism as a sort of provisional and emergent mode of governance. Neoliberal reason has its own form of logic, one that may not conform to or even seek to achieve earlier forms of consensus, stability and rationality. Given that neoliberal policy has so often failed on even neoclassical economic terms, it is worth exploring what the other goals of neoliberal policy have been. Fortunately, there are several decades of actual neoliberal policy to understand those goals, and *Captured* extends that analysis.

In the last decade, and especially in the wake of the Global Financial Crisis (2007–09) and its aftermath, the internal contradictions and destructive policies of neoliberal rule have generated their own escalating crises. There are crises not just in economic "performance" caused by low growth, stagnant wages, anaemic productivity, sustained low investment and corporate capture of the state, but there is also pervasive disillusionment with the legitimacy of and commitment to the entire present order of things, including a well-founded erosion of trust in almost all institutions and democracy itself. "Trust in business and institutions is at an all-time low, yet trust is critical to long-term economic growth, innovation and social wellbeing" (OECD 2019). So concerned is the OECD at this loss of trust it has created frameworks for measuring and enhancing trust in government (OECD 2021) and business (OECD 2023b).

During the neoliberal era the nation-state has not been able to ensure rising living standards, provision of essential services and adequate infrastructure necessary for reproduction of the system, *and* create and extend markets while supporting their profitability. It is primarily on this basis that neoliberal ideology demands state fiscal austerity (Mattei 2022). But there are multiple other demands on the state to increase spending as it is required to compensate the losers in industries and regions subject to rapid structural change, to respond to frequent financial crises caused by capital market deregulation and to commit more public resources to increasingly severe environmental crises. Herein lies one of the internal contradictions within neoliberal public policy and the prospect for alternatives.

The concluding chapter draws on the case studies in *Captured* to synthesise the several crises currently facing neoliberalism, the difficulties of enacting change to rectify the identified problems and briefly canvasses some possible non-neoliberal policy directions.[1]

---

1 It is certainly not the contention here that the pre-neoliberal era of public policy in Australia was wholly superior. One only needs to reflect, for example, on the earlier position of women and Indigenous people in the labour market. Moreover, Davidson in Chapter 8, for example, notes the previous system of disability service provision had multiple flaws and "no funding system or delivery system in human services can be perfect" given limited resources and the enormous diversity in human needs. Slattery and

Captured was written in response to the need to think through and stimulate discussion of the problems and possibilities of *actually existing* neoliberalism at this important juncture in the political economy in Australia. Specifically, *Captured* provides a compendium of detailed case studies demonstrating how neoliberal thought has effected profound change across an extraordinarily wide range of public policies: disability services, pricing of water, retirement policy, the operation of ports and the tax treatment of capital gains. *Captured* also describes how and why these changes delivered problematic and disappointing outcomes and neoliberalism failed in its own to terms to produce the efficiency, choice, transparency and accountability that many of its supporters promised. Finally, the contributors also offer guidance on alternative approaches to economic management, public sector governance and delivery of essential of goods and services. *Captured* is a testament not just to the extraordinary reach of neoliberal thought on public policy in Australia over the last 40 years, but also its effect on the broader culture and lives of individuals and how it has radically altered the relation between governments, citizens and markets.

The present volume follows an earlier collection of case studies, *Wrong Way: How Privatisation & Economic Reform Backfired* (Cahill and Toner 2018), which had similar objectives. Together, they constitute companion and complementary volumes, though each stands independently.[2] Yet, despite their scope and scale, these volumes far from exhaust a full exposition of neoliberal public policy in Australia and its transformation of the economy and society over the last four decades.

Captured is directed at a wide audience: academics, across a broad range of social sciences; public policy practitioners in government and the private sector; and the engaged reader who seeks to better

---

Johnson in Chapter 7 observe the earlier system for apportioning water entitlements to farmers on the Murray–Darling river system resulted in gross over-allocation and great environmental damage.

2 Combined these volumes comprise 32 discrete case studies of neoliberal policy formulation, implementation, outcomes and suggestions for change. They represent a unique resource for researchers and policy makers, both current and future.

understand one of the major influences on their social and economic lives in the last 40 years.

Many readers, certainly anyone born after the late 1970s, have spent their entire lives within a neoliberal regime and experienced how "neoliberal ideas become rooted in ... many facets of everyday life" (Mirowski 2013, 43). This volume may aid readers to form the broad outlines of an alternative social and economic order to the present.

What is neoliberalism?

Before outlining the key themes of *Captured* in more detail, we need to briefly define neoliberalism and consider its origins. Despite the risk that any summary of neoliberal thought will be too broad and somewhat reductionist, it is an unavoidable risk we must take. Some more extensive treatments of neoliberalism can be found in Peck and Tickell (1994), Jessop (2002), Peck (2010), Stedman Jones (2012), Cahill et al. (2018), Mirowski (2013), Brown (2015), Davies and Gane (2021), Gerstle (2022) and Mattei (2022).

It is a common observation that neoliberalism is a heterogeneous phenomenon and therefore difficult to precisely define (Mirowski 2013, 33–6; Vallier 2022). This is due, for example, to the fact that it is not a single unified theory or philosophy; rather, distinct but overlapping schools of thought are conventionally identified, producing a degree of incoherency and incompatibility in key assumptions and policy prescriptions. Indeed, the inconsistency and logical flaws of key aspects of neoliberalism were pointed to as early as the late 1960s, in a critique of Milton Friedman by C.B. MacPherson. In it he noted that almost all Friedman's opposition to the welfare state and regulatory state rests on the proposition that market capitalism has no coercive elements. In order to do so Friedman avoids:

> [recognising] the existence of a labour force without its own capital and therefore without a choice as to whether to put its labour into the market or not. Professor Friedman would agree that where there is no choice there is coercion. His attempted

> demonstration that capitalism co-ordinates without coercion therefore fails. (MacPherson 1968, 98).

MacPherson made these insightful observations before there was neoliberal support for explicit coercion and violent repression in countries like Chile in the early 1970s. There is also the vexed issue of differentiating neoliberalism from earlier and/or cognate doctrines such as "classical liberalism", with its emphasis on individual rights, a minimalist state and "laissez faire" economic policy (Jessop 2002).

We reject the common view that there are significant discrepancies between neoliberal theory and neoliberal state practice in advanced economies. In particular, the argument is often advanced that maintenance of a large and intrusive state (Maher 2021), growth of oligopolistic industries (Humphrys 2018, 11) and indifference of policy makers to the obvious market failures generated by neoliberal privatisations and contracting-out is anathema to neoliberal doctrine. Indeed, *Captured* is replete with examples of these three developments in the neoliberal era. It is misleading to characterise neoliberal public policy in Australia as essentially a neoclassical project directed at creating "free" markets intended to replicate or approach the conditions for "perfect competition". For example, the so-called Chicago school of neoliberalism, which was especially influential in Australia, associated with authors such as Milton Friedman, Gary Becker, George Stigler and James Buchanan argues that attempts to regulate oligopoly will cause more harm and be ineffective. "Government failure" is worse than "market failure" since government lacks information to make correct decisions and anyway the government is "captured" by private interests and thus subject to "regulatory failure". Cahill (2017) provides accessible summaries of the main schools of neoliberal thought. This misconception has been a source of confusion for those seeking to understand and challenge neoliberal public policy. The issue of neoliberal public policy failure is taken up in more detail below.

This misconception is understandable, as the explicit rationale for introducing neoliberal public policies was framed in neoclassical notions of efficiency, effectiveness and equity. A compelling list of claimed benefits that would flow from intensified competition, removing "distortions" to prices and sharpening of economic incentives included improved allocative efficiency (better aligning supply and demand with improved consumer choice), enhanced productive efficiency (higher productivity and innovation), lower prices, higher real incomes, transparency in decision making and accountability for outcomes: the Productivity Commission (1999) review of "micro-economic reform" provides a rich source for these claims. As the case studies in *Captured* show, virtually every "reform" enacted in Australia was justified with a selection from this compendium of purported benefits. We argue that simply pointing out that neoliberal practice has not attained those goals is an insufficient reading of neoliberal thought and practice as a form of critique. The reality has long ago proven that proponents have not even seriously attempted to achieve these goals.

It is important therefore to differentiate neoliberalism from what many people identify as its economic foundations in neoclassical economics. Neoclassical economics, with which many neoliberal thought leaders are associated, shares important attributes with neoliberalism including methodological individualism and the priority of markets. However, neoliberalism differs in important respects from neoclassical economics. Firstly, neoliberalism is both an economic ideology and a theory of the individual, society and government. Neoliberalism is as much a philosophical and moral creed as a theory of the economy or markets.[3] Philip Mirowski argued that neoliberalism, "is not simply or exclusively an *economic* doctrine; at a deeper level, it is primarily a *philosophical* credo, which then gets elaborated through a potpourri of economic and political doctrines depending on geography and political circumstance" (2019, 5).

A key point here is that neoliberalism is not a positivist scientific endeavour but a highly normative philosophical project. Similarly, Wendy Brown has recently noted neoliberalism is best understood as a universalising philosophy:

> [it is a] normative order of reason … [that] transmogrifies every human domain and endeavour, along with humans themselves, according to a specific image of the economic. All conduct is

3 The philosophical nature of neoliberalism is also emphasised by David Gordon (2020) of the Mises Institute.

> economic conduct; all spheres of existence are framed and measured in economic terms and metrics, even when those spheres are not directly monetized (2015, 9–10).

We can usefully outline the contrast between neoliberalism and neoclassical economics with the example of their contrasting conceptualisation of the individual and the state. These distinctions are especially important for understanding neoliberalism as a policy doctrine and state project.

Neoclassical economics conceptualises the individual economic agent as a rational maximising actor. Neoliberalism, on the other hand, does not require and indeed rarely entertains an *a priori* notion of rational individualism. Instead, the neoliberal individual has two key characteristics. First, perhaps reflecting the aristocratic background of some of the key neoliberal authors (notably von Mises and von Hayek) there is a characteristic elite disdain for the mass of individuals. The neoliberal standard issue individual needs to be made more rational by being made to be a market actor. As Mirowski has noted:

> The hallmark of the NTC [neoliberal thought collective] was that its members more or less accepted the inherited image of an addled and befuddled populace but thoroughly rejected any appeals to a scientific technocracy to instil some discipline in the masses …
>
> The primary way this would happen was through acknowledgment that "the market" was an information processor more powerful and more efficacious than any human being was or could ever be … In effect, the NTC believed if only the masses could learn to subordinate their ambitions and desires to market dictates, then their deficient understandings and flawed syllogisms would appear as convenient expedients smoothing the path to order (2019, 6).

In other words, neoliberal rationality is not an innate attribute, but is something that needs to be imposed on individuals by their participation in capitalist markets. The market is therefore not simply a sphere of exchange but also a disciplinary regime, where individuals subject or subordinate themselves to the rationality of the information-processing superiority of markets.

Related to this conception of the individual is the view that market participation is not a matter of simple exchange, but a form of life course entrepreneurialism – of risking, earning and learning. Wendy Brown has argued that this neoliberal market entrepreneurialism extends beyond being simply a 24/7 market actor. It also blurs the boundary between market actor and citizen where,

> political life and the state in particular ... are remade by neoliberal rationality. The replacement of citizenship defined as concerned with the public good by citizenship reduced to citizen as *homo economicus* also eliminates the very idea of a people, a demos asserting its collective political sovereignty (Brown 2015, 39).

This aspect of the neoliberal entrepreneurial individual is also stressed by Mirowski who, following Foucault, suggested that "the key to the process of spreading neoliberalism into everyday life involves recasting the individual into an entrepreneur of the self" (2019, 40).

This leads to a second point of contrast with neoclassical economics: namely, neoliberalism's theory of the state. Neoliberals do not conceive of markets in terms of the neoclassical "perfect competition" model; rather, markets are an ontological category conceived in terms of their information-processing capacity – something they can do, according to neoliberal doctrine, better than any other institutional form, including democratic institutions. Markets serve a normative societal-level organising role, in which individuals should accept (that is subordinate themselves) to markets' primacy in their social and economic affairs. Despite the primacy of markets, neoliberalism does not, paradoxically, promote laissez faire with a small, weak state. As Mirowski has explained:

> mature neoliberalism is not at all enamored of the minimalist night-watchman state of the classical liberal tradition: its major distinguishing characteristic is instead a set of proposals and programs to infuse, take over, and transform the strong state, in order to impose the ideal form of society (2013, 36).

Peck further argued that the lineage to the activist neoliberal state is characteristic not just of mature neoliberalism but can be traced back to its ideological origins: "what neoliberalism has *really* been about, ever since its birth as a transnational ideological project … has been the evolutionary development of *proactive* forms of liberal statecraft" (Peck 2010, 108).

Stedman Jones (2012) described how neoliberals did not rely on market spontaneity but conceived an insurgent project to take control of the state to remake existing markets and build new ones. A central priority, both initially during the crisis of stagflation in the 1970s and subsequently, was deploying the full resources of the state to reduce the influence of organised labour.

In summary, the broader literature and the case studies presented here reveal that neoliberal public policy has been directed at maintaining a strong state in order to effect their envisaged objectives of expanding and creating new "markets" with a view to both increasing the sphere of profitable investment opportunities for the private sector and subordinating the state and citizens to these imperatives.

Structure

To ensure consistency across the chapters the authors were asked to use the following template in their case study chapters: what was the situation in the specific field of public policy prior to the introduction of the neoliberal change; what was the case for change; how was change effected; what were the results and how did these outcomes accord with or differ from the original expectation and, if the latter, why. Authors were also tasked with identifying alternatives to current policy.

The essays in *Captured* fall naturally into three broad categories. The first Part, "The nation-state changes its mind", outlines key ideas in economic policy, public administration and law animating the "great transformation" of the social-democratic state from the 1970s with the ascendancy of the current neoliberal era. Part II, "Case studies: Neoliberal public policy", provides exemplars of neoliberal ideas reversing long-established bipartisan policies governing industrial relations, industry policy and taxation, and their adverse impact on many workers, the economy and wealth equality. One of the strengths of *Captured* is how expert analysis reveals the comprehensive invasion of neoliberal modes of thought and action into all aspects of economy and society. The final Part, "Case studies: Creation of neoliberal markets", offers 10 decisive examples of neoliberal public policy directed at creating or extending markets into an extraordinary and unexpected variety of government activity or industries. The chapters in this section of the book cover HECS financing for student fees, agricultural water pricing, vocational education and training pedagogy, electricity transmission, deregulated building inspection, privatisations of ports and roads, the National Disability Insurance Scheme (NDIS), women in the care labour market and superannuation.

Key findings on neoliberal public policy in Australia

On the persistence of neoliberal public policy

Taken as a whole, the essays in *Captured* reveal that the rise and persistence of neoliberal public policy in Australia is based on the interaction of three domains: *economic and political interests*, notably private capital; *ideas*, that is the ideological underpinning of neoliberal economic and political theory; and *institutions*, or the complex self-reinforcing set of organisations put in place during the neoliberal era that propagate neoliberal ideas and practice. We have already discussed ideas, so the focus of this section is briefly on interests and institutions.

The transformation of public policy in Australia from the 1970s reflected a fundamental shift in the composition and interests of capital that had been developing in Australia from the 1960s. First, as described by Jones' chapter on industry policy (Chapter 4), there was a realignment of economic and political interests within capital in Australia as increasingly important internationally oriented and capital-intensive mining, finance and agri-business came into conflict with domestically oriented industrial capital and the existing comprehensive system of "protection all-round". The former "fractions" of capital benefited from the deregulation of trade, capital and labour markets promoted by neoliberalism (Bell 1997, 232). Second, as shown by Jericho and Stanford in Chapter 6, the postwar boom (1947–74) with its rapid industrialisation and robust labour markets was favourable to the growth of powerful unions that, by the mid-1970s, had led to a peak in labour's share of national income. When international growth faltered in the mid-1970s, union power accentuated a "profit squeeze". A central objective of early neoliberal economic and public policy in Australia was abolishing national and state wage-bargaining systems, and diluting the legal rights that assisted collective union organisation and bargaining strength. Undermining organised labour is also identified as a key motivation for privatisation of shipping ports in Chapter 6 by Snell and Gekara, Chapter 9 by Macdonald on the care workforce and Chapter 8 by Davidson on the NDIS.

Against reductionism

The contributions also reveal the fallacy of a reductionist and functionalist interpretation of interest, especially one that treats capital as a uniform "lump" with homogeneous objectives. Rather, they reveal conflicting interests between different "fractions of capital" and ruling classes playing out in state policy. These insights follow from the case study methodology employed in many chapters that examine specific policies rather than deal with abstract categories. For example, Slattery and Johnson's chapter on water pricing shows deep divisions within different farming interests and between many farmers and the finance sector. Mountain's chapter on the mostly privatised national electricity market demonstrates incoherency in the application of marketisation to an integrated network that not only results in high costs to all users but also delays transition to renewable energy. O'Neill describes how indifference to oligopoly created a highly profitable private toll-road oligopoly with high-cost implications for all users, including the transport industry and its downstream customers. Hodge shows how the introduction of neoliberal pedagogy into vocational education and training reduced the quality of training and skills available to firms but opened up very profitable opportunities for private training providers. Macdonald similarly finds that neoliberal care policies have had the effect of reducing the quantity and quality of labour supply to the industry. Snell and Gekara highlight the high costs imposed on business users of privatised monopoly seaports, and the deregulation of building certification in New South Wales as described by Randolph and co-authors has caused buyer hesitation and great reputational damage to the whole building industry. Finally, also inconsistent with a simple functionalist interpretation of "interest", the large marketised publicly funded or subsidised health and welfare sector of the economy has an inescapable dual character, taking a commodified form to generate private profit but also attempting to serve, however inadequately. This duality is also noted for example in the chapters by Davidson on the NDIS, Macdonald on the care workforce and Richardson on superannuation.

A strong neoliberal state

It has been argued above that neoliberalism requires not only a strong but also institutionally transformed state, in which the state's form is more in harmony with its function of creating and extending markets. This is a state in which policy formation, program design and program delivery have been substantially contracted out, with the function of senior public sector managers being one of contract administration. Quiggin and Rundle detail this transformation in the mode of government operation, its damning effect on state capacity and the self-imposed restraint on acceptable policy options and courses of action to which it gives rise. But this incoherence has not resulted in a diminished state in terms of exercising either legislative and regulatory power, or its call on economic resources. Jericho and Stanford, for example, detail the decades-long revolution in legislation and state apparatus governing industrial relations designed to overturn 100 years of institutional precedence in regulating labour markets. In addition, privatisation of public monopolies, especially integrated networks, requires a new and intrusive regulatory apparatus as evident for example in Mountain's chapter on electricity transmission networks, with their labyrinthine system of state planning and incentives. Similarly, Slattery and Johnson describe the complex and ever-changing regulatory apparatus governing water markets and Davidson shows how the NDIS has grown to a scale of such bureaucratic complexity it is in danger of collapsing. These chapters reveal that a constant succession of inquiries into policy failures and incessant bureaucratic tinkering with regulation are a standard response to periodic crises. Such exposés and tinkering act to placate a restive electorate, and also preserve private markets, but these responses to market failures also frequently require increased state expenditure, undermining attempts at fiscal austerity.

Accounting for neoliberal public policy failure

As noted earlier, an explicit claim of neoliberals for market expansion is that it increases efficiency, productivity, innovation, incomes, quality, choice, transparency and accountability. These explicit objectives of Australian neoliberal public policy were enunciated in key foundation documents such as the *National Competition Policy* (1993) and the National Commission of Audit (1996).

Conventional analysis of the poor outcomes from neoliberal markets focuses on failure in the design and implementation of these markets to meet neoclassical preconditions to achieve these objectives: see, for example, Quiggin's (1996) rigorous economic analysis of the failure of these conditions to be met in privatisations, while Toner (2018) similarly applied orthodox economic techniques to explain the widespread fraud and diminished quality following contracting-out of publicly funded vocational education and training. Failure in these markets is ascribed to deficiencies such as incomplete contracts, information asymmetry, perverse incentives, disaggregating integrated networks, negative externalities and oligopolistic supply.

Captured is replete with examples of poorly designed policies and outcomes. These include privatisations transferring public monopolies into private hands without adequate pro-competitive regulation, including the case of Transurban, analysed by O'Neill (who, despite noting a great number of problems with the model, suggests extending this hybrid "state-capitalist" model to other infrastructure projects), or Mountain on electricity transmission, or Snell and Gekara on container ports. Contracting-out services occurred without specifying in detail the characteristics and quality of services to be delivered, allowing private contractors to act opportunistically to maximise profit. This critique also informs Randolph and co-authors on deregulating residential building certification; Rundle on the provision of quarantine accommodation during Covid-19; and Davidson on the NDIS. There are also many examples of wilful ignorance of, or indifference to, negative externalities. These include Richardson on growing wealth inequality facilitated by changes to capital gains tax; Slattery and Johnson on water pricing changing agricultural production leading to environmental damage; Mountain on the electricity transmission market inhibiting investment in renewable generation; and Quiggin on the loss of capacity within the public service due to the neoliberal doctrine of new public management.

Captured and its companion volume chart the failure of neoliberal public policy to meet its stated objectives. But why is failure and disappointment with outcomes such a common occurrence and why does it persist? Former head of the Australian Competition and Consumer Commission (ACCC), Rod Simms, suggested eagerness by government to maximise returns from privatisations created a disincentive to impose pro- competitive regulation that would make these assets less attractive to potential buyers. He is also critical of the powers available to the ACCC to remedy problems of oligopolistic pricing power (Simms 2020). Quiggin (1996, 64) argued that ideology dominated sound, rational decision making: "the standard of analysis would be greatly improved if economists ignored current policy fashions and based their work on mainstream economic theory rather than on popular prejudices about the merits or otherwise of competition or government intervention". Toner (2018) suggested naivety by decision makers, simply not understanding the corrosive effects of the profit motive unconstrained by competition, ethical standards and legal consequences. There are also disincentives for both bureaucrats and politicians to admit to problems and their role in causing them.

These orthodox and other explanations of disappointment with policy outcomes have considerable merit and contribute to our overall understanding of policy failure. But our argument, and one supported by the chapters in *Captured*, is that the neoliberal conception of markets is, in the main, incapable of delivering the promised outcomes; indeed, it stands in contradiction to these objectives. Neoliberal public policy is focused on creating and extending markets, but *not* attempting to replicate neoclassical models of perfect competition. This is partly because the real world simply does not conform to the impossibly rigorous conditions required for their operation but also, more importantly, because the creation and extension of markets and subjugation of the population to markets are ends in themselves. Neoliberalism is indifferent to the resulting market structure and whether outcomes conform to stated objectives. These factors are, we argue, important contributors to explaining indifference to problems of oligopoly, market failures and the discrepancy between promise and delivery that have beset Australian neoliberal public policies. Most recently, growth of oligopolies and their role in price inflation is identified as a factor in shifting national income from wages to profits (Stanford 2023) and in lower productivity growth (Treasury 2022).

The chapter by Susan K. Schroeder on the evolution and ascendancy of neoliberal economic ideas provides important insights into the causes of these outcomes. These ideas emphasised the removal of "wage and price rigidities, and other market imperfections" that in practice meant increasing the scope for "market forces", enduring fiscal austerity and an unbalanced reliance on monetary policy. Over the last four decades the outcome has been, argues Schroeder, the substitution of one crisis – stagflation – for a long period of relative stagnation, rising inequality and rolling financial crises without end.

The implications of neoliberalism's incapacity to resolve many of the conflicts within capital, deliver for the public good and sustain the economy and society are taken up in the concluding chapter.

Other studies of neoliberal public policy in Australia

There have been several book-length studies specifically on neoliberal public policy in Australia and it is important to know how *Captured* stands in relation to them. The following is not intended as an exhaustive guide to local literature on this topic. They were selected primarily because they highlight different methodological approaches to the study of neoliberal public policy and the different insights this imparts.

Perhaps the most similar to *Captured* in terms of scope and intent were a series of studies quite early in the Australian experience produced by the Public Sector Research Centre (PSRC), based at the University of New South Wales – not be confused with an identically named in-house think tank, created in 2007, within the global consulting giant PwC (while the first PSRC charted the loss of competence in government policy formation from contracting-out government activity, global consulting firms like PwC directly and indirectly profit from it). During the 1990s the PSRC was prolific in assessing the early implementation of neoliberal public policy in Australia with case studies on national competition policy, privatisation, contracting-out government services and free trade agreements. These studies were remarkably prescient in identifying the emerging problems with these policies such as reduced quality of service, lack of accountability, private oligopoly and cost reductions derived not from improved technical efficiency but simply cutting workers' wages and conditions. But more than a quarter of a century has elapsed, permitting a more complete assessment of what now must be regarded as mature policy changes. We argue *Captured* and its companion book (*Wrong Way* 2018) provide such an assessment.

Michael Pusey (1991) primarily employed a survey and ethnographic approach to understanding the rise and spread of neoliberal ideas, known at the time as "economic rationalism", by probing the attitudes of senior public servants within the federal bureaucracy. The key finding was that the social background, and especially the disproportionate share of senior bureaucrats with university degrees in orthodox economics, created a receptive audience for neoliberal ideas of monetarism and public choice. Of course, the extent to which even senior bureaucrats can actually influence, let alone determine, the direction of policy is unresolved in Pusey's book, but either way from the 1980s onwards many senior civil servants were in sympathy with neoliberal ideas and enthusiastic implementers of these policies. Pusey (2003) extended the ethnographic study of neoliberalism via a questionnaire, interview and focus group study of 400 randomly selected middle-income people across five capital cities. This study is important in that it investigated how Australians experienced "economic reform" over the previous decades in terms of its impact on the quality of working life, cultural values and the relation of citizen to government. Its main findings are a population feeling considerable anger and disquiet at declining life quality, the growing gap between winners and losers in income distribution, the unfairness of this trend and a perception of government causing these changes and problems but also being unwilling to correct them.

Pusey's work complements the present volume in explaining some key sociological factors behind the propagation of neoliberal thought and practice within the state and in the subsequent decline of state policy formation and program implementation capacity examined here by Quiggin and Rundle.

John Quiggin's (1996) critical assessment of the case for and the outcomes of micro-economic reform in Australia remains a *tour de force*. First, it details the orthodox economic case for the suite of policies associated with neoliberalism such as privatisation, contracting out government services, competition policy, tariff cuts and financial deregulation. It also describes the economic tools used to measure the gains from these policies, such as general equilibrium models. Second, Quiggin uses his profound knowledge of mainstream economics to detail the unsound assumptions, internal contradictions and plain misapplication of arguments to justify "reform". This is combined with a close critical empirical examination of the actual results of policy change to undercut the exaggerated claims of large gains in growth and productivity. Quiggin's book is a fascinating case study in ambiguity. On the one hand, "it is difficult to say with certainty whether the aggregate benefits of microeconomic reform so far have exceeded the costs" (Quiggin 1996, 221) but also "the benefits of microeconomic reform … are still positive and significant in many, perhaps, most cases" (Quiggin 1996, 222). This reflects the timing of the book: relatively early in the life of the policy shift. Recently Quiggin (2022) has produced a sophisticated and critical account of neoliberalism.

Captured differs in several substantial ways from Quiggin's earlier work. The present volume is much more critical of neoliberal change, primarily since – in the ensuing quarter-century – the failure of neoliberal economic reforms, privatisation, corporatisation, contracting out and competition policy to achieve their stated objectives has become more transparent. Most prominently, indices such as GDP and productivity growth, investment, innovation and real wages in the neoliberal era significantly underperform the prior Keynesian era. (Toner 2022, 6–11 provides an accessible summary of the data.) Moreover, the trend of capitalism to oligopoly has intensified.

The book by Gabrielle Meagher and colleagues (2022) provides a comprehensive set of case studies with a singular focus on the "marketisation of social services" in Australia dealing with child care, housing, employment programs, superannuation, aged care, disability and refugee settlement services. Given the centrality of "marketisation" of social services in Australian neoliberal public policy, there is necessarily some overlap between Meagher's book, *Captured* and its 2018 companion, *Wrong Way*.

Social services represent a dilemma for neoliberal governments as they are an essential provision for social reproduction and, by substituting family-based care for collective provision of care, free up labour for paid work. But, in the main, due to their high cost, they also cannot be fully privatised but are usually contracted out with continuing full or partial government funding. Governments also cannot divest themselves of ultimate responsibility for quality, equity of access and operational matters affecting the former like wages and conditions of employees in this sector. As Meagher explained, for decades governments have attempted to evade responsibility and accountability in social service delivery by hiding behind the "market veil" provided by contracting out, but ultimately without success.

Finally, Elizabeth Humphrys' (2018) book employed an explicitly Marxist approach to the rise of neoliberalism in Australia from the 1980s in that "capitalist class interests" are central to its program and the state is inherently "partisan" in that it must "defend and promote the stability and health of capitalist society on a national and international scale" (Humphrys 2018, 12). Humphrys' book is important in placing unions, the Australian Labor Party in government and the corporatist Accord (1983–96) as crucial "consensual" actors in implementing neoliberalism in Australia.

Some of these arguments are problematic. Any claim that the state acts by definition only in capitalist interests is subject to the logical fallacy of *petitio principii*: the conclusion is assumed in the premise. The conclusion is that trade unions, the Labor Party and Accord were *required* to enact neoliberalism. But does the fact that the Accord was instrumental in enacting neoliberal public policy also entail it was inevitable? Why is effective agency granted to neoliberals but not to those who oppose them or seek to moderate their excesses? The contributors to *Captured* certainly make the case that ideas, interests and institutions contributed to the rise and persistence of neoliberalism but equally that these are subject to human agency and particular historical circumstance.

Humphrys also does not satisfactorily define what is a "neoliberal" public policy. Are social programs such as Medicare, childcare, superannuation and the NDIS unambiguously neoliberal? This question is not directly answered (Humphrys 2018, 153).

We hope that this introduction provides a broader context for the fine essays on neoliberalism presented in the remainder of *Captured* by some of Australia's leading scholars on public policy. The book also offers an essay in conclusion offering some final reflections on key themes in the book and where neoliberalism and debates about it are currently tracking. It notes that there are increasing observations about the supersession of neoliberalism, although what sort of post/ill-liberal capitalism is emerging is still a matter of conjecture.

References

Balogh, T. (1978). Monetarism and the Oil Price Crisis, *Journal of Post Keynesian Economics*, Winter 1978–79, 1(2): 27–46.

Bell, S. (1997). *Ungoverning the Economy: The Political Economy of Australian Economic Policy*. Melbourne: Oxford University Press.

Brown, W. (2015). *Undoing the Demos – Neoliberalism's Stealth Revolution*. Princeton, NJ: Princeton University Press.

Cahill, D. (2017) *Neoliberalism*, Cambridge: Polity Press.

Cahill, D., M. Cooper, M. Konings and D. Primrose (2018). *The SAGE Handbook of Neoliberalism*. London: SAGE.

Cahill, D. and P. Toner, eds (2018). *Wrong Way: How Privatisation & Economic Reform Backfired*. Melbourne: Latrobe University Press.

Case, A. and A. Deaton (2020). *Deaths of Despair and the Future of Capitalism*. Princeton, NJ: Princeton University Press.

Center for Disease Control and Prevention (USA) (2023). *Suicide Data and Statistics*. https://www.cdc.gov/suicide/suicide-data-statistics.html.

Collier, P., D. Coyle, C. Mayer and M. Wolf (2021). Capitalism: what has gone wrong, what needs to change, and how it can be fixed. *Oxford Review of Economic Policy*, 37(4) 637–49.

Coombs, C. (2022). Explaining Gen Z's unsurprising adoption of nihilism. *Thred*, 2 May, https://tinyurl.com/2s3j9ddr.

Crouch, C. (2016). The paradoxes of privatisation and public service outsourcing. *Political Quarterly*, 86: 156–71. https://doi.org/10.1111/1467-923X.12238.

Davies, W. and Gane, N. (2021). Post-neoliberalism? An introduction. *Theory, Culture & Society*, 38(6): 3–28.

Edwards, L. (2019). *Corporate Power in Australia: Do the 1% rule*? Melbourne: Monash University Press.

Foa, R.S., A. Klassen, D. Wenger, A. Rand and M. Slade (2020*). Youth and Satisfaction with Democracy: Reversing the Democratic Disconnect?* Cambridge, UK: Bennett Institute for Public Policy, Cambridge University.

Gerstle, G. (2022). *The Rise and Fall of the Neoliberal Order*. Oxford, UK: Oxford University Press.

Gordon, D. (2020). *The Philosophical Origins of Austrian Economics*. Auburn, AL: Mises Institute.

Gough, I. (1979). *The Political Economy of the Welfare State*. London: Macmillan.

Gray, J. (1998.) *False Dawn: The Delusions of Global Capitalism*. Cambridge, UK: Polity Press.

Humphrys, Elizabeth (2018). *How Labour Built Neoliberalism: Australia's Accord, the Labour Movement and the Neoliberal Project*. Leiden: Brill.

Independent Committee of Inquiry (1993). *National Competition Policy* [the Hilmer Report]. Canberra: Australian Government Publishing Service. https://ncp.ncc.gov.au/; https://bit.ly/48PK6yW.

Innes, A. (2016). Corporate state capture in open societies: the emergence of corporate brokerage party systems. *East European Politics and Societies and Cultures*, 30(3): 594–620.

Innes, A. (2021). Corporate state capture: the degree to which the British state is porous to business interests is exceptional among established democracies. *LSE Politics and Society*, 22 April. https://tinyurl.com/y3s7eu68.

Jessop, B. (2002). Liberalism, neoliberalism, and urban governance: A state–theoretical perspective. *Antipode*, 43(3): 452–72.

Jones, O. (2021). Eat the rich! Why millennials and generation Z have turned their backs on capitalism. *Guardian*, 20 September. https://tinyurl.com/44jc2h8f.

Maher, H. (2021). The relationship between neoliberal ideology and state practice: corporate power in the Australian mining industry. *Australian Journal of Political Science*, 57(10): 1–16.

McFarlane, B. (1968). *Economic Policy in Australia – the case for reform*. Sydney: Cheshire.

McFarlane, B. (1977). Inflation – money, gold and Marx. *Journal of Australian Political Economy*, October: 62–9.

MacPherson, C.B. (1968). Elegant tombstones: A note on Friedman's freedom. *Canadian Journal of Political Science/Revue canadienne de science politique*, 1(1):95–106.

MacWilliam, S. (2023). Political impotence of the neo-liberal ideologues: the continuing primacy of customary land tenure in Papua New Guinea. *Journal of Contemporary Asia*, 53(4): 693–711.

Mattei, C. 2022. *The Capital Order – How Economists Invented Austerity and Paved the Way to Fascism*. Chicago: University of Chicago Press.

Meagher, G., A. Stebbing and D. Perche, eds (2022). *Designing Social Service Markets: Risk, Regulation and Rent-seeking*. Canberra: ANU Press.

Mirowski, P.(2013). *Never Let a Serious Crisis Go to Waste: How Neoliberalism Survived the Financial Meltdown*. London: Verso Books.

Mirowski, P. (2019). Hell is a truth seen too late. *Boundary*, 2(46): 1.

National Commission of Audit (Australia), and Officer, R.R. (1996). *Report to the Commonwealth Government/National Commission of Audit*. Canberra: Australian Government Public Service.

OECD (2014). *Focus on Inequality and Growth*. https://tinyurl.com/sbh24f6u.

OECD (2019). *Trust in Business Forum*. https://tinyurl.com/49dcm92c.

OECD (2021). *Trust in Government*. https://tinyurl.com/4vb2edhj.

OECD (2023a). *Trust in Business Initiative*. https://tinyurl.com/ycxzy9h4.

OECD (2023b). OECD Income (IDD) and Wealth (WDD) Distribution Databases. https://tinyurl.com/27kb4f9h.

Peck, J. (2010). Zombie neoliberalism and the ambidextrous state. *Theoretical Criminology*, 14(1): 104–10.

Peck, J., and A. Tickell. (1994). Jungle law breaks out: neoliberalism and global-local disorder, *Area 26*(4): 317–26.

Productivity Commission (1999). *Microeconomic Reform and Australian Productivity: Exploring the Links*. Research paper. Canberra: AusInfo.

Pusey, M. (2003) *The Experience of Middle Australia: The Dark Side of Economic Reform*. Cambridge, UK: Cambridge University Press.

Pusey, M. (1991). *Economic Rationalism in Canberra: A Nation-Building State Changes Its Mind*. Cambridge, UK: Cambridge University Press.

Quiggin, J. (2022). The evolution of neoliberalism. In S.J. Williams and R. Taylor, eds. *Sustainability and the New Economics Synthesising Ecological Economics and Modern Monetary Theory*, 89–106. Cham: Springer.

Quiggin, J. (1996). *Great Expectations: Microeconomic Reform and Australia.* Sydney: Allen & Unwin.

Reid, A. (2023). Rethinking democracy and disillusionment. *INDAILY*, 3 May. https://tinyurl.com/mtah5vyy.

Simms, R. (2020). Tackling market power in the COVID-19 era competition policy address to the National Press Club, 21 October. https://tinyurl.com/y6wth9v2.

Stanford, J. (2023). *Profit-Price Spiral: The Truth behind Australia's Inflation.* Canberra: Australia Institute/Centre for Future Work. https://tinyurl.com/2s3rz8f8.

Stanford, J. (2018). The declining labour share in Australia: definition, measurement, and international comparisons. *Journal of Australian Political Economy*, (81): 11–32.

Stedman Jones, D. (2012) *Masters of The Universe – Hayek, Friedman and the Birth of Neoliberal Politics.* Princeton, NJ: Princeton University Press.

Toner, P. (2022). *Lost at Sea: An Assessment of the Productivity Commission's Report on Container Port Productivity.* Canberra: Australia Institute/Centre for Future Work. https://tinyurl.com/4an7yrfe.

Toner, P. (2018). A tale of mandarins and lemons: creating the market for vocational education and training. In D. Cahill and P. Toner, eds. *Wrong Way: How Privatisation & Economic Reform Backfired*, 40–58. Melbourne: Latrobe University Press.

Tran, S. (2021). State capture: top corporations identified as members of both Liberal and Labor parties. *Michael West Media*, 11 March. https://tinyurl.com/3dtxm3yx.

Treasury (2022). Competition in Australia and its impact on productivity growth. *Treasury Round Up*, 14–20 October. https://tinyurl.com/4m8a633d.

Vallier, K. (2022). Neoliberalism. In E.N. Zalta and U. Nodelman, eds. *Stanford Encyclopedia of Philosophy Archive.* Winter edn. https://tinyurl.com/4j67mhfj.

West, M. (2023). Australia: high industry concentration, high profit margins, says UBS. *Michael West Media*, 19 January. https://tinyurl.com/5cf2x282.

Part I

The nation-state changes its mind

1

Contemporary monetary and fiscal policy

Susan K. Schroeder

The state we are in

New economic thinking is often stimulated by key moments or events where new insights and guidance are needed. The Great Depression of the 1930s was one of these moments. The prevalent economic thinking was at a loss to explain persistent, high unemployment. John Maynard Keynes' *General Theory of Employment, Interest and Money* (1936) was a *tour de force* not only for providing an explanation of this phenomenon but for also justifying an active role for government and fiscal policy to support aggregate demand, stimulate growth and alleviate unemployment. Another moment that concerns us here is the stagflation of 1970s. The revisions to conventional economic thinking and the neoliberal fiscal and monetary policies that emerged as a result have been found wanting today.

Stagflation is the combination of high unemployment and high inflation. Figure 1.1 illustrates the annual rates of inflation (consumer price index – CPI) for major economies from the 1970s through the 1980s. Inflation began to increase in 1973, spiked in 1974 and then began to decline. The United States of America, Canada and Germany experienced another bout in the early 1980s. The unemployment rate (aged 15 years and over) began to increase around 1975 (see Figure 1.2).

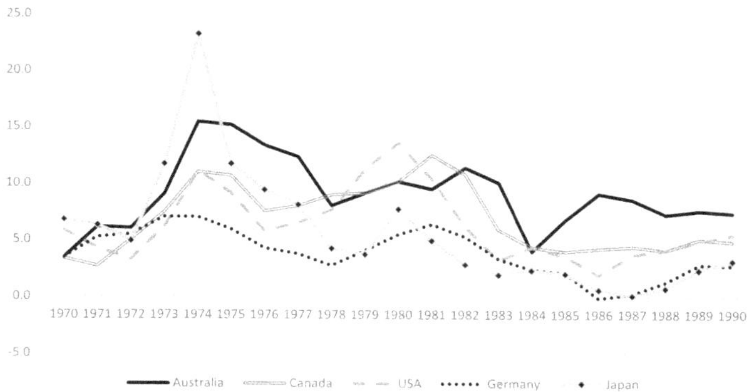

Figure 1.1 Annual rates of inflation (CPI) in selected advanced economies. Source: Organization for Economic Co-operation and Development (OECD, 2022a).

With the exception of Japan, the unemployment rates remained elevated into the early 1980s when they started to moderate. As late as 1990 the German, Canadian and Australian rates remained above levels experienced in the 1970s.

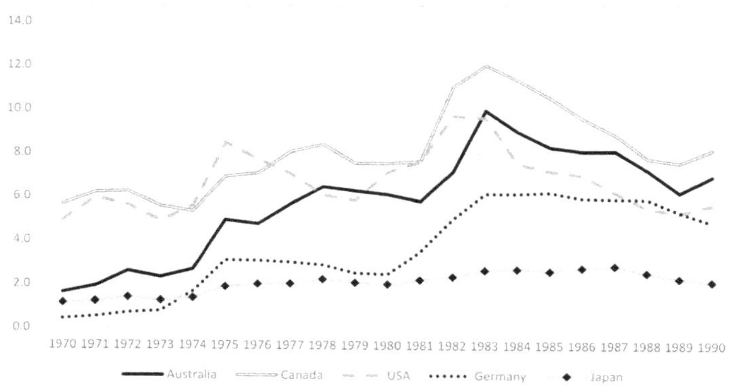

Figure 1.2 The unemployment rate (for those aged 15 and over) in selected advanced economies. Source: OECD (2022b).

At the time stagflation erupted, policy decisions were strongly influenced by a style of analysis (or school of economic thought) attributed to Keynes. If unemployment was a problem, expansionary fiscal policy such as increases in social welfare expenditure and social infrastructure (such as education) would support demand, boost productivity and growth. If inflation was a problem, taxes could be raised to cool demand or price controls could be implemented. If wage growth was attributed to strong unions, an incomes policy may be appropriate. If government spending was too strong, it should be cut back. There was a strong emphasis on fiscal policy. Monetary policy of the kind where a central or reserve bank could adjust the policy rate to cool demand and economic growth was possible but not preferred, as central banks were limited by the international financial architecture of Bretton Woods.

In the 1970s this approach became problematic. Fiscal stimulus to reduce unemployment seemed to exacerbate inflation. Raising taxes or implementing price controls to reduce inflation aggravated unemployment. The style of analysis – the neoclassical synthesis – was called into question. Methodological problems had surfaced before this point. The subsequent choices made by conventional economists to get around the problems enabled the emergence of ideas and justification of market-oriented policies: neoliberalism.

Over the next 40 years income and wealth inequality increased, private and public debt increased, and economic growth weakened. Governments continually function either near or in some form of fiscal crisis. As such, governments are constrained from doing more for their economies because of (perceived) budget constraints and threats of ratings downgrades that restrict access to funding. Monetary policy gravitated to ultra-low interest rates that stimulated the development of asset bubbles and a reliance on cheap credit by households and firms. Economies and financial systems are currently so fragile that raising interest rates may trigger crises central banks seek to avoid. These are hardly outcomes to crow about. The irony is that the methodological debates of the 1960s and 1970s were not actually resolved. Let's have a look.

The neoclassical synthesis and its limitations

Mainstream and non-mainstream economists largely agree that capitalism, as a system to achieve social reproduction, is prone to instability. Recessions, asset bubbles, income and wealth inequality, inflation, unemployment and underemployment all emerge at some point. The distinctiveness of economists' explanations hinges on what they identify as the underlying, persistent dynamics of capitalism. These distinctions lead to different explanations of how prices for products, inputs and assets are determined in a market system. In other words, variations in the explanations of prices are related to variations in the explanations of macro-economic aggregates (such as output, employment and inflation) and suggested policy recommendations. A deep dive into various price theories is not the objective of this chapter. Rather, as we will see, the shift towards neoliberal policies is related to issues associated with neoclassical price theory: that is, neoclassical theory's explanation of how the price of an item is determined by the balance of supply and demand.

The neoclassical synthesis is a school of thought that seemed to resolve a key issue with Keynes' *General Theory*. The *General Theory* provided an analysis of capitalism's dynamics at the level of the macro economy. That is, the arguments are conducted using macro-economic aggregates such as household consumption, investment by firms, government expenditure, trade balances and so on. There is no theory of how prices are determined in the marketplace (a theory of micro-economics). Occasionally, Keynes referred to the work of neoclassical economist Alfred Marshall for an explanation of how markets function and prices are determined. Keynes would have been aware of the limitations of Marshall's theory of price, as it had been critiqued by his colleague, the Italian economist Piero Sraffa, 10 years prior to the publication of the *General Theory*. (Sraffa identified a logical inconsistency with the construction of the firm's supply curve: the upward-sloping shape was at odds with the assumption of price-taking behaviour.) There was no ready replacement for Marshall's theory.

After World War II, a general equilibrium approach to price theory emerged as the dominant neoclassical price theory. The idea is, given consumers' preferences, inputs to production and the state of technology, a set of prices could be determined to balance supplies and demands for all markets at the same time. It was like Marshall's partial equilibrium approach – where each market or product is analysed individually – but all-encompassing and even more mathematical. (An early version of this approach is attributed to the French economist Léon Walras back in 1874.)

Interesting to note, the RAND Corporation was an important catalyst for the adoption of general equilibrium price theory. The RAND Corporation was established in 1948 as a non-profit think tank to generate research and analysis for the United States military. It provided an intellectual space where cutting-edge, abstract research could be dovetailed with real-world issues. Through the efforts of its contributors – Gérard Debreu, Kenneth Arrow and Paul Samuelson – an interpretation of Adam Smith's invisible hand emerged that could be captured in a mathematical model. It expressed a vision that society is made better off if individuals are free to make choices in their own interests (Abella 2008, 257–8). The markets need to be free for society to experience the best result from this method of social reproduction.

The neoclassical synthesis was a school of thought that combined Keynes' ideas with general equilibrium theory. Samuelson's economics textbooks were extremely popular for disseminating this school of thought throughout American colleges and universities for decades. It was a boon for bolstering the American myth regarding the spirit of individualism and countering the perception of a communist threat on American soil, and elsewhere.

The neoclassical synthesis conveyed several elements of the *General Theory* well. For example, the structure captured Keynes' vision that capitalism was a monetary system of production. That is, it is not possible to determine output and employment without the influence of the monetary/financial sector. Another element is aggregate demand being comprised of households' consumption, investment by firms, government expenditure and net foreign trade. Other elements include the balance of aggregate demand and aggregate supply (equilibrium output) being influenced by changes in output; the marginal propensities to consume and invest; the multiplier (or feedback) effect; and, to a lesser extent, the interest rate. The neoclassical synthesis conveys the idea that the equilibrium level of output is associated with a level of employment that is not necessarily full employment. The balance of the supply of and demand for money as an asset determining the equilibrium level of the interest rate in the monetary sphere is another feature.

The apparent precision of the apparatus gave the impression that a capitalist economy could be managed for stability and growth by fine-tuning policy. Mathematical modelling could evaluate the effectiveness of changes to fiscal and monetary policies. For a while, from the 1950s through to the 1960s, the neoclassical synthesis seemed to provide effective guidance to governments. Governments seemed to be able to fine-tune their economies to achieve stable investment, strong employment, good productivity and wage growth, low inflation and a growing middle class with the means to consume.

The emergence of stagflation in the 1970s lead to questions about this framework for guiding policy. Strong fiscal expenditure to alleviate high unemployment seemed to lead to high inflation. Weak spending to alleviate inflation stoked high unemployment. Governments – and voters – were increasingly frustrated. Government came to be seen as an impediment to improvements in social outcomes. While there was scepticism of Ronald Reagan's and Margaret Thatcher's assurances of a trickle-down effect with increased reliance on free markets, this is exactly what governments would eventually advocate.

Methodological issues with the neoclassical synthesis emerged over time. The first issue was while the synthesis was a good start, it did not fully capture the ideas in the *General Theory*. For instance, to achieve clarity the neoclassical synthesis quietly dropped Keynes' emphasis on the rate of profit of productive investment – the marginal efficiency of capital (MEC) – as a destabilising force. Keynes maintained that while the interest rate would have some influence over investment, it is the relationship between the interest rate (determined in the monetary sphere) *and* the profit rate (determined in the real sphere) that was the key driver of investment. If the profit rate is greater than the interest rate, the conditions are conducive to new investment; in a sense, the rate of return on new investment is greater than the financing cost of that investment. If the interest rate is greater than the profit rate, the conditions are not conducive to new investment. The two rates are determined in different, though related, spheres. Without the profit rate, a capitalist economy could be portrayed as being less prone to bouts of instability than is the case (if Keynes was correct).

Another issue is the explanation of inflation. Keynes had argued that, as an economy neared its full-employment level, there was a tendency for prices of inputs, including labour, to increase as they became scarcer. Their productivities would also decline. Rising prices of factors of production and declining productivities pressure the costs of outputs to increase. To protect profit margins, firms raise prices of their outputs – this generates inflation. In the neoclassical synthesis, inflation cannot be generated from the mathematical apparatus. Instead, the empirical relationship between unemployment and prices – the Phillips curve – is added to the system in an *ad hoc* way. Moreover, the Phillips curve was an empirical relationship; there was no theoretical explanation of it until Richard Lipsey's attempt in 1960. The relationship between inflation and growth is methodologically slipshod.

Yet another methodological issue is that general equilibrium theory was not logically sound. As he did with the partial equilibrium variant of neoclassical price theory, Piero Sraffa articulated a key logical inconsistency with the general equilibrium variant as well. The capital critique centred on the how "capital" is measured. Capital is problematic for neoclassical price theory, as it is an input to production that is also reproducible. It is an input and an output at the same time. To understand why this is a problem, we need to visit the concept of equilibrium.

A set of prices that constitutes a long-period equilibrium – sometimes referred to as natural or normal prices – requires the prices of non-reproducible inputs (determined at the balance of supply and demand curves) to reflect a uniform rate of return. If rates of return are unequal, a short-period disequilibrium position is present. Competition by self-interested individuals will adjust prices until uniform rates are attained. The long-period equilibrium prices of produced outputs will be equal to the outputs' respective costs of production.

It is not so simple with capital. On the one hand, if capital is defined as a lump of value, then to do so requires a unit or standard of value to amalgamate the capital goods. But having a standard of value for capital implies capital's price has already been determined. The logic is circular. On the other hand, if capital is defined as a set of physical quantities, a uniform rate of profit associated with a long-period equilibrium cannot be determined. Why? As inputs to production, the prices of capital goods, like other inputs to production, are determined by their respective supplies and demands. As capital goods are reproducible, their prices, in equilibrium, are also determined by their costs of production. There are two conditions that the prices of capital goods must satisfy. Mathematically, the system is said to be "overdetermined". Only by fluke will the two conditions be satisfied at the same time. One can avoid these issues by assuming the economy does not employ reproducible capital goods. But this is not realistic.

An implication is that the supply and demand curves for capital can behave perversely. That is, the supply curve is not guaranteed to be upward-sloping in the price–quantity space, and the demand curve is not guaranteed to be downward-sloping. As supply and demand curves in one market depend on the proper structure of curves in other markets, the determination of price of capital being without logical foundation implies the determination of prices in other markets is questionable. The idea of the (marginal) productivity of an input regulating its remuneration is invalidated. The old adage about higher productivity leading to higher wages or compensation is without a sound theoretical foundation, as is the idea that the marginal productivity of capital is equivalent to the interest rate in equilibrium.

The logical flaw associated with reproducible capital could be resolved in one of two ways: *either* keep the object of analysis as the determination of natural prices with uniform rates of return and recognise the analysis is not applicable to reproducible capital *or* redefine the concept of equilibrium. Conventional economists choose the latter option. The traditional concept of equilibrium was recast as intertemporal equilibrium where prices were determined by supply and demand at each point in time. The condition of uniform rates of return was relinquished. The equilibrium concept was recast to suit the needs of mathematical rigour rather than realism of the approach. Conventional theory attempts to deal with the realism problem by arguing market imperfections and asymmetric information exist to render the balance of supply and demand inefficient or suboptimal.

The problem here is that the methodological foundation of equilibrium remains unclear. If at every point in time markets clear without uniform rates of return, are we working with a short-period scenario or a long-period scenario? This has never been resolved. Conventional economists made a methodological choice to defer to mathematics for "intellectual rigour" and for the creation of models to supply empirical evidence to guide policy. In doing so, they rely on a micro-foundation that cannot explain the rate of profit (rate of return on capital) (Eatwell 2019). Without an explanation of the rate of profit, neoclassical theory does not have a robust explanation of the processes of capital accumulation and economic growth. It cannot explain the dynamics of capitalism. This is the basis of conventional fiscal and monetary policy.

The structure and policy recommendations that underpin neoliberalism (new Keynesianism)

The stagnation of the 1970s called into question the dominant approach to economics – the reinterpretation of Keynes' *General Theory* that jettisoned the role of the profit rate, slapped on the Phillips curve in an *ad hoc* way and introduced a questionable micro-economic underbelly. The close evaluation of this framework was a good thing. What emerged was a more mathematically-oriented approach that was more strongly related to the framework that Keynes sought to supplant.

New Keynesianism continues the tradition of combining Keynes' *General Theory* and elements of neoclassical price theory. It maintains asymmetric information, wage and price rigidities and other market imperfections that lead to market failures and disequilibria are endemic in capitalism. The presence of imperfections amplifies shocks to the system, which exacerbate bouts of instability and generate cycles. If prices and wages are sticky to adjust, output (and employment) bear the brunt of adjustment. An implication is imperfections need to be reduced or eliminated from the system. Prices and wages need to be made less sticky to improve the functioning of markets and absorb shocks.

The presence of general equilibrium theory can be found in the intertemporal nature of planned expenditures, such as household consumption, the importance of expectations about the future and the idea that disequilibria are the result of optimising behaviour. The New Keynesian school of thought, moreover, deepens the reliance on the interest rate. The consumption function is based upon the individuals' decisions regarding consumption in the present and consumption in the future. If the interest rate rises, an individual will postpone some consumption today to have more consumption tomorrow. As the interest rate rises, aggregate consumption can be expected to fall. Investment expenditures can also be expected to fall as the cost of capital (the interest rate and other expenses) rises and firms decide to postpone new investment. Trade will also weaken as the interest rate rises; the value of the domestic currency strengthens and makes the prices of exports less competitive (net exports contract).

The school's emphasis on the interest rate endows monetary policy more importance than Keynes had intended. During moments of instability, monetary policy could calm the markets and stabilise liquidity through managing the policy rate and balance sheet adjustments. Unfortunately, it has the side effect of stimulating asset bubbles. Monetary policy is influenced by a tension between the strength of aggregate demand and inflation. The greater the strength of demand, as represented by the narrowing of the output gap, the higher risk of inflation. As such, the policy rate should increase to soften aggregate demand (shorten or reverse the output gap). By confining inflation within limits, not only are the assets of wealth holders protected but inflationary expectations of firms are also stabilised, supporting their confidence to invest.

With respect to fiscal expenditure, short-term fiscal spending can alleviate immediate social suffering. But it is problematic because of the uncertainty over the public's reactions to changes in government spending and tax policies. For instance, if a government borrows to spend (and increases its debt burden) then the expenditure may have to be constrained later by trimming the social safety net or raising tax rates or both. The economy may not experience sustained growth with additional government expenditure if consumers decide to save (reduce consumption expenditure) in anticipation of higher tax rates.

In the long term, the recommendation for governments is to remove the inefficiencies within markets by reducing regulation. Reducing the presence of government enables markets to stimulate change and improvements in the economy and society, or so the story goes. The policies associated with the New Keynesian school facilitate a shift from the support for a social safety net for workers, via government expenditure (fiscal policy) to a safety net for financial capital, via support of asset prices and liquidity provision (monetary policy) (Palley 2021, 40).

The Australian experience

The Australian experience in the 1970s and 1980s was characterised by financial deregulation, floating of the foreign exchange rate, and the Prices and Incomes Accord. The Accord was intended to dovetail wage growth with productivity gains to stem inflation and promote labour market flexibility. Australia reduced tariffs to improve its current account imbalance and stimulate productivity improvements in domestic industries. While mining and agriculture industries benefited, manufacturing industries had more trouble competing on the international marketplace, (Berger-Thomson, Breusch and Lilley 2018). To promote the market's ability to reduce costs and prices, improve quality of products, and stimulate growth, several large state-owned enterprises were privatised: in transport (Qantas), financial services (Commonwealth Bank) and communication (Telstra). The idea was to use markets to restructure, streamline processes and incorporate new technologies through competition. The proceeds of privatisation – in combination with disciplining government's expenditures, broadening the tax base and increasing GST – meant Australia was able to reduce its net debt.

Prior to financial deregulation the Australian financial system entailed several controls that enabled better management of the economy in the context of Bretton Woods. Interest rates on loans and deposits were controlled. Banks were subject to liquidity and reserve ratios and limitations on the quantity of loans. Foreign exchange transitions were controlled. Financial institutions were highly specialised with specific goals. As a result, the exchange rate was stable; domestic savings were prevented from flowing cross-border (and supported domestic investment); there was a captive market for government securities; risk-taking by banks was limited and credit was directed to areas that needed development (housing and farming) (Battellino 2007).

Over time, the controls became less effective as international capital flows began to grow and challenge Bretton Woods. New financial instruments and institutions emerged to compete with the banks. Potential borrowers became frustrated with the lack of access to credit and, likewise, investors were frustrated with limited opportunities. Interest rates were the first to experience deregulation in 1973, and within 13 years "virtually all controls on banks had been removed, foreign banks had been allowed to enter the market and the exchange rate had been floated" (Battellino 2007, 79). Monetary policy became focused on controlling the context in which growth occurs, managing demand through the policy rate and the provision of liquidity.

While these adjustments seemed to provide initial benefits, the benefits would not last. According to the Productivity Commission (2020), labour productivity grew 1.8 per cent annually between 1974–75 and 2018–19. It has been declining since 2005, growing only 0.8 per cent between 2013–14 and 2018–19. Declines in manufacturing, agriculture, forestry and fishing, and gas, electricity, water and waste services explain most of the slowdown. According to neoclassical theory, enhanced productivity is supposed to lead to higher wages. For a while it did. Until 2012–13, wage growth outpaced labour productivity. From that point, it stagnated and fell below productivity growth. The culprits seem to be the increased presence of part-time work and casualisation, and lower rates of unionisation (bargaining power). The compensation of workers relative to gross operating surplus (profit) of private, non-financial firms is illustrated in Figure 1.3. Compensation was approximately four-and-a-half times greater than gross operating surplus in 1975–76 and declined to two times greater by 2020–21. More recently, companies' gross operating profit rose 10.2 per cent in the first quarter of 2022 relative to the prior quarter (seasonally adjusted); wages and salaries increased by a meagre 1.8 per cent (ABS 2022a). With interest rates so low, the situation suggests now is a good time to invest (profitability is greater than the interest rate) but uncertainty is so high businesses are not willing to do so.

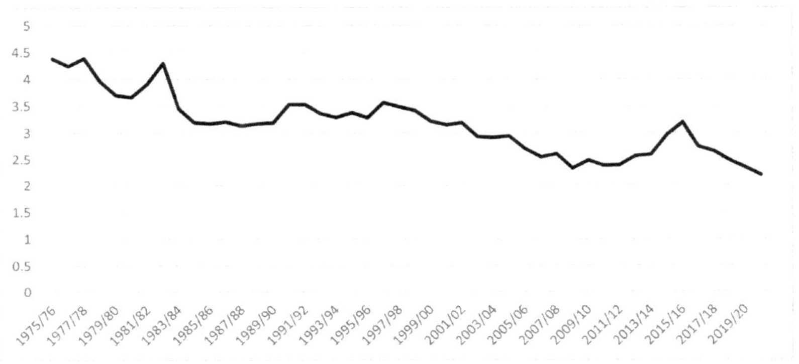

Figure 1.3 Compensation of workers as a proportion of gross operating surplus (Australia). Source: ABS, 2022b.

Not surprisingly, Australia has experienced rising inequality under neoliberalism. The Gini coefficient's long-term trend has been increasing, reflecting greater income inequality. In 1980 it stood at about 0.27 and rose to between 0.32 and 0.34 by the mid- to late 2000s. The Gini continues to fluctuate around 0.34 through to 2021 (Statista n.d.).

One of the ways that households offset sluggish income is with credit. At the end of 1988, liabilities of households (loans, accounts payable and securities) stood at $157.1 billion. At the end of 2021, liabilities had ballooned to $2634.0 billion – growth of approximately 1600 per cent (ABS 2022c, Table 35). In contrast, the financial liabilities of non-financial corporations grew 765.0 per cent: from $616.912 billion in December 1988 to $5337.203 billion by December 2021, (ABS 2022c, Table 6). Sovereign debt (bonds) increased from $37.930 billion at the end of 1988 to $883.519 billion by December 2021, for a rate of growth about 2100 per cent (ABS 2022c, Table 30).

Households turned to speculative activities to offset sluggish incomes with capital gains, particularly with housing as a vehicle for investment. The property market is valued at approximately $10 trillion. The most recent data from the ABS indicates approximately 87,100 households own at least four investment properties, excluding their current dwelling. 1,363,000 households own at least one investment property (ABS 2022d, Table 10). The property market has enabled those who hold wealth to earn passive income through capital gains. This effect exacerbates income and wealth inequalities and has been well documented by Thomas Piketty (2014) and researchers since.

What is next?

Could capitalism be reformed? An affirmative answer is provided by Mazzucato (2013), who suggests the state take a more entrepreneurial role to forge a better relationship between government and the private sector. That is, government ought to assume the risks associated with a space or conditions in which innovations emerge. Further, the state ought to create and shape markets. The United States government has done so in the past. Apple is an example of a firm that received government funding and state-funded technology to develop the iPhone. "From the development of aviation, nuclear energy, computers, the Internet, biotechnology and today's developments in green technology, it is and has been, state – not the private sector – that has kick-started and developed the engine of growth" (Mazzucato 2013, 13). The economic growth that is stimulated by innovations would lead to employment opportunities and stronger incomes. Government would be directly rewarded with a share of the returns according to its respective contribution, rather than simply rewarded, indirectly, through the tax system. There is scope to argue that full deployment of an IT revolution would bolster the green revolution through replacement of obsolete technology.

While this view has merit, it has yet to address the importance of national culture for entrepreneurial risk-taking. There have been numerous studies suggesting not all countries have national cultures that foster entrepreneurial spirit in the same way. For instance, using Geert Hofstede's cultural dimensions of individualism, uncertainty avoidance and power distance, Turkey's entrepreneurial culture is shown to lag that of the United States (Eroglu and Picak 2011). The vision of the entrepreneurial state may need to be adjusted to suit differences in national cultures. There is also the possibility that governments with entrepreneurial spirit for innovative projects may not have the managerial skill or oversight needed to see projects to successful fruition. The Victorian Economic Development Corporation, a venture-capital fund created by the Victorian government, was tasked to locate and invest in innovative projects. A key objective was to restructure the state's configuration of industries to support growth and employment. Poorly selected projects and mismanagement, however, lead to loses and the collapse of the Victorian State Bank. Inherent tension in the types of funding used, venture capital (equity) and development finance (debt), were also to blame (Rafferty 1993).

Do we need capitalism to support social reproduction? There have been two other ways societies have resolved issues regarding production, distribution, social maintenance and consumption. Societies have been organised around tradition, where tasks associated with social provisioning shifted from one generation to the next according to custom and usage. The structure is often reinforced by religion. A command or authoritarian system resolves these activities through a system of social planning and edicts of a collective or an individual. Here the structure was reinforced by penalties as stipulated by the authority (Heilbroner 1999, 19–20). The forms of governance are quite stringent and inflexible. Capitalism provided the opportunity for individuals to decide what is in their best interests. Social tasks are allocated by self-interested individuals through the lure of monetary gain. Unlike the other two methods, a market system did not ensure the stability of the system. While the drive for growth would stimulate demand for what was produced, its cyclical tendencies emerged. The low points of cycles are characterised by crises, recessions and progressive worsening of social ills. The push for unfettered growth has led to what is the likely the end game for this form of social reproduction – climate change.

Challenges posed by climate change and the ill effects of capitalism will likely require something different. While it is possible that capitalism could be reformed, more likely we face transitioning to some form of post-capitalism. However provisioning for social reproduction occurs, it will need to reconcile our self-centred natures with our need for social cooperation. Social cooperation will be key for this new form. Markets will still play an important part of our lives, but less so – as will the idea of social advancement through monetary gain. The role for government will need to shift from managing the context in which firms function and correcting market failures to coordinating the efforts of communities to improve local provisioning of what they need and foster self-sufficiency, resilience and environmental regeneration. Workers' self-directed enterprises, worker-owned enterprises and cooperatives would have a greater role (see Wolff 2012), as well as eco-villages and urban villages. An eco-village exists outside of the main society, whereas an urban village exist within the main society. While their internal structures and external linkages differ, they seek to promote reconnection to nature, development and mixed land use, and to contain social and economic activities within a limited space (Xue 2014), improving self-sufficiency and moderating growth.

Towards this end, the idea of a foundational economy is emerging. Here, society comes to an understanding of what its constituents need to subsist and what is needed to reproduce itself in future periods. Not every country will be the same because of its unique landscapes, vegetation, cultures and so on that underpin its social structures. Basic needs involve an optimal level of physical health and autonomy, and intermediate needs involve adequate nutritional food and water, protective housing, healthcare, and basic education (Doyal and Gough 1991; Gough 2017). As coordinator, the government monitors its industrial configuration to determine how well the activities within it can satisfy needs at the local level: that is, how well communities are able to produce goods and services within their geographic locale and how much they depend on a distribution network to access what they cannot produce. With this information, the government could determine where the industrial configuration is deficient, and how climate change may pose challenges to production and distribution.

Sovereign governments will also be in a better position to understand how to approach the United Nations' Sustainable Development Goals (SDGs), such as no poverty, good health and wellbeing, life on land, etc. (United Nations n.d.). The programs created to achieve SDGs will be rendered more strategic and targeted, and possibly more economical. There is a role for indigenous knowledge and informal economies for comprehending the ecosystems and managing how they are changing. The support for an ecological transition will be more effective.

Government, as a coordinator, will be pressed to reorient industrial policy and financing mechanisms. There has been renewed interest in industrial policy. This can be attributed to the apparently limited scope of fiscal and monetary policies as they currently exist. At the forefront of this interest are Justin Lin, Bruce Greenwald and Joseph Stiglitz. Their orientation is grounded in conventional economics. Lin (2014) for instance, has suggested that countries identify their comparative advantage, given resource endowments, to select industries that are the most competitive. Government should support them with infrastructure and let the market mechanism (free markets) take its course. Greenwald and Stiglitz have suggested learning and knowledge need to be better integrated into growth-enhancing investments. In this way the differences between average practice and best practices within industries (such as agriculture, services and manufacturing) are narrowed. Industrial policy must recognise "society's comparative learning and learning abilities (including its ability to learn)", particularly in relation to its competitors (Greenwald and Stiglitz 2013, 61). Moreover, "government must establish an environment that is conducive to creating a learning economy through public investments which support private-sector investment in learning sectors" (Greenwald and Stiglitz 2014, 426). According to this vision, government's management of industrial change boils down to fine-tuning labour markets. Industrial change occurs as learning by workers enhances their productivities and bolsters competitiveness in their associated industries (Schroeder 2015, 158).

The heterodox community has something different to offer. Rather than fine-tune labour markets and workers, government could reorient industrial policy to support programs such as a Green New Deal to slow climate change and ease an ecological transition. Features include upgrading transport systems and energy grids, creating green housing and food security, improving care for health, the aged and disabled, and guaranteeing jobs. Some variant of Mazzucato's *Entrepreneurial State* would be helpful to harness technology for these purposes. Programs could be funded through a variety of means such as wealth taxes, the use of central bank digital currencies and networks of community development banks. I have argued elsewhere (Schroeder 2021) that a modest wealth tax that not only maintains the sustainability of national debt for the United States can also generate substantial funds for a Green New Deal program. In this way, fiscal policy becomes less constrained.

Less reliance on markets for production and distribution implies the role and scope of economics will need to adjust. Conventional economics will likely have a smaller role to play in guiding the management of economic activities conducted through markets. There will need to be a paradigm shift to a mode of economic thought that justifies the state as coordinator of productive activities, where information technology stimulates the emergence of networks in which productive activities become more decentralised and collaborative in orientation. The approach will justify a role for the state that is not dissimilar to the pre-neoliberal era where governments provided utilities, public housing, telecommunications and transport through publicly owned entities. In our current historical context, such entities will have different forms, strategies and relationships to each other to facilitate better social outcomes. Public non-profit corporations, for instance, would lower the cost of necessities. Renationalisation of energy grids and fossil fuel firms would speed the transition to non-carbon sources of energy and lower their cost. Governments may want to establish new departments to promote collaborative productive activities that reduce the costs of outputs and to promote sharing of what is produced (Mason 2016).

This implies the style and status of analysis will be different. Adjusting general equilibrium frameworks to incorporate or absorb political, social and psychological phenomena, as conventional economics does, may yield interesting insights. But the efforts do not constitute a paradigm shift. The ideal of a free market system remains at the heart of it. Rather, a paradigm shift will entail economic analysis situating itself alongside the imprecise knowledge of the disciplines within social sciences and psychology (Heilbroner and Milberg 1995). A synthesis of economic sociology, political economy and heterodox economics could provide a foundation for this shift. In this context, the decisions of individuals reflect the sociopolitical essence of their historical setting. The methodology of political economy and heterodox economics is complementary to the methods found in the social sciences and other disciplines.

An important contribution by heterodox economics is the range of insights about how prices are determined. At present, they provide alternative price theories that underpin the post-Keynesian school of thought, such as theories formulated by Michael Kalecki, Piero Sraffa and Karl Marx. The post-Keynesian school has long maintained the neoclassical foundation for the *General Theory* was highly problematic. There is no consensus about how the strands relate to each other. But, there are methodological similarities than can be capitalised upon. For instance, the strands are part of the surplus approach that entails open systems of analysis and similar conceptions of time, uncertainty and equilibrium. There is a possibility that our understandings of "value" and "distribution" need to be recast for collaboratively produced commodities and outputs to something more socially or morally oriented.

Conclusion

Whatever societies decide as their direction for reproduction and provisioning, the role for the state will need to adapt. While markets will have their place, neoliberal fiscal and monetary policies have demonstrated themselves as counterproductive to the needs of just, equitable and democratic societies. Governments need to understand what their societies need and act to coordinate the outcomes with the tools at their disposal and, possibly, with the support of a range of multilateral agencies.

Fiscal policies to support social safety nets and goals will be bolstered with the adoption of a wealth tax to locate funding for expenditure and to service national debts. Possibilities here include the models suggested by Schroeder (2021) and Saez and Zucman (2020); the former's formulation is based on gross assets and the latter's formation is based on net assets. The political will to improve the location of taxable assets will be a challenge, but it is conceivable that this will occur as climate change progresses and governments are pressed into action.

Monetary policies will need to reorient themselves to support solutions to long-run supply conditions as climate change develops; this will be a shift away from the management of short-run demand conditions. It is possible; central banks have done it before. Central banks may be directed, as they have been in the past, to provide credit to activities deemed to be of importance. The use of central bank digital currencies would be a potential new instrument to achieve social goals.

In all, we have arrived at another historical moment. The new guidance and ideas on how to proceed begin to emerge. Let us hope for better times and just outcomes for the planet and future generations.

References

Abella, Alex (2008). *Soldiers of Reason: The RAND Corporation and the Rise of the American Empire*. New York, NY: Mariner Books (Houghton Mifflin and Harcourt).

Australian Bureau of Statistics (ABS) (2022a). *ABS Business Indicators, March 2022*, released 31 May 2022. https://tinyurl.com/2vdbks8b.

ABS (2022b). Australian National Accounts: National Income, Expenditure and Product. Cat. no 5204.0, Table 6. https://tinyurl.com/4tn77frk.

ABS (2022c). *Australian National Accounts: Finance and Wealth*. Cat. no. 5232.0. https://tinyurl.com/3my2ahwm.

ABS (2022d). *Housing Occupancy and Costs, Australia, 2019–2020*. Cat. no. 4130.0. https://tinyurl.com/3uvwm45z.

Battellino, Ric (2007). Australia's experience with financial deregulation: RBA deputy governor address to China Australia Governance Program, 16 July, Melbourne. *RBA Bulletin*, Reserve Bank of Australia, August, 77–81.

Berger-Thomson, Laura, John Breusch and Louise Lilley (2018). *Australia's Experience with Economic Reform*. Treasury Working Paper. Canberra: Australian Government, https://tinyurl.com/mbebbnhu.

Doyal, Len, and Ian Gough (1991). *A Theory of Human Need*. London: Macmillan.

Eatwell, John (2019). "Cost of production" and the theory of the rate of profit. *Contributions to Political Economy*, 38: 1–11.

Eroglu, Osman, and Murat Picak (2011). Entrepreneurship, national culture and Turkey. *International Journal of Business and Social Science*, 2(16): 146–51.

Gough, Ian (2017). *Heat, Greed and Human Need: Climate Change, Capitalism and Sustainable Well-being*. Cheltenham, UK: Edward Elgar Press.

Greenwald, Bruce, and Joseph Stiglitz (2014). *Creating a Learning Society: A New Approach to Growth, Development and Social Progress*. New York, NY: Columbia University Press.

Greenwald, Bruce, and Joseph Stiglitz (2013). Industrial policies, the creation of a learning society, and economics development. In Joseph Stiglitz and Justin Lin, eds. *The Industrial Policy Revolution I: The Role of Government Beyond Ideology*, 43–71. Basingstoke, UK: Palgrave Macmillan.

Heilbroner, Robert (1999). *The Worldly Philosophers: The Lives, Times and Ideas of the Great Economic Thinkers*, 7th edn. New York, NY: Touchstone.

Heilbroner, Robert and William Milberg (1995). *The Crisis of Vision in Modern Economic Thought*. Cambridge, UK: Cambridge University Press.

Lin, Justin (2014). Industrial policy revisited: a new structural economics perspective. *China Economic Journal*, 7(3): 382–96.

Mason, Paul (2016). *PostCapitalism: A Guide to Our Future*. London: Penguin.

Mazzucato, Mariana (2013). *The Entrepreneurial State: Debunking Public vs. Private Sector Myths*. London and New York: Anthem Press.

Organization for Economic Co-operation and Development (OECD) (2022a). Consumer Price Indices (CPI), OECD.Stat database, https://stats.oecd.org/.

OECD (2022b). Short-term Labor Market Statistics. OECD.Stat database, https://stats.oecd.org/.

Palley, Thomas (2021). *Financialization Revisited: The Economics and Political Economy of the Vampire Squid Economy*. Working paper 2110, Post-Keynesian Economic Society, June. https://www.postkeynesian.net/working-papers/2110/.

Piketty, Thomas (2014). *Capital in the Twenty-First Century*. Cambridge, MA: Belknap Press.

Productivity Commission (2020). *PC Productivity Insights, Recent Productivity Trends*. Canberra: Australian Government.

Rafferty, Michael (1993). The state, industry, and money capital: The case of the Victorian Economic Development Corporation. *Journal of Australian Political Economy*, 32: 75–105.

Saez, Emmanuel, and Gabriel Zucman (2020). *The Triumph of Injustice: How the Rich Dodge Taxes and How To Make Them Pay*. New York: W.W. Norton.

Schroeder, Susan K. (2021). A Kaleckian wealth tax to support a Green New Deal. *Economic and Labour Relations Review*, 32(2): 190–208.

Schroeder, Susan K. (2015). *Public Credit Rating Agencies: Increasing Capital Investment and Lending Stability in Volatile Markets*. New York, NY: Palgrave Macmillan.

Statista n.d. Gini index in Australia, 2013–2018, World Bank Survey. Statista database accessed through the University of Sydney.
United Nations (n.d.). *The 17 Goals*. https://sdgs.un.org/goals.
Wolff, Richard (2012). *Democracy at Work: A Cure for Capitalism*. Chicago, IL: Haymarket Books.
Xue, Jin. (2014). Is Eco-Village/Urban Village the Future of a Degrowth Society? An Urban Planner's Perspective. *Ecological Economics*, vol 105: 130–138.

2 New Public Management and the hollowing out of the state

John Quiggin

The world, including Australia, is beset with crises for which governments seem to have no adequate response. The most striking example has been the mismanagement of the COVID-19 pandemic. The COVID-19 crisis revealed huge gaps in state capacity (that is, the set of tools available to government to achieve its policy goals – to avoid confusion with state governments, I'll call it "nation-state capacity") at the federal level in Australia. In discussion of this failure, it was widely concluded that "the Commonwealth doesn't do things". The lack of nation-state capacity was presented as being inherent in our federal structure. In reality, the breakdown of nation-state capacity is a relatively recent development, reversing the trends that prevailed for most of the century following Federation.

The failure of nation-state capacity in the COVID-19 pandemic

Suppose that a Commonwealth government such as the one we had 50 years ago was in place when the pandemic began. It is highly unlikely that the crisis management would have been left to the states. (Chapter 3 in this volume examines the Commonwealth contracting out of quarantine services and reduced nation-state capacity from a constitutional law perspective). In the 1970s, the Commonwealth still operated quarantine facilities and had its own department of works, capable of building new facilities or expanding old ones. In the previous decades it had managed both the repatriation of hundreds of thousands of troops from World War II and the provision of housing to support an immigration program on an unparalleled scale.

The farcical situation today where Australians stranded abroad had to pay horrendous amounts for a handful of available seats on commercial flights would scarcely have occurred if, as in the 1970s, the Commonwealth owned its own airline (and, for that matter, rail and shipping businesses).

On the medical front, the Commonwealth ran its own network of repatriation hospitals and owned the Commonwealth Serum Laboratories, now privatised as CSL. The question of vaccine passports would certainly not have been controversial, since the government required a range of vaccinations for travellers (indeed, the scar from smallpox inoculation, required before overseas travel, served as a kind of permanent passport).

Above all, the Commonwealth government had confidence in its own capacity, employing the best and brightest graduates of the universities that had expanded massively thanks to Commonwealth funding beginning in the 1960s. The Commonwealth government saw itself as both more competent and less subject to interest group pressure than the states. Under both conservative and Labor governments, the Commonwealth had steadily expanded the scope and scale of its operations, reducing the roles of both state governments and the business sector.

The Commonwealth government of those times would have been far better equipped to deal with a pandemic and would have seen itself as having the obvious responsibility to do so. We might therefore have expected a national response, including requirements for QANTAS to repatriate Australians from overseas, a rapid expansion of dedicated quarantine facilities and a consistent national policy on lockdowns and movement restrictions.

Of course, we saw nothing like this. At almost every stage in the process, the Commonwealth sought to avoid responsibility, and transfer it either to the states or to private parties ranging from management consultants to hotel operators. To the extent that it took action of its own, the Commonwealth relied almost entirely on the military (and, more opaquely, on the advice of the quasi-military Australian Border Force).

The above examples of how governance has changed did not happen through accident or incompetence. Rather, the reforms of the 1980s and 1990s, still viewed through a rosy haze of recollection by much of the political class, were designed to produce this outcome. The reforms reduced nation-state capacity in order to make room for market forces and to unleash the untapped dynamism of the business sector.

The broader context in which these reforms took place is most commonly referred to as "neoliberalism".[1] While this term is often used loosely as a pejorative, it has a reasonably well-defined meaning in global discourse.

Neoliberalism first developed in the years after 1945. Classical liberalism, which prescribed a minimal role for the state, had been discredited by the disaster of the Great Depression, the success of wartime planning and, even more, by the social democratic welfare state. Theorists such as Hayek attacked both socialism and social democracy and sought to develop an alternative more consistent with economic freedom. The resulting theory of neoliberalism attracted little attention at first. But, when social democracy failed to provide an adequate response to the economic crisis of the 1970s, neoliberalism came to the fore.

In terms of economic policy, neoliberalism is constrained by the need to compete with the achievements of social democracy. Hence, it is inconsistent with the kind of dogmatic libertarianism that would leave the poor to starvation or private charity, and would leave education to parents. Neoliberalism seeks to cut back the role of the state as much as possible while maintaining public guarantees of access to basic health, education and income security. The core of the neoliberal program has three elements:

- to remove the state altogether from "non-core" functions such as the provision of infrastructure services

1 In Australia, the term "economic rationalism" was more common in the late 20th century.

- to minimise the state role in core functions (health, education, income security) through contracting out, voucher schemes and so on
- to reject redistribution of income except insofar as it is implied by the provision of a basic "safety net".

The term is used somewhat differently in the United States, reflecting the different usage of the term "liberal" there. Broadly speaking, it is used primarily to describe followers of the "Third Way", most notably in the Clinton and Obama administrations. US-style or "soft" neoliberalism maintains the emphasis on markets, but is more favourable to policies of income redistribution and to a substantial public sector.

New Public Management

As far as pandemic policy is concerned, the most relevant aspect of the neoliberal reform process was "New Public Management" (also described, in more pejorative terms, as "managerialism"). While much of the reform agenda was drawn from the policies of the Thatcher government in the United Kingdom, New Public Management drew more heavily on those of the United States and shares the "soft neoliberal" approach dominant there.

The foundational text of this approach was *Reinventing Government: How the Entrepreneurial Spirit is Transforming the Public Sector* by consultants David Osborne and Ted Gaebler (1992). The book's chapter titles are a set of snappy slogans that encapsulate both the spirit of New Public Management and the reasons for its failure. The first of these is "Catalytic government: steering rather than rowing". The basic idea is that, rather than delivering services directly, governments should fund private (for-profit or non-profit) organisations to perform such tasks, while confining the public role to high-level policy management. It effectively foreshadowed the notion that the government doesn't do things, it pays other people to do them. Privatisation takes this a step further.

The logic of steering not rowing comes to the fore when policy advice is contracted out to consulting firms. By their nature, these firms are poorly placed to advise governments to reverse the process of which they are part and from which they directly benefit.

Osborne and Gaebler themselves pointed to a crucial problem here: "When governments separate policy management from service delivery, they often find that they have no real policy management capacity. Their commerce departments, welfare departments, housing authorities – all are driven by service delivery" (1992, 39–40).

The New Public Management solution is to bring in generic managerial skills, to formulate strategies that can then be specified in contractual forms. The reality, though, is that, for most public services, policy management cannot be separated from service delivery in the way Osborne and Gaebler imagined. Much of the knowledge required for policy management is tacit and shared by the professional and vocational employees who actually do the work.

When the same organisation designs and delivers policy, there is a natural feedback loop between design and delivery, leading to potential for learning by doing. Planners and designers increase their understanding of the policy by interacting with the delivery process. Contracting out breaks this loop.

The result is that, having adopted the "steering not rowing" approach, public sector organisations frequently find themselves incapable of steering. This task, in turn, is contracted out to consulting companies such as McKinsey & Company and Accenture, which provide policy advice that typically involves even more outsourcing.

A crucial cost of outsourcing policy advice is the loss of institutional memory. While the consulting companies have plenty of institutional memory, it concerns the process of consultancy, not the concerns of individual clients. Consultants need to develop the flexibility to move quickly from one contract, and one team, to another. Such flexibility inevitably involves an element of amnesia (see Morton 2021).

All of these failings were on full view during the pandemic. According to internal leaks from the government, designed to show Prime Minister Scott Morrison as a decisive leader hampered by incompetent underlings, the advice to go slow on ordering vaccines came from McKinsey consultants (BioPharma Dispatch, 2021). McKinsey rejected this version of events, but, as this exchange illustrates, one of the important motives for outsourcing policy advice is the potential for blame-shifting when things go wrong.

Reliance on external consultants for highly priced, but apparently useless, advice was a consistent theme during the pandemic. Often this was taken to absurd extremes: for example, *Guardian Australia* revealed that the federal health department, which has its own media and communications team, had been paying a public relations firm to take a copy of its daily document of vaccination data (which is already on the department's website), attach it to an email, and send it to media outlets. The government's 2019 decision to let an inquiry into its use of consultants lapse without issuing a report did nothing to allay concerns about the misuse of public funds, and the outsourcing bills have continued to balloon.

Further into Osborne and Gaebler's book there's "Customer-driven government: meeting the needs of the customer, not bureaucracy". The crucial feature here is the idea that services such as health and education are provided not to patients and students but to "customers". The implication is that the market relationship between sellers and buyers (or "customers") is the archetype for the provision of services, and that any other relationship is an imperfect substitute.

But if, as customers, people can assess the relative merits of alternative offerings of essential services, choosing the one that appears to meet their needs and switching to another if the first proves unsatisfactory, there is no obvious need for governments to get involved. This assumption, however, does not stand up to scrutiny. Patients and students are not customers. Patients want to get well and students want to learn, but they rely on the health and educational professionals to judge the best options for them.

The idea of students as customers found its fullest expression in the costly fiasco of the VET FEE-HELP scheme. The idea was that consumer choice would lead to the provision of the most appropriate educational offerings in the most efficient possible way. In practice, the "market" was dominated by education firms that offered up-front incentives like free iPads to students, but delivered nothing in the way of value. A review of VET FEE-HELP by the federal department that conceived and administered the program found:

> an essential challenge to the scheme has been dealing with uninformed, poorly informed or misinformed consumers who may not understand their options or the implication of these options. Critical to understanding this is the scale and breadth of unethical practices undertaken by some providers and brokers employed to attract and enrol students (Department of Education and Training 2016, 24; see also Australian National Audit Office 2016).

An echo of this thinking can be seen in the vaccination advice from the Australian Technical Advisory Group on Immunisation (ATAGI). All of the calculations put forward were from the perspective of an individual judging what would be best from them personally, with no apparent concern about the need to restrict the spread of the pandemic. Even the qualification that the advice would change in the presence of an outbreak referred only to the change in the individual balance of risks, with no weight at all on the public health need to control the outbreak.

Another chapter of *Reinventing Government* pushes the idea of "Market-oriented government". In the early 1990s, the collapse of the Soviet Union and the strong performance of the US economy produced a wave of market triumphalism. No one wanted to be seen to support bigger government, even in areas where existing market systems had clearly failed. As Osborne and Gaebler observed:

> In health care, the debate about universal health care is really a debate about how to restructure the marketplace. No-one recommends a British-style public health system in which government administers the entire system and doctors and nurses are public employees (1992, 283).

In the midst of the pandemic, no doubt, many would question this assertion. Despite immense challenges, the UK's National Health Service stood up to the challenge of the pandemic much better than the (massively more costly) US system.

In the Australian context, the most striking contrast is between the private market in aged-care services, administered by the

Commonwealth, and the public system in Victoria. During the difficult second-wave Melbourne COVID-19 outbreak, the inadequacy of the private aged-care system become horribly evident, as it accounted for the vast majority (82 per cent) of total COVID-related deaths. Understaffing and reliance on casuals working across multiple facilities were crucial factors. State-run facilities had only a handful of cases. While this outcome was partly due to geographical factors (the state-run facilities are more heavily concentrated in regional areas less exposed to the pandemic), the recent Royal Commission into aged care exposed systematic deficiencies, particularly in the for-profit sector.

Finally, and perhaps worst of all, has been Osborne and Gaebler's idea of "Injecting competition into service delivery". The logic of New Public Management, interpreting public services in terms of customers and markets, leads inexorably to a focus on competition. The desire for competition in the provision of public services has been a constant theme in Australia since the 1995 National Competition Policy reform. The results have ranged from mediocre to disastrous. The replacement of the public Technical and Further Education (TAFE) system by private operators under the VET FEE-HELP scheme was the most spectacular failure, but there have been many others. The National Disability Insurance Scheme (NDIS), for instance, a crucial initiative in expanding access to health services, has been pushed to the edge of failure by the insistence on framing policy in terms of a competitive market. (See Chapter 8, which examines in detail the causes of failure.)

A hollow state

After decades of hollowing out, the nation-state capacity of the Commonwealth has largely been reduced to two elements: financial and military. In more vernacular terms, all the government does is sign cheques (preferably oversized, novelty ones) and send in the military. In many cases, even these functions have been reduced to theatre.

Section 96 of the Constitution states that "the Parliament [of the Commonwealth] may grant financial assistance to any State on such terms and conditions as the Parliament thinks fit". At the high point of national ambition, under the Whitlam government, the Commonwealth's grants power was used as an instrument to bypass state governments seen as obstructing policy goals. It has gradually degenerated into the worst form of pork-barrel politics, enabling the handing out of carefully targeted bribes for projects that ought to be the realm of state or local government.

The first public, detailed exposure of this kind of malpractice was the original "sports rorts" affair, at the end of 1993, in which, according to the disarmingly candid evidence of then sports minister Ros Kelly, an office whiteboard was used to decide which marginal electorates should receive sports grants. Although Kelly took the rap for this process, resigning from the ministry and then parliament, it had been initiated by the apostle of "whatever it takes", Labor powerbroker Graham Richardson. The whole episode was repeated on a larger scale in 2020, with Nationals MP Bridget McKenzie in the Ros Kelly role, and Scott Morrison's office pulling the strings. Corruption of this kind is now open and routine.

Despite its regular abuse, the power to spend as much money as needed for public purposes turned out be essential in the pandemic. The one big policy success of the Commonwealth (admittedly under plenty of pressure from unions and employers) was the rapid introduction of the JobKeeper and JobSeeker schemes in March 2020. More often, stimulus measures and disaster-style payments have been made in an *ad hoc* manner, formulated and announced by the prime minister according to their immediate political requirements.

The misuse of the armed forces for exhibitionist display is another matter. In the absence of wartime operations, the Australian Defence Force (ADF) is commonly seen by government as a convenient source of workers who can be directed to just about any goal imaginable, particularly those involving ill-defined policing tasks. This kind of thinking has always been common, but until relatively recently it was successfully resisted by military leaders who wanted to keep personnel focused on their traditional tasks, with limited exceptions such as for disaster relief, where the armed forces have useful special equipment and skills.

But as the capacity of the civilian arms of the Commonwealth has been hollowed out, the appeal of calling in the military has increased. The Howard government's "Intervention" in the Northern Territory, which began in 2007 on the basis of dubious claims about the prevalence of sexual abuse in Indigenous communities, was an important step in this process. The fact that armed forces were ill equipped to solve complex social problems quickly became apparent, and the ADF personnel were withdrawn a year later.

The militarisation of border security took the process a step further. The political success of "stopping the boats" was used as the basis for creation of Australian Border Force, which has turned the civilian functions of customs and immigration into a quasi-military outfit.

Unsurprisingly, Border Force proved almost entirely useless in keeping us safe against COVID-19 when the outbreak first struck our shores, allowing thousands of returning travellers to cram airports with no possibility of social distancing. Once the international border was closed, Border Force acted as an unaccountable bureaucracy, making decisions that were essentially impossible to review. It is just about impossible to determine who was responsible for a situation where, after more than a year of the pandemic, tens of thousands of Australians were still stranded overseas. But clearly Border Force did not help to solve the problem.

The debate about the use of ADF personnel to provide security for hotel quarantine was central in the Victorian inquiry into Melbourne's second-wave outbreak in 2021. In retrospect, this debate turned out to be a waste of effort. As we saw, hotel quarantine did not work regardless of whether police, soldiers or private firms provide security.

In August 2020, the federal government banned Australians who normally lived overseas from returning to their overseas homes without special government permission. The amendment was justified on the grounds it "will reduce the pressure on Australia's quarantine capacity", presumably by discouraging expat Australians from visiting for any reason. Australia was alone in the world in banning its citizens, temporary visa holders, permanent residents and dual citizens from leaving the country – simply because it had not built adequate quarantine facilities.

The reliance on military uniforms as props continued with Prime Minister Morrison eagerly offering to send troops to south-western Sydney to help control the outbreak that began in June 2020. Given the small numbers involved (300 ADF soldiers compared to thousands of police deployed, and thousands more State Emergency Service and other workers who could be called upon), and the fact that the work mostly involved doorknocking to check on lockdown compliance, this exercise can only be understood as a piece of symbolism (or, less politely, street theatre).

The instinct to hide behind army uniforms, most notably that of Lieutenant General John Frewen, nominal head of the national vaccine rollout, reflected not just an unwelcome politicisation of the military but a lack of nation-state capacity. Sending in the troops, whether or not they serve any purpose, is the one way remaining for the Commonwealth government to show that it is doing something. And although soldiers have none of the enforcement powers available to state police, or even health officers, their deployment makes the government look tough. But in reality, the troops have no more authority in such operations than would ordinary civilians dressed in camouflage gear.

New Public Management and the federation

The destructive impact of New Public Management has been felt throughout the developed world. In Australia, it has been much more evident at the national than at the state level. The nation-state capacity of the Commonwealth government is a shadow of what it was in the mid-20th century. By contrast, the states have maintained their core services, such as health and education, and have, if anything, upgraded their policy capacities.

What explains this outcome? The Australian federal system has long been characterised by vertical fiscal imbalance. The Commonwealth raises most of our tax revenue through income taxes and the goods and services tax (GST). Some of this is returned to households through pensions and benefits. But the majority of actual expenditure on service provision is undertaken by state governments, largely financed by transfers from the Commonwealth.

The GST was supposed to "belong" to the states, thereby fixing this problem, but this has proved to be nothing but accounting cosmetics. Federal Treasurers, including Scott Morrison, have regularly threatened to change GST allocations to keep state governments in line on their tax policies, and even on issues only tangentially related to tax, such as gas fracking proposals and bank levies.

For most of our history, the Commonwealth's control of revenue went hand in hand with an expansion in the scope and ambition of national government. But once government came to be seen as the problem rather than the solution, it was easier for the Commonwealth to shift tasks seen as peripheral back to the states, or hand them over to the private sector through privatisation and contracting. Given the focus of the political class on big-picture issues such as foreign policy and macro-economic management, the Commonwealth found relatively little difficulty in doing this.

By contrast, state governments have found it much more difficult to escape their responsibilities. Privatisation has proved politically toxic, bringing down a string of governments that have attempted or undertaken such deals. For a time, it seemed that public–private partnerships might represent a magic pudding, allowing governments to deliver schools, hospitals and other services at low cost and without taking on debt. But this hope proved illusory. Numerous deals of this kind failed, with hospitals, in particular, being returned to public operation in around half of all cases in Australia. Existing models, based on the now-abandoned private finance initiative in the United Kingdom, are widely seen as broken. As a result, whatever their inclinations, state governments have retained most of the core responsibilities they had before the advent of New Public Management.

Outlook for the future

The COVID-19 pandemic was just one of many recent difficult challenges facing Australia as a nation, including the pandemic's economic aftermath, climate change, the crisis of democracy in the United States, and the rise of a powerful authoritarian regime in China. A restoration of nation-state capacity is urgently needed. But our starting point is not promising.

The Liberal–National Party government that held office from 2013 to 2022 allowed nation-state capacity, already weakened by decades of managerialism, to atrophy even further. This was not initially evident, simply because the government had no real policy agenda beyond the gesture politics of the culture wars. A succession of attempts to produce a coherent policy on climate change went nowhere, as did the frequently restated goal of returning the Commonwealth budget to surplus.

Having approached the 2019 election with every expectation of defeat, the government started its unanticipated fourth term in office with hardly any policy agenda. The political commentariat largely endorsed this, focusing on the supposed electoral appeal of Prime Minister Morrison to "quiet Australians". It was not until the series of crises that began with the catastrophic bushfires of late 2019 and 2020 that the hollowness of the government became truly evident.

The change of government brought about by the 2022 election has, so far, produced only modest improvements. Shell-shocked by a narrow but unexpected defeat in 2019, Labor has tied its hands by ruling out all the revenue measures proposed at that election. In addition, Labor voted to support the massive tax cuts for high-income earners legislated in advance by the Coalition. These cuts were originally supposed to be financed by a decade of strong economic growth, but are being implemented at a time when the budget is already in deficit.

In the absence of the financial resources needed to enhance nation-state capacity, Labor can offer little more than improvements in processes, as far as the core business of government is concerned. Modest progress has been made in some areas, such as the processing of visa and citizenship applications. The government has announced plans to improve the capacity of the public service, and aims to reduce the use of external workers by 10 per cent over its first term in office.

There is more scope for action in relation to government business enterprises, which are off-budget in the sense that their borrowings are not included in measures of gross and net government debt. Labor's largest initiative in this respect is the Rewiring the Nation Corporation, which offers low-cost funding for investments in electricity transmission needed to complete the transition to carbon-free energy. So far state government enterprises have been the main recipients.

Concluding comments

The enthusiasm with which New Public Management was greeted in the 1990s has dissipated, as its failures have been recognised. But in the absence of a clear reassertion of the role of government, backed by investment in publicly provided services, inertia and the power of the vested interests created by the reform process will carry New Public Management into the future. It remains to be seen whether such a reassertion will be forthcoming.

Nature abhors a vacuum, it is said. So, as the national government has retreated, the states have stepped up their own activity, not just on the pandemic but also in areas such as energy and climate policy. This is better than nothing, but it forgoes many of the advantages that led our forebears to combine six fractious colonies into a federal nation 120 years ago. Perhaps some improved version of national cabinet will provide us with a way forward. Then again, perhaps not.

References

Australian National Audit Office (2016). *Administration of the VET FEE-HELP Scheme*. https://tinyurl.com/2afh8wd2.

BioPharma Dispatch (2021). *Exclusive: PM was forced to intervene on vaccine after months of inaction*, 27 July. https://tinyurl.com/4vawkyux.

Department of Education and Training (Commonwealth) (2016). *Redesigning VET FEE-HELP: Discussion Paper.* Canberra: Commonwealth of Australia. https://tinyurl.com/44dr66ky.

Morton, Rick (2021). How private management consultants took over the public service. *The Saturday Paper*, 9–15 October. https://tinyurl.com/42suepwb.

Osborne, David, and Ted Gaebler (1992). *Reinventing Government: How the Entrepreneurial Spirit is Transforming the Public Sector*. New York, NY: Addison-Wesley.

3
Outsourcing and neoliberal constitutionalism

Kristen Rundle

At a time when more than half the country has had the COVID-19 disease at least once, and some have been vaccinated against it five or six times, the conditions in which the 2020 Victorian COVID-19 Hotel Quarantine Inquiry played out might seem the stuff of distant memory. That we once went to extreme lengths to keep every shred of the novel coronavirus contained is almost surreal in the "Covid normal" era.

This chapter is not about public health policy in the COVID-19 era, nor about the now forgotten national policy of hotel quarantine. It is about what we learned from the quest to uncover who made the decision to contract out the frontline of Victoria's first hotel quarantine enforcement to private security guards, from whom that state's second wave of COVID-19 infections had seeded. The inquiry struck to investigate this and other questions yielded a range of helpful insights for managing a public health emergency. But on the puzzle of who had made the decision to outsource such an important and novel role, it could ultimately shed no light. There was no such decision to be found, nor anyone who could be said to have made it.

The aim of what follows is to explain what this puzzle taught us about the extent to which the entrenchment of outsourcing as a core governmental practice has upended the operation of Australia's constitutional systems. Using the failure of Victoria's first experiment with hotel quarantine as its case study, its purpose is to show why there is a pressing need to pay much more attention than has been the case so far to the interface between outsourcing and the principles of Westminster constitutionalism on which Australia's systems of government are built. Not everything to be learned on this point can be taken from what was revealed before the Victorian COVID-19 Hotel Quarantine Inquiry ("the inquiry") struck to investigate the causes of that failure. Still, the attention given by that inquiry to the interface between outsourcing and the constitutional commitments to which government action in this country is meant to be answerable offered critical insights for the overarching conversation about the appropriateness of outsourcing that we are largely yet to have.

Outsourcing: the basics

Observers of government over the past three decades will be familiar with the basics of outsourcing, or contracting out, as a particular neoliberal governmental technique. Outsourcing uses the legal device of contract to separate the delivery of a government function "out" from the public sector for performance by private sector providers. At the heart of the practice is the assumption that government functions can be translated into "services" capable of forming the subject of contractual arrangements between government entities and private sector providers. While the outsourcing contract is in place, the role of the government party is typically limited to contract management and monitoring. Direct control over the performance of the activity is relinquished.

Outsourcing has become the go-to tool for the performance of government functions across all Australian jurisdictions. In this country at least, functions thought suitable for discharge through this technique have ranged from garbage collection to detention services. An outsourcing arrangement may attach to a particular government function in full or in part: an example of full provision is the Commonwealth government's outsourcing of immigration detention services. In all instances, the practice is founded on the assumption that the functions and responsibilities of government can be performed by anyone with the training skills necessary to perform them.

Neoclassical economic arguments have been central to the justification of outsourcing as a more efficient means of delivering quality public services through the creation of market conditions in which public and private providers of services can compete. The primary critique of outsourcing so far has come from opponents of neoclassical economics who have questioned the assumptions underpinning and justifications for the practice as it has manifested in particular settings of governmental activity. The "transaction cost critique" has been especially well developed in this context, questioning the reframing of government functions as "commodities" and the assumptions made about the conditions in which efficient outsourcing occurs (Toner 2014). Among the arguments levelled at outsourcing by proponents of the transaction cost critique is that outsourcing contracts are inherently "incomplete contracts" due to the difficulty or impossibility of achieving a precise contractual specification for the delivery of at least some governmental "commodities" or "services" (Toner 2014; Holden 2020).

By contrast, the critique of outsourcing by legal scholars remains a work in progress. From the perspective of the private law of contract, outsourcing is just another commercial contract practice among others, though some at least have tried to point out the relevant sites of tension (Seddon 2018). In keeping with the inherited premises of English contract law, Australian legal practice as it stands does not subscribe to the idea that there is anything distinct, in terms of the application of a different type of contract law, about contracts in which government is a party. The ordinary private law of contract applies.

The critique of outsourcing from a public law perspective specifically similarly remains in development and orients primarily to concerns about the implications of outsourcing for the transparency and accountability of government action generally (Aronson 1997; Davies 2001, 2008; Freedland 2003; Vincent-Jones 2006; Freeman and Minow 2009; Cane 2016; McLean 2016). The exemption of outsourced service providers from freedom of information requests on grounds of "commercial in confidence" is frequently cited by public law commentators as an example of how the protection of contractual rights within outsourcing arrangements has been permitted to trump statutory rights held by the public. But little has been said so far about why outsourcing might be specifically problematic for the performance of complex or novel statutory functions. Sharing similar concerns as the transaction cost critique in its emphasis on the complexity of the "commodities" or "services" that are contracted for in an outsourcing arrangement, the concern here is directed to the often difficult to anticipate and interconnected responsibilities that attach to the performance of public functions specifically.

The nub of that concern is that the whole might simply be larger than the sum of its parts (Rundle 2020, 2021). Indeed, justifications for outsourcing appear to be premised on the idea that there is no such "whole" in the first place. The belief that everything can be broken down and re-described as a service capable of being provided by the private sector presumes not only that this is conceptually and descriptively possible, but that the work of government and the work of the private sector is essentially the same. There is no conceptual or operational accommodation within the ideology of outsourcing for the idea that public functions are distinctive. Everything instead comes down to the task of specifying the service with sufficient precision that it can form the subject matter of a contract. The question of whether something important might be lost in translation – especially in relation to functions reposed and delineated by statute – is not considered (Rundle 2021).

Victoria's (first) hotel quarantine program

The policy of hotel quarantine emerged from a consensus decision by Australia's newly formed National Cabinet in late March 2020 that this was how we would contain the threat of the novel coronavirus at the point of its entry into Australia. The burden of implementing this policy fell most heavily on New South Wales and Victoria as the two states that receive the highest number of international passenger arrivals. The idea was that each state would use existing statutory powers from relevant public health legislation to detain such persons in designated hotels under administrative orders. In Victoria's case, this was authorised by direction and detention notices issued under the *Public Health and Wellbeing Act 2008* (" the Act") by the Chief Health Officer. (Amendments to the Act legislated in December 2021 have since vested "pandemic powers" of this kind in the Premier or the Minister for Health, rather than in the Chief Health Officer as applied during the peak of the COVID-19 pandemic in 2020–21.)

The window available for designing and launching the hotel quarantine program was extremely tight: the system needed to be up and running within a matter of days. Two Victorian government departments were involved in launching the operation – the Department of Health and the Department of Jobs, Precincts and Regions – which was also to operate within an emergency management structure that had been triggered.

To understand how it came to pass that the frontline of this operation was assigned to private security contractors, it is necessary to appreciate what quarantine is: namely, a form of civil imprisonment in service of the control of an infectious disease. A detention operation of this kind requires enforcement, which those charged with designing and instituting the Victorian hotel quarantine program interpreted as requiring "security services". From there, it seems, the question to be answered was who should perform this "security services" role: public sector officers (Victoria Police) or private sector providers. The choice to be made between the two, to the extent that it was ever entertained, appears to have come down to a calculation of what would be the most efficient use of police resources in the circumstances. Those designing the program also decided that there would be no Victoria Police presence at the quarantine hotels, unless requested.

The task of entering into the contracts for the provision of security services was assigned to the Department of Jobs, Precincts and Regions. The kind of security service specified in the contracts was an "observe and report" brief directed to ensuring that those detained remained in their rooms. Contracts were made with several security services providers who in accordance with the prevailing business model in the industry subcontracted and sub-subcontracted the performance of the service to others. Again in accordance with the industry's business model, those ultimately employed were drawn from a largely casualised workforce, and many were recruited through an informal call-out communicated through the messenger service WhatsApp. All were asked to complete a short online training course in infection control, though evidence to the inquiry suggested that this requirement was not met in all cases.

An "authorised officer" (an existing Victorian public service employee) appointed under the Act was also present at each hotel to help coordinate the operation by managing requests for exemption from quarantine and other administrative matters. The authorised officer did not however possess any coercive powers. This meant that the system accordingly was one in which the task of ensuring that those detained did not leave their rooms landed on the subcontracted or sub-subcontracted security guards stationed in the corridors of the quarantine hotels.

As a matter of fact and law, none of the security guards contracted to perform this function could actually "ensure" that detainees remained in their rooms. The contracts with head contractors made clear that the security guards had no legal authority to physically restrain, or to touch, any detainee. Such would have required additional statutory authorisation that was not sought in this instance. The guards' actions were therefore limited to the use of verbal de-escalation techniques in which, as holders of security licences under relevant Victorian legislation, it was assumed they were trained.

It is important to grasp what this meant in practice. If a detainee sought to leave their room without permission, and verbal de-escalation techniques deployed by the security guard proved ineffective, that guard would need to escalate the matter to their shift supervisor whose mobile phone number was provided at the beginning of each shift. This shift supervisor might in turn seek the advice of the onsite departmental authorised officer, or further escalate the matter directly to Victoria Police who were to be contacted in the ordinary way: by phoning 000.

It was therefore incorrect to say, as many media reports did at the time, that private security contractors were "running" Victoria's hotel quarantine operation. They had in fact been contracted to perform no more than an "observe and report" security service with backup from Victoria Police on request. But, for those detained in the hotel rooms, it was impossible to tell the difference. Positioned in the corridors of the hotels, the contracted security guards stood, literally, at the frontline of the operation. They were the human face of quarantine in both its detention and infection control aspects, despite having no authority over those detained and holding no expertise in infection control beyond the short online course that some did not complete.

Evidence before the inquiry suggested the contractors found these arrangements complex and confusing. Being early in the COVID-19 pandemic experience, health advice was changing regularly and ensuring clear and effective communication about this aspect of the role with a large and diffusely organised workforce was difficult. The tasks that head contractors and subcontractors were asked to perform under the "observe and report" brief soon also evolved to include a range of other activities such as taking detainees on fresh-air breaks and searching the bags of incoming guests. While evidence from the head contractors indicated that they did their best to adapt to an unfolding situation, maintaining clarity about what, precisely, was the service for which they had been contracted was an ongoing problem (COVID-19 Hotel Quarantine Inquiry 2020, Transcript, Head contractors' evidence, 3 September 2020).

Outsourcing meets Westminster constitutionalism

Such was the landscape from which Victoria's disastrous (by standards then holding) "second wave" of COVID-19 infections seeded into a wholly unvaccinated population, precipitating a four-month lockdown and costing Victorian taxpayers tens of millions of dollars. In July 2020 Premier Daniel Andrews struck a judicial inquiry to get to the bottom of what had gone wrong. Why had Victoria's attempt to contain the spread of the novel coronavirus through the mechanism of hotel quarantine crashed so badly while the same endeavour in other states seemed to have gone relatively smoothly?

It was in pursuit of insight into this question that the inquiry's chair, retired judge Jennifer Coate AO, sought evidence about who had made the decision to contract-out the frontline of hotel quarantine enforcement to private security contractors. This straightforward question proved to be anything but. To understand why, it is necessary to understand how things are meant to work in a constitutional system built upon the Westminster principles of responsible government.

In a Westminster constitutional system, a government is answerable to the parliament, and through the parliament to us, the electors. In this model a government holds office only if parliament is prepared to support it. At the centre of this arrangement is the doctrine of ministerial responsibility. In the event of government failure in an area within their assigned portfolio, ministers of government are expected to demonstrate their responsibility to parliament through a range of actions from pledging to undertake a positive program of reform through to resigning or being dismissed from office. The idea behind this accountability mechanism is that the authority entrusted to a government must be used in the ways that parliament intended or can accept.

Within this set of interlocking constitutional conventions, it is uncontroversial that governments remain legally, morally and politically responsible for the performance of their functions irrespective of whether this is done by public officers or by private contractors. That this remains the operating assumption even if such functions are outsourced explains why so much of the inquiry's time was spent attempting to ascertain who made the decision to assign frontline responsibility for maintaining the quarantine system to private security providers. This effort soon became a spectacle in itself. Witness after witness, from ministers to emergency services commissioners to senior police officers to departmental secretaries to Premier Daniel Andrews himself, denied any association with the decision. This was, by any measure, bewildering. But by all indications, no one was hiding anything. They were just each unable to answer the question.

Coate's description in her Final Report of the decision to engage private security contractors as "an orphan" was an apt use of metaphor (COVID-19 Hotel Quarantine Inquiry 2020, Final Report, 20). As she elaborated the point, a highly consequential decision about how to design and operate Victoria's first hotel quarantine program had been made "without proper analysis or even a clear articulation that it was being made at all", with no "contemporaneous rationale" and "with no person or department claiming responsibility for having made it" (COVID-19 Hotel Quarantine Inquiry 2020, Final Report, 20, 158, 20). All of this, Coate emphasised, was "at odds with any normal application of the principles of the Westminster system of responsible government" (COVID-19 Hotel Quarantine Inquiry 2020, Final Report, 20).

Unravelling the riddles

It is not every day that a quest to find out who made a particular decision must arrive at the unsettling conclusion that there was neither a "who" nor a "decision" to be found. Like all riddles, this conclusion requires some unravelling.

We need to begin by reflecting further on how outsourcing works as a particular kind of government practice. To its private sector party, an outsourcing contract is just a contract in the sense that it is a commercial medium of exchange through which a specified service is provided in return for payment. The parameters of that service and the performance obligations attaching to it are defined by the terms of the contract. The position of the government party, by contrast, is very different. Though bound by the same obligations and constraints as the private party when participating in the contractual relationship, for the government party these private law responsibilities coexist with prior legal and political responsibilities derived from the government party's status as an entity of government. These include the publicly mandated responsibility for discharging the relevant government function to which the proposed outsourcing arrangement will attach. Any such responsibilities must in turn be discharged in accordance with the overarching demands of the constitutional system with which all practices of government in this country are meant to be compatible, and to which they are also meant to be answerable.

Evidence given to the inquiry by numerous senior government officials suggested that the notion that outsourcing could interrupt or impair the carriage of these responsibilities had never occurred to anyone. Once it was settled that the "security" aspect of hotel quarantine would be performed by private contractors, the task of creating those contracts was assigned to an agency (the Department of Jobs, Precincts and Regions) otherwise unconnected to the agency that supported the statutory officers who held the legal powers of quarantine (the Department of Health and Human Services).

This immediately produced an unacknowledged problem for the operation of the basic precepts of Victoria's Westminster constitutional system. Separating the business of contract creation from the agency responsible for the discharge of the quarantine function ensured that the frontline of hotel quarantine enforcement could only ever be tenuously tethered to the possibility of ministerial responsibility. A different minister presided over the department that entered into the contracts from the minister who presided over the department responsible for the administration of the Act through which the authority to detain those in the hotel quarantine hotels derived (COVID-19 Hotel Quarantine Inquiry 2020, Final Report, 20, 202). Those who negotiated and supervised the contracts therefore did so "without any clear understanding of the role of security in the broader Hotel Quarantine Program" and with "no experience in security issues or infection prevention and control" (COVID-19 Hotel Quarantine Inquiry 2020, Final Report, 20). Coate went on in her Final Report to comment (under the heading "Contract development and management") that "DHHS was the appropriate body to manage those contracts and should have done so as control agency with overall responsibility for the Hotel Quarantine Program" (COVID-19 Hotel Quarantine Inquiry 2020, Final Report, 22). The reference to "control agency" relates to the emergency management framework that overlaid the departmental framework: another piece of the institutional design puzzle that there is not space to address here.

While the remedy to this part of the picture would be to insist that the business of contracting-out take place within the same portfolio agency that is responsible for a particular government function, even here there are other features of outsourcing to overcome before the channels of political responsibility for government action can operate coherently. Motivated by a concern to avoid conflicts of interest, it is standard practice for a departmental "wall" to go up between the minister politically responsible for a particular government function and any process of contract creation associated with it. Speaking to this norm, the Minister for Jobs, Precincts and Regions, Martin Pakula, told the inquiry that it was not typical – indeed it was rare – for him to be aware of contracts made by his department (COVID-19 Hotel Quarantine Inquiry 2020, Transcript, Pakula evidence, 23 September 2020). Pakula did not seem concerned when giving this evidence because this was and is simply how things work, even if the effect is to render any idea of ministerial responsibility for outsourcing theoretical at best. Indeed, the one minister who did resign in response to the failure of the first hotel quarantine program – the Minister for Health, Jenny Mikakos – was at none of the meetings in which the design of the hotel quarantine program was settled.

These are just some of the features of the incoherent political accountability landscape that surrounded Victoria's first experiment with hotel quarantine. Yet another worrying aspect was the consistency of evidence across all of the high-ranking political and government officials who appeared before the inquiry that confirmed that no one had thought to question the suitability of outsourcing such a novel and high-stakes operation, at least not at the time. Minister Mikakos told the inquiry that she had no cause to turn her mind to the question of precisely who was stationed outside the doors of those detained under the quarantine orders (COVID-19 Hotel Quarantine Inquiry 2020, Transcript, Mikakos evidence, 24 September 2020); Emergency Services Commissioner Andrew Crisp said he had thought that "well trained and well supervised private security in this type of role would have been efficient and effective" (COVID-19 Hotel Quarantine Inquiry 2020, Transcript, Crisp evidence, 15 September 2020); while the Minister for Police Lisa Neville similarly explained that she had seen some combination of police and private security work well at major events like the AFL Grand Final (COVID-19 Hotel Quarantine Inquiry 2020, Transcript, Neville evidence, 23 September 2020).

All of this evidence was given in good faith – indeed, all government witnesses presented as committed, competent and more than willing to assist the efforts of the inquiry. Yet ultimately no one managed to get to the nub of the problem in the kind of clear terms needed to understand what exactly had gone on and why its implications were so serious. No one made the decision to contract out the frontline of hotel quarantine enforcement because there was not anything one could call a "decision" to do so at all. Outsourcing had (and has) become so standard within the everyday practice of government in Victoria that no one thought to question its application in this novel circumstance. It was business as usual, because this is business as usual. And no one had thought about what this meant for the discharge of the dual infection control and detention aspects of the quarantine function, or for the principles of Westminster responsible government around which all of Australia's constitutional systems are built (Rundle 2021).

Framing the conversation we have never really had

As noted earlier, the starting assumption from which the operation of Victoria's first hotel quarantine program was born was that the functions of government can be performed by anyone with the training and skills necessary to perform them. What unfolded before the inquiry made more than clear that it is well past time to interrogate this assumption more critically, and to do so with an eye on the constitutional ground rules within which all government action in this country is meant to occur.

The terms of reference against which Jennifer Coate conducted her inquiry did not call for suggestions about how to reform the conduct of government in Victoria *per se*, or the place of outsourcing within it. The most she could credibly do within the confines of her role is caught in her recommendation 76 that the Victorian Public Sector Commissioner examine "the lines of accountability and responsibility as between departmental heads and ministers and give guidance across the public service as to the obligations, both in law and in practice, on heads of department and senior public office holders" (COVID-19 Hotel Quarantine Inquiry 2020, Final Report, 47, 313).

It is accordingly up to the rest of us to determine the content of the conversation about outsourcing that we need to have from here. Some of the worries to be dealt with are obvious: the prescription that the contracting aspect of a proposed outsourcing arrangement should take place within (or at the very least in close consultation with) the portfolio of government responsible for the discharge of the function in question is an example. Other worries are more subtle, requiring changes in directions of thought and the order of questions asked. But all can profit in the first instance from asking in what circumstances outsourcing might be appropriate or inappropriate, and why.

The absence of this conversation of principle has bred chaos and confusion alike. In the Victorian hotel quarantine example, few concessions were ever made on this question of appropriateness, beyond some observations made with the benefit of hindsight that the highly diffuse and casualised workforce characteristic of private security service provision was "the wrong cohort" for this kind of endeavour (COVID-19 Hotel Quarantine Inquiry 2020, Transcript, Sutton evidence, 16 September 2020). Evidence before the inquiry did reveal that not everyone at close range at the inception of the hotel quarantine program had considered outsourcing the frontline of enforcement to be a sensible strategy. One witness from the Department of Jobs, Precincts and Regions, which had been assigned responsibility for entering into the contracts, attested that she had advanced the view that Victoria Police should maintain a 24/7 presence at the hotels because it was a significant undertaking to detain people in this way and the risks were unclear (COVID-19 Hotel Quarantine Inquiry 2020, Transcript, Febey evidence, 27 August 2020).[1] Evidently, interjections of this kind were either overridden or simply not taken seriously at the time.

This goes to show why it is so crucial to develop a framework of principle in which objections and speculations of this kind might find stronger articulation and support. The basic building blocks of such a framework are not hard to conjure and could include questions such as the following: What is the government function to be performed? Is it novel? What kinds of public interest considerations might it engage? To what extent can it be broken down into specified tasks so as to form the subject matter of an outsourcing contract? What gaps or contingencies might be encountered if this is done? What is the character of the workforce that should be assigned? What lines of vision will be required? What is the rationale for engaging private contractors rather than public sector personnel?

A hunger for answers to questions of this kind – and that such questions be asked at all – might go some way towards explaining the immense level of public interest in the ultimately futile "whodunnit" exercise that occupied so much of the inquiry's time. True, there was a need to find out who had made the decision to outsource the frontline of Victoria's first hotel quarantine operation because options for

---

1 See further paragraphs 56 and 57 of Exhibit HQI0032a_P: https://www.quarantineinquiry.vic.gov.au/exhibits.

assigning responsibility depended on it. But answering this question was never, at least on its own, going to explain *why* outsourcing was inappropriate in this instance. That question required a different conversation, yet one got the sense that many held the expectation that finding out who had made the decision would simultaneously reveal what was wrong about it.

That there should be an appetite for critical appraisal of the extent to which we should be allowing, accepting or endorsing outsourcing in a particular sector of governmental activity is understandable in a country in which such critical appraisal has, so far, been vanishingly rare. Most disturbingly given the scale of the reach of outsourcing across all kinds of government functions, those who are responsible for doing so on our behalf – our parliamentarians – have done disturbingly little to contest the appropriateness of outsourcing in different contexts. This is precisely why public inquiries like that examined here are so important. They lift the veil to offer rare insight into the governmental logics prevailing at a particular historical moment, and what can go wrong within them.

Yet even here it is important to recognise that the efforts of public inquiries can only take us so far if not guided by a framework of principle capable of disrupting the patterns of thought and practice that have entrenched outsourcing as the paradigm tool of government in an era committed to the prescriptions of neoliberalism. Rather than call for a head-on engagement with whether the practice itself is appropriate, in instances where a public inquiry does illuminate how outsourcing contributed to the relevant governmental or regulatory failure under examination, recommendations for reform tend primarily to appeal to standards internal to the practice itself, such as calling for better service specification or improved monitoring arrangements. An example can be found in the recommendations of the 2005 Report on the Inquiry into the Circumstances of the Immigration Detention of Cornelia Rau. Though highly critical of the relevant outsourcing arrangement and its contribution to the alarming instance of government failure with which that inquiry was dealing, all recommendations pertaining to this aspect of the picture remained embedded within a framework of outsourced service delivery (see especially section 7.5, "Contracting and government policy outcomes" and recommendations 7.5, 7.6 and 7.7, Commonwealth of Australia 2005, 176–82).

Recommendations of this kind are of course still valuable for their effort to diagnose a problem and suggest ways to respond to it. Nonetheless, it is important to recognise that recommendations made in this spirit are, in effect, a call to perfect rather than to challenge outsourcing as a practice. Absent any appeal to external standards beyond those constitutive to the practice itself – standards, for example, drawn from the foundational demands of the constitutional system with which all government action is meant to be consistent and to which it is meant to be answerable – the animating logics of neoliberal government escape unscathed. And continue to be reproduced.

If this last thought is sobering, it is worth asking whether we are telling the tale to be told here in a way that makes these logics and their implications sufficiently clear. Analyses of the hotel quarantine example, including the present one, primarily tell a derogation story. Our Westminster system of constitutional government requires certain things of its actors, and these requirements were not met. Yet the trouble with a derogation story is that it tells us more about what is not happening than about what is. What, therefore, might we learn if we instead describe what is being built to replace that which most of us thought still held, and in whose service we head regularly and compulsorily to the ballot box in an effort to reproduce and maintain?

In this alternate story – which we might call neoliberal constitutionalism – the question of who made the decision to outsource the frontline of hotel quarantine enforcement would not need asking because it would no longer be a relevant question to ask. Alongside a relentless pull towards executive centralism, a corresponding view of representative democratic institutions and their legislative outputs as nothing more than a rubber stamp on predetermined executive action, a refusal of the notion that public authority is distinctive, and an unshakeable faith in contract as the governing legal form of political order, in this alternate story the commitments of principle that underscored the quest of the Victorian COVID-19 Hotel Quarantine Inquiry to answer the question of who made the decision to outsource the frontline of hotel quarantine enforcement to private security operators would be irrelevant. For some of us at least, it is a frightening spectre. Yet still more frightening is the thought that we may already have arrived there – without ever having had a say about whether this is the kind of political order to which we, as a polity, are willing to sign up.

Conclusion

The collapse of Victoria's first experiment with hotel quarantine will be remembered above all for the months of lockdown that it precipitated and for the scores of COVID-19 infections and deaths that followed, especially in the aged-care sector. But, and perhaps unexpectedly, the inquiry struck to investigate that collapse also showed how the foundational principles of Australia's constitutional systems can be rendered dysfunctional, by design, in service of the ascendance and consolidation of a particular neoliberal governmental technique. The thought that this critically important offering of the Victorian COVID-19 Hotel Quarantine Inquiry might get filed away in the COVID-19 archives is tragic. Yet residing as it did within an exceptional epoch of national collective life, it seems unlikely that this moment in the history of Australia's handling of the pandemic will be remembered for how it provoked us to notice the frameworks of everyday thought and practice within which contemporary public policy failures occur and continue to be reproduced.

Whether what has been examined here is to be described as a "public policy failure" is itself an instructive question. The latter tends more typically to be associated with matters of substance than with matters of form, or technique. Yet both the embrace of neoliberalism as the animating political philosophy of contemporary Australian statecraft and the consolidation of its institutional design prescriptions as the go-to tools for doing the work of government *are* matters of public policy. They frame how governments govern in our name, as well as how our individual relationships with government are structured.

The time for questioning Australia's versions of the neoliberal project at their inception has long past, if indeed such can be pinned down to a moment at all. A relentless and all-consuming creep might be a better description. Whether those awake at the time could see – or should have seen – that the foundational demands of our constitutional systems would lie in the balance is a question on which we can only speculate. But we are in a different place now, one in which we are entitled to replace speculation with evidence. And the evidence is telling us that a whole lot of the picture is not working as it is meant to work, and precious little is being done about it.

If we imagined our way into neoliberal constitutionalism, we can imagine our way out of it. Reminding those who need reminding that we have a set of constitutional ground rules that are and were never up for grabs is a good place to start. Pointing out that there is nothing neutral about the choice of legal and institutional forms through which government does its work is equally important. Because until these wisdoms have been (re)internalised, we should only expect to see more from neoliberal constitutionalism and its debasements of what we thought we had.

References

Aronson, Mark (1997). A public lawyer's responses to privatisation and outsourcing. In Michael Taggart, ed. *The Province of Administrative Law*, 40–70. London: Hart Publishing.

Cane, Peter (2016). *Controlling Administrative Power: An Historical Comparison*. Cambridge, UK: Cambridge University Press.

Commonwealth of Australia (2005). Inquiry into the Circumstances of the Immigration Detention of Cornelia Rau. https://www.homeaffairs.gov.au/reports-and-pubs/files/palmer-report.pdf.

COVID-19 Hotel Quarantine Inquiry (2020). *Transcripts*. https://tinyurl.com/y4jsbfzu.

COVID-19 Hotel Quarantine Inquiry (2020). *Final Report*. Melbourne: Victorian Government Printer. https://tinyurl.com/ycxysvkx.

Davies, Anne C.L. (2001). *Accountability – A Public Law Analysis of Government by Contract*. Oxford, UK: Oxford University Press.

Davies, Anne C.L. (2008). *The Public Law of Government Contracts*. Oxford, UK: Oxford University Press.

Freedland, Mark (2003). Government by contract re-examined – some functional issues. In Carol Harlow, Paul P. Craig and Richard Rawlings, eds. *Law and Administration in Europe: Essays in Honour of Carol Harlow*. Oxford, UK: Oxford University Press.

Freeman, Jody, and Martha Minow (2009). *Government by Contract: Outsourcing and American Democracy*. Cambridge, MA: Harvard University Press.

Holden, Richard (2020). Vital signs: Victoria's privatised quarantine arrangements were destined to fail. *The Conversation*, 24 July. https://tinyurl.com/2wb75ksp.

McLean, Janet (2016). The unwritten Constitution and its enemies. *International Journal of Constitutional Law* 14(1): 119–36.

Rundle, Kristen (2020). *Reassessing Contracting-out: Lessons from the Victorian Hotel Quarantine Inquiry*. Melbourne School of Government *Governing During Crises* Policy Brief no. 7, 20 September.

Rundle, Kristen (2021). Orphaned responsibility: contracting out the duties of government. *Griffith Review* 73: 81–92.

Seddon, Nicholas (2018). *Government Contracts: State, Federal and Local*. Sydney: Federation Press.

Toner, Philip (2014). Contracting out publicly funded vocational education: A transaction cost critique. *Economic and Labour Relations Review* 25(2): 222–39.

Vincent-Jones, Peter (2006). *The New Public Contracting: Regulation, Responsiveness, Relationality*. Oxford, UK: Oxford University Press.

Part II

Case studies: Neoliberal public policy

4

The big country that can't

Evan Jones

This chapter is devoted to the relatively low rank and status of the manufacturing sector in Australia and the political and ideological culture that has produced that situation. I have refrained from dealing with the armaments domain. Armaments production for national "defence" is a necessary evil. But armaments production inevitably comes with odious baggage, especially when facilities are privately owned. A lobby is created, exports are pushed with governmental support, employment-generating pressure is brought to bear (witness South Australia), all magnified with Australian politics subordinate to US imperatives (notably the AUKUS project) against manufactured enemies. Sadly, pressure to foster armaments production is a ready default strategy for the manufacturing sector when an industry policy for manufacturing in general is rendered ideologically impossible.

Australian manufacturing employment has experienced relative long-term decline – from 1,096,200 in November 1984 (new series) to 948,300 in August 2023, respectively 16.7 per cent and 6.8 per cent of the labour force (ABS 2023a, Table 4). However, the subcontracting of ancillary activities, involving a reclassification of such as services, implies an (unknowable) overstatement of employment decline. Atypically, absolute numbers increased during 2023. The long-term decline is common to Western countries, but manufacturing in Australia now has the smallest share of employment of all OECD members. It would have been even lower without the partial success of industry policies pursued against the grain.

Consultant economist Jim Stanford (2020) has laid out the parlous present status of manufacturing in the Australian economy. Stanford highlighted the peculiar importance of manufacturing and the costs of its continuing policy marginalisation – the centrality of manufacturing for technology innovation and diffusion, for employment across all states and regions, and for offsetting the significant and growing trade gap of elaborately transformed manufactures. Stanford noted that, as a consequence of bipartisan ignoring of the core role of manufacturing, the Harvard indicator of country "economic complexity", as of 2017, has Australia in 93rd place.

Australia is in the top 10 countries in terms of gross domestic product (GDP) per capita. Yet under the bonnet it looks more like a banana republic, with economic priorities determined in default mode. Albeit Australia is not yet a republic, highlighting that a comparable courage is lacking in both the political and economic spheres.

The unsatisfactory character of the Australian economy

What is the essence of Australia's economic structure? Regarding international trade, exports are dominated by unprocessed mineral and fuel extraction. In 2021–22, primary products constituted 84 per cent of merchandise exports (73 per cent of which were unprocessed) (Department of Foreign Affairs and Trade 2023). Minerals and fuels accounted for $422.6 billion (up dramatically in the last several years), 71 per cent of merchandise exports. By contrast, manufactures constituted 74 per cent of merchandise imports (90 per cent of which were elaborately transformed manufactures).

Mining exports have been sustained by ill-considered mining concessions (in valuable farming land and environmentally sensitive areas), gross subsidies to the sector (compare Peel et al. 2014), low royalty payments and minimal corporate tax payments. Behind these giveaways has been an omnipresent mining lobby embodied in well-funded think tanks, ministerial staffing, revolving door employment and hefty political party donations.

The power of the mining sector in Australia is reflected in the Howard government spying on impoverished Timor Leste for the benefit of Woodside Petroleum. Add Rio Tinto's wilful destruction of the 46,000 year-old Indigenous sacred site in the Pilbara's Juukan Gorge in May 2020.

Economists defend this mining sector dependence as conforming to a country's "comparative advantage". Strange then that a country's comparative advantage requires so many public resources to sustain it. These pampered mining exports have adverse impacts elsewhere. They drive up the Australian dollar and impede the global competitiveness of other sectors. Manufacturing has been further hit by the appropriation of gas production for export and the denial to domestic users of a gas reservation requirement.

Within the domestic economy, the driving force is the construction sector, in the erection of residential and commercial buildings – in scale and placement regardless of urban amenity. Developer business is coupled with large-scale immigration totals, the influx locating predominantly in the already stressed areas of Sydney, Melbourne and south-eastern Queensland.

Another distortion of the economy comes from a bloated finance sector. Finance sector income as a percentage of total corporate income has grown from 5.8 per cent in 1959–60 to 20.0 per cent (it has been higher) in the first three quarters of 2018–19 (ABS 2023b, Table 7; latest figures available). The finance sector employs 539,000 people (ABS 2023a, Table 4). This process of an increasingly disproportionate role of the finance sector is called financialisation. (There has been some recent rationalisation of employment numbers, but ironically contrary to the public interest.) Much of the finance sector is oriented to speculative mediation. The banking sector itself is not fit for purpose. It is predominantly oriented to housing finance (pushing up the cost of accommodation to unaffordable levels), depriving communities of banking services through ongoing branch closures (with attendant employment cuts), and its treatment of non-corporate commercial borrowers is perennially predatory (Jones 2018b).

The anti-intellectual stance of successive Coalition governments has been responsible for the parlous state of Australia's education institutions. The underfunding of tertiary education (forcing reliance on foreign fee-payers), the systematic dismantling of technical and further education (TAFE) and the privatisation of vocational education and training (VET) belie any claims for Australia becoming a "smart country".

For over 40 years the workforce has been dramatically bifurcated, with significant numbers reduced to casual employment (Peetz 2020) and the capacity of unions to improve working conditions limited by restrictive regulations. Surprisingly, officialdom applauds this tawdry structure (Berger-Thomson et al. 2018). Of significance is that an ideologically driven "reform" *process* is considered more important than substantive *outcomes*. The resulting structure of the Australian economy is considered, de facto, inevitable, with the relative downsizing of manufacturing seen as a hallmark of progress. Politics is adapted to countering at the margin the most damaging dimensions of these changes to appease a dissatisfied electorate. Politics is driven not by vision but by expediency.

Embedded liberalism

Australia is immersed in a particular political philosophy – that of liberalism. It implicitly shapes how the corpus of political and bureaucratic decision makers conceive their role and the possibilities for action. The liberalist culture was inherited from the mother country, the United Kingdom – as also occurred in Canada and New Zealand.

Liberalism entails a self-restraint by the political class in conceptualising state capacity. Regarding policy development, it is conducive to a narrowed pragmatism, reactive to pressures. It limits the capacity of political leaders to think strategically about major projects and fundamental economic or social transformations – conceiving, developing, implementing, monitoring, remediating and thus controlling the process to finality. (One might surmise that such a liberalist harness inhibits governments from engaging in pharaonic wasteful projects. Yet the recent excursions of successive Coalition governments in New South Wales into gigantic transport projects, with no control over functionality or costs, proves otherwise.) The short-sighted vision is embedded in the mentality of individuals and institutions and in institutional interrelations.

There have been rare exceptions to this incapacity generalisation, not least at the conclusion of World War II. The most striking exception is the Snowy Mountains Scheme. The atypical conditions that facilitated this exception included the long-time pressure (at least since the 1880s) to sustain decentralised (White) settlement by overcoming low rainfall and perennial drought; an effective post-World War II can-do mentality embodied in seasoned public servants with planned economy experience; the extraordinary technical acumen acquired over decades by state water and electrical engineers; the lessons from successful implantation of hydro-electric schemes overseas and in Tasmania; and the leverage by the Commonwealth of a defence preparation imperative (Wigmore 1968). The Snowy Scheme aimed to facilitate a dramatic increase in sustainable primary production: a succession of World Bank loans totalling over US$400 million between 1950 and 1956 were oriented predominantly to related land development and greater settlement.

Strategic federal government initiative was also embodied in the establishment of the Bureau of Mineral Resources, Geology and Geophysics in June 1946 under geologist Harold Raggatt as a vehicle for government-sponsored resources exploration and documentation. The Menzies government Department of National Development became, de facto, a resources department under Raggatt's directorship from 1951. The 1957 Australia–Japan Commerce Agreement provided the key market for minerals exports in the 1960s and beyond.

In 1945, the Chifley government also established the first federal bureaucracy devoted specifically to the manufacturing sector – the Secondary Industries Division (renamed the Division of Industrial Development in 1948) within the Department of Post-War Reconstruction. The division had staff with firsthand experience in a war economy administration, capable of detached and big-picture thinking (Jones 2002a).

Thus the Chifley government had a postwar vision that encompassed more stable, balanced economic development involving primary production, resources extraction and manufacturing. Two world wars provided the imperative and legitimacy for an expanded manufacturing sector. It employed a significant percentage of those who came in large-scale post-World War II immigration, driven domestically by a bipartisan-felt necessity to increase the population for national security reasons.

Despite of these developments, a prime example of the liberalist incapacity phenomenon was the failure of the Chifley Labor government after 1945 to implement its agenda for reconstruction and social change (Jones 2021). Notable was the failure to direct appropriate resources into infrastructure and capital equipment needs in the face of surging demand for consumer goods. By contrast, (authoritarian) governments in West Germany and Japan successfully implanted comparable structural priorities – with US blessing in a Cold War milieu.

The issue runs deeper than the division of powers and the fragmentation of institutional power centres (compounded in federations like Australia and Canada). I am unaware of any literature that addresses Australia's policy culture at a fundamental level. (Tim Rowse (1978) has, rarely, placed liberalism at the centre of White Australia's cultural consciousness, but his important book doesn't cover the dimension of interest here.) The catchphrase "laissez faire" is unsatisfactory. One is confronted with a state whose actions are channelled to inhibit long-sighted strategic action that diverges from the status quo.

This inhibiting political culture provides insight into why significant national problems remain in the too-hard basket – such as Australia's ongoing subordination to US imperatives, climate change and its associated natural disasters, recognition of First Nations peoples, and the integrity of the Murray–Darling basin. Here we deal with the political treatment of the manufacturing sector following the demise of the protective tariff regime.

Why it matters: the current account as policy objective

A substantive indicator of the national economy's character is that of the balance on current account – showing a country's net economic relationship with the rest of the world. A range of developed countries exhibit near permanent surpluses on their current accounts. This list includes Germany, Japan, the Netherlands, Denmark, Sweden, Switzerland, Austria and Singapore (International Monetary Fund

1948–). These nations evidently ensure that the current account does not present problems for other domestic priorities.

Australian policy makers were long concerned with the balance on the current account. This was inevitable in the era of fixed exchange rates, and when the rural sector was the dominant source of merchandise exports. But rural produce markets were notoriously unstable, making such dependence unsustainable.

The resolution of this dilemma came in the form of mineral and fuel exports (facilitated by government initiative, as noted above). The resulting long-term resources export bonanza dependent upon successive Asian countries' industrialisation was unexpected. The phenomenon has become entrenched as natural and permanent. The potential impact of climate change acknowledgement in reducing demand for coal and China's curtailment of Australian imports for geopolitical reasons have not dented the belief in the endless bounty to be earned from resources exports. A reckoning is inevitable.

The imprint of social liberalism: the rise of "the Australian settlement"

Arguably, the move in the late 19th century to "reform" the autocratic structure of White Australia embodied a strategic vision and action – one that enjoyed a significant measure of success. (The movement was, of course, equally complicit in the dispossession and deprivation of First Nations peoples.)

Domestic economic development inevitably meant support for a local manufacturing sector. This drive was strongest in Victoria where the post-gold rush population had swelled considerably. The vehicle was the then-common protective tariff, carried over after Federation in compromised form.

If this movement is deemed strategic, because of its conscious vision, purposive implementation and towards substantive ends, it was nevertheless contained within a liberalist framework. These people were self-consciously "new" or "radical" liberals – afterwards labelled "social" liberals. They drew on, and in some respects went further than, a comparable momentum in Britain.

In Australia, the growing manufacturing sector relied almost exclusively on the tariff to consolidate and sustain its presence.The sector expanded further with foreign capital (especially British) catering to the domestic market behind the tariff. The Tariff Board, created in 1922, aimed to imbue the still controversial tariff regime with legitimacy by judging the merits of claims for assistance. An informal committee, comprising academic and bureaucratic heavyweights (J.B. Brigden, D.B. Copland, E.C. Dyason, L.F. Giblin and C.H. Wickens) provided intellectual defence of the regime (Committee on Economic Effects of the Tariff 1929). Its analysis centred on the claimed capacity of the export-oriented rural sector to handle partial re-distribution of the surplus to a predominantly urban-centred manufacturing population. A more assertive and strategic approach to the sector's development could not be conceived within the country's mindset.

Tariff protection threatened then vanquished

As early as 1960 an ongoing crisis loomed. Long-time Trade and Customs bureaucrat Alf Rattigan was appointed head of the Tariff Board in 1963, and he soon saw fit to dismantle the prevailing tariff regime (Jones 2018a). In 1973, the Whitlam Labor government replaced the Tariff Board with the Industries Assistance Commission (IAC), installed Rattigan as head and institutionalised his agenda. Myriad reports were produced that were drenched with a purist line on the evils of the tariff regime. Scorched-earth recommendations were coupled with utopian claims of a smooth adjustment for employment possibilities.

The IAC's anti-tariff push was concomitant with the global surge of an ideology directed to "freeing up" markets – a product of forces of capital seeking new domains and means to recover profits after the end of the long postwar boom. In Australia, the ascendancy of the resources sector, with international linkages, generated an evolving material base for institutionalising domestically a policy regime conducive to its interests.

The rise in unemployment after 1975 prompted the Whitlam government and then the Fraser government to doubt the IAC's optimistic prognostications. The Whitlam government responded with the Jackson report (Committee to Advise on Policies for Manufacturing Industry 1975–76). The Fraser government responded with the Crawford report (Study Group on Structural Adjustment 1979). The latter concluded that the long boom was over and that tariff reductions were inevitable but it emphasised that new structural policies were essential for smoother adjustment and the long-term viability of domestic manufacturing industries. The IAC and its supporters remained undaunted.

After the Hawke Labor government came to office in 1983, the union movement pushed for a critical investigation into the IAC. The government complied by establishing the Uhrig inquiry (Review of the Industries Assistance Commission 1983). The report was critical, but the government nevertheless gave the IAC a pass to continue operations unrestrained. Industry Minister John Button appointed Bill Carmichael, Rattigan adviser and collaborator, as the new IAC chairman in 1985. It was to be business as usual. The government moved the IAC from the Industry Department to Treasury in July 1987. In March 1990 the Labor government attached two ancillary organisations to the unreformed IAC, renaming it the Industry Commission (IC) and giving it a comprehensive brief regarding public policy.

An extended battle over a post-tariff industry policy

Ambitions to support a substantial manufacturing sector not dependent on tariffs were met with a perennial headwind. Jenny Stewart (1994, Ch. 3) noted that each industry had its own character in confronting imports exposure, but there were problems in common: sourcing finance, management culture, capital–labour relations, the training of appropriately skilled personnel and harnessing the self-interest of foreign-owned firms to the national interest (the latter never achieved).

As noted above, a federal industry bureaucracy had been established in 1945 to put the manufacturing sector on a firmer footing. But, during 1951–53, the newly empowered Treasury under Secretary Roland Wilson, without formal authority, emasculated the Division of Industrial Development (Jones 2002a). Treasury wanted no alternative sources of expertise or opinion. The depleted division, staff-wise and intellectually, was moved to the new Department of Trade in 1956 (renamed Department of Trade and Industry in 1963) where it became subordinated within that department's protectionist agenda.

Union initiatives

The economic malaise of the late 1970s was compounded in Australia by the global recession induced by the Volcker Shock of higher interest rates in Reagan's USA. Significant unemployment resulted during the early 1980s. Some Australian unions were directly active in the late 1970s, in conjunction with Labor in Opposition, in proposing means to reverse the decline. It is noteworthy that the celebrated Australian Council of Trade Unions (ACTU)–government Accord itself accorded nominal priority to industry policy but marginalised it substantively; jobs were to be secured indirectly through wages control (and increased expenditure on the social wage).

A significant union initiative was the 300-page Metal Trades Federation of Unions' (MTFU's) *Policy for Industry Development and More Jobs* (1984; Stilwell 1984). The MTFU document was possibly the first serious effort to propose a respectable conceptual apparatus for assertive industry policy for a post-tariff regime. The report posited a post-Keynesian rationale for industry policy, reflecting lessons learned by contributor Colin Edwards from Nicholas Kaldor at Cambridge University. Metals and engineering industries are deserving of selective support, argued the report, because they are a repository of disproportionate technological development and skilled workforce deployment. Their technology is diffused throughout the economy. Growth, centred initially on domestic growth, is regarded as the means to greater scale economies and higher productivity (Verdoorn's law).

Peter Brain, of Melbourne University's Institute of Applied Economic and Social Research (IAESR) provided complementary econometric modelling. (In early 1984, the IAESR was subject to a coup and reoriented towards a mainstream economics agenda with the appointment of general equilibrium modeller Peter Dixon as its head). Brain's model took countenance of substantial contemporary constraints (such as the balance of payments and budgetary constraints) that inhibited purely macro-economic expansion options. Rather, sustainable development was to be achieved by import replacement, in turn facilitated by strengthening purchase–supplier networks – by that time demonstrating their capacity to enhance domestic production.

The MTFU document sank like a stone (although it gained momentary publicity in a vituperative exchange in the *Australian Financial Review* between critic Gary Sampson and co-authors Peter Brain and Nixon Apple, 2 April, 8, 9, 22 and 28 May 1985). So did a substantial parliamentary inquiry and 200-page report, *Manufacturing Industry Revitalisation* (Senate Standing Committee on Industry, Technology and Science 1988 – the Childs report). Australian Democrat Senator John Coulter wrote a Minority Report to the latter, presciently noting that the relation of the increase in output for the quality of life should be the relevant criterion, and asking what the environmental impact was.

A similar fate befell the dense 200-page report *Australia Reconstructed* (ACTU–Trade Development Council Mission to Western Europe 1987).*Australia Reconstructed* received hysterical critical treatment in the media (Jones 1997). Evidently voices emanating from the workforce are unacceptable *per se*. Strange also that the policy gatekeepers would show no interest in the policy structures of the diverse developed economies of Austria, Norway, Sweden, the United Kingdom and West Germany.

The Australian Manufacturing Council

A potential vehicle for change was the Australian Manufacturing Council (AMC), established in 1977 after the Fraser government's White Paper response to the Jackson report. The AMC was refashioned from the Manufacturing Industry Advisory Council (1958–77). After Labor was returned to office in March 1983 the AMC was reconfigured, albeit not until March 1984.

Industry councils were established (initially 11) with tripartite (business, union and government) membership. Further delays occurred with a demonstrable clash between management and union expectations (Stewart 1994, 196). Ultimately, each council produced reports, drawing from firsthand experience, on the state of play in each industry and the potential to enhance its viability. The councils generated bottom-up experience and facilitated better management–union understanding and co-operation.

But the AMC lacked formal authority and it had no organic relationship with the Industry Department. After several years the AMC moved into sponsoring studies of varying quality from consultancies. The most significant of these reports was the 1990 *The Global Challenge* (Pappas Carter Evans and Koop 1990). In spite of personnel interviews, the report has a schematic character, lacking an organic relationship with Australian manufacturing sector conditions. For example, *Global Challenge* treated only obliquely the impact of foreign-owned corporations and restrictions on their Australian branches' export orientation. Whatever its weaknesses, the report faced an innately hostile environment. The Industry Commision was of the opinion that, post-tariff elimination, no industrial development mechanisms of any kind were acceptable.

Instead, the "correct-liners" found their champion in Ross Garnaut's *Australia and the Northeast Asian Ascendancy* (1989). Garnaut's general proposition was that Australia's economic salvation lay in engaging with Asia (it was already doing so, with the responsible trade bureaucrats unacknowledged). But Garnaut's recommendation for successful integration was that Australia must move to zero tariffs pronto – an argument drawn essentially from aprioristic principles. As Northeast Asia develops, said Garnaut, it will engage in mutual trade liberalisation – again from aprioristic principles. Such was the standard of acceptable opinion.

The AMC's later years, in the early 1990s, were given over predominantly to a best-practice program. The AMC's tripartite structure was marginalised in favour of the Business Council of Australia's (BCA's) agenda of the displacement from union-centred collective bargaining to non-union enterprise bargaining. The best-practice project was subtly reoriented to a "lean production" project oriented towards labour shedding. The AMC had lost its moorings and was readily disbanded by the Howard government in March 1996.

The Bureau of Industry Economics

Another potential vehicle for new ideas was the Bureau of Industry Economics (BIE), created in 1977 as an analytical arm of the Industry Department and the AMC. Labor in office made much use of the BIE but staffed it predominantly with mainstream economists. The BIE reports were of varying quality, some being ill informed and even antagonistic to assertive industry policy.

The BIE's dry credentials were on display early when it mounted an immediate and abrasive critique of the above-named MTFU document (Chapman et al. 1984). Who motivated this hostile attack? The BIE critique was inconsistent – it admits and denies the sense of the Kaldorian vision. It is ignorant of the factors behind East Asian industrial success, citing mainstream American sources as authoritative. The study acknowledged that such countries had created a "dynamic comparative advantage" but claimed without evidence that such a route was not available for Australia because of its high wage levels and relative affluence.

Representative of the BIE's restricted capacity is a series on industry policies of select countries – *Studies in Industrial Development and Innovation Policy* (1987–88). They provided useful statistical detail and were far in advance of the IAC mentality but remained ill informed on the key historical role of industry policy in a country's national development.

By the early 1990s, the BIE was forced to act as a consultant (peculiarly, in collaboration with the BCA), a role for which it was manifestly unsuited. Opposition leader John Hewson promised to abolish the BIE if elected to office. The Labor government duly initiated a review of the BIE (to which I made an invited submission in October 1992, my views being ignored). The Labor victory in the federal election of March 1993 gave the BIE a temporary reprieve. In April 1998 under the Howard government, the BIE was incorporated into the IC (i.e., abolished) and the IC renamed as the Productivity Commission.

Industry plans

After 1983 the Labor government engaged in structural adjustment plans in three significant tariff-dependent industries under the aegis of Industry Minister Button: steel; motor vehicles; and textiles, clothing and footwear (Capling and Galligan 1992). The incoming Labor government had little choice but to deal specifically with these industries. They were variously important in terms of material and technological significance and the scale and diverse regional location of employment. The IAC, whose expertise was automatically sought as official gatekeeper, recommended scorched-earth treatment for the industries. The plans were administered in Button's office, not the Industry Department. Tariff reductions were delayed, giving the industries an extended life, but the tariffs were reduced and the industries became atrophied.

Labor initiated another plan – for heavy engineering. Here was an essential industry subject to perennial instability. This was not tariff-related but driven by the industry crisis after the 1982 recession. Facilitated by relevant AMC industry councils, some gains were made, not least in workplace cultural transformation, but the dominant dry bureaucratic environment inhibited greater success (Jones 1993).

During the 1980s, the promises of the North West Shelf resources off the Western Australian coast, firstly under Woodside Petroleum, offered prospects for trickle down benefits to Australian industry and employment in the context of the impasse resulting from the early 1980s recession. A 1989 hard-hitting preliminary parliamentary inquiry report on "Australian Industry Participation" (*The North West Shelf: a sea of lost opportunities?*) was ignored. A second parliamentary inquiry was initiated in 1995, to which I made two submissions. I made a third in July 1997 after the secretariat invited me to give feedback on the Industry Department's submission. The department's submission, late and perfunctory, was essentially a catalogue of existing programs with no account of their functionality or cognisance of the colonial cringe at play with Australian industry being structured out of participation in this burgeoning offshore gas sector. The submissions from the departments of Primary Industry and Energy and of Foreign Affairs and Trade were no better. The second report, *A sea of indifference* (House Standing Committee on Industry, Science and Technology 1998 – the Reid report) was equally hard-hitting and ultimately equally inconsequential.

Technology and science

A 1983 report under mining engineer Frank Espie, initiated by the Australian Academy of Technological Sciences, highlighted the problem of facilitating the prospect of high-tech start-ups evolving into larger sustainable businesses. Subsequently, in 1984, the Labor government established the Management and Investment Companies (MIC) scheme to facilitate the financing of risky ventures. The MIC scheme had perennial administrative problems, and the key problem of sustainable evolution has never been satisfactorily resolved. Of course, fundamental structural inhibitions exist, as for all manufacturing, in the form of a small domestic market and the tyranny of distance from North Atlantic markets and finance sources (compare Thompson et al. 2011).

And the CSIRO? From 1977 onwards, this iconic institution was subject to a series of reviews and subsequent dramatic restructuring (Upstill and Spurling 2007). The general thrust involved moving CSIRO from a pure-science orientation to cooperative interaction with other researchers and with commercialising agents. A key change was the 1988 requirement to source 30 per cent of its funding from commercial sources. That ratio was achieved fairly readily, but the forced change and a contemporaneous imposition of a managerialist hierarchy generated widespread disgruntlement – indeed bitter hostility from some personnel to the changes. (The 30 per cent requirement was abandoned in 2002.)

Labor's retreat into orthodoxy

Comprehensive financial deregulation brought Australia crippling interest rates and "the recession we had to have" in 1990. Those macro-economic settings destroyed many businesses and farms and generated significant unemployment, rendering questionable Labor's entire policy program. There has never been a mea culpa, although Australian Democrat Senator Sid Spindler initiated an inquiry (Independent Parliamentary Inquiry into Tariffs and Industry Development 1993) that attracted many submissions and witnesses from businesses and councils, attempting to counter neoliberal orthodoxy and testifying to the adverse effects on business closures and employment of the combined impact of the recession and the top-down tariff reduction regime.

Subsequently, a succession of policy statements was issued: *Building a Competitive Australia* (the "March Industry Statement"), 1991; *One Nation*, 1992; *Investing in the Nation*, 1993; *Working Nation*, 1994; *Creative Nation*, 1994; and *Innovate Australia*, 1995 (Jones 2005). There were desirable elements in these packages, such as research and technology subsidisation, collaboration and diffusion. But the pace of reduction in tariffs across the board was quickened.

In the midst of this policy pragmatism came the National Competition Policy (NCP). Its conception and implementation is an exception to the strategic incapacity policy regime argued here, and the origins of its virulent promotion remain unexamined. NCP was developed strategically and implemented brutally. Save for the New South Wales Greiner government, with neoliberal adviser Gary Sturgess as NCP proselytiser, the states were threatened and bribed into compliance. One New South Wales senior bureaucrat later noted:

> The national competition policy was introduced, not through democratic processes, but by subverting them in the form of what is not unfairly described as an extra-Constitutional coup. Not only was the policy never the subject of debate in the course of an election, but nor was it ever properly considered by any of our parliaments. Rather, the policy is a product of "executive federalism" (Sheil 2001).

A Commonwealth parliamentary inquiry was held but after the legislation had been passed; critical feedback was ignored. The formal agenda was to introduce competition to state enterprises and utilities and to abolish rural commodity marketing schemes that were hindering so-called micro-economic reform and to subject those bodies to the *Trade Practices Act*. The real agenda was to facilitate access of profit-oriented capital, including via privatisation, to public services previously out of bounds.

The Hilmer report (Independent Committee of Inquiry into Competition Policy in Australia 1993) provided the NCP's defence. It crudely dismissed government *per se* as inefficient while praising "competition" as the universal elixir. It displays no understanding of the inevitable historical ascendancy of public provision, and no understanding of competition itself (Jones 1995). The report was written by junior Treasury bureaucrats, with management academic Fred Hilmer as titular overseer. Hilmer had elsewhere bizarrely opined that governments should be run like businesses. The Industry Commission was enlisted to defend the indefensible.

The Howard government and beyond

After the election of John Howard's Coalition government in March 1996, several years were lost in pandering to the "scorched earth" National Commission of Audit under Robert Officer (Jones 2005). Howard's 1996–97 budget cuts hit Labor's labour force programs predominantly and its industry support programs were cut indiscriminately. A backlash from the business community led to the inept 1997 Mortimer review of business programs (*Going for Growth*), followed by the equally hastily constructed package *Investing for Growth*. After two years of contradictory action, the Coalition resurrected and tweaked Labor's potpourri of industry programs.

Discontent from the scientific community led to a flurry of reports and statements – *Knowledge and Innovation* (1999), *Unlocking the Future* (2000), the Chief Scientist Robin Batterham's *The Chance to Change* (2000) and *Backing Australia's Ability* (2001) (Jones 2006). Extra funding went into research infrastructure and existing programs were reshuffled. But the claimed emphasis on education and training within these mooted programs was illusory, as noted above.

Probably the most significant development in the Howard era was further restructuring of the CSIRO. In 2004, the government introduced the Flagships program, with resources to be devoted to six areas. The flagship resources were to be extracted from non-included divisions. The program was introduced without consultation and generated marked bitterness from detractors. In the meantime, the corporatisation of CSIRO had set in, with dysfunctional management, inflated remuneration of some executives, more resources devoted to marketing and public relations, and increasing casualisation of scientific and technical staff.

Labor was returned to office in December 2007. The Rudd government initiated reviews in four areas (innovation; motor vehicles; defence procurement; and textiles, clothing and footwear). Only the textiles, clothing and footwear review (Green 2008) appears to have had a long-term impact.

With Prime Minister Julia Gillard came the Manufacturing Task Force and the *Report of the Non-Government Members* (August 2012). Surprisingly, the prime minister, with Industry Minister Greg Combet, dictated that a sovereign wealth fund and a gas reservation policy were off the table (Prime Minister, Minister for Industry and Innovation 2012). Regardless, the task force and any influence of the report disappeared with the Coalition's electoral victory under Tony Abbott in September 2013.

The 2014–15 Senate Economics References Committee inquiry and report, *Australia's Innovation System*, was initiated by Labor's Senator Kim Carr in Opposition. When Malcolm Turnbull became prime minister in September 2015, he enthusiastically embraced the report, a key component of which was the claimed necessity to centralise the administration of innovation-associated program and budgetary measures. But Turnbull's narrow victory in the July 2016 election had him reconsidering the innovation agenda as an electoral liability, and his ardour rapidly cooled.

Research funding was cut under the Abbott government (with no science minister and the word "innovation" made taboo as it smacked of Labor initiatives) and during the Turnbull government's post-election phase. In 2016 a central agency, Industry Innovation and Science Australia, was established within the Industry Department but the associated cultural foundations, institutions and funding remain non-existent, fragmented and insufficient. The subsequent period of government under Scott Morrison was a policy vacuum save for indirect spin-offs from its orientation to fossil fuel development.

Embedded liberalism revisited

After the dismantling of the tariff regime, statements, inquiries and reports regarding the manufacturing sector have succeeded each other with monotonous regularity. Some programs have achieved modest success. But grand labels never match the impoverished substance of what follows. Behind the litany of start–stop and pragmatic fixes lies an immutable infrastructure that is antagonistic or indifferent to manufacturing on Australian soil.

At the centre of the problem is the bureaucratic hierarchy and its cultures. The Department of Prime Minister and Cabinet is the formal bureaucratic core, but it imbibes the hegemonic liberalist Kool-Aid and always faces short-term pressures. Treasury, with the like-minded Department of Finance in tow, sits at its centre. Treasury was historically the keeper of the public purse but, during the 1960s, accountants had been replaced by university-trained economists. David Charles, then head of the Industry Department, claimed: "The IAC and Treasury are illiterate about the realities of Australian industry. They have no real involvement with it. They don't get out there and meet industry like we do …" (Gray 1987).

All ancillary economic institutions, save for the "independent" Reserve Bank, are within the Treasury umbrella. Treasury formally oversees the Productivity Commission, probably the most ideologically pure official think tank in the world and with a comprehensive brief. Line departments have been allocated secretaries of lower status and colonised by "dries" from the central agencies to keep them from straying from the orthodoxy.

There has been the odd attempt to restructure the bureaucratic hierarchy for more forceful deliberation. The Coombs Royal Commission found Treasury's influence unpalatable:

> It was argued that the Treasury held a substantial monopoly as the source of economic and financial advice and that … it had

> developed an almost doctrinal attitude about the theoretical basis on which policy should be developed …
>
> we consider it necessary that there should be within the administration a focus of knowledge and understanding of the structure of the economy as a whole which will balance and complement that of the Treasury. At present no such focus exists.
>
> We recommend therefore that there be a department, which might be named the Department of Industries and the Economy (DINDEC). (Royal Commission on Australian Government Administration 1976, 299, 302)

No such establishment transpired. Prime Minister Fraser, irritated by Treasury's dogma, created a separate Department of Finance in 1977. But, by the early 1980s, Finance had become an ideological sibling of Treasury and has since remained so.

In 1983 Hawke's Labor government created the Economic Planning Advisory Council (after 1994, Commission – EPAC). Formally EPAC had a big-picture brief, but it was created as a diversionary talking shop. Labor expanded the IAC into the Industry Commission, as above. Labor also first neutered then killed off the independently minded Department of Trade in 1987, not least because it saw it as a bailiwick of the Country/National Party.

Treasury reigns unqualified. Treasury personnel are predominantly those with tertiary economics training. Yet the economics syllabus is remarkably bereft of tuition on how capitalist economies work and how the most successful have achieved that status (Jones 2002b). In June 1990, when interviewing a senior member of the BIE, I claimed that its output might be more robust if it hired more non-economists. The staffer replied that if the BIE did that it would become more marginalised in Canberra and could not attract "the best and brightest".

Any dissidence from orthodoxy in the economics profession has mostly centred on adherence to a post-1930s Keynesianism, which aims for progressive social ends through purely macro-economic policies still within a (modified) liberalist framework. Economic structure is thus left to be monopolised by orthodoxy whose only program is a commitment to an abstract textbook ideal – thus "micro-economic reform".

So entrenched is the arrogance of ignorance that when informed sceptics have claimed that East Asian industrial successes had a significant discriminatory statist component, considerable resources were expended to claim the contrary. This imperative for "paradigm maintenance" (Wade 1996) meant that Western establishment institutions (World Bank, IMF, OECD) and like-minded academics have been the only authorities accorded intellectual legitimacy.

When the bodies dedicated to considering industry policy possibilities in Australia couch their analyses in terms like "market failure", one readily appreciates the contorted spectrum of acceptable opinion.

"Paradigm maintenance" is of the highest priority in Australia. The financial media has played a significant role – particularly prominent during the 1980s and early 1990s when the general policy direction of the Labor government was evolving. The pressure on the Labor government to pursue "micro-economic reform" was brutal and relentless. (There were some exceptions to this agenda – notably Peter Roberts in the *Australian Financial Review* and Kenneth Davidson in the Melbourne *Age*.) Labor faced a barrage of ill-informed to ludicrous claims as to the source of then economic dilemmas, not least regarding the origins of the problematic current account deficit. Treasurer Keating's garbled "banana republic" outburst on 14 May 1986 (he was right but for the wrong reasons) backfired on the government itself.

The neoliberal ascendancy in Australia had fertile ground. Political discourse and institutional construction are rooted in liberalism. The edifice that the neoliberal forces sought to dismantle, "the Australian Settlement", was itself a social liberalist construct.

At the federal level, Australia has not merely ensconced itself in a neoliberal mould, but its policy orientation is stamped with a colonial cringe. Representative of the latter has been a succession of eight bilateral free trade agreements in which asymmetric benefits accrued to the other party. The 2005 agreement with Thailand, for example, contributed to nails in the coffin of the Australian motor vehicle industry. Manufacturing industry has long been used as a sacrificial lamb ("coin") to gain access to highly protected agricultural markets overseas. Whatever results is always on the other's terms.

Is a more supportive environment possible?

Will the analysis of Stanford and other contemporaries – Green (2022), for example, posits the components of a desirable institutional structure to underpin a viable and sustainable manufacturing sector for Australia – fall on deaf ears, as per myriad comparable earlier analyses?

The election of the Albanese Labor government in May 2022 offered more positive prospects. It is conscious of the vulnerability of Australian society during the Covid-19 pandemic due to a lack of essential supplies in the health sector. There is an acknowledged imperative to marginalise the powerful fossil fuel lobby and to provide the manufacturing basis for a greener economy.

Albanese Labor has an Industry and Science Ministry (albeit penultimate in the hierarchy) and an Assistant Industry (and Trade) Minister. To date, the Industry and Science Ministry is inert. But Labor also has a Ministry for Defense Industry which is anything but inert. Minister Pat Conroy has claimed that AUKUS-related developments will involve "the greatest industrial undertaking Australia has ever attempted" (Scrafton 2023). This hyperbole foreshadows a boondoggle of misdirected resources that will do nothing for a functioning and sustainable manufacturing sector in Australia.

The constraining policy parameters and the underlying political culture are deeply entrenched. The bulk of the political class and of the bureaucracy are not even conscious of such constraints to which they are subject. A thoroughgoing cultural and institutional transformation is an essential prerequisite to give manufacturing in Australia an appropriate place.

References

Australian Bureau of Statistics (2023a). *Labour Force, Australia*. Cat. no. 6291.0. Canberra: Australian Bureau of Statistics, August.

Australian Bureau of Statistics (2023b). *Australian National Accounts*. Cat. no. 5206.0. Canberra: Australian Bureau of Statistics, September.

ACTU–Trade Development Council Mission to Western Europe (1987). *Australia Reconstructed*. Canberra: Australian Government Publishing Service, July.

Berger-Thomson, Laura, John Breusch and Louise Lilley (2018). *Australia's Experience with Economic Reform*. Treasury Working Paper, October. Canberra: Department of the Treasury.

Capling, Ann, and Brian Galligan (1992). *Beyond the Protective State: The Political Economy of Australia's Manufacturing Industry Policy*. Cambridge, UK: Cambridge University Press.

Chapman, David, et al. (1984). *A Review of the Report by the Metal Trades Unions, "Policy for Industry Development and More Jobs"*. Background Paper, December. Canberra: Bureau of Industry Economics.

Committee on Economic Effects of the Tariff (1929). *The Australian Tariff: An Economic Enquiry*. Melbourne: Melbourne University Press/Macmillan & Co. [Brigden report]

Committee to Advise on Policies for Manufacturing Industry (1975–76). *Policies for Development of Manufacturing Industry: A Green Paper*. 4 vols. Canberra: Australian Government Publishing Service. [Jackson report]

Department of Foreign Affairs and Trade (2023). *TRIEC [Trade Import and Export Classification] 1989–90 to 2021–22*. Cat. no. 5368.0. Canberra: Australian Bureau of Statistics.

Garnaut, Ross (1989). *Australia and the Northeast Asian Ascendancy*. Canberra: Australian Government Publishing Service.

Gray, Joanne (1987). Industry revitalisation plan runs out of steam. *Times on Sunday*, 29 November.

Green, Roy (2008). *Building Innovative Capacity: review of the Australian textile, clothing and footwear industries*. 2 vols. Canberra: Commonwealth of Australia. https://hdl.voced.edu.au/10707/123610.

Green, Roy (2022). Roy Green on the urgency of the task ahead. *The Innovation Papers*, https://tinyurl.com/24vbdt5p.

House Standing Committee on Industry, Science and Technology (1998). *A Sea of Indifference: Australian Industry Participation in the North West Shelf Project*. Canberra: Australian Government Publishing Service. [Reid report]

Independent Committee of Inquiry into Competition Policy in Australia (1993). *National Competition Policy*. Canberra: Australian Government Publishing Service. [Hilmer report]

Independent Parliamentary Inquiry into Tariffs and Industry Development (1993). *Final Report*. Canberra: The Inquiry. [Spindler Report]

International Monetary Fund (1948–). *International Financial Statistics*. Washington DC, International Monetary Fund. https://tinyurl.com/4ctzc6ns.

Jones, Evan (1993). The heavy engineering adjustment and development program: origins, process and outcomes. *Australian Journal of Public Administration* 52(1): 40–52.

Jones, Evan (1995). Submission. *Inquiry into Aspects of the National Competition Policy Reform Package*. No. 49, October, Submissions Volume 5, Canberra: House of Representatives Standing Committee on Banking, Finance and Public Administration.

Jones, Evan (1997). Background to *Australia Reconstructed*. *Journal of Australian Political Economy*, 39(June): 17–38.

Jones, Evan (2002a). Post–World War II industry policy: opportunities and constraints. *Australian Economic History Review* 42(3): 312–33.

Jones, Evan (2002b). The ascendancy of an idealist economics in Australia. *Journal of Australian Political Economy* 50(December): 44–71.

Jones, Evan (2005). Industry policy in the 1990s: *Working Nation*, its context and beyond. *Journal of Economic and Social Policy* 9(2): 25–53.

Jones, Evan (2006). The evolution of industry policy under Howard. *Australian Review of Public Affairs*, 23 February.

Jones, Evan (2018a). Australian trade liberalisation policy: the Industries Assistance Commission and the Productivity Commission. *Economic and Labour Relations Review* 27(2): 181–98.

Jones, Evan (2018b). Financial deregulation exposes banking's antisocial character. In Damien Cahill and Phillip Toner, eds. *Wrong Way: How Privatisation & Economic Reform Backfired*, 186–201. Melbourne: La Trobe University Press and Black Inc.

Jones, Evan (2021). Macroeconomic and structural policies: economic policy in post–World War II Australia. *Journal of Australian Political Economy* 88(Summer): 98–123.

Metal Trades Federation of Unions (1984). *Policy for Industry Development and More Jobs*. Sydney: Metal Trades Unions.

Pappas Carter Evans and Koop (1990). *The Global Challenge: Australian Manufacturing in the 1990s*. Melbourne: Australian Manufacturing Council.

Peel, Mick, Rod Campbell, and Richard Denniss (2014). *Mining the Age of Entitlement: State government assistance to the minerals and fossil fuel sector.* Canberra: Australia Institute.

Peetz, David (2020),.The truth about much "casual" work: it's really about permanent insecurity. *The Conversation*, 11 December. https://tinyurl.com/3xp9vn49.

Prime Minister, Minister for Industry and Innovation (2012). Government Welcomes Manufacturing Task Force Report, *Media release*. Canberra: Department of the Prime Minister and Cabinet, 16 August. https://tinyurl.com/29pnjt7t.

Review of the Industries Assistance Commission (1983). *Report*. Canberra: Australian Government Publishing Service. [Uhrig report] https://www.pc.gov.au/__data/assets/pdf_file/0009/195561/thirtyyearhistory.pdf.

Rowse, Tim (1978). *Australian Liberalism and National Character*, Melbourne: Kibble Books.

Royal Commission on Australian Government Administration (1976). *Report*, Canberra: Australian Government Publishing Service.

Scrafton, Mike (2023). AUKUS: Conroy's justification of the "greatest industrial undertaking" falls short. *Pearls and Irritations*, 13 August.

Senate Standing Committee on Industry, Technology and Science (1988). *Manufacturing Industry Revitalisation: Making It Together*. Canberra: AGPS. [Childs report]

Sheil, Christopher (2001). What do we expect of government? *Evatt Journal* 1(2): October. https://tinyurl.com/2h24txnw.

Stanford, Jim (2020). *A Fair Share for Australian Manufacturing: Manufacturing Renewal for the Post-COVID Economy.* Canberra: Centre for Future Work, Australia Institute.

Stewart, Jenny (1994). *The Lie of the Level Playing Field: Industry Policy and Australia's Future.* Melbourne: Text Publishing Company.

Stilwell, Frank (1984). A platform for industry development. *Journal of Australian Political Economy* (17): 61–72.

Study Group on Structural Adjustment (1979). *Report March 1979*, Canberra: Australian Government Publishing Service. [Crawford report]

Thompson, Lyndal-Joy, Michael Gilding, Thomas H. Spurling, Greg Simpson, and Ian R. Elsum (2011). The paradox of public science and global business: CSIRO, commercialisation and the national system of innovation in Australia. *Innovation: Management, Policy and Practice* 13(3): 327–40.

Upstill, Garrett, and Thomas H. Spurling (2007). Adjusting to changing times: CSIRO since the 1970s. *Innovation: Management, Policy and Practice* 9(2): 113–24.

Wade, Robert (1996). Japan, the World Bank, and the art of paradigm maintenance: the "East Asian Miracle" in political perspective. *New Left Review* 217: 3–36.

Wigmore, Lionel (1968). *Struggle for the Snowy: The Background to the Snowy Mountains Scheme*. Melbourne: Oxford University Press.

5 Capital gains and wealth

David Richardson

The aim of this chapter is to point to the rapid growth in wealth and capital gains in Australia as well as potential for increasing the tax on wealth and capital gains. The failure to adequately tap these revenue sources is becoming increasingly obvious as wealth has massively increased relative to household income as traditionally measured, while capital gains on that wealth have been outpacing traditional income measures. The discussion below outlines what we mean by this and provides the relevant facts and figures. With that in mind the chapter turns to consider how we might better tax capital gains and wealth. The neoliberalism arguments against taxing wealth are also canvassed.

The problem

Capital gains in Australia are booming and massively adding to household wealth (Richardson 2021). In the financial year 2020–21 household income in Australia without including capital gains was $1,767 billion (Australian Bureau of Statistics – ABS 2022c). Capital gains accruing to households added another $1,934 billion and so more than doubled household income (ABS 2022b). (Capital gains are calculated by deducting the closing value of net wealth at June 2020 from its value at end June 2021. From that figure we also deduct household savings as conventionally measured: that is, by deducting consumption – plus minor other items – from net disposable income.) By December 2021 total net worth for households rose to $14,677 billion or 8.4 times annual household income (ABS 2022b). As we shall see, Australia only taxes capital gains and wealth very lightly. That means a tax base of some $14 trillion is barely touched by the tax system yet even just a 0.5 per cent average tax on that would raise $70 billion.

Piketty (2014) has made the theoretical argument that there is a tendency for increasing inequality in all societies (subject to the condition that the return on capital exceeds the rate of growth in national income, which tends to be the case historically). In Australia, with lower economic growth in recent years, we have witnessed rising inequality. Figure 5.1 shows how the fruits of economic growth have been shared between the top 10 per cent of the income distribution and the rest. The periods chosen are the six periods of upswings over the economic cycles experienced in Australia since 1950. The fruits of economic growth in Figure 5.1 are calculated as the increase in per capita real income for the periods in question. Figure 5.1 shows that, for the first time, the fruits of economic growth in the decade before Covid-19 have gone exclusively to the top 10 per cent of income earners. This seems to have been a fundamental change in the operation of the Australian economy. Since World War II the majority of the benefits of economic growth have flowed to the bottom 90 per cent of income earners but, as shown in Figure 5.1, between 2010 and 2019 the top 10 per cent received all of the gains of the latest recovery, and then some.

Figure 5.1 clearly shows that Australians outside the top 10 per cent of income earners were not sharing in the fruits of economic growth over the period 2010 to the eve of the pandemic. As a result, income itself is being distributed more unequally as can be seen in Figure 5.2.

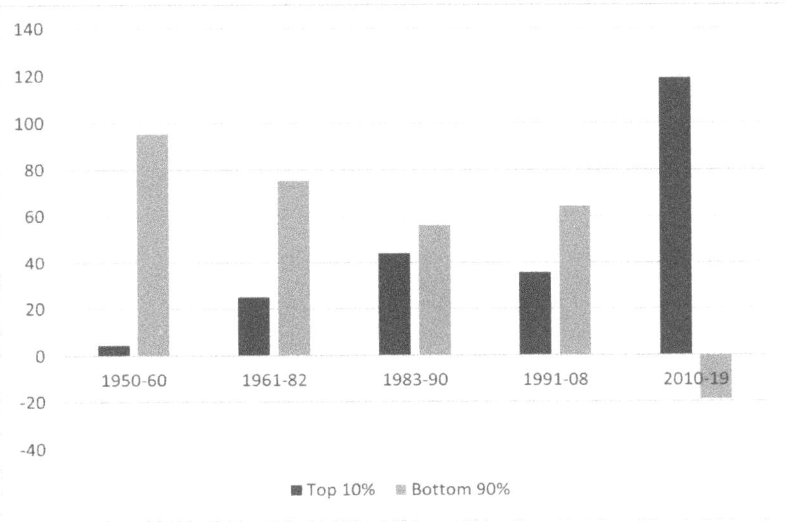

Figure 5.1 Share (%) of postwar economic growth going to top 10 per cent and bottom 90 per cent of adults. Source: Author's calculations based on World Inequality Database, https://wid.world/.

Figure 5.2 shows a V-shaped trend with falling incomes for the top 1 and 10 per cent to just before 1980 and increases in those top income groups since then. The top 1 per cent experienced a sharp upward increase in their income, which peaked in about 1950, perhaps as a result of agricultural commodity booms about then. The recent data in Figure 5.2 show that the top 1 per cent received 12.9 per cent of the income and the top 10 per cent received 33.6 per cent of the income. Figure 5.2 also shows that since around the mid-1970s the share of income going to the top 1 per cent and top 10 per cent has increased substantially. Even so, these figures do not include capital gains income, which is important to our discussion below.

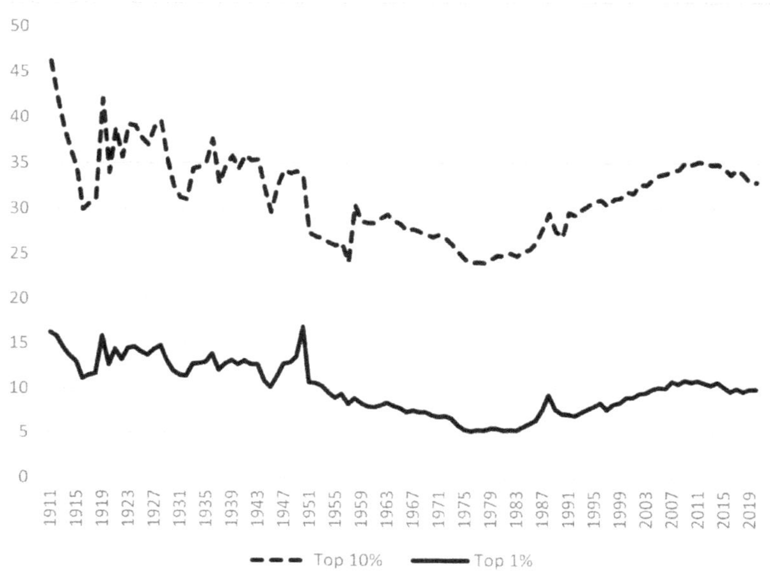

Figure 5.2 Share of national wealth for the wealthiest 10 per cent and top 1 per cent of Australian adults, 1912–2021. Source: World Inequality Database, https://wid.world/.

Wealth is even more concentrated. We cannot show similar figures to those presented in Figure 5.2 that gives the top 1 per cent and 10 per cent shares by individuals but we do have ABS data for the top quintile (20 per cent) of households, who have 41.6 per cent of total equivalised income (the ABS adjusts household income for household size to produce a series for equivalised income), while the top quintile of wealth owners have 62.3 per cent of the wealth (ABS 2021a). The ABS also gives Gini coefficient estimates for income and wealth. The Gini is a measure of inequality that falls within the range of zero to one. The higher the value, the worse the inequality. For the 2017–18 financial year, the ABS gave Gini estimates of 0.439 for gross household income and 0.621 for household net worth (ABS 2019). The Gini for income has become marginally worse over time but the Gini for wealth has substantially worsened.

Just as wealth holdings are more unequal than incomes, so are capital gains, which have been very large in recent years (Richardson 2021). Even if wealth inequality grew no worse over time, the *growth* in wealth means capital gains on wealth make the distribution of income so much worse than is suggested by the ABS data. In the next section, I argue that capital gains should be included in definitions of income. Moreover, the distribution of income plus capital gains is getting worse as capital gains loom larger. The ABS income distribution data do not include capital gains as income and we have to add that ourselves. When they *are* included, the distribution of income appears so much worse. This is evident when appropriate adjustments are made to the ABS data as shown in an earlier paper (Richardson 2021): for example, it showed that the top 20 per cent of households had ordinary gross income (excluding capital gains) at 3.4 times that of the bottom 20 per cent. But, for capital gains, the ratio was 108.4 times. Capital gains boosted the income of the bottom 20 per cent by 4.4 per cent but boosted the incomes of the top 20 per cent by a massive 144 per cent (Richardson 2021). Those figures show very clearly how capital gains on the unequal wealth holdings imply a much worse income distribution than is suggested by the traditional measures of income that exclude capital gains.

Equity means taxing capital gains

A fundamental principle of the Australian tax system is that similar income be taxed the same no matter what the source of that income. Public finance textbooks have stressed for generations that fiscal policy discussions should be using a comprehensive definition of income. The review of taxation, chaired by Ken Henry, the Treasury Secretary at the time, referred to the pure definition of income under which income represents the increase in a person's stock of assets in a period, plus their consumption in the period (Australian Government 2010 – note that since consumption plus savings/investment will exhaust income then that becomes a useful definition of income). Most discussions refer to the Haig–Simons income concept, which is simply defined as "consumption plus changes in net worth" (Staff of the Joint Committee on Taxation 2012, 3). The references are to works by the economists Robert Haig (1921) and Henry Simons (1938). While tax systems tend to include realised capital gains for practical reasons, the Haig–Simons definition definitely includes capital gains on an accrual basis (Armour, Burkhauser and Larrimore 2013). This reflects the view that capital gains are a resource to the income unit whether or not they are realised.

When the Hawke government decided on a capital gains tax, it argued "because real capital gains represent an increase in purchasing power similar to real increases in wages, salaries, interest or dividends, they should be included in any comprehensive definition of income" (Australian Government 1985). The view here is that equity considerations demand the taxation of capital gains, ideally as they accrue. An important subsidiary argument can also be made for taxing capital gains to stem tax avoidance, since a good deal of avoidance takes place by disguising other incomes as capital gains. Tax avoidance is not pursued further here but is worth keeping in mind.

Capital gains are something now added to the tax system almost as an afterthought and only to the extent of including some realised capital gains. But capital gains have not been incorporated into general macro-economics.

The taxation of capital gains in Australia

If you buy and sell anything within 12 months, then any resulting income is treated as a trading profit, which should be declared as income and is taxed at the taxpayer's ordinary tax rate (there are exemptions such as in the case of a trading income made in the course of pursuing a hobby such as stamp collecting; corporations and other taxable entities are also taxed on trading profits). This is not what we mean by capital gains taxation, even though in ordinary discourse a trading profit might well be described as a capital gain. Rather, capital gains generally refer to the "profit" made on selling an item that has been held for a year or more. The distinction seems to be a pragmatic way of distinguishing between income produced by second-hand dealers and other traders as compared with investors looking for long-term benefits from holding property, shares, art and other assets. In Australia, capital gains are taxed on realisation at the taxpayer's marginal tax rate but there are many tax concessions or tax expenditures given to taxpayers.

In 2022–23 the government expects to raise revenue of $22.4 billion through the capital gains tax (CGT) (Australian Government 2021). That figure suggests the government will collect CGT of about 1.2 per cent of total household capital gains (this compares the 2021–22 budget estimate for CGT with the household capital gains figure for 2020–21 and so may be a slight overestimate). A good deal of the CGT is paid by corporations, so the actual tax paid by households is an even lower share of capital gains received by households. Part of the reason the CGT is so low is the various concessions that apply. The annual statement giving tax expenditures (Australian Government 2021) provides an estimate of the value of the various concessions. For example, the family home is exempt from CGT and that exemption alone is valued at $47 billion (that figure is due to the family home being exempt from ordinary capital gains tax that applies to individuals as well as the 50 per cent discount usually available to individuals). The other main reason the CGT is so low is that it only applies on realisation: when the asset is sold.

The Henry Review (Australian Government 2010) gave the theoretical reasons for taxing capital gains but the review did not pursue further efforts in that regard. Its failure to do so probably reflects Henry's view that capital incomes should be lightly taxed, if at all. The Henry Review wanted to tax labour income much more heavily than what used to be known as "unearned income", the income from investments, or income on capital, as opposed to personal exertion. The Henry Review wanted income on capital to be discounted by 40 per cent compared with income on the part of someone who works for a living. Henry made it clear in a number of speeches during the review (e.g., Henry 2008 and 2009) that he had in mind a model in which people earn an income and have to decide how to allocate it between present and future consumption. Earmarking income for future consumption is the act of saving.

For the Henry Review, the question about taxing unearned income was one of how to tax the "reward" for "savings". All property income is seen as a tax on savings. The model used by Henry is typical of the models economists use to try to understand how households allocate their income over their lifetime. At first the household's only source of income is from working and their problem is to allocate income over their whole life, including retirement. That is reflected in the way Henry has talked about the tax on savings elsewhere:

> individuals make an initial choice about how much to save. This is affected by several factors, ranging from holding some funds to pay for everyday needs or some "lumpy" purchases such as a vehicle, through to decisions to save for a future family home or for retirement. Much of the analysis of savings and investment is based on an analysis of incentives between spending earnings now (consumption) and deferring that spending to some future point in time (saving) (Henry 2008).

Henry portrayed the process of investment and the acquisition of wealth in Australia as the result of hardworking individuals salting away their hard-earned, delaying consumption today for consumption on a rainy day later in their lives. Tax on that investment income frustrates that process. But the idea that wealth in Australia is deferred consumption on the part of households saving for retirement is frankly bizarre. By far the bulk of wealth in Australia is old wealth that will persist well beyond the current generation and the facts show that any current accumulations by households are a small fraction of total wealth. It is reported that the Treasury Secretary, Steven Kennedy, has a salary of $892,290 (Johnson 2022). To such a Treasury Secretary, the world may well look like the myth promoted in the Henry Review.

Household savings over the decade before the pandemic averaged $89.9 billion per annum (ABS 2022b) and some of that will be savings on the part of unincorporated business. The total household net worth in Australia is $14,677 billion (as shown above). The latter figure does not come about as a result of a bunch of workers saving part of their income for use in retirement. Our calculations suggest household savings as traditionally defined accounted for only 19.2 per cent of the increase in household wealth. Moreover, household savings as traditionally defined are only 19.4 per cent of the total savings for

Australia (calculations based on ABS 2022b; savings for the whole economy are defined as gross domestic product, or GDP, less total consumption). Even then, 43 per cent of household income is non-wage income and 69 per cent of the household savings are made by the top income quintile, which receives 56 per cent of the property incomes and mixed incomes (calculated from ABS 2022a). This suggests something like half of household savings and perhaps a lot more are derived from non-wage incomes. Furthermore, a good deal of the savings taking place on the part of households would be compulsory superannuation contributions, which are now running at $76 billion (the figure for the year to December 2021, referring to just the super guarantee contributions; when voluntary contributions and defined benefit contributions are included the figure is $139 billion – see Australian Prudential Regulation Authority 2022).

Evidently the story told by the Henry Review refers to a small part of the issue when it uses the analogy of workers' savings as the basis for not taxing the income on wealth or taxing it lightly.

A tax on wealth

Taxing wealth is a good idea even if only because there is a lot of it and it is relatively easy to tax. When asked why he robbed banks, the bank robber replied "because that's where the money is" (Quote Investigator 2013). Historically that has been a good enough reason to impose taxes on various income streams, expenditure streams and various assets. They are where the money is. But we have much better arguments for imposing taxation or more taxation on wealth in Australia.

Arguments in favour of taxing wealth

There are strong arguments in favour of taxing capital gains at the same rate as other income as was argued above. The fact that it has not happened to date means that a good deal of the accumulated wealth in Australia derives from income that has never been taxed. A wealth tax would address that to some extent. As Atkinson (2015) pointed out, while the increasing inequality due to capital gains suggests that tighter capital gains taxes may be warranted, in fact a good deal of the capital gains have already taken place and dramatically increased the wealth of the wealthy. For example, capital gains that have not been realised have never been subject to income tax. Past capital gains that skipped the tax system can only be captured by a wealth tax of some sort. Included in that would be a large amount of capital gains that accrued as a result of income disguised as capital gain. (Capital gains are taxed more lightly than other incomes if they are taxed at all, hence disguising income as capital gains can be used as a tax avoidance mechanism.)

Notice too that a wealth tax with a relatively high threshold, say fifteen times average weekly earnings – approximately $1.35 million as this is being written (ABS 2021c) – would not involve amounts that could reasonably be accumulated by ordinary income earners in Australia without assistance from large capital gains, inheritances, lottery prizes and the like.

Thomas Piketty (2014) argued that to address the creeping inequality throughout the world we need "new tools, adapted to today's challenges". He suggested the ideal is a global tax on capital or wealth. Piketty admitted that the ideal is utopian but put it as the reference point against which alternative proposals might be judged. When Piketty wrote, such an idea may well have been utopian but recently we have seen agreement among countries of the Organisation for Economic Co-operation and Development (OECD) for a co-ordinated approach to company taxation. That countries can come to some agreement on company tax suggests international approaches to such issues are not as utopian as might have been thought. Moreover, it may be more difficult to hide income overseas following recent OECD initiatives on the international coordination of tax monitoring and administration (OECD 2021). To the extent that those initiatives make it harder to hide income abroad, there is less need for international agreements on taxing wealth.

The OECD (2018) report on wealth taxes should be seen in that light. The report documented existing approaches to taxing wealth while also presenting the arguments for taxing wealth and tightening up existing tax arrangements. Among other things, the OECD reinforced the need for wealth taxes to tackle growing inequality. A wealth tax is more critical in the absence of taxes on capital, death duties and the like. The OECD did not suggest that there is any particular need for international coordination of wealth taxes even though that may well be desirable.

In many ways a wealth tax is less distortive than a CGT based on the realisation of asset values because the latter provides an incentive not to realise capital gains. The CGT can lock in particular assets, as their owners do not want to trigger CGT by selling particular assets. But wealth taxes do not incentivise the locking in of capital gains. Nor are they affected by taxpayers' tax-planning strategies. A tax on wealth cannot be avoided by changing the composition of that wealth.

The OECD (2018) argued for directly dealing with wealth inequality through the tax system. It pointed out that "wealth inequality is far greater than income inequality" and getting worse. Moreover, the OECD argued, "wealth accumulation operates in a self-reinforcing way and is likely to increase in the absence of taxation". To begin with, high earners are able to save and invest more, which means accumulating more wealth. Wealthy taxpayers are in a better position to invest in riskier assets that will tend to generate higher returns. That may be due to their "financial expertise and more lucrative investment opportunities" as well as their ability to obtain loans, so as to invest more and accumulate more wealth. The OECD also mentioned that wealth may confer more economic and political power that helps the rich get even richer. Citing Meade (1978), the OECD (2018) pointed out that wealth may bestow social status, power, greater opportunities, satisfaction or provide an insurance value against unexpected future needs. Unfortunately, these non-monetary considerations are not further developed by the OECD. Other observers are less blunt. For example, Richard Wolff, Emeritus Professor of Economics at the University of Massachusetts, said:

> Elon Musk, Jeff Bezos and other U.S. billionaires decide alone and unaccountably how to spend hundreds of billions. The decisions of a few hundred bring economic development to some regions, industries, and enterprises and lead to the economic decline of other regions. The many millions of people affected by those spending decisions are excluded from participating in making

> them. Those millions of people lack the economic and social power wielded by unaccountable, obscenely wealthy tiny minorities. That is the opposite of democracy (2021).

The obscenely rich have also used the power they yield from their wealth to successfully undo taxes threatening their obscene wealth or its dynastic transmission through inheritance.

The examples here are American but we know there are numerous Australian examples of the exercise of private power including through bodies such as the Business Council of Australia, the Mining Council of Australia and so on.

It might be thought that a wealth tax is politically difficult to implement. We can anticipate resistance from the wealthy themselves. Moreover, most Western countries seem to have reduced their taxes on the rich elites and shifted the burden to lower- and middle-income households. Aspects of that in Australia include eliminating inheritance taxes, reducing top marginal rates from around 67 per cent under the Menzies government to 45 per cent now (excluding the Medicare levy), integrating company and personal income tax to substantially reduce the total tax on dividend income, and so on. Against that we have observed state governments gradually increasing taxes on property owners without much of a backlash. State and territory taxes on property have increased steadily from 1.3 per cent of GDP in 2001–02 to 1.7 per cent in 2019–20 (ABS 2021d).

Australian wealth taxation

Australia does not have a national tax on wealth or net worth. Instead, there are local government rates on some properties, which look like a tax but could almost be regarded as a fee-for-service that pays for rubbish collection and sundry other services (Australian Local Government Association 2021), and some state taxes on some types of property. The current land tax rates in various states and territories are summarised in a document prepared by the multinational business consultancy PwC (PwC 2021). The Henry Review claimed the land tax is "efficient" in the sense that land cannot be moved or otherwise altered in attempts to change the tax liability. This is not the place to enter a full critique of this notion of efficiency, but note that a tax on short people would be more "efficient" than an income tax in that sense because the former cannot be easily evaded while income can be altered by changing behaviour or disguising it – although that does not make a tax on short people a good idea. But it could be argued that a tax on land makes it relatively more attractive to hold wealth in alternatives to land, so there are spill-over effects that may well reduce economic efficiency. In any case, efficiency is not the sole criteria for a good tax arrangement.

A tax on land alone would not be a bad thing if land holdings were highly correlated with a person's or household's wealth. As it happens, the share of land in a household's net wealth falls as the net worth increases. For example, in 2018–19, the second quintile of wealth holders held 88 per cent of their net worth in land holdings while the top quintile held a smaller 39 per cent of their wealth as land (figures calculated based on ABS 2021a). We would expect that figure to fall further if we had good statistics on the top 10 per cent and 1 per cent of wealth holders. These considerations suggest that property rates do not perform well on the equity criterion.

Australia used to impose estate duties on deceased estates at both the state and federal levels, but in the 1970s there was a classic race to the bottom among state governments initiated by Queensland in 1977 that abolished estate duties (see Reinhardt and Steel 2006). A recent editorial in the *Weekend Australian Financial Review* (2021) called for a "modest inheritance tax". That followed the publication of a report by the Productivity Commission (2021) on the large magnitude of inheritances in Australia. The *Weekend Australian Financial Review* argument included the generous tax concessions for super as well as the booming prices of shares and real estate: the baby boomers have been lucky with all that and an inheritance tax would be a way for the government to get some of that back. In an earlier Australia Institute paper it was argued that estate duties have a major role to play in addressing the increasing inequalities in Australia (Richardson 2016). Many tax specialists worry about the incentive effects of taxes and ask, with regard to particular taxes, whether they would make people work harder or less hard. They may also be interested in other behavioural effects such as how investment behaviour might change. Estate or inheritance taxes are usually said to have no incentive effect on the person whose wealth is to be distributed nor to the beneficiaries of any will. As one observer put it: "the tax liability comes at a point where those who did have the money no longer need it, and those who are about to get the money have managed quite well so far without it" (Truman 2006).

Discussion and conclusions

Australia has experienced high and worsening inequality in income and wealth. Wealth has been increasing rapidly in Australia to the extent that just the increase in household wealth, the capital gains, is running higher than household income itself as conventionally defined in the national accounts. Wealth inequality is much worse than income inequality as conventionally measured. That means increases in wealth are experienced as capital gains and, when these are added to conventional measures of income, they have the effect of more than doubling total income but making the distribution of income even more unequal.

These features of the Australian economy mean that people complain about the burden of taxation yet tax falls mainly on conventional measures of income with capital gains income being mostly exempt from tax (unless it is realised). People who work for a living are taxed but the wealthy receive tax-free capital gains. We might wonder how this ever came to pass, but this chapter has pointed out that there is a lot that can be done to address these inequities while the scope of the problem makes it rather urgent those inequities are dealt with.

The equity arguments for taxing capital gains are overwhelming. It is simply wrong and discriminatory to tax two different forms of income at different rates. In the year to December 2021 capital gains were 19 per cent of wealth on average. Even with a 10 per cent capital gain, someone with a modest wealth of $402,000 is making in capital gains an amount equivalent to the minimum wage in Australia ($772.60 a week as this is being written). PAYG tax on the minimum wage is around $80 a week or $4,175.25 per annum but nothing for most recipients of the equivalent income in the form of capital gains.

The Australian tax system presently taxes capital gains at half the rate for "normal" income and then only on realisation and with a lot of exemptions. Some of those exemptions could be closed, which would give an immediate revenue boost of perhaps $10 billion per annum. That would make a small contribution towards properly including capital gains into the Australian tax system. If the system could impose just an average 2.5 per cent tax on capital gains as they accrue, there would be additional revenue of around $34 billion.

To use the "lifters and leaners" language of former Liberal Treasurer Joe Hockey, the conventional definition of income in the national accounts can be thought of as the income resulting from the activities of the "lifters". Meanwhile we have a class of "leaners" who passively receive income mainly in the form of capital gains and who pay almost no tax on it but accumulate it into massive fortunes. The leaners receive more than the lifters but the latter do the work and pay the taxes.

Taxing wealth is at least as important if not more important than taxing capital gains. A lot of wealth is created through capital gains that have never been taxed. The amounts involved are far from trivial as we have seen. An average wealth tax of just 0.5 per cent would raise some $65 billion per annum. A progressive system with higher rates on bigger wealth holdings would also be useful in tackling inequality in Australia.

Taxes on inheritances should also play a large part of any tax system. These taxes are almost perfect in that they apply to people who no longer need the wealth and to people who have not become used to it. These taxes should be good for close to $20 billion based on the Productivity Commission (2021) estimates of the value of inheritances. These and other measures need to be discussed as a start towards a fairer tax system.

The above revenue sources are available by including unearned income in the case of capital gains as well as the fruits of unearned income in the case of wealth. For those who want to balance the budget, the alternative to these easy revenue sources is to impose tax burdens on those whose income derives from personal effort. It seems urgent that Australia thinks creatively about capital gains and wealth. It is not too extreme to suggest Australia's fiscal system is broken, in that there has been a fundamental change in the nature of Australia's household income. It is analogous to scientists discovering that there is a vast amount of dark matter that accounts for the behaviour of the universe. Similarly, there is a vast amount of "dark income" without which it is virtually impossible to explain the Australian economy and the magnitude of the inequality and inequities in the system.

Part of the neoliberal mindset includes the view that the wealthy should be left alone to pursue their interests in business and so add to national output and employment, hence the rich need encouragement to save and invest. The view from the executive suite in the federal Treasury is only slightly more sophisticated. Wealth in Australia is seen as the result of people finding work and saving for their retirement out of their post-tax income – people who should be encouraged to save with low tax rates on any income earned on their savings. But this myth is a smoke screen that hides the Australian rich who make little contribution to the revenue while those with more visible income pick up the tab.

References

Armour, P., R.V. Burkhauser and J. Larrimore (2013). *Levels and Trends in United States Income and its Distribution: A Crosswalk from Market Income towards a Comprehensive Haig–Simons Income Approach*. National Bureau of Economic Research (USA). Working Paper 19110, June. https://www.nber.org/papers/w19110.

Atkinson, A.B. (2015). *Inequality: What Can Be Done?* London: Harvard University Press.

Australian Bureau of Statistics (ABS) (2019). *Household Income and Wealth, Australia*, 12 July. https://tinyurl.com/338s6hv8.

ABS (2021a). *Australian National Accounts: Distribution of Household Income, Consumption and Wealth, 2003–04 to 2019–20*, 18 June. https://tinyurl.com/2na3jf2

ABS (2021b). *Australian National Accounts: National Income, Expenditure and Product, September 2021*, 1 December. https://tinyurl.com/5fhnkuzn.

ABSs (2021c). *Average Weekly Earnings, Australia, May 2021*, 19 August. https://tinyurl.com/2s3s8ymx.

ABS (2021d). *Taxation Revenue, Australia, 2019–20 Financial Year*, 27 April. https://tinyurl.com/3mbcmdnu.

ABS (2022a). *Australian National Accounts: Distribution of Household Income, Consumption and Wealth, 2019–20*, 18 June. https://tinyurl.com/2na3jf2

ABS (2022b). *Australian National Accounts: Finance and Wealth, December 2021*, 2 March. https://tinyurl.com/bvhz694n.

ABS (2022c). *Australian National Accounts: National Income, Expenditure and Product, December 2021*, 31 March. https://tinyurl.com/easf943k.

Australian Government (1985). *Reform of the Australian Tax System*. Draft White Paper. Canberra: Australian Government Publishing Service.

Australian Government (2010). *Australia's Future Tax System: Report to the Treasurer*, Part Two Detailed Analysis. 2 vols. Canberra: Australian Government Publishing Service. [Henry Review]

Australian Government (2021). Statement 5: Revenue. Budget Paper No 1, Budget 2021–22. https://tinyurl.com/wtewfdt9.

Australian Local Government Association (2021). *Facts and Figures*. 21 December. https://alga.asn.au/facts-and-figures/.

Australian Prudential Regulation Authority (2022). *Quarterly superannuation performance statistics: September 2019 to December 2021*. https://tinyurl.com/mvv8nk4x.

Haig, R.M. (1921). The concept of income – economic and legal aspects. In R.M. Haig, ed. *The Federal Income Tax*. New York, NY: Columbia University Press.

Henry, K. (2008). *Architecture of Australia's tax and transfer system*, August. https://tinyurl.com/ycywxhyh.

Henry, K. (2009). *Taxation reform and fiscal federalism – Implications of Australia's Future Tax System Review*, August. https://tinyurl.com/32ynnn9b.

Johnson, S. (2022). How Australia is home to the world's richest public servants – with taxpayers funding salaries three times larger than those in Britain and the U.S. *Daily Mail*, 4 May.

Meade, J.E. (1978). *The Structure and Reform of Direct Taxation: Report of a Committee Chaired by Professor J.E. Meade*. London: Allen & Unwin.

Organisation for Economic Co-operation and Development (OECD) (2018). *The Role and Design of Net Wealth Taxes in the OECD*. Report. https://tinyurl.com/2e8atefv.

OECD (2021). *130 countries and jurisdictions join bold new framework for international tax reform*. Media release. https://tinyurl.com/3ryjexmr.

Piketty, T. (2014). *Capital in the Twenty-First Century*, trans. A. Goldhammer. Cambridge MA: Harvard University Press.

Productivity Commission (2021). *Wealth Transfers and Their Economic Effects*. Research paper. Canberra: Productivity Commission.

PwC (2021). *Australian stamp duty and land tax maps*. 30 June. https://tinyurl.com/yn83jpd9.

Reinhardt, S., and L. Steel (2006). *A brief history of Australia's tax system*. Treasury Economic Roundup (Winter). https://tinyurl.com/55wfk2j2.

Richardson, D. (2016). *Surprise Me when I'm Dead: Revisiting the Case for Estate Duties*. Discussion Paper, February. Australia Institute. https://tinyurl.com/45y8hz7b.

Richardson, D. (2021). *The Intergenerational Report Ignores Booming Wealth and Capital Gains*. Discussion paper. 25 August. https://tinyurl.com/2s3pk5jx.

Simons, H.C. (1938). *Personal Income Taxation: The Definition of Income as a Problem of Fiscal Policy*. Chicago, IL: University of Chicago Press.

Staff of the Joint Committee on Taxation (2012). *Overview of the definition of income used by the staff of the Joint Committee on Taxation in distributional analyses*. Congress of the United States. Committee Document JCX-15-12, 8 February. https://tinyurl.com/d6yx9wz6.

Truman, M. (2006). A perfect tax? *Taxation*, 2 March. https://tinyurl.com/3cc9n638.

Weekend Australian Financial Review (2021). Is it now time for a modest inheritance tax? Editorial. 11 December.

Quote Investigator (2013). I rob banks because that's where the money is. https://tinyurl.com/4aunude3.

Wolff, R. (2021). *A critique of obscene wealth*. 19 December. Blog post. https://bit.ly/4bGMvhj.

6

Neoliberal labour market policy in Australia: The "fair go" is long gone

Greg Jericho and Jim Stanford

At the dawn of the neoliberal era, Australia possessed one of the most egalitarian labour markets in the world. After three decades of postwar economic development and social policy innovation, by the 1970s Australian wages were high and relatively equal, workplace rights and protections were extensive – and workers felt empowered to keep demanding more.

Of course, while this postwar prosperity was relatively inclusive by historical comparison, it was never equally accessible to all. Deep traditions of sexism and racism in Australia (the latter reinforced by discriminatory immigration policies) framed this prosperity around a working class largely understood in white, male terms. Indeed, the terminology "Harvester Man" was used to describe the basis for wage setting in Australia through the first 75 years of the 20th century (Buchanan et al. 2006). This referenced the pivotal Arbitration Commission 1907 "Harvester Judgement" which established a "living wage" based on the assumption of a male family breadwinner.

Despite these omissions and inequalities, it was in this context of regulated, egalitarian postwar growth that the Australian ethos of a "fair go for all" was defined and cemented in popular consciousness. Rising living standards, relative equality and a strong culture of working-class opportunity underpinned an era of inclusive prosperity unprecedented in the history of Australian capitalism.

However, these gains of workers, accompanied by other constraints on business (like higher taxes, intrusive regulations and public ownership), sparked a backlash from business and financial elites (in Australia and globally) that led to the birth and consolidation of neoliberalism. Everywhere it has been practised, a primary goal of neoliberalism was to disassemble the institutions underpinning workers' postwar gains: rolling back the power of unions, reestablishing job insecurity, suppressing labour costs and reinforcing labour discipline in workplaces. Australia was no exception: the remaking of Australia's labour market was a top priority for neoliberal policy makers from the outset.

The neoliberal restructuring of labour markets and labour policy has had a unique trajectory in Australia. This is in part because there was more distance for neoliberal policy to travel in Australia to achieve a solidly employer-friendly labour regime, given the relatively egalitarian state of affairs at the end of the postwar expansion. It also reflects the unique configuration of Australian party politics, in which much initial neoliberal change was implemented by the Australian Labor Party (rather than from right-wing parties, as in most other industrial countries).

This chapter will review the history and dimensions of the neoliberal restructuring of Australia's labour market. In contrast to past emphasis on "fair go" egalitarianism, today's labour market is now marked by a very lopsided balance of power between business and workers, relatively high levels of inequality and job insecurity, and an industrial relations system that can only be described as repressive. The first major section briefly reviews the history of the dismantling of the postwar labour regime, and its replacement by a labour system marked by employer dominance and permanent insecurity. The next section interrogates the misleading and one-sided ideological narrative that accompanied neoliberal labour policy – founded on shallow and manipulative conceptions of "flexibility" and "productivity". The third section reviews several empirical indicators of Australia's current labour market. Evidenced by the suppression of labour costs, de-unionisation and soaring profitability, it is clear that this neoliberal restructuring has been remarkably successful for employers – although it has not translated into improved capital investment, innovation or productivity, all of which have stagnated in neoliberal Australia. The conclusion considers the prospects, at time of writing, for reversing some of the extremes of this neoliberal employment regime.

Ratcheting down: the evolution of Australian labour market policy under neoliberalism

Australia's tradition of innovative and egalitarian labour policy was established early in its colonial history. Important labour struggles (like the campaign for an eight-hour day) featured centrally in pre-Federation economic and political developments. Soon after Federation, the Commonwealth Conciliation and Arbitration Court was established to apply the "rule of law" to labour disputes, hoping to avoid industrial confrontations in favour of reasoned argument – equivalent to the peaceful settlement of other legal disputes. A national industrial relations system based on judicial conciliation and arbitration then developed, with most workers eventually covered by industry-wide awards. Unions were empowered to bargain for workers across entire sectors; union membership expanded rapidly, reaching over 60 per cent of employment by the mid-1950s. In the latter years of the postwar boom, stronger unions could negotiate superior, over-award terms with particular companies, which they then tried to extend across entire sectors through the Awards. Real wages grew rapidly, and wage gaps between different groups of workers were relatively modest. The postwar expansion of social welfare and income support programs reinforced income equality. The income share captured by the richest 1 per cent of the population was halved through the postwar era, falling to 4 per cent by 1980 (among the lowest of any industrial country) from 9 per cent at the end of the war.

But opposition by businesses and their owners to this relatively egalitarian model of growth intensified as the postwar era continued, and Australia (like other countries of the Organisation for Economic Co-operation and Development, or OECD) confronted financial and political instability. Neoliberalism began with a powerful attack on Australia's labour relations system, complemented by other business-friendly reforms (including a flexible exchange rate, international trade liberalisation, stricter monetary policy and the privatisation of public assets).

One unique feature of Australian neoliberalism was the role of Australian Labor Party governments in its initial introduction (Humphrys and Cahill 2017). After the election of a Labor federal government in 1983 led by Bob Hawke (former President of the Australian Council of Trade Unions), the first of several prices and incomes accords was implemented. It restrained wage increases below the rate of inflation, in return for improvements in social programs – including the introduction of universal health-care benefits and compulsory superannuation, which was originally conceived as a method of channelling labour compensation into a non-spendable pool of assets, in order to reduce the assumed inflationary effects of wage increases (Philips 2013). Subsequent accords further reshaped labour relations and employment policy during Labor's 13-year tenure. Wage increases were restrained and linked to measures to boost productivity and enhance management prerogative in workplaces (Stewart 2004). In effect, the Accord and its associated policies represented a form of "constrained neoliberalism" (Peetz and Baily 2011). While the strategy was intended as a compromise to trade off wage restraint for social welfare enhancements, later Coalition governments imposed stricter constraints on collective bargaining and union power – while abandoning accompanying commitments to expanding the social wage.

Another important labour market legacy of Labor's time in office during the early neoliberal era was a shift to enterprise-based collective bargaining. The Keating government's *Industrial Relations Reform Act* of 1993 reduced the ambition of sector-wide awards (repositioning them as backstops for wages and conditions, rather than as a leading edge of industrial progress) and created a new system whereby collective bargaining occurred mostly at the enterprise level. Unions initially supported this shift through the seventh (and final) Accord in 1991 (Forsyth and Holbrook 2017), hoping it would allow more generous wage increases (at least in some workplaces) than had been permitted under previous accords. Industry-wide awards were relegated to a second-tier or fallback status; breakthroughs in wages and conditions then depended on stronger unions winning them at specific companies. Keating's legislation recognised a legal right of workers to strike for the first time, protected from lawsuits by employers (McCrystal 2010) – but set strict boundaries limiting the exercise of that right.

In 1996, a new employer-friendly Coalition government under John Howard introduced numerous changes in labour law, including the *Workplace Relations Act* of 1996 (Fenwick and Howe 2009; Riley and Sheldon 2008). These changes reduced the arbitration powers of the Industrial Relations Commission, prohibited closed-shop agreements and preferential union hiring systems, restricted access to workplaces by union officials and required the provisions of enterprise agreements to be made equally available to all workers in a workplace (whether union members or not). It also extended the scope for enterprise agreements to be implemented without unions, through non-union agreements. The Howard legislation also allowed enterprise bargaining to establish terms lower than minimum standards in some areas, so long as workers were compensated by superior provisions in other areas; this dilution of minimum labour standards was justified by the supposed need for "flexibility" across individual workplaces (Mitchell et al. 2005).

During its last term in power, the Howard government introduced more aggressive anti-union measures bundled in the *Work Choices Act* of 2005, although the 1996 *Act* was the source of the more far-reaching restrictions on union security and union activity, including its prohibitions of union preference and membership clauses, and strong restrictions on union right of entry to workplaces (Fenwick and Howe 2009; see also Riley and Sheldon 2008). *Work Choices* expanded federal industrial rules through the takeover of former state powers. Individual contracts (even in workplaces with enterprise agreements) were permitted – supposedly underpinned by five basic minimum standards (which were often ignored in practice). *Work Choices* also limited what matters could legitimately be discussed during collective bargaining, narrowing negotiations to core matters directly tied to the employment relationship, and excluding many other workplace issues (Stewart and Riley 2007). Employers' power to dismiss workers was enhanced (especially for smaller businesses). Other measures enacted during the Howard government's last term included creating the Australian Building and Construction Commission to police union activity in construction. This multidimensional assault on union rights was opposed by a powerful " Your Rights at Work" campaign, led by the Australian Council of Trade Unions, contributing to the electoral defeat of Howard's government in 2007 (Wilson and Spies-Butcher 2011).

Hopes were high for a major shift in labour market and industrial relations policy under the subsequent Labor government, but those hopes were ultimately disappointed. Labor oversaw the streamlining and consolidation of the awards system: dramatically reducing the number of awards and affirming explicitly they would now function solely as a "safety net" of minimum standards. The *Fair Work Act* of 2009 created a new Fair Work Commission. It had power to determine awards and minimum wages, but unlike its predecessor industrial commission, it had limited power to conciliate or arbitrate collective bargaining disputes (which, except in exceptional circumstances, were left to employers and unions to settle). The *Fair Work Act* also established 10 National Employment Standards (stronger than the five minimums created under the Howard government). Most features of previous Coalition labour law, including limits on unions' right of entry, prohibitions of union preferences in hiring, and strict limits on industrial action, were retained.

A series of three Coalition governments, under three different prime ministers, was elected beginning in 2013. Their anti-union rhetoric remained aggressive, but without full control of the Senate the Coalition's industrial relations legislative agenda was relatively incremental – including a Royal Commission into alleged union corruption, which set the stage for more initiatives to regulate and police union activity. In sum, during the Coalition's nine-year term (ending in 2022), union membership and collective bargaining coverage continued to erode, and wage growth stagnated at historic lows (Stewart, Stanford and Hardy 2022).

It is clear from this brief history that labour and industrial relations policy in Australia under neoliberalism has followed a ratchet pattern (for fuller accounts of the evolution of labour law and policy during the neoliberal era, see Buchanan and Considine 2007; Peetz and Baily 2011; Bray and Stewart 2013; Fair Work Ombudsman 2017; Stanford 2018). Labor governments set the initial, important neoliberal reforms in motion – including the erosion of industry-wide wage regulation, its partial replacement with decentralised enterprise bargaining, deliberate efforts to suppress wages, and restrictions on union activity. Later Coalition governments enhanced those measures with more intrusive and punitive restrictions, with special focus on undermining the long-run institutional, financial and social base of trade unionism. Intervening Labor governments under prime ministers Kevin Rudd and Julia Gillard relaxed some of the most extreme of these measures but preserved their overall effect. Later Coalition governments tightened the ratchet a bit further, with more suppression and vilification of union activity, pay caps on public sector workers, and policies that entrenched the growth of insecure work. The overall trend of de-unionisation, the weakening of the awards system, and the individualisation of employment relations continued, regardless of which party was in power. This integrated, multidimensional strategy to enhance the power of employers over work and employment has been a key part of the overarching neoliberal effort to restore business power in all areas of Australian life. As described in the following sections, from the perspective of employers this strategy has clearly been successful.

"Design features" and neoliberal ideology

The essence of neoliberal labour market policy was inadvertently revealed with surprising clarity in 2019 by Finance Minister Mathias Cormann. He was responding to a question on *Sky News* about why average wage growth in Australia had been so weak over the previous several years:

> The whole reason why it is important to have flexibility in the labour market … is to ensure that wages can adjust in the context of economic conditions to avoid massive spikes in unemployment, which are incredibly disruptive. That is a deliberate design feature of our economic architecture (Murphy 2019).

"Flexibility" is a striking euphemism to describe a decade marked by the weakest sustained wage growth in Australia's postwar history (for historical data on the historic weakness of wage growth in Australia after 2013, see Stewart, Stanford and Hardy 2022). But for a politician to confirm that suppressing wages was a deliberate goal of policy was nevertheless revealing. Soon after, Cormann's colleague Linda Reynolds unwittingly confirmed how unusual it was that the bare truth of neoliberalism should be spoken out loud, when she suggested (in an exchange reported by Murphy 2019) to *Sky News* journalist David Speers that the words must have been said by the leader of the Opposition, Bill Shorten:

> David Speers: Do you agree flexibility in wages and keeping wages at a modest level is a deliberate feature of our economic architecture?
>
> Linda Reynolds: No, absolutely not. For Bill Shorten to even suggest that ...
>
> David Speers: I'm quoting Mathias Cormann.

Cormann's statement (and Reynolds' confusion) revealed not only the true purpose of neoliberal policies, but also how much it has become accepted conventional wisdom. Cormann clearly assumed that the theory behind austere neoliberal labour policy was self-evident and should be taken as given. So accepted has the ideology become that elected politicians can now brag about how successful they have been in suppressing labour costs.

And yet the 2022 Australian election revealed the continuing divide between this accepted conventional wisdom among media and political elites, and the reality experienced by those at the sharp end of neoliberal policies. An important debate over wages broke out when Labor Party leader Anthony Albanese suggested that minimum wages should be lifted to keep up with inflation, accelerating in the wake of the COVID-19 pandemic. His Coalition opponents seized on his remarks, seeing them as an opportunity to discredit Labor's economic competence. How unthinkable, they fumed, that a prospective prime minister suggest that the real living standards of low-wage workers should be protected against surging prices. But the attack on Albanese backfired. Most voters (most of whom, after all, are workers) agreed that real wages should not go backward. Exit polling showed an overwhelming majority of voters in that election (including 79 per cent of Coalition supporters!) agreed wages should at least keep up with inflation (Raynes 2022). Where Coalition leaders assumed the logic of wage suppression should be self-evident, public support for higher wages ultimately enhanced Labor's winning campaign.

Empirical dimensions of neoliberal policy in practice

The impact of neoliberal policies on labour market functioning in Australia is starkly evident. The ratcheted restructuring of labour market institutions, laws and practices over the past 40 years has resulted in reduced union size and power; the erosion of collective bargaining; the near-disappearance of industrial action; the widespread replacement of standard employment (full-time, permanent, waged jobs) with precarious work in many different forms (including part-time, casual, labour-hire, contracted-out and now gig jobs); slow wage growth and declining real wages; steady erosion of the share of national income going to labour; slower productivity growth (not faster); and an unlinking of real wages from whatever productivity growth was achieved. The overall impact has been a historic shift of national income towards profits and away from labour. And that, as evidenced by occasional moments of honesty from Mathias Cormann and others, was precisely the point.

Neoliberalism arose in the wake of high-inflation years of the 1970s, and its restrictive policies are often framed as necessary to prevent a return of high inflation. This narrative theme has been resuscitated after the COVID-19 pandemic, when a combination of supply disruptions, energy price shocks and opportunistic profit-taking by businesses pushed the inflation rate up again. But while fear of inflation is positioned as the primary impetus for these policies, it requires little unpicking to see their true goal is actually to transfer national income from workers to companies (and the high-income individuals who own and direct them). In other words, the true goal of neoliberal labour policy is less to control inflation than to control workers.

Making the workplace relations system more "flexible", along with other so-called micro-economic reforms, was justified by claims that productivity growth (presumably handcuffed by government and union interference) would be unleashed by neoliberal policies. In turn, proponents argued, that would lead to improved living standards. Indeed, this is the core assumption embedded in trickle-down economics. Now, some 40 years into the experiment, evidence of any productivity benefit from neoliberal policies is still lacking. As illustrated in Figure 6.1, real labour productivity growth has deteriorated steadily since 1983 (after the first neoliberal measures included in the accords). In fact, Australia experienced much stronger productivity growth in pre-neoliberal times – despite supposedly productivity-disrupting inflation, regulation and strikes – than since. Productivity growth has been especially miserable since the waning of the mining investment boom in 2013, and the election of three successive Coalition governments: equalling just 0.5 per cent per year since then, much slower than the OECD average. If the goal of neoliberal policy were indeed to better grow the economic pie, it has failed miserably: on a cumulative basis, productivity growth since 1983 (under 1.2 per cent per year) has been one-third slower than during the two previous decades.

A seeming productivity surge in the latter 1990s is often attributed to neoliberal micro-economic policies (including deregulation and privatisation). In contrast, Quiggin (2004) attributed the temporary improvement in productivity growth to reduced investment, job cuts and work intensification. For a while, output could increase with fewer inputs, causing measured productivity to rise. In newly privatised utilities, for example, private investors recouped often excessive prices paid for formerly public infrastructure assets by cutting capital budgets and downsizing staff. But these gains could only be temporary, eventually offset by deferred investments and hiring (often for wasteful marketing and administration roles) in subsequent years (Richardson 2019). In any event, productivity gains in the 1990s did not even make up for the productivity slowdown in the latter 1980s. And since then, Australian productivity growth has slowed down considerably.

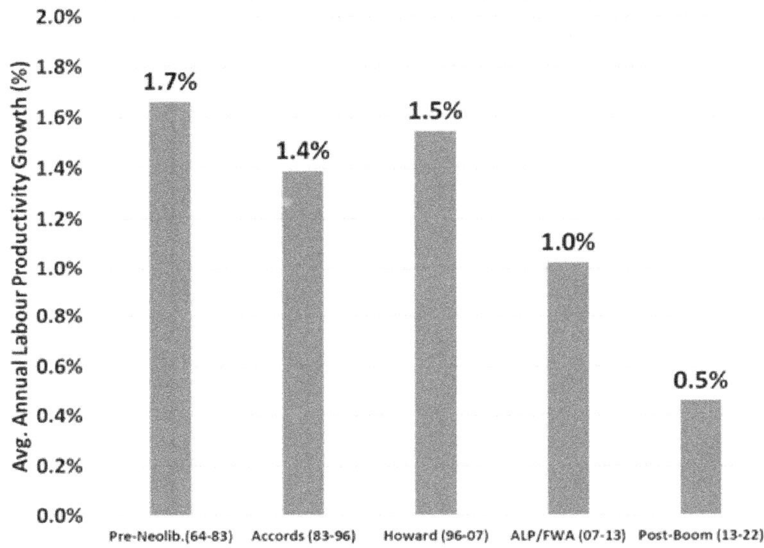

Figure 6.1 Labour productivity growth by decade. Source: Calculations from OECD Economic Outlook data, labour productivity in total economy.

In 2015, the Productivity Commission investigated the productivity effects of the workplace relations framework. It acknowledged that "surmise aside, there is little robust evidence that the different variants of workplace relations systems over the last 20 years have had detectable effects on measured economywide productivity" (Productivity Commission 2015, 9). The Commission hurriedly stressed "this does not mean there are no effects, but simply that they apply at the enterprise and industry level and are hard to identify in the aggregate economy given the myriad of other factors shaping productivity" (Productivity Commission 2015, 9). In other words, when the evidence to support neoliberal policy is lacking, the problem must be with the evidence, not the policy.

While there is no evidence of productivity improvements during the neoliberal era (in fact, productivity growth since the mid-1980s has slowed), there is clear evidence of a lasting and deliberate redistribution of output toward profits. Figure 6.2 documents the long-term shift of income from labour to capital in Australia since the mid-1980s. During the postwar expansion, thanks to strong wage growth and rapid industrialisation, the share of gross domestic product (GDP) paid to workers had grown steadily, reaching a peak of 58 per cent of GDP by the mid-1970s. Eventually higher labour costs (combined with other restrictions on private corporations) squeezed profits, which fell to 15 per cent of GDP (in gross terms, before depreciation). A similar profit squeeze occurred in most other OECD economies in the latter years of the postwar expansion, contributing to the emergence of global neoliberalism; Glyn (2006) reviewed those global trends. In Australia, backlash from the corporate sector then led to the introduction of neoliberal labour market policies to boost employer power and reduce labour costs (supplemented by complementary measures in other realms, including monetary policy, trade liberalisation and privatisation). The quick and intended result was a long rise in corporate profitability (already evident by the mid-1980s) and a corresponding erosion of labour compensation.

In the wake of the COVID-19 pandemic and its aftermath, this redistribution from workers to owners reached new extremes. By 2022, labour compensation fell to 45 per cent of Australian GDP – lower than any previous time in postwar history, and down 13 percentage points from the peak of the mid-1970s. The mirror image has been an almost-equal expansion in the share of GDP going to business profits, which virtually doubled since the mid-1970s, and reached almost 30 per cent of national output during the pandemic. For those who accepted at face value claims about a "wage overhang" in the mid-1970s (purportedly the result of excessive wage demands by strong unions), that concern clearly has no relevance today. The labour share of GDP has fallen lower than any time in postwar history. Instead, the problem today is clearly a wage underhang – or perhaps a profit overhang?

Arithmetically, a decline in the labour share of GDP is caused by a divergence between real labour productivity and real labour compensation. At the micro level, real wage growth that lags behind productivity growth produces a decline in real unit labour costs. Alternatively, in nominal terms, nominal unit labour costs will fall if nominal wages grow more slowly than the sum of labour productivity growth and inflation; Jericho (2022, 57–9) discussed this further. At the macro level, the analogue is a decline in the labour share of GDP (which is in effect a macro-economic measure of unit labour cost; for more detail on the theory and measurement of labour shares, see Flanagan et al. 2018). A divergence between labour productivity and labour compensation arose early in the neoliberal era, and has worsened subsequently – to the point where it is difficult to ascertain any relationship between productivity and wages at all. This is a devastating failure in the logic of trickle-down economics: in neoclassical labour market theory, an automatic link between wages and productivity is supposed to give workers a direct incentive to boost productivity. But that promise has been doubly disproved (see Figure 6.3). First, productivity growth has slowed (not accelerated) under neoliberal policy. And second, even the modest productivity gains that have been achieved had little effect on labour compensation.

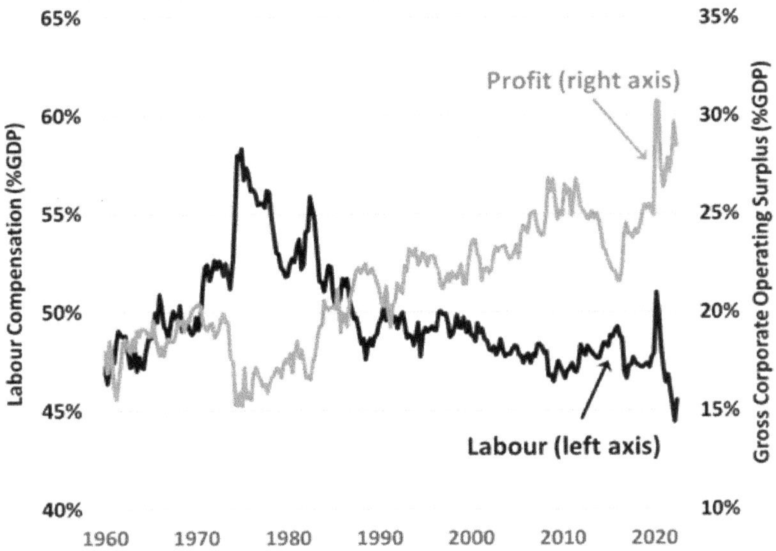

Figure 6.2 Shares of national output. Source: Calculations from ABS Australian National Accounts data.

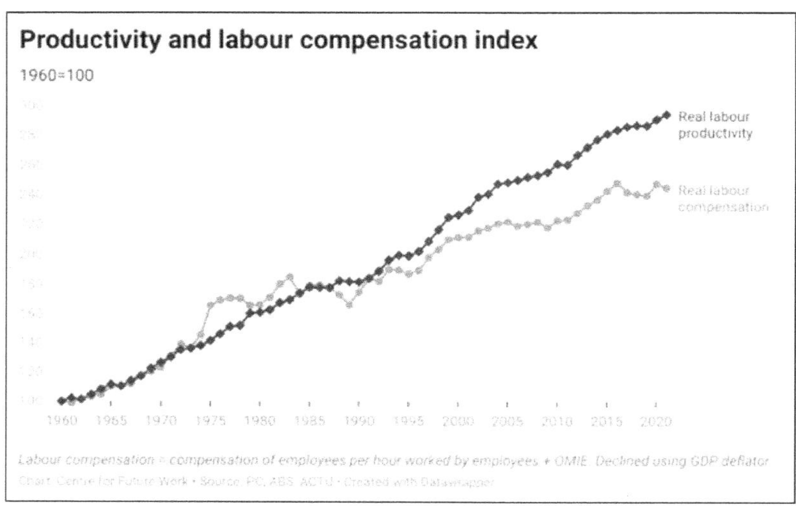

Figure 6.3 Productivity and labour compensation index.

From the early 1990s onwards, real wages have consistently lagged behind real labour productivity growth. This divergence reflects many factors. Wage growth was suppressed by the shift to enterprise bargaining, the erosion of minimum wages and the awards, and restrictions on union activity. Corporate profits were boosted by lower unit labour costs, privatisation of once-public assets, and increasing financial activity and financial profit: financial corporations' gross operating surplus more than tripled as a share of the economy, from an average of 1.35 per cent of GDP from 1960 through to the end of 1984 (when the banking system was opened to foreign entities), to an average of 4.7 per cent since the turn of the century (calculations from ABS 2023, Table 7). Since 2014, there has been virtually no real wage growth at all in Australia – despite continuing (modest) productivity growth. More recently, with the surge in post-pandemic inflation, real wages have begun to decline rapidly.

In sum, after decades of labour market policy aimed deliberately at restricting union power, suppressing wages and giving employers more unilateral power over the organisation and conditions of work, it cannot be credibly argued that this agenda has anything to with lifting productivity and wages. Neither has it boosted business capital spending, which has languished (apart from a short-lived boom in capital-intensive resource extraction projects in the 2000s). Nevertheless, in terms of its true goal, neoliberal labour market policy has clearly been "successful": the power and profits of employers, and the capital-owning class more generally, have been lifted spectacularly. But that success has come at the cost of stagnant living standards, growing inequality and permanent insecurity among workers.

Several obvious policy interventions have been central to achieving this redistribution of power and income from workers to capital. These include de-unionisation, a dramatic weakening of collective bargaining, restrictions on industrial action, the expansion of non-standard and precarious work, and the erosion of minimum wages and the awards system.

- *De-unionisation*: Howard-era legislation prohibited union preferences in employment and hiring, in a direct assault on union membership. Later changes also prohibited arrangements such as bargaining fees, which would collect resources from non-members covered by a union-administered enterprise agreement. The terms of enterprise agreements must apply to all workers in a covered workplace; benefits or entitlements cannot be restricted to union members. The end result is full ratification of free-riding for non-union members: they are entitled to access any benefits negotiated by unions, without contributing to the cost of negotiating or administering them. The intended result is that narrowly rational individuals see no personal incentive for union membership (Stanford 2021a provides a full discussion of the impacts of free-riding in industrial relations, and a catalogue of potential remedies). Union recruitment efforts, emphasising the importance of solidarity and collective action, resist this individualistic logic, but have been unsuccessful in stopping the decline in membership. Restrictions on union access to workplaces, legal controls over union representatives, and other anti-union rules further inhibit organising. In 2022 union membership fell to 12.5 per cent of employees, an all-time low (and just 8 per cent in the private sector); as recently as 1990, the share of employees who belonged to unions had been more than 50 per cent. Along with New Zealand, Australia has experienced the most dramatic de-unionisation of any industrial country.

- *Collective bargaining coverage*: Before the introduction of enterprise bargaining, most workers in Australia were covered by some combination of a collective agreement (usually negotiated at the sectoral level) and an award. Coverage declined notably under the new enterprise-based system. In the early 2010s, even after the introduction of the *Fair Work Act*, federally regulated enterprise agreements covered less than one-quarter of all employees; another 10 per cent were covered by state-regulated enterprise agreements. (Other than in Victoria, which integrated its industrial system with the federal structure, most state and local public sector workers are covered by state industrial relations laws.) More recently, bargaining coverage plunged further after 2013 – suppressed by employer resistance, the limited organisational capacities of unions, and government vilification of unions. By 2022 barely 10 per cent of private sector workers in Australia were covered by an enterprise agreement, down almost half since 2013 (calculations from Department of Employment and Workplace Relations 2023); individual employment contracts are now the most common form of employment relationship, followed by awards and then enterprise agreements. The rapid erosion of collective bargaining has been an important cause of record-slow wage growth experienced during this time. Empirical analysis in Stanford, Macdonald and Raynes (2022) suggests over half of the slowdown in wage growth in Australia after 2013 can be attributed to the decline of collective bargaining coverage.
- *Industrial action*: Australia has some of the most severe restrictions on industrial action of any industrial country. Workers can only strike in limited windows related to enterprise agreement negotiations. The rapid erosion of both union membership and collective bargaining automatically reduces strike frequency. This has been exacerbated by onerous restrictions on strike activity: unions must give full notice of planned actions, each action must be ratified by membership ballots, and even then legal strikes are regularly banned by industrial regulators on grounds they are too

disruptive – which is, after all, the point of a strike (see McCrystal 2010, 2019 for useful overviews of the barriers to legal strike action). Proportionate days lost to industrial disputes have declined 99 per cent compared to turbulent pre-neoliberal times, in recent years representing an average of just 0.01 per cent (one-hundredth of 1 per cent) of total working time. The near disappearance of industrial action in Australia is both a consequence and cause of the erosion of workers' bargaining power under neoliberal governance.

- *Non-standard and precarious work*: Neoliberal labour policy has promoted the emergence of more flexible (from the employers' perspective) employment forms, which allow businesses to fluidly and costlessly match labour inputs to fluctuating customer demand. These strategies include part-time work, casual jobs, labour hire, outsourced and contracted-out work, and (more recently) platform-mediated gig work. A clear majority of employment in Australia now incorporates one or more of these dimensions of precarity (see Stanford 2021b) and Australia exhibits one of the highest incidences of non-standard work of any OECD country (Australian Council of Trade Unions 2018, 5). Labour law encourages this insecurity in several ways: allowing regular use of casual and temporary arrangements (even in steady work situations), endorsing abuse of contractor status by gig platforms and other businesses, and limiting the coverage of minimum standards (such as the minimum wage) to those with formal employment status. Two High Court decisions in 2021 opened the door fully to employer use of non-standard arrangements in almost any job, ruling that any contract designated as casual or independent will be treated as such, regardless of the real circumstances of the job (see Whitson 2021). Workers in non-standard roles have lower wages, higher turnover and underemployment and much lower union representation; the steady growth of precarious work in all its forms has been a crucial factor undercutting workers' bargaining power.
- *Minimum wage*: Australia invented the concept of minimum wages with the famous Sunshine Harvester arbitration in 1907 (see Fair Work Commission n.d.). During the postwar era, strong minimum wages, extended through the awards system, complemented collective bargaining in ongoing efforts to both lift and equalise wages. With the reconstitution of awards as a weaker "safety net",

minimum wages have fallen significantly in relative terms. Measured as a share of the prevailing median wage (known as the minimum wage "bite"), Australia's minimum wage fell from 65 per cent of median wages in 1991 to 53 per cent in recent years. Ironically, most other industrial countries significantly strengthened minimum wage policies at the same time. Thus Australia regressed from having one of the highest minimum wage bites in the world as recently as 2000 to one that now only matches the median of industrial countries. Given the erosion of other wage-supporting institutions, the minimum wage has become more critical in wage determination (Stanford 2019) and its erosion has clearly contributed to broader weakness in wages.

- *Public sector pay suppression*: Australia's public sector accounts for around 15 per cent of total employment, and these workers benefit from higher unionisation and collective bargaining coverage than in the private sector. But neoliberal governments have taken a more direct approach to suppressing wages for their own employees: imposing direct caps on wage growth, and completely circumventing normal collective bargaining rights. The Liberal state government in New South Wales pioneered this practice in 2012, imposing an austere cap (then 2.5 per cent per year) on pay raises in state-funded public services. The cap was supposedly intended to help eliminate modest deficits after the Global Financial Crisis, but it was maintained even as the state soon ran up large surpluses. Other states (including some Labor governments) and the Coalition Commonwealth government mimicked this practice. As a result, public sector wages and conditions were suppressed alongside private sector trends, despite a stronger union base (see Henderson 2018 for more discussion of the spill-over effects of public sector pay restrictions on wage trends in the broader economy). Even the Reserve Bank has highlighted the perverse effect of public sector wage suppression in hampering overall wage growth (Karp 2019).

Together, these measures have created an unforgiving labour market in which individual workers are left increasingly to their own devices in an ongoing struggle to attain decent, stable work. As Quiggin (2019) summed up: "For more than forty years, both the architecture of labour market regulation and the discretionary choices of governments have been designed with the precise objective of holding wages down". We should hardly be surprised, then, to see that these policies have "worked".

Conclusion: pushing back

Neoliberalism has overseen a profound restructuring of economic and political power in Australia's labour market over the past four decades. This agenda has weakened statutory supports for wages and job quality, aggressively rolled back union power and suppressed labour costs. This shift in the balance of power in favour of employers has not translated into improved economic performance, measured by indicators such as capital accumulation, productivity or growth. But it has certainly translated into higher profits and management authority.

This far-reaching reorientation of the labour market has been met with resistance from workers, unions and other progressive movements. The basic expectation that working people deserve a fair go retains an important degree of cultural and political resonance. The union movement, despite reduced numbers and constrained resources, has conducted feisty campaigns in both the economic and the political arenas: fighting for better terms and conditions with individual employers, and improvements in labour, macro-economic and social policies to improve the wellbeing and power of workers. Despite the entrenchment of neoliberal policies and structures, therefore, Australian workers continue to push back for something better.

The 2022 federal election saw the Labor Party win an outright majority in the House of Representatives, and the possibility to pass progressive legislation through the Senate (contingent on sufficient support from the crossbench). This opens possibilities for easing some of the most repressive aspects of neoliberal labour policy. For example, pressed by the union movement, the new Labor government passed amendments to the *Fair Work Act* in 2022 that allow new possibilities for collective bargaining on a multi-employer basis, along with other measures to strengthen bargaining and wage growth (see Stanford, Macdonald and Raynes 2022 for a review of these changes). Subsequent reforms implemented by the government tackled other problems like the misuse of casual labour and outsourcing; exploitation in gig jobs; and wage theft.

But these important reforms are not likely to alter the fundamental nature and direction of Australia's labour market. The entrenched structural power of private business, reinforced by the full spectrum of neoliberal measures (including privatisation, globalisation and financialisation), constrains the potential of the union movement and collective bargaining, even with these helpful shifts in industrial relations laws, to correct the power imbalance of the present labour market. To build an economy that genuinely reflects the values of a fair go, more ambitious efforts to regulate corporate power and assert the interests of workers and broader society in all economic decision-making will be necessary.

References

Australian Bureau of Statistics (2023). *Australian National Accounts: National Income, Expenditure and Product*. Canberra: Australian Bureau of Statistics, https://tinyurl.com/yc7jtcp5.

Australian Council of Trade Unions (2018). *The Rise of Insecure Work in Australia*. Melbourne: Australian Council of Trade Unions.

Bray, Mark, and Andrew Stewart (2013). From the arbitration system to the *Fair Work Act*: the changing approach in Australia to voice and representation at work. *Adelaide Law Review* 34: 21–41.

Buchanan, John, Ian Watson, Chris Briggs and Iain Campbell (2006). Beyond voodoo economics and backlash social policy: where next for working life research and policy? *Australian Bulletin of Labour* 32(2): 183–200.

Buchanan, John, and Gillian Considine (2007). *The Evolution of Australian Workplace IR 1987–2007: Making Sense of Recent Policy and Practice*. Sydney: Workplace Research Centre, University of Sydney.

Department of Employment and Workplace Relations (2023). *Trends in Federal Enterprise Bargaining* Canberra: Department of Employment and Workplace Relations, 21 December. https://tinyurl.com/mpc3eec5.

Fair Work Commission (n.d.). Harvester case. https://tinyurl.com/2nvcu922.

Fair Work Ombudsman (2017). Australia's Industrial Relations Timeline. https://tinyurl.com/4vy25pzp.

Fenwick, Colin, and John Howe (2009). Union security after Work Choices. In Andrew Stewart and Anthony Forsyth, eds. *Fair Work: The New Workplace Laws and the Work Choices Legacy*, 164–85. Sydney: Federation Press.

Flanagan, Francis, Frank Stilwell, Jim Stanford, David Peetz, Margaret McKenzie and Shaun Wilson (2018). Exploring the decline in the labour share of GDP: a symposium. *Journal of Australian Political Economy* 81: 5–94.

Forsyth, Antony, and Carolyn Holbrook (2017). The prices and incomes accord. *The Conversation*, 24 April.

Glyn, Andrew (2006). *Capitalism Unleashed: Finance, Globalization, and Welfare.* Oxford, UK: Oxford University Press.

Henderson, Troy (2018). Public sector austerity and its spill-over effects. In Andrew Stewart, Jim Stanford and Tess Hardy, eds. *The Wages Crisis in Australia: What it is and What to Do About it*, 115–27. Adelaide: University of Adelaide Press.

Humphrys, Elizabeth, and Damien Cahill (2017). How Labour made neoliberalism. *Critical Sociology* 43(4–5): 669–84.

Jericho, Greg (2022). *Inflation: A Primer.* Canberra: Centre for Future Work.

Karp, Paul (2019). RBA governor endorses lifting public sector wage caps to stimulate economy. *The Guardian*, 9 August, https://tinyurl.com/5n8e5j2z.

McCrystal, Shae (2010). *The Right to Strike in Australia.* Sydney: Federation Press.

McCrystal, Shae (2019). Why is it so hard to take lawful strike action in Australia? *Journal of Industrial Relations* 61(1): 129–44.

Murphy, Katharine (2019). Linda Reynolds stumbles on wages growth in TV interview. *The Guardian*, 10 March, https://tinyurl.com/yc9kbhtz.

Peetz, David, and Janis Baily (2011). Neo-liberal Evolution and Union Responses in Australia. In Gregor Gall, Adrian Wilkinson and Richard Hurd, eds. *The International Handbook of Labour Unions: Responses to Neo-Liberalism.* Cheltenham: Edward Elgar.

Philips, Keri (2013). Australia's Strange History of Superannuation. *Rear Vision, ABC News.* 23 April, https://tinyurl.com/mpe5t3cs.

Productivity Commission (2015). *Workplace Relations Framework.* Inquiry Report, No. 76, 30 November. Canberra: Productivity Commission.

Quiggin, John (2019). Ultra low wage growth isn't accidental. It is the intended outcome of government policies. *The Conversation*, 17 March. https://tinyurl.com/yc4xs59v.

Raynes, Lily (2022). *Wages, Prices, and the 2022 Federal Election.* Canberra: Centre for Future Work.

Richardson, David (2019). *The Costs of Market Experiments: Electricity Consumers Pay the Price for Competition, Privatisation, Corporatisation and Marketization.* Canberra: Australia Institute.

Riley, Joellen, and Peter Sheldon, eds (2008). *Remaking Australian Industrial Relations*. Sydney: CCH Australia Limited.

Stanford, Jim (2018). "Fair go" no more: Australian neoliberalism and labour market policy. In Damien Cahill and Phillip Toner, eds. *Wrong Way: The Legacy of Reform*, 166–85. Melbourne: La Trobe University Press and Black Inc.

Stanford, Jim (2019). *The Importance of Minimum Wages to Recent Australian Wage Trends*. Canberra: Centre for Future Work.

Stanford, Jim (2021a). International approaches to solving the "free rider" problem in industrial relations. *Labour and Industry* 31(3): 278–300.

Stanford, Jim (2021b). *Shock Troops of the Pandemic: Casual and Insecure Work in COVID and Beyond*. Canberra: Centre for Future Work.

Stanford, Jim, Fiona Macdonald and Lily Raynes (2022). *Collective Bargaining and Wage Growth in Australia*. Canberra: Centre for Future Work.

Stewart, Andrew (2004). The AIRC's Evolving Role in Policing Bargaining. *Australian Journal of Labour Law* 17(3): 247–75.

Stewart, Andrew, and Joellen Riley (2007). Working Around WorkChoices: Collective Bargaining and the Common Law. *Melbourne University Law Review* 31(3): 903–37.

Stewart, Andrew, Jim Stanford and Tess Hardy (2022). *The Wages Crisis – Revisited*. Canberra: Centre for Future Work.

Whitson, Rhianna (2021). Bosses win in High Court rejection of backpay for casuals, Uber and Deliveroo could too. *ABC News*, 4 August. https://tinyurl.com/yjt33dkk.

Wilson, Shaun, and Ben Spies-Butcher (2011). When Labour Makes a Difference: Union Mobilization and the 2007 Federal Election in Australia. *British Journal of Industrial Relations* 49(s2): s306–s331.

Part III

Case studies: Creation of neoliberal markets

7

Murray–Darling Basin water market

Maryanne Slattery and Bill Johnson

This chapter is about water markets in the Murray–Darling Basin, with an emphasis on the New South Wales southern basin. It outlines a brief history of irrigation and the evolution of water markets. Despite widespread claims that the water market is an overall success, the policy intent of water markets has not been evaluated. Claimed measures of success overlook the costs the water markets have placed on some industries, communities and the environment. Early policymakers designed a suite of policies necessary for a functioning market. Most of these have either not been implemented as intended, or not implemented at all. Finally, alternate policy objectives to manage and share water are suggested.

Brief history

Large-scale irrigation in Australia began in the late 1880s with irrigation settlements at Mildura in Victoria, followed by Renmark in South Australia. These were subsidised by governments, and privately managed and constructed. Both went into liquidation in the 1890s and hundreds of settlers faced foreclosures (National Museum Australia 2022). The Victorian and South Australian governments passed legislation that converted the schemes to irrigation trusts managed by a Board of Commissioners on behalf of the irrigators (Renmark Irrigation Trust n.d.; Wilkinson 1997).

After this, the first irrigation schemes in New South Wales in the early 1900s, on the Murrumbidgee and the Murray rivers, were funded and controlled by the state government. It constructed the irrigation channels, designated and allocated land to be irrigated, built and managed nurseries and manufacturing plants, issued irrigation licences, delivered the water and even built towns. Water was attached to land titles, and each irrigator was issued one water licence per title, to irrigate 162 hectares (400 acres). There was no limit to the volume of water that could be applied (Wilkinson 1997, 11, 41).

The system of mostly government-controlled and -subsidised irrigation that had evolved over the 20th century achieved significant agricultural development. By the 1970s and 1980s, several problems were becoming evident. Salinity was threatening irrigation and it was clear that the levels of water extractions were damaging downstream users and aquatic ecosystems. By the 1970s, the fruit industry started by governments in the Murrumbidgee was no longer viable and the governments funded a large-scale "tree-pull scheme" over the following 20 years to bail the industry out (Wilkinson 1997, 37–8). Irrigation infrastructure was ageing and needed major refurbishment, but there was no provision set aside by governments to fund it (Working Group on Water Resource Policy 1994, 1).

At the same time, farmers, particularly emerging large-scale agribusiness, were pushing for more autonomy and control over water (Wilkinson 1997, 40–1).

By the early 1990s, governments acknowledged that significant reforms to the water industry were needed (Working Group on Water Resource Policy 1994, 1). This coincided with governments' shift towards privatisation and market-based reforms at the end of the 20th century. The National Competition Policy, released in 1993, was Australia's landmark micro-economic reform program (National Competition Council 2007). A key principle was that competitive markets generally best serve the interests of consumers and the wider community (Independent Committee of Inquiry into Competition Policy in Australia 1993). This translated into the principle that water going to its highest value use would generate maximum public benefit

(Council of Australian Governments 1994; Working Group on Water Resource Policy 1994; Australian Competition and Consumer Commission 2021). To enact this principle required the creation of a "water market".

In 1995, the Australian, New South Wales, Victorian and South Australian governments agreed to the Murray–Darling Basin Cap. This sought to limit surface water extractions in the basin to the level of development that existed on 30 June 1994 (Murray–Darling Basin Commission 2000). While it was implemented to deal with over-extraction of water, it was a necessary foundation for a cap-and-trade water market (Australian Competition and Consumer Commission 2021).

In New South Wales the handover of control to private independent irrigation organisations was complete by about 2000.

The 2004 National Water Initiative replaced the water reforms of the National Competition Policy. While recognising the need for sustainable levels of take, and for water for Indigenous and cultural values, it was fundamentally an economic reform to increase efficiency of water use, provide investor confidence and improve water security (Department of Climate Change, Energy, the Environment and Water 2022).

In 2004, with the creation of water shares, New South Wales made water an asset, separate from the land title (National Water Commission 2006). These shares are a right to a volumetric share of water in a valley under a statutory Water Sharing Plan (like a share in a company). Water shares receive an annual allocation of water, based on water availability. The average amount of allocation received is known as reliability.

The creation of water shares set the foundation of a water market to allow the trade of both water shares and allocations.

Governments renewed efforts to facilitate water trade and remove barriers to trade under the National Water Initiative, including trade between states and valleys in the southern Murray–Darling Basin (Wheeler 2022). By 2021, the average annual value of trade was reported to be more than $1.8 billion (Australian Competition and Consumer Commission 2021).

The intent of the water market

The water market is intended to move water to its highest value use, which it is claimed generates maximum public benefit (Australian Competition and Consumer Commission 2021). Maximum public benefit is also referred to as the "national interest" (Commonwealth of Australia 2019a; Simpkins 2020).

The water market is considered by many to be an overall success, delivering substantial net benefits to the irrigation sector (Productivity Commission 2021; Quinlivan 2022; Wheeler 2022).

The market is claimed to be a valuable risk management tool, and to encourage efficient water use. It is said to be beneficial to irrigators during droughts by allowing trade of water from flexible demands (annual crops) to inflexible demands (permanent crops), and to improve irrigators' access to finance (Productivity Commission 2021).

Problems with the definition of "highest value use"

There is some acknowledgement that the benefits of the market are not even across the basin and communities. This was a finding from a review commissioned by the former Commonwealth Water Minister, Keith Pitt: "there is clear evidence that market reforms have had uneven impacts, with some communities feeling like the collateral damage of improved outcomes in another region" (Panel for Independent Assessment of Social and Economic Conditions in the Murray–Darling Basin 2020, 59).

Others, however, point to fundamental problems caused by acceptance of the National Competition policy principle of allocating water to its "highest value use". A New South Wales parliamentary inquiry and the peak New South Wales irrigation body argued that the policy of moving water to its highest value use in the national interest is a threat to Australia's food security:

> we are persuaded by those who raised concerns about the growth in permanent plantings of "high-value" crops such as almonds, at the expense of others. It is our view that if this trend continues, New South Wales will face a serious loss in agricultural diversity.

> This presents a risk to our food security, and to the health and prosperity of all the local communities that rely on irrigated agriculture. (Select Committee on the status of water trading in New South Wales 2022, 45)
>
> a principle of water policy in Australia is that the water should go to the highest value use . . . As consistent as that is with a free market approach, it may not necessarily be in the National Interest . . . It is not the intention of the NSWIC [New South Wales Irrigators Council] to undermine public confidence in food security matters with any public statements, however it is clearly the responsibility of Australian governments to understand the implications of their policies and to ensure that there is a plan in place to ensure food staples are not under threat from external or internal factors (Simpkins 2020, 2).

The view that the market is an overall success, while at the same time threatening communities, industries and Australia's food security, can partly be explained by how we define and measure highest value use.

The term "highest value use" is frequently employed but rarely defined. It sometimes seems to mean no more than a purchaser with the ability to pay the highest price for water access (Wheeler 2022). Highest value use rarely includes broader economic and financial values, such as supply chains, regional employment, value-added agricultural processing, taxation or tourism. As a purely financial measure it also overlooks non-financial values such as culture, robust regional communities, health, social benefits, food security and the environment (Simpkins 2020; Arrojo Agudo 2021; Select Committee on the status of water trading in New South Wales 2022).

Information provided as evidence of success of the market includes the amount of water traded in a given period; participation in the market by irrigators; the total financial value of water entitlements, and an increase in the gross value of irrigated agriculture (Productivity Commission 2017, 2021; Australian Competition and Consumer Commission 2021; Quinlivan 2022).

These criteria are quantitative and do not demonstrate the performance of the market against its intended outcome of maximising public benefit, or even if water has moved to its highest value use. It is worth looking at each of these criteria in turn.

The amount of water traded simply demonstrates there is a market, not that the water market has maximised public benefit.

Secondly, participation in the market as a measure of success assumes that participation is a choice. But there is no substitute for water, so participation is compulsory when an irrigator needs water. This is explained by the CEO of Duxton Water, the only publicly listed water trader in Australia (Peters 2021):

> There are certain things in life one can't make up and one of the things for me, that brought my attention to the water market is we've got one of the economics 101 supply demand imbalances that is so perfect, you couldn't make a better story . . . So, we've got a declining pool of water and on the other side of this, we've got an increasing amount of plantings . . . So we've got one of these unbelievably beautiful stories, where we're going to have the next drought, it's not if, it's when, and there's going to be one heck of a fight for the marginal supply of water for those people who don't have it already (Foote 2021).

Participation in the market is increasing, but this does not reflect farmers' attitudes to the market. In 1999, more than 80 per cent of farmers surveyed in the Goulburn–Murray Irrigation District agreed or strongly agreed that water trade was a good idea. By 2015–16, more than half of irrigators surveyed in the southern Murray–Darling Basin disagreed or strongly disagreed that water markets have been good for farming (Wheeler et al. 2020).

Thirdly, the value of water entitlements is silent about whether the market is achieving intended outcomes.

Finally, the growth in the gross value of irrigated agriculture, on its own, does not demonstrate that the market is maximising public benefit. Total gross value is influenced by many factors, including water availability, seasonal conditions, commodity prices, domestic and international markets and supply chains. This measure also overlooks that gross value is not a reliable indicator of farm profitability (Meyer 2005), or that irrigation generates more economic activity to a region than selling water (Panel for Independent Assessment of Social and Economic Conditions in the Murray–Darling Basin 2020).

These measures start with the narrowest definition of highest value use and then only attempt to measure the gross benefit side of the maximum public benefit equation. They ignore costs incurred moving water from one use to another. It is a cost–benefit analysis without counting the costs.

Design and implementation

Early policymakers envisaged the water market as one component of water reforms. These reforms included integrated catchment management, pricing based on full cost recovery (including environmental externalities and transparent subsidies), consistent pricing and trading across jurisdictions, clearly defined institutional arrangements, structural adjustment for farming businesses and community involvement (Working Group on Water Resource Policy 1994; Council of Australian Governments 2004).

Most of these policies survived the next round of formal intergovernmental policy development, the 2004 National Water Initiative. But many of the features foreseen by policymakers as necessary for water markets were not implemented or were later watered down during implementation. These include inadequate governance, the removal of a valley cap, and inadequate water accounting and trade registers. These components are examined below.

Inadequate governance

During the drought of 2018–19 and 2019–20 there were many rumours of price manipulation and general anti-competitive behaviour (Hunt, 2019a, b).

In early 2019, the Almond Board of Australia, concerned by apparent anti-competitive behaviour, issued a public statement calling for reform in the water markets. This call included elements necessary for any market, such as an appropriate and enforceable compliance regime, the registration and regulation of water brokers, consistent trading rules and a single water register and clearance platform. The Almond Board also asked for a moratorium on new water use licences for new irrigation developments, and that the Australian Competition and Consumer Commission (ACCC) review the water market, including non-competitive behaviour by non-water users (Almond Board of Australia 2019).

The federal Treasurer then directed the ACCC to conduct a review of the water market, guided by terms of reference that directly considered the Almond Board's concerns (Frydenberg 2019).

The ACCC found that there were "significant deficiencies in current water trading arrangements. Basin water markets lack many features that make markets work effectively" (ACCC 2021, 13). These deficiencies included an absence of effective governance arrangements, an incomplete and fragmented regulatory framework, different trading arrangements, rules and platforms across three states, preferential rules for a small number of water licences within a state, some information not publicly available and information asymmetry, inability to detect anti-competitive behaviour or market manipulation, reliance on water availability affected by complex, interconnected inter-jurisdictional arrangements and river operations where the effects were not intuitive (ACCC 2021).

Added to these deficiencies is that there is no substitute for water in an irrigation business, making most water market participants price takers (Hamilton and Kells 2020; Peters 2021).

In such an environment the opportunities for arbitrage, speculation and insider trading are so abundant it would be surprising if they weren't occurring. Hamilton and Kells (2020) outlined this argument by analysing the water market policy framework. The ACCC heard similar claims while undertaking its review but was unable to determine whether anti-competitive practices were occurring:

> The ACCC considered these concerns, but due to deficiencies in the available data the ACCC was unable to determine whether there was behaviour of concern. Without adequate and complete data, it would not be possible for any regulator to properly investigate allegations of insider trading (ACCC 2021).

This finding has been widely reported as a lack of evidence of speculation or insider trading, the implication being that there is none, or that any occurrences are minor and not of concern (Simmons 2021; Thompson 2021; Quinlivan 2022; Wheeler 2022). What has been mostly unreported is that the ACCC said the lack of data means that it is simply not possible to investigate if anti-competitive activities are taking place.

The ACCC (2021) made 29 recommendations and proposed 70 actions to improve the water market, focusing on governance, market integrity and conduct, trade processing, market information and market architecture (the framework of laws, rules, policies and arrangements for water markets).

The most significant recommendation was the creation of a statutory water market agency, to be responsible for the following:

- market regulation and surveillance
- market information
- market evaluation
- advice and advocacy (ACCC 2021).

Six months after the ACCC review was published, federal Water Minister Keith Pitt announced that Daryl Quinlivan had been appointed to develop a plan for implementing water market reforms, considering the ACCC's recommendations. He would be informed by an advisory panel. On the day of the announcement, before the advisory panel was appointed, and well before the review commenced, Mr Quinlivan said his focus was not to add unnecessary costs or regulatory burdens on users (*CountryNews* 2021).

The Quinlivan Report adopted and prioritised most of the ACCC recommendations. It did not include the water market agency, citing that it would be a regulatory burden and not cost-effective. Instead, it recommended those functions be shared between existing Commonwealth agencies and the yet-to-be created National Water Commission (Quinlivan 2021; Albanese 2022). The sharing of regulatory functions will not address the fragmentation of the governance of the water market, which was one of the ACCC's key criticisms of governance arrangements.

The ACCC and the Quinlivan Report both touched very lightly on the governance of the irrigation schemes. This deserves further scrutiny.

Governance of the independent irrigation operators

The New South Wales Government privatised its irrigation schemes in the Murrumbidgee and Murray (New South Wales side) rivers in the 1990s (Souris 1994; New South Wales Parliamentary Research Service 2017). The schemes were transferred, at no cost, to new irrigation companies, known as independent irrigation operators (IIOs). The irrigators in each scheme became shareholders of that irrigation company (Souris 1994).

These IIOs are responsible for delivering water within an irrigation scheme. They own and maintain the delivery infrastructure, and own the bulk water entitlements (the water shares held by the IIOs – irrigators within the schemes have a contract with the IIO for their share of the bulk water entitlement). They allocate water to individual irrigator accounts, record use by individual irrigators, maintain the individual irrigator accounts, approve and account for trades within the irrigation scheme and in or out of the irrigation scheme, and issue and manage delivery shares.

This is an unusual, perhaps unique, relationship between the company and its shareholders. After water is allocated to the IIO by government, the company has complete control over it. It creates a power imbalance in favour of the company.

Allegations have been made that some IIOs have exploited their shareholders, including insider trading, over-recording water use, borrowing or appropriating water, and issuing or withdrawing delivery shares in ways that are discriminatory (Commonwealth of Australia 2019b; Heffer 2020, 2022; Murray Irrigation Limited 2022).

IIOs reject these allegations, claiming that internal controls prevent these types of activities (Murrumbidgee Irrigation Limited 2020, 2022).

It seems there are no regulatory arrangements in place, or proposed, to detect, deter, prohibit or prosecute these types of allegations.

The Natural Resource Access Regulator is responsible for the enforcement of water laws in New South Wales but it has no jurisdiction within the IIOs for compliance with metering or water use (Pavey 2021). That is, the IIO is responsible for compliance within its scheme. This is obviously problematic when allegations of non-compliance are being made against the IIO itself.

The IIOs own between 50 and 60 per cent of the water in the New South Wales Murray and Murrumbidgee rivers (WaterNSW 2023). Only the IIO can see its internal trades, prices paid and individual water account balances. Governments do not have access to information within the IIO unless provided by the IIO (Australian Competition and Consumer Commission 2021). This means there is no visibility by government or market participants of any trades within the IIOs. Yet the IIOs have access to the public information on trades, as well as the trades and account balances within their scheme. This is a significant information asymmetry.

Some IIOs hold separate companies to trade water (Murrumbidgee Irrigation Limited 2022). In a financial context, this could present the IIOs with opportunities for insider trading, as the IIOs enjoy a unique advantage against other market participants.

But tradeable water rights are explicitly excluded as a financial product (Clause 2BC of the Australian Securities and Investments Commission Regulations 2001). The provisions relating to insider trading of financial products under the *Corporations Act*, and their regulation by the Australian Securities and Investment Commission, therefore do not apply to water. The Basin Plan includes insider-trading rules, but these are narrow and only deal with information around allocation announcements (Murray–Darling Basin Authority n.d.), which can be calculated without insider information. The Quinlivan Report (2022) recommended replacing the existing insider trading rules with a legislated insider trading prohibition. This would include a broader definition of insider trading to relate to all material information and not just water announcements. It would include an explicit carve-out for individuals or corporations (like IIOs) acting on their own business plans (Quinlivan 2022). It remains to be seen if this will adequately tackle the current opportunities for insider trading type that exist within the IIOs.

Removal of a valley cap

The foundation of any natural resource market is a limit or cap on use set by government. The volume within this cap is shared between licence holders. The trade of these shares can occur within the limits set by the cap (ACCC 2021). It is self-evident, but needs to be emphasised, that a natural resource market will not work if there is no limit or cap.

The Murray–Darling Basin cap is being replaced by a Sustainable Diversion Limit under the Murray–Darling Basin Plan. The Sustainable Diversion Limit in five northern basin valleys has increased by approximately 350 gigalitres, or 10 per cent of the original Sustainable Diversion Limit, since the Basin Plan was made in 2012 (Select Committee on Floodplain Harvesting 2021; Murray–Darling Basin Authority 2023).

The increase is outside the statutory process and without parliamentary oversight (Slattery and Johnson 2022). Bret Walker SC advised Southern Riverina Irrigators this approach is unlawful (Walker 2019; Walker and Hartford-Davies 2021). The Commonwealth government maintains that the long-term average Sustainable Diversion Limits can be changed at any time (Slattery and Johnson 2021). This means that water extractions are no longer restricted to a quantitative limit. That is, the "cap-and-trade" water market is operating with an increased cap that can change at any time – a cap-and-trade without a cap.

Inadequate water accounting and trade registers

Governments made early progress on water accounting and developed a Water Accounting Conceptual Framework (2009), a Water Accounting Standard 1 for the preparation of water reports (2010) and a Water Accounting Standard 2 for the Assurance of water reports (2014) (Godfrey and Chalmers 2012; Bureau of Meteorology n.d.).

The Bureau of Meteorology and the New South Wales government have both prepared annual water accounts based in part on the Water Accounting Standard 1 since 2010 (Bureau of Meteorology n.d.; New South Wales Government 2024). Neither is wholly consistent with the Water Accounting Standards. It is unclear if Water Accounting Standard 2 has ever been applied.

A test of the adequacy of accounting information is whether it is useful for making decisions (Water Accounting Standards Board 2009; Cordery and Sinclair 2016). Despite accounting standards being in place, and reported on for more than a decade, there are gaps in relevant and reliable accounting information. The federal Water Minister, Tanya Plibersek, outlined a five-point plan to reset water management in the Murray–Darling Basin. This included a commitment to better understand water availability and use (Plibersek 2022). In other words, accounting for water.

Several protracted disputes could have been resolved by proper water accounting. These include the volumes of water historically extracted by floodplain harvesting (New South Wales Irrigators Council 2021; Brown et al. 2022), the contribution that the northern basin makes to the southern basin (Keelty 2020; Slattery 2020), the volume of water savings from government-funded efficiency projects (Grafton et al. 2018; Wang et al. 2018; Wheeler et al. 2020) and the cause of the decline of inflows into the Murray River (Interim Inspector-General of Murray–Darling Basin Water Resources 2020; Grafton et al. 2022).

Water accounting in Australia has a strong theoretical basis but reporting only partly follows the water accounting standards, and there has been no assurance in accordance with the accounting standards against those reports. Water accounting has not supported the water market as intended.

The *Water Act 2007* requires that all trades are recorded on water registers that are compatible, publicly accessible and reliable. The Commonwealth government committed $30 million dollars for the basin states to implement transparent water registers. This project was terminated, unfinished, in 2014. The National Water Commission reported: "it is unclear which actions have been implemented and what, if any, objectives have been achieved" (Productivity Commission 2017).

Despite the requirements under the *Water Act*, state water registers are not consistent in the information they disclose, have different levels of accessibility (ACCC 2021) and are incomplete. For example, the New South Wales trade register recorded only 13 to 30 per cent of the sales price of trades between 2017–18 and 2021–22 (WaterNSW 2023).

In addition, as noted earlier, the *Water Act* does not require the trade registers to disclose transactions within an IIO. The New South Wales IIOs hold a water access licence, known as a bulk water entitlement, for the scheme. Irrigators within the scheme have a contract with the IIO for their share of the bulk water entitlement. The New South Wales Register does not record or disclose transactions between irrigators with a share of the bulk entitlement. Trade from within the IIO to outside the IIO is disclosed as trade with the bulk entitlement and not the individual water holder (ACCC 2021).

Because the IIOs hold between 50 and 60 per cent of water shares in the New South Wales Murray and Murrumbidgee rivers (WaterNSW 2023), any trade with at least half of the water shares is not publicly reported. Of the trades that are reported, up to 87 per cent do not include sales data.

That is, the majority of transactions are not recorded, or only partly recorded, in the New South Wales trade registers.

The physical environment

During the design of the water market, the physical limitations of the system were ignored.

Moving water to its highest value use is an economic objective that ignores the physical limitations of the system. Early policymakers envisaged water moving towards high-value crops like fruit and nuts, and away from low-value crops like pasture (Council of Australian Governments 1994). This has happened as intended. The Australian almond industry has grown from around 3,500 hectares in 2000 to more than 60,000 hectares in 2021 (Almond Board of Australia 2022). Nut and fruit trees are perennial and need water every year to survive, while crops like pasture, cotton or rice are annuals and can be forgone for a season if there are water shortages.

The Victorian government commissioned a study of water supply and demand in the Murray River. It estimated how much water the permanent plantations in place in 2019 would need when they reach maturity. It found that, in a drought, all the water available in the southern connected basin will only meet 40 per cent of the water demand for the 2019 permanent plantations (Aither 2019). Despite this, permanent plantings have increased in all jurisdictions since 2019 and the industry expects further growth (Almond Board of Australia 2019, 2022).

The water needed to deliver irrigation water through a river is called system conveyance water. System conveyance water increases with the distance irrigation water is delivered.

Two-thirds of the almond plantations are on the Murray River, near the South Australian border (Almond Board of Australia 2022). This is a shift in irrigation demand from the upstream Murray River to approximately 1,000 kilometres downstream. The increase in permanent plantings downstream in the Murray River increases system conveyance water.

System conveyance water used is socialised across all water holders before water is allocated to individual accounts. If water is traded from Yarrawonga to Wentworth, a distance of approximately 1,100 kilometres, that additional system conveyance is shared amongst all water holders and is not borne solely by the water buyer in Wentworth. This reduces the amount of water available for allocations, so therefore decreases all water holders' reliability. The growth of permanent plantations in the lower Murray River is exacerbating this problem. The ACCC identified this as a market distortion that is particularly affecting holders of lower priority water shares (ACCC 2020).

The lowest channel capacity in the Murray River is the Barmah Choke, also known as the Choke, in the upstream Murray. It is difficult to deliver enough water through the Choke to meet increasing downstream demand (Murray–Darling Basin Authority 2022).

To overcome this, governments are exploring options to move water around the Choke (Murray–Darling Basin Authority 2021). These include large-scale engineering solutions, such as new or enhanced channels to bypass the Choke or dredging (Murray–Darling Basin Authority 2022). Government has argued that limiting or reducing irrigation downstream is an unacceptable policy option because that would be interfering in the water market (Commonwealth of Australia 2019a; Middleton 2020).

The Barmah–Millewa Forest is located around the Choke. It is listed as an iconic environmental site (Murray–Darling Basin Authority 2009) and a wetland of international significance under the Ramsar

Convention (Hale and Butcher 2011). The volume and timing of water deliveries through the Choke damage that environment, risking the ecological characteristics that made the site eligible for a Ramsar listing (Sinclair Knight Merz 2011).

Downstream water users do not incur the cost of environmental damage created by deliveries through the Choke, either as an externality or direct remediation costs (ACCC 2021).

The water market has increased permanent plantings, but there will not be enough water to keep more than half of these alive in a drought. It has also moved irrigation downstream, which has reduced the reliability of all water holders in the Murray. Governments are investigating large engineering projects to meet the increased downstream demand, and it seems the cost of these will be borne by taxpayers. Increased downstream demand causes environmental damage, the cost of which is not borne by the downstream irrigators.

Comments on implementation

The Quinlivan Report contended that some of the problems with the water market are a result of it being young and without international guidance (Quinlivan 2022). The inference is that policymakers are still learning how best to design a policy framework for water markets.

That the water market lacks "many features that make markets work effectively" (ACCC 2021) is not a consequence of immaturity, poor planning or lack of foresight. Most of the components necessary for a water market were identified by policymakers 30 years ago under the National Competition Policy, and reiterated 20 years ago under the National Water Initiative. These components have simply not been implemented as intended.

There could be many explanations for this. Samnakay (2020) argued that the Commonwealth exhibits indifference and waning enthusiasm for implementing environmental reforms after the initial commitment. Matthews (2017, 2018) observed that when there is a strong impetus for water reform, and clear identification of what that reform should look like, there is corresponding resistance to that reform.

It is clear the power structures that benefit from an unregulated market, arbitrage, insider trading, growth in extractions, a lack of public information and information asymmetry have outweighed governments' willingness or capacity to implement a regulated and properly functioning market.

The Quinlivan Report (2022) is yet to be implemented, so perhaps the missing features that make markets work effectively will be instated. Before this is attempted, it seems necessary to first understand why the efforts over the last 30 years have failed. The latest water market reforms should also be broadened, as many of the criticisms raised in this chapter are not considered in Quinlivan's road map.

An alternate policy objective

When questions about highest value use and national interest are raised, the responder often assumes this is an argument for a centralised agricultural system:

> Senator Patrick: You say the object is to get the best value out of the water. But, in certain circumstances, that's against the national interest. We see dairy farmers really struggling now, getting to the point where it's either borderline or we are now importing more milk; we're a net importer of milk. Surely, you have to then take that principle of best value use of the water, and reconsider.
>
> ...
>
> Senator Canavan: But what I'm saying here, Senator Patrick, is I don't think our nation's farms can be managed from a room in Canberra. That would be a recipe for disaster (Commonwealth of Australia 2019a).

Another response is that the critics are ignorant: "Such arguments against water markets are not always grounded in truth and facts, have not read the extensive academic literature that exists and ignore all the many varied benefits that markets provide" (Wheeler 2021).

Neither of these responses fosters public debate about whether the original policy intent of water markets was sound, the extent to which water markets have achieved their original policy intent or why the implementation of the components necessary for a water market has been so poor. Without an intellectually honest and inclusive discussion, it seems that Stage III of the Water Markets Readiness Framework of reinforcement, improvement and identification and reform of problems (Wheeler 2021) is impossible.

Even National Party MPs, while in government, with a National Party Minister responsible for the combined water and agriculture portfolio, seem to despair that there is no policy alternative to the water market. National Party senators Davey and McKenzie frequently interjected in Senate Estimates to complain to their own executive that the water market was harming farming industries and have made several public statements around this (McKenzie 2020; Commonwealth of Australia 2020).

> While the water market is working economically and water is being purchased for highest value, is highest value best use? ... The risk is that we are going to reach peak almond and then when the almond industry recalibrates, as has happened with olives [and other crops], the collateral damage on the way is our broad-acre industries – rice, corn, wheat and dairy (Middleton 2020).

It is curious that even the government of the day seems to feel powerless to change a policy it disagrees with and that its believes is causing harm to its constituents.

After 30 years, it is time to reconsider the original policy intent of water markets.

Water policy in Australia should always be viewed through the lens of drought. In wet years, the tensions about how we share water dissipate. In drought years, the past decisions about how we share water are tested. The first water policy question should be: what do we want to irrigate during a drought?

In the Murray–Darling Basin in the last drought (2018–19 and 2019–20), irrigation of annual crops declined, as expected. This reduced feed available for dairy, beef and sheep and those herds dramatically reduced through export or slaughter (Australian Bureau of Statistics 2021; Beef Central 2021; Australian Bureau of Agricultural and Resource Economics and Sciences 2023). While industries recover somewhat after drought, there is an attrition of farmers and a contraction of those industries. For example, the Australian Dairy Industry Council has warned, "it's likely that we will see the progressive elimination of the dairy industry in the Basin as one of the unintended consequences of the current market" (Australian Dairy Industry Council Inc. 2020, 3).

Meanwhile, a lot of the water we did have for irrigation was being used to keep young almond trees alive that weren't yet producing nuts and at least 60 per cent of which will not survive the next drought (Aither 2019). This does not seem like our water is being used in the national interest.

The second water policy question is: what do we want our irrigated industry to produce?

Do we want to grow what we eat? Do we want industries like beef, dairy and rice as permanent, and secure, features of our agriculture? Do we want to grow fodder to maintain our dryland beef and sheep industries? Do we want resilient regional communities? If so, we have to find a way for those industries to survive during the next drought.

References

Aither (2019). *Water Supply and Demand in the Southern Murray–Darling Basin.* Melbourne: Victorian Water Register.

Almond Board of Australia (2019). *Murray–Darling Basin: Water Policy Position.* Loxton, SA: Australian Almonds.

Almond Board of Australia (2022). *Almond Insights 2021/22.* Loxton, SA: Australian Almonds.

Arrojo Agudo, P. (2021). *Risks and impacts of the commodification and financialization of water on human rights to safe drinking water and sanitation: note by the Secretary-General.* Report of the Special Rapporteur on the Human Rights to Safe Drinking Water and Sanitation series. United Nation Human Rights Council. https://digitallibrary.un.org/record/3936723.

Australian Bureau of Agricultural and Resource Economics and Sciences (2023). *Sheep meat.* [Online] https://tinyurl.com/58afyntc.

Australian Bureau of Statistics (2021). *Agricultural Commodities, Australia.* Statistics on the production of agricultural commodities including cereal and broadacre crops, fruit and vegetables and livestock on Australian farms. https://tinyurl.com/582k23z6.

Australian Competition and Consumer Commission (2021). *Murray–Darling Basin Water Markets Inquiry – Final Report*. Canberra: Australian Competition and Consumer Commission.

Australian Dairy Industry Council Inc. (2020). *ADIC Submission: ACCC Murray-Darling Basin Water Markets Inquiry*. Canberra: Australian Competition and Consumer Commission.

Australian Government (2004). *Intergovernmnental agreement on a national water initative*. [Online] https://tinyurl.com/ycys96b6.

Beef Central (2021). *National herd rebuild underway following two years of drought-induced decline, says MLA projections*. [Online] https://tinyurl.com/3vm33v7f.

Brown, P., M. Colloff, M. Slattery, W. Johnson and F. Guarino (2022). An unsustainable level of take: on-farm storages and floodplain water harvesting in the northern Murray–Darling Basin, Australia. *Australasian Journal of Water Resources* 26(1): 43–58.

Bureau of Meteorology (n.d.). *Australian Water Accounting Standards*. https://tinyurl.com/jha8vx5n.

Commonwealth of Australia (2019a). Senate: Rural and Regional Affairs and Transport Legislation Committee: Estimates, 25 October 2019, Canberra: Australian Parliament.

Commonwealth of Australia (2019b). Multijurisdictional Management and Execution of the Murray-Darling Basin Plan: Public Hearings, Griffith, 11 December 2019. Griffith: Australian Parliament.

Commonwealth of Australia (2020). Senate: Rural and Regional Affairs and Transport Legislation Committee: Estimates, 6 March 2020. Canberra: Australian Parliament.

Cordery, C., and R. Sinclair (2016). Decision-usefulness and stewardship as conceptual framework objectives: continuing challenges. *SSRN (Social Science Research Network) Electronic Journal*. https://tinyurl.com/wvudcyss.

Council of Australian Governments (1994). COAG *Communique 25 February 1994, Attachment A – Water Resource Policy*. Canberra: National Competition Council.

CountryNews (2021). *Adviser on water market panel*. [Online] https://tinyurl.com/48szcbsb.

Department of Climate Change, Energy, the Environment and Water (2022). *National Water Initiative*. https://tinyurl.com/2a6vkkah.

Foote, C. (2021). Going nuts: Murray Darling's "unbelievably beautiful story" for investors a nightmare for farmers, environment. *Michael West Media*, 21 August. https://tinyurl.com/5xst3ktu.

Frydenberg, J.L.D. (2019). *ACCC Water Inquiry*. Joint media release with David Littleproud, 7 August. https://tinyurl.com/spd4fcwt.

Godfrey, J., and Chalmers, K. (2012). *Water accounting: international approaches to policy and decision-making*. Cheltenham: Edward Elgar Publishing Limited.

Grafton, Q., J. Williams, C. J. Perry, F. Molle, C. Ringler et al. (2018). The paradox of irrigation efficiency. *Science* 361(6404): 748–50.

Grafton, Q., C. Long, R. Kingsford, G. Bino and J. Williams (2022). Resilience to hydrological droughts in the northern Murray-Darling Basin, Australia. *Philosophical Transactions of the Royal Society* 380(2238).

Hale, J., and R. Butcher (2011). *Barmah Forest Ramsar Site: Ecological Character Description*. Canberra: Department of Sustainability, Environment, Water, Population and Communities.

Hamilton, S., and S. Kells (2020). *Submission from Scott Hamilton and Professor Stuart Kells in Response to the ACCC's Murray-Darling Basin Water Markets Inquiry – Interim Report*. Canberra: Australian Competition and Consumer Commission.

Heffer, K. (2020). Email Re water trading submission. Canberra: Australian Competition and Consumer Commission.

Heffer, S., and K. Heffer (2022). *Submission to the Inquiry on the Status of Water Trading in New South Wales*. Sydney: New South Wales Parliament.

Hunt, P. (2019a). Basin speculators: Coalition would call in ACCC to review water trades. *Weekly Times*, 3 May [Online]. https://tinyurl.com/3bvb9s97.

Hunt, P. (2019b). Irrigation water prices spike as speculators buy up big. *Weekly Times*, 30 January [Online]. https://tinyurl.com/33vrp3w4.

Independent Committee of Inquiry into Competition Policy in Australia (1993). *National Competition Policy*, Canberra: AGPS. [Hilmer report]

Interim Inspector-General of Murray-Darling Basin Water Resources (2020). *Impact of Lower Inflows on State Shares under the Murray–Darling Basin Agreement*. Canberra: Inspector-General of Water Compliance.

Keelty, M. (2020). *Clarification of evidence provided at the 12 May 2020 public hearing, received from Mr Mick Keelty, Interim Inspector-General of Murray-Darling Basin Water Resources on 13 May 2020*. Canberra: Australian Parliament House.

Matthews, K. (2017). *Independent Investigation into New South Wales Water Management and Compliance: Advice on Implementation*. Sydney: New South Wales Department of Industry.

Matthews, K. (2018). *Water Management in Australia – Time for a Re-think.* Canberra: Australian Water Association.

McKenzie, B. (2020). *Get Serious on Water, Back Moratorium.* Media Release [Online]. https://tinyurl.com/mvbhpapc.

Meyer, W. (2005). *The Irrigation Industry in the Murray and Murrumbidgee Basins.* Cooperative Research Centre for Irrigaton Futures.

Middleton, K. (2020). *Shortfalls in the Murray–Darling Basin.* Sydney: Roy Morgan.

Murray Irrigation Limited (2022). *Select Committee on the status of water trading in New South Wales: Other Documents: 15/09/22, Answers to Questions on Notice, Murray Irrigation.* Sydney: New South Wales Parliament.

Murray–Darling Basin Authority (2009). *The Living Murray Program.* Canberra: Murray–Darling Basin Authority.

Murray–Darling Basin Authority (2021). *Barmah–Millewa Feasibility Study.* Canberra: Murray–Darling Basin Authority.

Murray–Darling Basin Authority (2022). *Water Demand and Shortfalls.* https://tinyurl.com/bdcm9ez3.

Murray–Darling Basin Authority (2023). *Current diversion limits for the Basin.* [Online]. https://tinyurl.com/34m57cn7.

Murray–Darling Basin Authority (2024). *Water trading rules of the Basin Plan.* [Online]. https://tinyurl.com/4383r28j.

Murray–Darling Basin Commission (2000). *Review of the Operation of the Cap: Overview Report of the Murray–Darling Basin Commission, including the Four Companion Papers.* Canberra: Murray–Darling Basin Commission.

Murrumbidgee Irrigation Limited (2020). *Additional Documents: Response to potential adverse reflections arising from the 11 December 2019 public hearing, received from Murrumbidgee Irrigation on 25 February 2020.* [Online] https://tinyurl.com/xz7a5bky.

Murrumbidgee Irrigation Limited (2022). *2022 Annual Report.* Griffith, NSW: Murrumbidgee Irrigation Limited.

National Competition Council (2007). *Timeline of the National Competition Policy.* www.ncp.ncc.gov.au/pages/timeline.

National Museum Australia (2022). *Murray River irrigation begins.* [Online] https://tinyurl.com/4ytnsep3.

National Water Commission (2006). *2005 National Competition Policy Assessment of Water Reform Progress.* Canberra: National Water Commission.

New South Wales (2022). *Report on proceedings before the Select Committee on status of water trading in NSW.* Griffith: New South Wales Parliament.

New South Wales Government (2024). *New South Wales General Purpose Water Accounting Reports.* https://tinyurl.com/bdh4mpab.

New South Wales Irrigators Council (2021). *Inquiry into Floodplain Harvesting.* Sydney: New South Wales Parliament.

New South Wales Parliamentary Research Service (2017). *Privatisation in NSW: a timeline and key resource,* Sydney: New South Wales Parliament. https://tinyurl.com/4rstcscv.

Panel for Independent Assessment of Social and Economic Conditions in the Murray–Darling Basin (2020). *Final Report: Independent Assessment of Social and Economic Conditions in the Murray–Darling Basin.* Melbourne: Panel for Independent Assessment of Social and Economic Conditions in the Murray–Darling Basin. https://tinyurl.com/3pehebxs.

Pavey, M. (2021). *Letter to Senator Perin Davey on behalf of Mr Stuart and Mrs Katrina Heffer.* [Online] https://tinyurl.com/b5xdyvb6.

Peters, E. (2021). *Duxton Water Ltd: MST small cap conference,* 15 June 2021. Stirling, SA: Duxton Water.

Plibersek, T. (2022). *River Reflections Conference address,* 1 June 2022. [Online] https://tinyurl.com/2p6j5mbd.

Productivity Commission (2017). *National Water Reform.* Canberra: Productivity Commission.

Productivity Commission (2021). *National Water Reform.* Canberra: Productivity Commission.

Quinlivan, D. (2022). *Water Market Reform: Final Roadmap Report.* Canberra: Department of Climate Change, Energy, the Environment and Water. [Quinlivan report]

Renmark Irrigation Trust, n.d. *History: the first irrigation trust in South Australia.* [Online] https://rit.org.au/history/.

Samnakay, N. (2020). Understanding design and implementation attributes for strategic policies: the case of Australia's national environmental policies. *Policy Studies* 43(4): 715–37.

Select Committee on Floodplain Harvesting (2021). *Floodplain Harvesting.* Sydney: New South Wales Parliament.

Select Committee on the Status of Water Trading in New South Wales (2022). *Status of Water trading in New South Wales.* Sydney: New South Wales Parliament.

Simmons, M. (2021). Muddying the waters. Review of Hamilton and Kells: *Sold Down the River. Inside Story,* 31 August. https://insidestory.org.au/muddying-the-waters/.

Simpson, L. (2020). Water recovery and food security. Sydney: Obtained under Freedom of Information Request LEX 20393 (Document 8). https://tinyurl.com/2w2axx36.

Sinclair Knight Merz (2011). *Barmah Choke Study: Individual Options Phase.* Canberra: Murray–Darling Basin Authority.

Slattery, M. (2020). *Multi-Jurisdictional Management and Execution of the Murray-Darling Basin Plan: Correspondence regarding evidence provided at a public hearing on 12 May 2020, received from Ms Maryanne Slattery on 3 June 2020.* Canberra: Australian Parliament House.

Slattery, M. and W. Johnson (2022). *Licensing floodplain harvesting in Northern New South Wales: analysis and implications.* Sydney: New South Wales Parliament.

Souris, H. G. (1994). *Irrigation Corporations Bill: Second reading.* Sydney: New South Wales Parliament.

Thompson, B. (2021). ACCC wants independent watchdog for $1.8bn Murray Darling water trade. *Australian Financial Review*, 26 March. https://tinyurl.com/395w26pd.

Walker, B. (2019). *Murray–Darling Basin Royal Commission Report.* Adelaide: Government of South Australia.

Walker, B., and Hartford-Davies, S. (2021). *Joint memorandum of advice to Southern Riverina Irrigators.* [Online] https://tinyurl.com/s3cur5h6.

Wang, W., Glen W. and A. Horne (2018). *Potential Impacts of Groundwater Sustainable Diversion Limits and Irrigation Efficiency Projects on River Flow Volume under the Murray–Darling Basin Plan.* Canberra: Murray-Darling Basin Authority.

Water Accounting Standards Board (2009). *Water Accounting Conceptual Framework for the Preparation and Presentation of General Purpose Water Accounting Reports.* Canberra: Bureau of Meteorology.

WaterNSW (2023). NSW Water Register. https://waterregister.waternsw.com.au/water-register-frame.

Wheeler, S.A. (2021). Assessing water markets around the world. *Global Water Forum*, 16 November. https://tinyurl.com/27v3fu74.

Wheeler, S.A. (2022). Debunking Murray-Darling Basin water trade myths. *Agricultural and Resource Economics* 66(4): 797–821.

Wheeler, S.A., E. Carmody, R.Q. Grafton, R.T. Kingsford, and A. Zuo (2020). The rebound effect on water extraction from subsidising irrigation infrastructure in Australia. *Resources, Conservation and Recycling* 159.

Wheeler, S.A., A. Zuo, Y. Xu, J. Haensch and C. Seidl (2020). *Water Market Literature Review and Empirical Analysis.* Canberra: Australian Competition and Consumer Commission.

Wilkinson, J. (1994). *Briefing Note: Irrigation in Southern NSW: The Irrigation Corporations Bill 1994.* Sydney: New South Wales Parliament. https://tinyurl.com/5ywvwswd.

Wilkinson, J. (1997). *Water for Rural production in NSW: Grand designs and changing realities*. Sydney: New South Wales Parliamentary Library Research Service.

Working Group on Water Resource Policy (1994). *Report of the Working Group on Water Resource Policy to the Council of Australian Governments*. Canberra: Australian Parliamentary Library.

8

Neoliberalism and human services: the National Disability Insurance Scheme (NDIS)

Bob Davidson

Increasingly over the last four decades, publicly funded human service programs have had to operate in a context shaped by neoliberalism. This chapter looks at disability services in Australia to examine how neoliberalism has framed the design, development and operation of the National Disability Insurance Scheme (NDIS). As part of this, we also consider whether and how neoliberalism has been responsible for the problems that engulfed the NDIS within its first decade. The Australian Labor government under Anthony Albanese set up a review of the NDIS in October 2022. This chapter was largely written before the Interim Report of that review (NDIS Review 2023), which identified many, but not all, of the issues raised in the chapter.

The next section gives a brief overview of how neoliberalism and marketisation have been applied to human services in general. After that, we consider the origins and development of the NDIS, before looking at the impact of neoliberal ideas on the NDIS. A brief account of alternative approaches to the design and management of the scheme is then provided. Davidson (2023) has further detail on the issues and developments outlined in the chapter.

Neoliberalism and marketisation in social policy

Neoliberalism

Drawing on both neoclassical economics and libertarian philosophy, the concept of neoliberalism is ostensibly based on a belief in personal liberty and responsibility, the power of markets, and the need to limit state and collective action. It promotes the idea of a minimal state, claiming that government action distorts the preferences and freedoms of individuals (Friedman 1962; Hayek 2007), and that the state will inevitably be captured by vested interests (that is, public choice theory, as espoused by Buchanan 1978).

An important effect of neoliberalism on human services (including the NDIS) and government more generally over the last four decades has been the hollowing out of government competence in policy formation and service administration due to factors such as contracting out policy and program delivery; the growth of managerialism, which discounts disciplinary expertise and prioritises generic management skills; and an ideological hostility to public-sector capacity building (see Chapter 2 for a detailed discussion of managerialism). As part of this, there appears to be little capacity to consider any issue or need other than through a neoliberal lens. The former editor of the *Canberra Times* and long-time Canberra watcher, Jack Waterford (2022) has noted:

> [with] departmental memory, experience and expertise having been run down by ideology and finance departments, and policy work subcontracted out to consultants and interest groups, there is hardly anyone equipped to point out the shortcomings of an undisciplined idea.

This has been starkly revealed in recent times with the widely reported Robodebt and PwC consulting scandals.

The marketisation of human services

Neoliberalism has taken many forms, but in human services it has primarily been implemented via *marketisation*, which involves the introduction or expansion of a range of market mechanisms to replace or reduce direct control or intervention by government in the planning, allocation and delivery of services. This has been justified by its proponents primarily in economic terms, based on a belief in the power of markets to improve the operation and outcomes of these services in a range of ways (see below).

Over time, marketisation has led to seismic changes in the public–private interface in human services. In general, it has not led to reduced government funding for services – indeed, the experience of the last 40 years in many human service sectors has been quite the contrary, with substantially increased funding (Spies-Butcher 2014; Davidson 2015) – but it has substantially changed the way that funds are distributed, and the way that services are delivered. Quasi-markets have been created in many human service sectors. The defining characteristic of a quasi-market is that some entity other than the user or their family (usually government) pays a significant proportion, possibly all, of the total cost of the services. Flowing from this and from the extensive intrinsic asymmetries of information and other market failures in the sectors in which they are used, quasi-markets have a number of features that are either unique or more likely to be present than in conventional markets (Davidson 2015, 2016, 2022).

On the supply side, government funding has become more contestable with the use of non-government providers (both not-for-profit and privately owned for-profit) to deliver services, with these providers competing for government contracts or individual service users as "customers". On the demand side, there has been a movement to enable service users to have a greater say in determining their services and who provides them through the use of choice and exit mechanisms (Hirschman 1970; Simmons, Powell, and Greener 2009; Yeandle, Kroger and Cass 2012), together with various means of giving users subsidies that represent quasi-vouchers that are portable between providers. Much greater pressure and responsibility have been put on service users to find, manage and assess providers and services. Users are also more likely to face a means test in accessing public funds and to be required to make a substantial co-payment (financial contribution) for their services than in the past. While both means-testing and co-payments have long existed, their use has been increased substantially under marketisation. There is also often a strong relationship between them in that means testing may (but not necessarily) influence whether an individual needs to make a co-payment and the size of their co-payment.

The market mechanisms that constitute marketisation can take many forms depending on the specific case, but most can be characterised as introducing or extending one or more of 10 elements (which can be summarised as C4MP3ID) – contestability, competition, (user) choice, co-payments, means-testing, prices, profit motive, privately owned providers, individualisation of users (encompassing both the cashing out of program funding into quasi-vouchers for each user, and requiring individuals to be more responsible for arranging, managing, and assessing the services they receive) and the deregulation of provider behaviour. These mechanisms are intended to have a range of positive effects on services, providers and users. For example, it is argued that more competition among providers and more choice for users will, among other things, lead to more responsive providers, greater allocative and productive efficiency, lower costs, more innovation, improved transparency and accountability, a better matching of supply and demand for services, and more control by users over their services and who provides them.

In practice, however, a range of problems have emerged in highly marketised sectors, often leading to a decline, not just in the quality and equity of services, but also, ironically, in choice and efficiency, two of the key goals of marketisation. At the heart of the problems of many quasi-markets has been a simplistic understanding and application of the mechanisms by program designers (Davidson 2015). The power of large corporations has been an issue in some sectors (e.g., childcare, aged care and vocational education), but more prevalent in the NDIS have been problems arising from multiple smaller providers responding to the freedom and perverse incentives caused by the excessive use of market mechanisms.

A core contention of this chapter is that government's prime obligation with publicly funded human services is to ensure the supply of quality and affordable services to all people and communities that need them and to ensure that people can have easy access to those services, rather than simply establishing a market and *hoping* those goals will be achieved. Alongside that, however, some use of the 10 market mechanisms listed above is desirable in many human services, with some level of contestability and user choice of services being essential. Choice of services does not necessarily imply a choice of providers but could in principle be achieved by enhancing the flexibility, responsiveness and capability of a single monopoly provider, and ensuring that users are able to have an effective "voice" within the provider (Hirschman 1970; Yeandle, Kroger and Cass 2012). All 10 of the mechanisms can potentially have a positive effect if applied strategically and in moderation, but it has been their excessive and unevaluated use – to chase an ideological fantasy, to remove pressure on governments, to feed vested interests or any combination of these – that has led to many of the major problems in human services in recent decades (Davidson 2016, 2018).

Complexity of providing human services

It is important to note at the outset that there are intrinsic difficulties involved in providing *any* publicly funded human service program, irrespective of marketisation. Most important are the inevitable constraints on funding, workforce shortages, and the intrinsic and unavoidable complexity in designing and delivering human service systems (Davidson 2023). Each of these is significant in the NDIS. A core message from these factors is that *no* funding system or delivery system in human services can be perfect, a situation that is complicated further when markets are used to provide services. Even in the best possible case, the provision of human services is a constant "choice between imperfect alternatives" (Wolf 1988), in a world where the "theory of the second best" is ever present (Lipsey and Lancaster 1956).

Clearly, some programs and managers meet these challenges better than others, and how a program is designed, governed and managed will determine the ultimate effect of any external and pre-existing factors. The designers, governors and managers of the NDIS had the opportunity to absorb the lessons of over a quarter-century of marketisation of human services and take their own directions in response to the initial conditions they faced. As it was, they chose to go further down the road of marketisation – with inevitable results.

NDIS – establishment and history

Establishment of the NDIS

The NDIS is widely considered to have been the biggest single social policy reform in Australia in the last 50 years (since Medibank in 1975). It represented the consolidation under the national government of the funding and regulation of all disability services for people with significant and permanent disabilities, replacing an incomplete patchwork of state-based services; a major increase in funding for these services; and a transformation of the way in which the services were funded and delivered aimed at giving people with disability greater choice and control over the services they receive and who delivers those services.

The public life of the NDIS is generally regarded as having begun at the 2020 Summit convened in 2008 by the new Australian Labor Party government headed by Kevin Rudd. In fact, this built on work by Brian Howe (former Labor minister and deputy prime minister) and Bruce Bonyhady (a businessman, father of two boys with a disability, and chair of a not-for-profit provider) (Miller 2017). From 2007 on, Bill Shorten (Parliamentary Secretary for Disability) provided support from within government. Subsequently, the government asked the (strongly pro-market) Productivity Commission to examine disability services and its report came out in 2011. The NDIS was established in March 2013, with the scheme to be administered by the National Disability Insurance Agency (NDIA).

While the Commonwealth government is responsible for administering the scheme, the states and territories continue to provide significant funds and have a say at a strategic level, while they are also supposed to have modified their other programs to ensure access for people with a lower level of disability who are ineligible for the NDIS. This is a large number of people and far more than are under the NDIS. Australian Bureau of Statistics (ABS) data indicates there are over 4.4 million people in Australia with a disability (ABS 2019), of whom about a third (1,464,415 in 2022) require assistance with core activities (ABS 2022), yet only half a million of these are NDIS participants. As well, a significant number of the people who have never been under the NDIS had previously received support from state or territory disability programs or the Commonwealth Home and Community Care (HACC) program.

The NDIS began operating pilot projects in 2013, but was not fully rolled out until 2020. It is widely accepted that the scheme began operating before it was fully ready, with an oft-used analogy that they "had to fly the plane while it was still being built".

Key features of the design of the NDIS in its first decade

The goal of the NDIS is to ensure that all people with "significant and permanent" disabilities receive "reasonable and necessary" support services subject to the services being "value for money" (NDIA 2021). The NDIA sets the definitions for each of these key terms and its assessors decide whether they apply in each case. (It is important to note that the NDIS does not cover the needs of all people with a disability. It does not include people with lower support needs nor people 65 years old and over who did not receive NDIS support before they turned 65; while some provisions for people with disabilities are covered by other programs, notably disability pensions and employment assistance.) On the demand side, an assessor employed by the NDIA meets (briefly) with each applicant to determine their eligibility and to establish an Individual Support Plan for each eligible person ("participant") that specifies in precise detail the services and amount of financial subsidy they can receive. In effect, each participant is given a set of quasi-vouchers which they can use to "purchase" approved services from providers via a fee-for-service model. Participants can choose to have their services and funding managed by a service provider or by the NDIA or to "self-manage". There are no means tests or co-payments (client contributions) in the scheme.

On the supply side, service providers are no longer given block grants by government, their revenue now coming from the aggregate of payments received from clients who choose them and then use their quasi-vouchers to "buy" services. Providers can be unincorporated sole traders or family members and not all providers even need to be registered, especially for self-managing participants. The profile of disability service providers has changed hugely since the beginning of the NDIS. There has been a major increase in the number of entities that provide services, with a more than five-fold increase between 2016 and 2022, from 3,519 providers at 30 June 2016 (ANAO 2016, 68) to 18,347 by 30 June 2022 (NDIA 2022). Much of this increase has come from more privately owned for-profit providers, which now represent more than 90 per cent of the total providers, although not-for-profit providers continue to receive the majority of funds and to support the majority of participants. In many locations, public providers and small not-for-profit providers have been closed, privatised or downsized, representing a major loss of choice for many NDIS participants. Most providers are relatively small, and most are limited to larger urban areas.

The increasing cost of the NDIS

One of the major issues confronting the NDIS is that the actual and projected numbers of participants and total cost of the NDIS have continued to grow over the decade since the scheme was first mooted. The 2011 Productivity Commission report estimated that when the NDIS was fully rolled out, there would be an annual cost of $13.6 billion, but by 2022–23, the estimated annual cost was $35.8 billion for that year with a forecast that it would rise to over $60 billion by 2030. As a consequence, while the Productivity Commission (2011) estimated that the cost of the scheme would be 1 per cent of gross domestic product (GDP), by 2022 it was estimated that it will eventually be 3 per cent of GDP (Clun 2022), making it the highest cost social program in the Commonwealth budget.

Both the number of participants and average cost per participant have kept increasing. The reasons for this include a lack of caps on individual plans; no obvious macro mechanisms to limit total expenditure; the extension of both eligibility and benefits since the original conception of the scheme; a much greater take-up by some groups than was envisaged (e.g., in 2022, 36 per cent of NDIS participants had autism, while many more children than planned are now participating); major leakages of funds incurred by individual service providers as business overheads that primarily result from marketisation (e.g., advertising, other marketing, management fees, consultants, IT, accounting costs, legal costs, "satellite services" and profits); overpricing; and fraud.

The promise and positives of the NDIS

The NDIS promised to give people with disabilities more funds for services and equipment; greater certainty; higher quality services; customised services; greater choice and control over their services; more service and provider options; and new opportunities to live more independent and fuller lives.

Nearly a decade later, many people have benefited greatly from the scheme, receiving services that have transformed their lives. As at 30 June 2022, there were 534,655 NDIS participants, 59 per cent of whom had not received any support from a state or commonwealth disability program before the NDIS (NDIA 2022). More public funds have been allocated to disability services and there is a more coordinated and consistent approach nationally. Moreover, disability is now a frontline issue on the public policy agenda and recognised as a prime moral and financial responsibility of government.

Problems of the NDIS

Despite these promises and positives, when the incoming Labor national government took over in May 2022, the NDIA was being overwhelmed by a multitude of deep-set problems. The NDIS may be working reasonably or very well for large numbers of people who are supported by the scheme, but gaps and problems are now so great as to throw into question key aspects of the scheme. The major problems include:

1. *financial issues*, including concerns that the scheme is financially unsustainable in the longer term; reduced contributions from states and territories; arbitrary cuts to participant plans; claims that the NDIA pays unnecessarily high prices for items; and a range of inefficiencies and major leakages of the service dollar away from actual services
2. *issues with the processes for determining the support needs and financial and service entitlements for each individual participant*, including rigid and centralised decisions that reduce users' control and require repeated reassessments; a lack of certainty and security of entitlements over time, as reflected in the cuts to plans;

inequities between participants; and the use of a medical rather than social model of disability to assess some participants

3. *poor decision-making processes in the NDIA*, with many documented instances of people waiting unduly long times for approvals; a lack of transparency and lack of compassion in decisions; and many people being forced into legal battles with the NDIA
4. *some services are not available at all in some communities* (in so-called thin markets with few or no providers or suitable staff), especially in regional areas, yet *in other areas there is a confusing multitude of options*
5. *eligible individuals cannot obtain services* for which they have been approved and funded because of their location or the nature and complexity of their needs
6. *no or inadequate services for the many people with disabilities who have been deemed as ineligible for the NDIS*, but still need support. This particularly includes older people who did not apply for the NDIS before they turned 65 and people with less disabling conditions who have relatively low external support needs (including many people who received some assistance prior to the NDIS). In general, the states and territories have not met their original commitment to modify mainstream programs to the extent necessary
7. *increasing concerns about the capability and quality of service providers* in the wake of both the loss or downsizing of many long-established good public and community providers, and the increasing influx of poor and opportunist providers, many of which have little experience in human services (let alone disability services), little infrastructure, and are primarily motivated by commercial goals and priorities. The outcomes of this range from poor-quality services to financial fraud. As yet though, large corporations have not become excessively powerful
8. *difficulties obtaining the required workforce*, in regard to both the *quantity* of staff (with shortages long felt in some localities now extending to being a more widespread problem) and the *quality* of staff (with significant numbers lacking the necessary skills, experience, or personal suitability for the work)

9. *poor working conditions for many support workers,* with an increasing number employed under gig work conditions (van Toorn 2022), an issue that also contributes to staff shortages
10. a number of concerns about the *accommodation and living situation* for a significant number of participants, including young people who have to live in aged care homes; residents subject to abuse; and funding models that reduce the choice and control of participants and their access to appropriate care
11. *inadequate support for group, community and team approaches* in delivering services, due to the overriding emphasis on individualising entitlements, service delivery and payments, rather than a core focus on the unique needs, social connectedness and overall wellbeing of each individual person
12. lack of capacity (financial and logistic) to cater for *groups of people whose extensive use of the NDIS was unanticipated* (e.g., children, people with psycho-social disabilities)
13. increasing prevalence of *fraud* with professional criminals exploiting the fee-for-service payment models and reduced regulation of providers.

These problems are well known and well publicised. No single document covers all of these issues, but see Tune 2019; Per Capita 2021; van Toorn 2022 and NDIS Review 2023. There are many media articles covering the issues; links to a wide range of these articles can be found at Wikipedia.

The influence of neoliberalism on the NDIS

We now consider in turn the origin, design, governance and management of the NDIS to identify the influence of neoliberalism on the scheme at these key stages of its development and operation.

Origin of the NDIS

Neoliberalism was not the main driver of the original desire to reform disability services that culminated in the decision to create the NDIS. Rather, it was primarily a social reform, initially driven by disability advocacy groups (concerned about inadequate funding and people with a disability having little control over the services they received) who were subsequently supported in achieving their aims by people experienced and influential in politics and government (Miller 2017; van Toorn 2022). The moral imperatives were powerful, and the NDIS was substantially sold to the public on this basis.

The social case for reform and the efforts of disability advocacy groups had always been present, but there were also new elements that gave powerful impetus to the cause and helped ensure that the NDIS was accepted after disability had been in the policy and funding wilderness for so many years. First, it had support from influential people within and outside government. Second, it was marketed well, presented as a radically new approach via an insurance scheme rather than a welfare program, with everyone required to pay a "premium" (via taxes) and able to make a "claim" if they need assistance. (In reality, however, it is little different from the arrangements that have underpinned many long-term government programs that have provided universal coverage for a service, both in Australia and elsewhere since the 19th century: Mulino 2022). Third, it was partially framed as an economic measure, as an investment that would generate a financial return to society greater than its cost. Fourth, the fact that the scheme was to be largely operated on a market basis made it more acceptable to decision-makers steeped in over three decades of neoliberal ideology. Van Toorn (2022) describes the linkages between disability advocates and key government agencies that led to marketisation becoming central to the creation of the NDIS.

Finally, and critically, there is a strong alignment between the human rights focus on individual rights and the neoliberal championing of the rights of individuals to exercise greater choice or sovereignty in their consumption of government-funded services. A core tenet of contemporary disability theory is that each person should be treated as an individual. The reasons for this approach are clear and undisputed, in the light of a history of abusive institutionalisation of people with a disability and the failure by government and society to recognise the humanity of people with a disability and their human rights as individual people. Thus, two philosophies – human rights and neoliberalism – poles apart in their origins and many other respects, came together in their strong support for individuals to be able to decide their services and providers. As Glendinning (2009, 178), writing in the United Kingdom about such schemes, has noted:

> [There is] an uneasy synergy between … "bottom-up" user movements and the "top-down" ambitions of successive governments to [extend] … market mechanisms in the public sector, … a synergy [that] reflects a convergence between a civil rights or social justice discourse and a neoliberal approach.

The result of such a strong focus on the individual, however, is that all too often there can be an undue pressure on vulnerable people with a disability to arrange and assess their own services; greater isolation of the people; and the individualisation of entitlements, payments and delivery modes in ways that limit the use of group, community and team approaches that should be part of a suite of services to best meet the needs of each individual.

Design of the NDIS

While the NDIS was justified primarily by human rights arguments, it was implemented using a neoliberal market-based strategy and mechanisms. From the outset, the NDIS was very consciously framed to operate as a market. Early documents (e.g., NDIA 2016) envisaged a sector that operated similarly to a conventional consumer market once people had been given their funding entitlements, while also reading in part like a prospectus for profit makers.

There are two major ways in which the design of the NDIS embodies a market-based approach: the overall strategy and the various specific market mechanisms that were adopted.

Strategy

As noted earlier, the core strategy underpinning the design and operation of the NDIS is based on a faith in the market and on public choice theory that distrusts the motivation and capability of long-term not-for-profit and public providers in the sector. Rather than planning to ensure the availability of services to all places and people that need them, coupled with relatively easy access of participants to these services (as, for example, underpins the public school and public hospital systems in Australia), NDIS relies on the market to achieve these goals.

The NDIS is based on the assumption that existing providers will expand or new providers will be established in response to the opportunities presented by the growing number of approved participants in each area. In practice, the result of this approach is that in some areas participants face a "confusopoly" (Adams 1997 has used this term for the unmanageable plethora of options that buyers face in many markets) with a multitude of providers from which to choose, yet in other areas there are no services for some people. Moreover, there may be more provider options to choose from, but there has been a major narrowing of the *types* of organisations that provide services, especially public and not-for-profit providers. Nor does the approach guarantee all providers meet some minimum level of capability and quality, while many participants have no meaningful guide as to which providers have a record of good service or which would be most appropriate for them. While there is an NDIS Quality and Safeguards Commission, in practice it has limited direct oversight of unregistered providers and can give only limited guidance to individual users about particular providers.

Central to the NDIS strategy is encouraging new entities to enter the sector and promote competition in order to reduce the alleged monopoly power and complacency of long-term providers. Thus a curious implicit assumption in the NDIS is that the operation and outcomes of services will somehow be improved by replacing some long-established, experienced and proven social-maximising not-for-profit and public providers with commercially focused providers that often have little or no experience in human services.

Specific mechanisms

There are three market mechanisms that have been particularly important in enabling the NDIS to operate as a market – individualised approaches for participants (via entitlements, delivery, and/or payments); the use of a fully fee-for-service model of payments for providers; and limited regulation of the entry of new providers. Each of these three mechanisms has a valid policy rationale and may well, in some situations, improve outcomes, but due to a number of factors (notably the unreal economic assumptions underlying these mechanisms and the intrinsic constraints in providing any human service), the actual outcomes are frequently perverse.

Davidson (2023) has outlined the rationale and the potential problematic outcomes of each of these three mechanisms. The problems include, for example, greater funding volatility and uncertainty for providers, which can lead to underinvestment in people and equipment and ultimately threaten the viability of a provider; less control and flexibility for participants in determining and changing their services; the atomisation and commodification of participants and services; less incentive for people to work in the sector; and major leakages of the service dollar. In particular, relaxing entry requirements has been one of, if not the, major cause of debacles in human service markets over recent decades. (Toner in 2014 and 2018 has shown how these sorts of problems emerged in the contracting-out of vocational education and training in Australia.)

Thus market mechanisms generate new problems, but it is also common for marketisation to inadequately respond to critical aspects of the reality of human services, or even to remove measures that have previously worked well. A notable design gap in the NDIS is the failure to ensure a provider-of-last-resort (van Toorn 2022) to ensure all people and places can obtain services, nor is there any mechanism to ensure a public provider in most places, despite the clear benefits such bodies can have in making human services markets work better (Davidson 2022). Another gap with reality is that while people with physical or sensory disabilities may have the personal agency and capacity to operate as the relatively well-informed and rational consumers of market theory (*Homo economicus*), the majority of NDIS participants are either children or adults with a cognitive disability that substantially (and in many cases totally) limit their capacity to make informed choices.

On the other hand, it is important to note that three features commonly linked with neoliberalism have not been present in the

NDIS. Total funding for the scheme has not been limited by arbitrary budget limits, nor are any means tests or co-payments required. Indeed, the initial failure to recognise the financial implications of the planned scheme and to have no obvious macro mechanism to constrain total expenditure has been a major problem of the NDIS. It has created a potential fiscal time bomb that led the former Coalition government to implement a series of de facto rationing devices by stealth (e.g., via delays in decisions and lower entitlements for some participants). While the NDIS is ostensibly an uncapped, demand-driven scheme, in practice even these sort of schemes are usually managed by ongoing variations to eligibility rules (which limit the number of users); and benefit levels (which limit the cost per user); queues; or a combination of these, undesirable as they all may be in terms of maximising access.

In summary, the NDIS has been a market where a majority of service users have no or limited personal agency to assess and make decisions about the quality of services and the capability of providers; someone else other than the user is actually paying for services (government); there is easy and often unregulated entry for many new providers; and there are extensive asymmetries of information between providers and the consumers (both users and payers). What could possibly go wrong?

Some paradoxes and perversities with neoliberalism and the NDIS

The NDIS has been a curious mixture of neoliberal market-based approaches and heavy-handed central control, with a number of consequent paradoxes and perversities in its design and operation.

First, there has been an excessive faith in market mechanisms in situations where strong control is essential, such as in the regulation of the entry of new providers. Conversely, there has been excessive central control where a more decentralised approach is desirable, for example, where government assessors have determined the precise services a client receives, a process that is also at odds with the strong philosophical underpinning of neoliberalism and marketisation that people know what is best for them rather than government officials. Second, despite marketisation ostensibly promoting efficiency and choice, the marketised elements of the scheme significantly work against these goals in a number of ways. For example, efficiency is reduced by the high transaction costs imposed on all parties and the extensive leakages of funds for non-service items, while the loss of public and not-for-profit providers has significantly reduced choice for many people.

An implicit Faustian pact

The NDIS was justified to the public by human rights arguments, but then implemented via neoliberal strategy and mechanisms. There is some irony that, despite the intrinsic dangers and problems that have resulted from neoliberalism, those features were probably a necessary condition for the initial acceptance of the NDIS by a bureaucracy and political class so heavily influenced by a neoliberal mindset. The reality is that in the contemporary world, the NDIS may have been impossible unless it embodied these neoliberal ideas. This can be seen as an implicit Faustian pact, whereby the neoliberal features that were a necessary condition for initial acceptance of the NDIS have inevitably led to inherent and critical flaws in the design and operation of the scheme. This sort of pact has characterised human services more generally in recent decades, where greater marketisation has often been the price that has to be paid for additional funding.

Governance and management of the NDIS

There have been many examples of poor governance and management of the NDIS in the decade since it was established. This has been at all senior levels, from those who have dictated the overall tenor of the government through to ministers, the NDIA Board and senior NDIA managers. This was especially so after the NDIS came under the control of the newly elected Coalition government in September 2013, within six months of its establishment.

The Coalition government replaced the Board and chairman, which in turn had spillover effects into senior management with the appointment of various CEOs and senior managers with little or no background running government programs, or no lived experience of disability, or both. As the projected costs kept increasing, ministers took or supported a series of actions to reduce expenditure, including capping the number of NDIA staff; overseeing action by NDIA assessors to reduce the amount of funding being offered to individual participants; and attempting to introduce so-called independent assessors, in part because the government believed that, as stated by the then Health Minister, Linda Reynolds, the NDIS was "relying ... too much on individual public servants' ... *natural empathy*" (Commonwealth Hansard, 2021, emphasis added). These actions created or contributed to many of the problems listed earlier.

Alternatives

What should be done to remove or reduce the problems in the NDIS outlined above, especially in relation to the ones deriving from the neoliberal features of the scheme?

When the Albanese government was elected in May 2022, a multitude of reforms to the NDIS were necessary. Broadly these reforms could be grouped under three main elements, which are essentially the reverse image of much of what has been described above.

First, rectify the poor governance and management of the scheme, including changing the people at the top so that the scheme is overseen by people with a deep knowledge and experience of disability and managing human service programs; clarifying the total funding available for the NDIS and identifying macro mechanisms to better constrain the many funding pressures facing the scheme; and making explicit and public any decisions about the scheme (such as changes in the basis for determining entitlements).

Second, there are a number of necessary policy changes unrelated to marketisation, including clearer definitions of "permanent and significant" (disability) and "reasonable and necessary" (support); holding state and territory governments to account for facilitating access to mainstream services for people with relatively low support needs; and reconsideration of the case for (otherwise eligible) people 65 years old and older to be able to access the scheme.

Third, there needs to be action that makes the scheme *less* marketised, including giving precedence to overall planning above a simple reliance on market mechanisms; supporting proven providers; returning to some level of block-grant funding for high-quality providers; returning to tighter regulation of the entry of providers; and government identifying high quality proven providers to assist participants in making their choices. Overall, it is important to reduce the extent of commercialisation, commodification, atomisation and marketing in the scheme, all of which work against quality and efficient services (Davidson 2023). On the other hand, there is a need for some action that would be a move towards *more* neoliberal and marketised approaches by accepting the inevitability of constraints on total funding; giving greater discretion for clients within approved parameters; and giving consideration to the introduction of some limited means testing and co-payments.

The net result of these alternatives would be to ensure supply of quality services for all who need them while still drawing on the benefits of market-based processes.

Conclusion

This chapter has revealed that, in relation to neoliberalism, the NDIS has been influenced by three broad sets of factors: ones that would have affected the scheme regardless of neoliberalism, ones deriving from the wider impact of neoliberalism on the body politic, and ones deriving from explicit decisions to adopt a neoliberal market strategy and mechanisms for the NDIS. In turn, the major problems of the scheme can also be explained on this basis.

The NDIS has been captured by neoliberalism at the level of ideology via the broad strategy and mechanisms on which the scheme is based, but it has not yet moved to the stage that has been reached in other human service sectors where large profit-maximising corporations have substantially captured the scheme in terms of their influence on key policy and program parameters.

The NDIS has been a striking success in a number of ways, but it is also beset by a variety of major problems. Some of these problems may have arisen whatever funding and delivery models had been chosen, but others are self-inflicted, a direct result of decisions made in the design, governance and management of the scheme, especially in relation to supporting excessive marketisation. A decade after its establishment, the funding base of the NDIS still needs to be resolved, the governance and senior management of the scheme need to be revamped, and the government needs to revise other core aspects of the scheme.

Importantly, some of the major problems of the NDIS are not unique to the NDIS. They have arisen in other human services, but the lessons of some four decades of extensive marketisation of human services have not been learned. The NDIS illustrates the potential value of market-based approaches, but also the limits of these approaches.

References

Adams, Scott (1997). *The Dilbert Future: Thriving on Business Stupidity in the 21st Century*. New York, NY: Harper Collins.

Australian National Audit Office (ANAO) (2016). *National Disability Insurance Scheme – Management of Transition of the Disability Services Market*, Auditor General Report No 24 of 2016–17, 9 November. https://tinyurl.com/dbc35axt.

Australian Bureau of Statistics (2019). *Disability, Ageing and Carers, Australia 2018*. Cat. no. 4430.0. Canberra: Australian Bureau of Statistics.

Australian Bureau of Statistics (2022). *Disability and carers: 2021 Census*. https://tinyurl.com/2pcjwdx5.

Buchanan, James M. (1978). From private preferences to public philosophy: the development of public choice. In *The Economics of Politics*, 15–25. IEA Readings 18. London: Institute of Economic Affairs.

Clun, Rachel (2022). The $60 billion question: how to fund and run the NDIS. *Sydney Morning Herald*, 16 October. https://tinyurl.com/3jexyync.

Commonwealth Hansard (2021). Joint Standing Committee on the National Disability Insurance Scheme, 18 May 2021, 32.

Davidson, Bob (2015). Contestability in human services – a case study of community aged care. PhD thesis, University of New South Wales, Sydney. https://tinyurl.com/bdz9wzvc.

Davidson, Bob (2016). Marketisation and human services providers: an industry study. In Frederic S. Lee and Bruce Cronin, eds. *Handbook of Research Methods and Applications in Heterodox Economics*, 364–87. Cheltenham UK: Edward Elgar.

Davidson, Bob (2018). The marketisation of aged care in Australia. In Damien Cahill and Phillip Toner, eds. *Wrong Way: How Privatisation & Economic Reform has Backfired*, 101–16. Melbourne: La Trobe University Press and Black Inc.
Davidson, Bob (2022). Public providers: Making human service markets work. In Gabrielle Meagher, Adam Stebbing and Diana Perche, eds. *Designing Social Service Markets: Risk, Regulation and Rent-seeking*, 331–76. Canberra: Australian National University Press.
Davidson, Bob (2023). *Lessons from the marketisation of human services for the future use of markets in the NDIS*, Submission to the Review of the National Disability Insurance Scheme, SUB-K1S6-003892, https://www.ndisreview.gov.au/submissions/sub-k1s6-003892.
Friedman, Milton (1962). *Capitalism and Freedom*. Chicago, IL: Phoenix Books.
Glendinning, Caroline (2009). The consumer in social care. In Richard Simmons, Martin Powell and Ian Greener, eds. *The Consumer in Public Services: Choice, Values and Difference*, 177–96. Bristol, UK: The Policy Press.
Hayek, Friedrich A. (2007[1944]). *The Road to Serfdom*. Chicago, IL: University of Chicago Press.
Hirschman, Albert O. (1970). *Exit, Voice and Loyalty: Responses to Decline in Firms, Organisations and State*. Cambridge, MA: Harvard University Press.
Lipsey, Richard G., and Kelvin Lancaster (1956). The general theory of the second best. *Review of Economic Studies* 24(1): 11–32.
Miller, Pavla (2017). "The age of entitlement has ended": designing a disability insurance scheme in turbulent times. *Journal of International and Comparative Social Policy* 33(2): 95–113.
Mulino, Daniel (2022). *Safety Net: The Future of Welfare in Australia*. Melbourne: La Trobe University Press.
National Disability Insurance Agency (NDIA) (2016). NDIS Market Approach: Statement of opportunity and intent. November. https://tinyurl.com/bdd9aunw.
NDIA (2021). *NDIA Annual Report, 2020–2021*. https://tinyurl.com/4zvnp5rc.
NDIA (2022). NDIS National Dashboard as at 30 June 2022. https://tinyurl.com/5h36y948.
NDIS Review (2023). *What We Have Heard: Moving from Defining Problems to Designing Solutions to Build a Better NDIS*. NDIS Review Interim Report, June. https://tinyurl.com/y4aecwjn.
Per Capita (2021). *False Economy: The Economic Benefits of the National Disability Insurance Scheme and the Consequences of Government Cost-cutting*. Report. https://tinyurl.com/yus4cwff.

Productivity Commission (2011). *Disability Care and Support*. Report no. 54. Canberra: Productivity Commission.

Simmons, Richard, Martin Powell, and Ian Greener, eds (2009). *The Consumer in Public Services: Choice, Values and Difference*. Bristol, UK: The Policy Press.

Spies-Butcher, Ben (2014). Marketisation and the dual welfare state: neoliberalism and inequality in Australia. *Economic and Labour Relations Review* 25(2): 185–201.

Toner, Phillip (2014). Contracting out publicly funded vocational education: a transaction cost critique. *Economic and Labour Relations Review* 25(2): 222–39.

Toner, Phillip (2018). A tale of mandarins and lemons: creating the market for vocational education and training. In Damien Cahill and Phillip Toner, eds. *Wrong Way: How Privatisation & Economic Reform Has Backfired*, 59–84. Melbourne: La Trobe University Press and Black Inc.

Tune, David (2019). *Review of the National Disability Insurance Scheme Act 2013: Removing Red Tape and Implementing the NDIS Participant Service Guarantee*. Report. https://tinyurl.com/3ku8fv9k.

van Toorn, Georgia (2022). Marketisation in disability services: a history of the NDIS. In Gabrielle Meagher, Adam Stebbing and Diana Perche, eds. *Designing Social Service Markets: Risk, Regulation And Rent-seeking*, 185–214. Canberra: Australian National University Press.

Waterford, Jack (2022). Marketing an economic plan must appeal to the heart as much as the head. *Pearls and Irritations*. https://tinyurl.com/ye237c97.

Wikipedia (n.d.). National Disability Insurance Scheme. https://en.wikipedia.org/wiki/National_Disability_Insurance_Scheme.

Wolf, Charles, Jnr (1988). *Markets or Governments: Choosing Between Imperfect Alternatives*. Cambridge, MA: MIT Press.

Yeandle, Sue, Teppo Kröger and Bettina Cass (2012). Voice and choice for users and carers? Development in patterns of care for older people in Australia, England and Finland. *Journal of European Social Policy* 22(4): 432–45.

9

Neoliberal care policies and women's economic inequality

Fiona Macdonald

This chapter places care at the centre of an analysis of the ways in which recent neoliberal reforms have influenced economic outcomes for women. Formal care services are core supports of the welfare system and care policies are critical in shaping women's access to waged work and opportunities to gain good-quality employment. The chapter analyses care services as direct employers of women and also indirectly, as the cost, quality and availability of care services also affect women's labour market participation.

The majority of care work, both unpaid and paid, continues to be undertaken by women. Women do most of the unpaid care work undertaken in families, whether that be as parents providing care for children or as family members caring for adults who need support due to disability or old age. The paid care workforce is also overwhelmingly female. In the past 30 years, there has been some progress – as a result of targeted action – to reduce gender inequalities via better work/care reconciliation policies and via better working conditions and pay in care sectors and other feminised sectors. But the adoption and extension of neoliberal care policies continue to generate pressures that push in the opposite direction, entrenching and deepening inequalities in work and care.

Australia's care systems have been transformed by neoliberal policies that have created so-called quasi-public or managed markets for these essential publicly funded human services. Neoliberal ideology has been a key driver of policy for early childhood education and care (ECEC) (Hill and Wade 2018), disability support and care through the National Disability Insurance Scheme (NDIS) (Macdonald 2021) and aged care (Davidson 2018; see also Chapter 8). While there are many differences in the design and operations of these essential care systems they share some key aims, dynamics and effects that reflect their neoliberal character.

Many of the tensions and pressures around the availability, costs and quality of formal care play out in ways that have implications for gender equality through their impacts on women as unpaid carers and paid care workers. Gender equality should be advanced by growth in formal care services that allow women to increase their engagement in paid work. Yet Australia's neoliberal markets for care do not provide equitable access to care services; they are often least accessible and affordable for those women and families who are most likely to experience labour market disadvantage. Growth in the feminised care workforces should also be a positive development for gender equality, but only if jobs offer decent working conditions, fair pay and career pathways but all the evidence points to neoliberal policies that have marketised care acting as countervailing forces against equality, including through degrading the quality of care jobs and creating barriers to equitable access to care. Neoliberal ideologies have underpinned major labour market and family and welfare policy reforms over the past 30 years, although policies do not necessarily adopt processes or conform to ideas understood to be central to neoliberalism. The labour market reforms of the 1990s and 2000s certainly had a strong deregulatory bent but they were also highly interventionist in disciplining unions (Stanford 2018). Under conservative Coalition governments welfare reforms have insisted on greater individual responsibility and self-reliance while, simultaneously, family policies created disincentives for women's economic participation in a bid to uphold conservative family values.

This chapter considers the consequences of neoliberal policies for formal care in the context of trends and reforms in these other policy areas. The next section describes the dimensions of economic inequality for women in Australia. After this is an examination of neoliberal welfare and family and labour market policies and their effects on women's economic (in)equality, focusing on work and care. The discussion then turns to neoliberal policies of marketisation, whereby markets and market mechanisms are used to deliver publicly-funded services, in three key formal care systems: ECEC, aged care and disability support and asks, "how well does marketised care support working carers?" and "how has marketisation of care affected paid care workers?"

Women, work, care and inequality

On most measures of economic security, in Australia, women fare worse than men. While women's education attainment is similar to men's, their labour force participation and employment rates are lower, and they work fewer hours in paid employment. Women's incomes are lower than men's, as are their savings at retirement age.

From the 1980s to the present, women's labour market employment has risen sharply while men's has declined very slightly, shrinking what had been a large gender gap in labour force participation. In late 2022, the female participation rate among 15- to 64-year-olds was 76.5 per cent compared with a rate of 83.6 per cent for males. In 1978 the comparable rates were 50.6 per cent for women and 88.1 per cent for men (Australian Bureau of Statistics – ABS 2022c, Table 01). For many years female labour force participation in Australia lagged behind similar anglophone countries, although it is now comparable. In 2021, among 15- to 64-year-olds, female labour force participation rates were, in Australia, 75.1 per cent; the United Kingdom, 74.7 per cent; Canada, 75.6 per cent; and New Zealand, 77.5 per cent (Organisation for Economic Co-operation and Development 2022).

Aggregate labour force participation rates hide some significant gender inequalities associated with women's continuing role as primary carers of children. In particular, there remain large gender gaps in participation and employment during the prime child-rearing ages. In the 30–34 and 35–44 year age groups, around eight in ten women participate in the labour force compared with more than nine in ten men (ABS 2022). Among parents in couple families with a youngest child aged under five years, nine out of ten fathers are employed, while only two-thirds of mothers are employed. Mothers' labour force participation increases with the age of the youngest child but remains about 10 percentage points lower than fathers', whatever the age of the youngest dependent child (up to 24 years) (ABS 2022d). Further, the large shift away since the 1980s from one-earner male breadwinner households with fathers in full-time employment and mothers who stay at home has not involved any large change in the employment patterns of fathers with dependent children, as the vast majority continue to be employed full-time (Baxter 2019). Among the one in five families that is a sole-parent family, 82.8 per cent are headed by women and these sole-parent mothers are much less likely to be in employment (67.3 per cent) than fathers in sole-parent families (75.8 per cent) (ABS 2022d).

Gendered impacts of care on labour market participation and economic security also arise from women undertaking the greater share of informal care for adult family members and others who require support due to old age or disability. One in ten Australians is an informal carer and a third of carers are "primary" carers who provide the most assistance to a person. Most primary carers are of working age (73.4 per cent) and seven of every ten are women (ABS 2019). Among primary carers aged 15 to 64 years in 2018, 58.8 per cent were in the labour force, compared to 81.5 per cent of people who provide no informal care and 76.6 per cent of people who provide some informal care but are not primary carers. Informal caring is highest among people aged 55 to 64, with almost one in five people in this age group providing care (Furnival and Cullen 2022).

Informal care prevents women in mid-life from increasing their workforce participation. Informal care of 10–15 hours a week is likely to lead to women reducing their working hours, and care of 20 hours or more care is associated with women exiting from the labour market or entering early retirement (Moussa 2019). Being a carer increases the risk of involuntary retirement (Welsh et al. 2018). Carers are more likely than non-carers to report that their households are poor or just getting by financially; they are likely to earn less and are more likely to be receiving government income support payments (University of Canberra 2021).

There are long-term effects from women's time spent in part-time work or out of the labour force due to caring, especially when caring is in the early years of women's working life, when much caring for children takes place. Career and employment opportunities and lifetime earnings are reduced. Women retire with lower levels of superannuation, with a 20 per cent gender gap in median superannuation balances at age 65 (ABS 2022b). It is also the case that women living in all household types are more likely than men to live in poverty (Australian Council of Social Services and UNSW Sydney 2020).

Women are twice as likely to be in part-time employment than men (43.2 per cent compared with 18.5 per cent in late 2022), and women are also more likely to be underemployed (7.1 per cent compared with 4.9 per cent) (ABS 2022b). Caring for children is the main reason given by women who want to work more hours or who are not working but want a job. For men wanting more work, the main reason for not being available is long-term sickness or disability. Where child care is a barrier to workforce participation or increased work hours, 30 per cent of women cite either childcare costs or lack of availability of child care in their locality (ABS 2022a).

In employment, high levels of occupational gender segregation and comparatively poor and more insecure conditions in part-time work also contribute to gender inequalities. First, gender segregation is one of the key means by which the undervaluation of women's work is perpetuated. The undervaluing of paid care work is central, with some of the lowest paid jobs in the economy in direct care occupations in the highly feminised, large and growing care sectors (National Skills Commission 2022). Women comprise around 80 per cent of employed care workers in Australia, including around nine out of ten childcare workers and four out of five workers in the "long-term care" or "social care" sectors of aged care and disability support (National Skills Commission 2021, 51–2). Second, inferior conditions prevail in jobs with part-time hours – the jobs in which women are concentrated due to families' unequal sharing of unpaid care. Casual employment – employment without paid leave entitlements – is more common among female employees (26.4 per cent) than among male employees (22.5 per cent). It is highest among younger women (36.3 per cent among 15 to 34 year olds) while for men it is highest among those aged 65 years and over (38.1 per cent). Casual employment is often on-demand work with insecure hours (i.e., unpredictable and variable, with no guaranteed minimum). The healthcare and social assistance industry, along with retail trade, accommodation, and food services industries, accounted for just under a half (48.6 per cent) of all casual employees in August 2020 (Gilfillan 2021).

Care in context: gender equality, family and welfare policies and labour market reforms

During the 1970s and 1980s Australia was regarded as at the forefront of the development of policy machinery for achieving women's equality, with central high-level mechanisms in place supporting whole-of-government approaches to assessing gender impacts of policy (Sawer 2007). Working in alliance with the women's movement and the Australian Council of Trade Unions (ACTU), Australian Labor Party federal governments under Gough Whitlam in the early 1970s and Bob Hawke in the 1980s developed childcare, employment and income support policies that supported women's economic equality (Brennan 2007). But, from the 1990s on, successive governments dismantled arrangements for building a national framework on gender equality and failed to develop comprehensive women's policies (Harris Rimmer and Sawer 2016). Where commitment to gender equality was concerned, neoliberal agendas somewhat blurred the differences between Labor and conservative governments. Over the 1990s and 2000s changes were made in gender-equality policy machinery and in income support and labour market policies, despite predicted negative gender effects of the changes. Some changes were part of neoliberal economic reforms; other policies were expressions of conservative views of gendered household labour relations.

Contradictions in neoliberal family and income support policies

Neoliberal assumptions of individualism and self-reliance as the basis for welfare have been embedded in Australia's income support policies since at least the 1990s. These assumptions are reflected in the treatment of sole-parent mothers, as outlined below. But family and childcare policies paradoxically contain some strong disincentives for women in couple families with dependent children to engage in employment equally with their partners.

Neoliberal critiques of the welfare state promoted in the United States in the 1980s included arguments that the welfare system had produced a problem of welfare dependency among people who could be expected to support themselves (Saunders 2000). Australia's first "activation" strategies, designed to make income-support recipients more active job seekers, were Labor government initiatives, introduced in the early 1990s to address long-term unemployment. These were followed by more onerous and punitive work-first approaches and increased welfare conditionality under Coalition governments. While applied in the most punitive fashion to First Nations people in the form of compulsory income-management policies, these policies also targeted young people and sole parents.

Under Coalition federal governments led by John Howard from 1996 to 2007, neoliberal welfare-to-work measures were extended from unemployed people to sole parents in receipt of income-support payments. Since that time sole parents' eligibility for parenting payments has been further restricted by both Coalition and Labor governments, with many sole parents who are not in paid employment transferred to Newstart (to become JobSeeker): unemployment allowances that are paid at lower rates than parenting payments and have stricter income tests and requirements for economic participation (McKenzie, McHugh and McKay 2019, 19). The proportion of sole parents who receive the lower unemployment payment, JobSeeker, increased from 0 per cent in 2000 to 28 per cent in 2021 (Australian Council of Social Services and UNSW Sydney 2021, 7).

From the 1990s, the expectation was established in income-support and family policies that sole parents should combine care for young children with paid work. Yet the family benefits payments system supported partnered parents in single-income families to choose not to work and retain benefits. Family payments and tax were structured so that couple families with a primary breadwinner who earned 80 per cent of the household income in a one-and-a-half earner family received greater financial benefit than families in which partners' earnings were more equal (Hill 2007). Strong disincentives for women in low- and middle-income households to increase their participation in paid work were built into the system. While the neoliberal theme of choice has been prominent in childcare policy, under Coalition governments, this has always been combined (and often in tension) with the promotion of conservative family values (Brennan 2007).

Tax and parenting-payment arrangements continue to create disincentives for women with children to participate in the paid workforce to the same extent as full-time partners. All else being equal, more benefit is paid when a family's income is earned by one person, rather than by two (Broadway 2021). In addition, childcare subsidies – the primary mechanism by which the government assists families with the costs of childcare – also create disincentives for equal workforce participation by women. If a mother (as the lower-paid partner in a couple) works full-time, the family will be worse off due to the higher costs they have to pay for formal child care. This disincentive to work also exists for sole parents (Stewart 2018). To the present time, Australia's arrangements for paid parental leave provide little incentive for leave to be shared by fathers (Scott, Grudnoff and Fleming 2021).

Carers of older people and people with disability can also have their participation in work and study curbed by income support requirements. Eligibility for Carer Payment, the main income support measure for carers, allows employment for up to 25 hours a week only. While women are more likely to need to stay in the workforce longer, they are far more likely to retire early due to caring responsibilities. In paid work, gender inequalities persist, with neoliberal labour market reforms playing an important part in this.

Neoliberal industrial restructuring through a gender lens

Although formal barriers to women's labour force participation were largely removed in the 1970s and 1980s, most female workers entering the labour force did not benefit equally from the employment protections that underpinned the Australian "wage earners" welfare state in the postwar decades (Castles 1994). As women's integration into the paid workforce proceeded in the 1980s, a combination of neoliberal restructuring and conservative welfare and family policy left a modified male breadwinner model partially intact. Over the past three decades, women's workforce participation has continued to grow but women still occupy very different positions in employment from men. There has been some policy intervention to support workers who are also carers (working carers), with many of the important gains made as a result of unions running test cases in the industrial relations tribunal – including parental leave and carers' leave – rather than through the initiative of governments (Chapman 2018). But work and care/family provisions have favoured workers who are in "standard" full-time continual employment, while women's employment has been concentrated in "non-standard" part-time and casual jobs (Cooper and Baird 2015).

Good-quality part-time jobs have been regarded by feminists as one key to gender equality in employment under a dual-breadwinner, dual-carer couple household model. But, as part-time work has grown, an increasing proportion of part-time jobs have been insecure casual jobs that have no paid leave entitlements and often no certainty of work. In mid-2022, while about one in every ten (11.3 per cent) full-time employees was engaged as a casual, more than half (51 per cent) of all employees in part-time work were casual (ABS 2022e). In addition, long-standing inferior conditions continue to exist in many permanent part-time jobs in comparison to conditions in equivalent full-time jobs, and even these standards have been eroded under neoliberal industrial relations regimes (Chalmers, Campbell and Charlesworth 2005; Charlesworth and Heron 2012). Many workers with care responsibilities are in jobs with little security of working time, making it very difficult for them to combine work and care (Charlesworth and Heron 2012). The trend to insecurity in part-time jobs in particular commenced in the 1980s and was hastened under neoliberal labour market reforms.

With the 1993 introduction of enterprise-based bargaining by the Keating Labor government, many women (and men) in the lower-paid services industries, including care sectors, were excluded from collective bargaining. While the new enterprise focus was promoted as allowing work and family matters to be negotiated at the workplace level (Brennan 2007), fears of potential negative impacts on female workers were largely borne out (Charlesworth 1997; van Wanrooy, Wright and Buchanan 2009). With bargaining shifting to the individual workplace level, the pay and conditions set down in sector-wide industrial awards became safety-net minimums only. Care workers were particularly poorly placed to participate in and benefit from enterprise-based bargaining. These workforces had high levels of part-time employees in small, mostly not-for profit organisations with a long-standing reliance on and ethos of voluntary mission and high levels of dependence on government funding. Levels of union membership were not high.

Subsequent labour market reforms under Coalition governments in the 1990s and 2000s further undermined low-paid workers' pay and conditions and working carers' ability to combine work and care (Pocock et al. 2008). Labor's *Fair Work Act 2009* did not live up to hopes that it would return a balance to the industrial relations system, and it provided no effective support for working carers (Charlesworth and Macdonald 2015, 2017; Macdonald, Charlesworth and Brigden 2018). During Labor's time in office in the early 2010s, Prime Minister Julia Gillard committed the government to funding large pay increases for social and community services workers, a commitment that was seen as critical to the subsequent success of a historic equal-pay case fought by unions in the sector (Macdonald and Charlesworth 2013). In late 2022 the Albanese Labor government was quick to put forward reforms that are intended to reverse some of the effects on workers of 30 years of neoliberal industrial relations policies, including reforms directed to increasing gender equality and improving pay and conditions for low-paid workers in care sectors (Department of Employment and Workplace Relations 2022). There are no immediate fixes among these reforms and any impacts may not be seen for a number of years. The reforms are not radical and it will take further changes to reverse the effects of 30 years of neoliberal labour market reforms that have enabled the growth of insecure work with poorer conditions, protections and entitlements – especially in part-time jobs.

Neoliberal policies and the marketisation of formal care systems

Before the introduction of neoliberal policy changes, the state directly funded and operated early childhood education and care (ECEC), disability support and aged care providers, or made grants to generally long-established not-for-profit operators (Fine and Davidson 2018; Hill and Wade 2018; Macdonald 2021). Neoliberal policies for formal care and other social services were introduced in Australia in the 1980s and were framed within narratives of increasing personal responsibility and choice, while also being strongly driven by ideas of increased efficiency and limiting the role of government (Brennan et al. 2012). This saw the introduction of competitive market-based models where financing of formal care shifted away from the supply-side to demand-side funding. In all three care systems, public funding is in the form of allocations to individual care "consumers" who purchase services from their preferred providers in quasi-public or managed markets.

Through these changes, the role of government has been transformed from service provider to market manager. Most recently, the government's role (in the NDIS context), had been referred to as one of "market stewardship", involving setting the "rules of the game", constantly monitoring market development and adjusting the rules to "steer the system" to achieve high-level policy aims (Gash et al. 2013, 6, 35). The service provider landscape has been reconfigured so there is no longer much public service provision at all, depleted not-for-profit provision and significant growth in for-profit provision in all care systems. Underpinning the competitive market model is the idea that consumer choice leads to innovation and diverse service models that meet the preferences and needs of all care users. The achievement of this requires that there be limited regulatory intervention. Individual consumer funding, promoted to maximise individual choice and control over services, also provides governments with a means to control the growth of care spending. The government has no infrastructure or operational costs and is distanced from accountability for meeting the full costs of services that are provided in a market. An important context for the neoliberal reforms to all care systems is the growing demand for formal care services, which is contributing to pressures for governments to find ways to curb costs.

Governments face a range of constraints to the effective management of care systems once they are marketised. In Australia common issues in marketised social services include loss of operational expertise within government; fraud and gaming of rules by providers; decline of the not-for-profit sector – involving loss of local expertise and social capital; and creation of a political problem as powerful firms are able to successfully resist policy or regulation that would be unfavourable to them (Brennan 2007; Considine 2022).

In ECEC, for-profit providers dominate in the parts of the market to which most government money flows. Large for-profits, including national and international chains and publicly listed companies, have replaced the traditional small- and medium-sized family-run centres (United Workers Union 2021; Grudnoff 2022). They pay higher CEO and executive salaries, and have been found to offer inferior services compared to not-for-profits and public providers (Grudnoff 2022). In aged care, providers have used public funding to buy property and grow their businesses (Centre for International Corporate Tax Accountability and Research 2022). In the NDIS, the market is still developing. State and territory governments have rapidly moved out of service provision. Thousands of private for-profit firms have entered the new market, many of them very small. Mergers and acquisitions have created some very large providers. The NDIS has provided many people with support that meets their needs for the first time but there are also many indications of emerging significant problems with the highly unregulated system. There are signs of some providers moving to concentrate service provision in the most lucrative parts of the market while people with more complex needs, in disadvantaged communities and in regional and remote areas cannot access services to meet basic needs (Malbon, Carey and Meltzer 2019). There is emerging evidence that provider fraud is an important factor in rising NDIS spending (Dickinson 2022). Detailed investigations of the workings and effects of Australia's marketised care systems identify some common failings for the people they are supposed to support, including overall shortages in services, inequity in access and affordability, and significant problems with quality (Hill and Wade 2018).

How well does marketised care support working carers?

Access to affordable formal care services is critical for women's equal participation in the workforce. When the costs of care are high the proportion of unpaid care increases (Vuri 2016).

Australia invests less (relative to gross domestic product) in ECEC services than most OECD countries and yet has one of the most expensive ECEC systems globally (Grudnoff 2022). Services are unaffordable for almost 40 per cent of families (Gromada and Richardson 2021). Lack of access and unaffordability limit children's participation in early learning and prevent women from participating in the labour force.

The market basis of ECEC contributes to women's relative economic disadvantage, with service availability poorest in lower socio-economic areas and providers clustering in more affluent areas where there is greater opportunity to profit. Some of the families most likely to benefit from formal care, including families with parents with irregular work, casual jobs with variable hours or shift work, are poorly provided for by the service offerings in the ECEC market. For someone earning minimum wages, the out-of-pocket costs can be so high that it is not worth working at all. In sum, the ECEC system is not successful in meeting one of the key objectives of the system: to support all women with preschool children to participate as fully as they wish to in the workforce.

Under the NDIS, there has been an overall expansion of support for people with significant disabilities that has benefited many unpaid carers. At the same time, individual consumer funding models in both aged care and the NDIS provide new potential for increased reliance on family members and other informal carers to make up for shortfalls in formal care services. This is especially so in the context of the significant relocation of care from institutional residential settings to private homes. This relocation is driven in part by changing social norms and preferences, but it also reflects government efforts to control public spending. One way in which spending is reduced when care is home-based is through increased dependence on family members and others for unpaid care provision.

In aged care and the NDIS, the ability of carers to participate in employment has been undermined by individual consumer funding in at least three ways. First, separate programs and supports for carers have been wound back. Second, the individualised funding schemes are not directed to supporting carers. Where support is directed to carers, it is to assist them in their roles *as carers*. A carer's desire or need to take up paid work may not be factored into their family member's support plan or care package; rather the plan or package is built around assumptions of their availability to care. Third, much of the administration and management of care is undertaken by consumers (or their carers) in individualised direct funding systems, including locating, purchasing and managing care. In effect what used to be funded work has been outsourced to people eligible for care and their unpaid family and other informal carers. With the individual consumer at its heart, marketised care has led to a "lack of informal carer visibility and recognition in policy" (Hamilton, Charlesworth and Macdonald 2024, 124).

Paid care work in marketised care

Increased recognition of the complexity of care work and the skills it requires have been part of slow progress towards better working conditions and pay for care workers in Australia. But marketisation and individualisation of care systems have generated pressures that pull strongly in the opposite direction, towards more degraded working conditions and low pay in informalised jobs. For example, on the one hand, in 2012 pay increases that partially remedied gendered undervaluation were won by unions in the social and community services equal pay case. On the other hand, in individualised consumer markets, flexible services are being achieved by reshaping the workforce to provide labour on-demand at the lowest possible cost. This has fragmented care workforces and leads to individualised employment arrangements.

In the NDIS and in home-based care for the aged, most frontline care and support jobs offer only part-time hours, often short hours. In the NDIS workforce, 80 per cent or more of workers are employed part-time, compared with about 30 per cent of workers in the Australian labour force overall. An early trend to increased casualisation under individualised funding continues with about 40 per cent of employees in the NDIS in casual employment, compared with 23 per cent across the economy (ABS 2022e; National Disability Services 2022, 34). Low pay and poor working conditions are associated with high levels of turnover and intention to quit. In ECEC, high turnover is associated with overwork, stress and low pay. Understaffing and underinvestment are more common in for-profit than not-for-profit centres (Chifley Research Centre 2020).

In the growing home-based aged care and disability support sectors, workers have little certainty of working time and income. Unpredictable work schedules and long workdays of short, broken shifts are common. At the same time, these workforces have high rates of underemployment and multiple job-holding. It is not unusual for care workers to hold multiple short-hours jobs and work over six or seven days to make up just 25 hours' work for the week. These working patterns leave workers exhausted, stressed and unable to plan or engage in any regular non-work activities (Macdonald, Bentham and Malone 2018). Profit maximisation may be the motivation for some service providers for organising work as on-demand labour. In aged care and the NDIS, it is also the case that individualised, billable-hours funding regimes that contain little or no provision for employees' training, supervision or peer support provide a strong incentive for employers to minimise labour time and invest as little as possible in staff.

New for-profit business models and employment practices are evident in individualised disability and aged care markets. With the appearance of digital labour platforms in these markets, there is now a workforce of solo, self-employed care workers, including low-paid and inexperienced workers. Platforms can exert considerable control over workers' behaviour and their pay, while they maintain they are neither service providers nor employers but merely provide a "marketplace". Poorly regulated market platforms have a significant cost advantage over traditional service providers that derives entirely from devolving the costs, risks and responsibilities of employment and of service provision, including service quality and safety, to individual workers and to care users. Care workers are placed completely beyond the reach of minimum wages and employment standards and most other labour protections. In the NDIS, platforms and independent contracting are promoted by scheme managers as responding to consumer needs and preferences for flexibility, choice and control over services, while also providing cheaper and better value for money care (Macdonald 2021).

Conclusion

Australia's quasi-markets for care are far from success stories in as far as they support a reduction in women's economic inequality. All systems maintain or increase unpaid work for some groups of women most likely to benefit from the opportunity to participate or increase their participation in waged work. While the ECEC system excludes some participants, the directions being taken in the aged care and NDIS systems are towards systems that rely on the unpaid work from carers to function at all.

The experience of the Covid-19 pandemic appeared to open up a space for recognition of care as an essential public good and as key to women's economic disadvantage. The new Albanese Labor government has placed pay and conditions in the feminised care and community sectors on the agenda. But there are few signs that privatisation, marketisation and individualisation of care are to be challenged any time soon, despite the mounting evidence of some fundamental problems with these approaches to the provision of a public good.

References

Australian Bureau of Statistics (ABS) (2019). *Disability, Ageing and Carers, Australia: Summary of Findings, Australia.* https://tinyurl.com/3jspv8js.

ABS (2022a). *Barriers and Incentives to Labour Force Participation, Australia.* https://tinyurl.com/5n9xtss2.

ABS (2022b). *Gender Indicators 2022.* https://tinyurl.com/mum8s7v7.

ABS (2022c) *Labour Force Australia, Detailed,* October 2022. https://tinyurl.com/4nymxwcy.

ABS (2022d). *Labour Force Status of Families.* https://tinyurl.com/2ubea5rt.

ABS (2022e). *Working Arrangements,* August 2022. https://tinyurl.com/h37sn6um.

Australian Council of Social Services and UNSW Sydney (2020). *Poverty in Australia 2020: Part 2 – Who is affected?* Sydney: Australian Council of Social Services in partnership with the University of New South Wales.

Australian Council of Social Services and UNSW Sydney (2021). *Australian Income Support since 2000: Those Left Behind.* Sydney: Australian Council of Social Services in partnership with the University of New South Wales.

Baxter, J. (2019). *Fathers and Work: A Statistical Overview.* Research summary. Melbourne: Australian Institute of Family Studies.

Brennan, D. (2007). Babies, budgets, and birth rates: work/family policy in Australia 1996–2006. *Social Politics: International Studies in Gender, State and Society* 14(1): 31–57.

Brennan D., B. Cass, S. Himmelweit, and M. Szebehely (2012). The marketisation of care: rationales and consequences in Nordic and liberal care regimes. *Journal of European Social Policy* 22(4): 377–91.

Broadway, B. (2021). Time to reform Australia's unfair family support system. *Pursuit*, 16 March. https://tinyurl.com/mt5fyjev.

Castles, F.G. (1994). The wage earners' welfare state revisited: refurbishing the established model of Australian social protection, 1983–93. *Australian Journal of Social Issues* 29(2): 120–45.

Centre for International Corporate Tax Accountability and Research (CICTAR) (2022). *Careless on Accountability: Is Federal Aged Care Funding Siphoned Away*? https://tinyurl.com/2jad5khh.

Chalmers, J., I. Campbell and S. Charlesworth (2005). Part-time work and caring responsibilities in Australia: towards an assessment of job quality. *Labour and Industry: A Journal of the Social and Economic Relations of Work* 15(3): 41–66.

Chapman, A. (2018). Work-and-care initiatives: flaws in the Australian regulatory framework. *Journal of Law and Equality* 14: 115–44.

Charlesworth, S. (1997). Enterprise bargaining and women workers: the seven perils of flexibility. *Labour and Industry* 8(2): 101–15.

Charlesworth, S. and A. Heron (2012). New Australian working time minimum standards: reproducing the same old gendered architecture? *Journal of Industrial Relations* 54(2): 164–81.

Charlesworth, S., and F. Macdonald (2015). Women, work and industrial relations in Australia in 2014. *Journal of Industrial Relations* 57(3): 366–82.

Charlesworth, S. and F. Macdonald (2017). Employment regulation and worker-carers: reproducing gender inequality in the domestic and market spheres? In D. Peetz and G. Murray, eds. *Women, Labor Segmentation and Regulation*, 79–96. New York: Palgrave Macmillan.

Chifley Research Centre (2020). *Investing In Australia's Early Childhood Infrastructure.* Kingston, ACT: Chifley Research Centre.

Considine, M. (2022). *The Careless State: Reforming Australia's Social Services.* Melbourne: Melbourne University Press.

Cooper, R. and M. Baird (2015). Bringing the 'right to request' flexible working arrangements to life: From policies to practices. *Employee Relations* 37(5): 568–81.

Davidson, B. (2018). The marketisation of aged care in Australia. In D. Cahill and P. Toner, eds. *Wrong Way: How Privatisation & Economic Reform Backfired.* Melbourne: La Trobe University Press and Black Inc.

Department of Employment and Workplace Relations (2022). Legislation to improve Australia's workplace relations system has received royal assent from the Governor-General. https://www.dewr.gov.au/secure-jobs-better-pay.

Dickinson, H. (2022). NDIS fraud reports reveal the scheme's weakest points. *The Conversation,* 16 August. https://tinyurl.com/yckc72j4.

Fine, M., and B. Davidson (2018). The marketization of care: Global challenges and national responses in Australia. *Current Sociology* 66(4): 503–16.

Furnival, A., and D. Cullen (2022). *Caring Costs Us: The Economic Impact on Lifetime Income and Retirement Savings of Informal Carers.* Canberra: Carers Australia.

Gash, T., N. Panchamia, S. Sims and L. Hotson (2013). *Making Public Service Markets Work: Professionalising Government's Approach to Commissioning and Market Stewardship.* London: Institute for Government.

Gilfillan, G. (2021). Recent and long-term trends in the use of casual employment. *Research Paper Series, 2021–22.* Parliament of Australia, Parliamentary Library.

Gromada, A., and D. Richardson (2021). *Where Do Rich Countries Stand on Childcare?* Innocenti Research Report. Florence, Italy: UNICEF Office of Research – Innocenti.

Grudnoff, M. (2022). *The Economic Benefits of High-Quality Universal Early Child Education.* Canberra: Centre for Future Work at the Australia Institute.

Hamilton, M., S. Charlesworth and F. Macdonald (2024). Informal care policy: Needs of older people and people with disability or chronic illness. In M. Baird, E. Hill and S. Colussi, eds. *At a Turning Point: Work, Care and Family Policies in Australia,* 121–44. Sydney: Sydney University Press.

Harris Rimmer, S., and M. Sawer (2016). Neoliberalism and gender equality policy in Australia. *Australian Journal of Political Science* 51(4): 742–58.

Hill, E. (2007). Budgeting for work-life balance: the ideology and politics of work and family policy in Australia. *Australian Bulletin of Labour 33*(2): 226–45.

Hill, E. and M. Wade (2018). The "radical marketisation" of early childhood education and care in Australia. In D. Cahill and P. Toner, eds. *Wrong Way:*

How Privatisation & Economic Reform Backfired, 21–39. Melbourne: Latrobe University Press and Black Inc.

Macdonald, F. (2021). *Paid Care Work in the New Gig Economy*. Singapore: Palgrave Macmillan.

Macdonald, F., and S. Charlesworth (2013). Equal pay under the *Fair Work Act 2009*: mainstreamed or marginalised? *UNSW Law Journal*. 36(2): 1–24.

Macdonald, F., and S. Charlesworth (2016), Cash for care under the NDIS: shaping care workers' working conditions? *Journal of Industrial Relations* 58(5): 627–46.

Macdonald, F., E. Bentham and J. Malone (2018), Wage theft, underpayment and unpaid work in marketised social care. *Economic and Labour Relations Review* 29(1): 80–96.

Macdonald, F., S. Charlesworth and C. Brigden (2018). Low-paid workers and collective bargaining: the issues. In B. Creighton, A. Forsyth and S. McCrystal, eds. *Collective Bargaining under the Fair Work Act: Evaluating the Australian Experiment in Enterprise Bargaining*, 206–27. Sydney: Federation Press.

McKenzie, H.J., C. McHugh and F. McKay (2019). Life on Newstart allowance: a new reality for low-income single mothers. *Journal of Family Studies* 25(1): 18–33.

Malbon, E., G. Carey and A. Meltzer (2019). Personalisation schemes in social care: are they growing social and health inequalities? *BMC Public Health* 19(1): 805.

Moussa, M.M. (2019). The relationship between elder care-giving and labour force participation in the context of policies addressing population ageing: a review of empirical studies published between 2006 and 2016. *Ageing & Society* 39(6): 1281–310.

National Skills Commission (2021). *Australian Jobs 2021*. Canberra: National Skills Commission.

National Skills Commission (2022). *Care Workforce Labour Market Study Final Report*, 30 September 2021. Canberra: National Skills Commission.

National Disability Services (2022). *State of the Disability Sector Report 2022*. Sydney: National Disability Services.

Organisation for Economic Co-operation and Development (2022). OECD Statistics, Labour force statistics by sex and age indicators. https://stats.oecd.org/Index.aspx?DataSetCode=lfs_sexage_i_r.

Pocock, B., J. Elton, A. Preston, S. Charlesworth, F. Macdonald, M. Baird, R. Cooper and B. Ellem (2008). The impact of "Work Choices" on women in low paid employment in Australia: a qualitative analysis. *Journal of Industrial Relations* 50(3): 475–88.

Sawer, M. 2007. Australia: The fall of the femocrat. In J. Outshoorn and J. Kantola, eds. *Changing State Feminism*, 20–40. London: Routledge.

Saunders, P., ed. (2000). *Reforming the Australian Welfare State*. Melbourne: Australian Institute of Family Studies.

Scott, A., M. Grudnoff and J. Fleming (2021). Boosting workforce participation and wages. In A. Scott and R. Campbell, eds. *The Nordic Edge: Policy Possibilities for Australia*, ch. 6. Melbourne: Melbourne University Press.

Stanford, J. (2018). Fair go no more: neoliberalism and Australian labour market policy. In D. Cahill and P. Toner, eds. *Wrong Way: How Privatisation & Economic Reform Backfired*, 166–185. Melbourne: La Trobe University Press and Black Inc.

Stewart, M. (2018). *Personal income tax cuts and the new Child Care Subsidy: Do they address high effective marginal tax rates on women's work?* Tax and Transfer Policy Institute – Policy Brief, 1/2018. Canberra: Australian National University.

University of Canberra (2021). *Caring for Others and Yourself: The 2021 Carer Wellbeing Survey*. Report by Centre for Change Governance and NATSEM, University of Canberra. Canberra: Carers Australia.

United Workers Union (2021). *"Spitting off Cash": Where does all the money go in Australia's early learning sector?* Melbourne: United Workers Union.

van Wanrooy, B., S. Wright and J. Buchanan (2009). *Who Bargains?* Report prepared for the NSW Office of Industrial Relations by the Workplace Research Centre. Sydney: University of Sydney.

Vuri, D. (2016). Do childcare policies increase maternal employment? *IZA World of Labor*. https://tinyurl.com/3n94u3v5.

Welsh, J., L. Strazdins, S. Charlesworth, C.T. Kulik and C. D'Este (2018). Losing the workers who need employment the most: how health and job quality affect involuntary retirement. *Labour and Industry: A Journal of the Social and Economic Relations of Work* 28(4): 261–78.

10

The national electricity market 25 years on: outcomes and prospects

Bruce Mountain

More than 25 years has passed since the *National Electricity (South Australia) Act 1996*, created the national electricity market (NEM), a series of interconnected regional markets for the sale of bulk electricity production, and an access regime for the transmission and distribution networks in the participating jurisdictions.

In its authorisation of the National Electricity Code in 1997 (Australian Competition and Consumer Commission - ACCC 1997) the Australian Competition and Consumer Commission (ACCC) summarised the rationale for the creation of the NEM, and drew attention to factors that might mean its benefits fall short of hopes. Competition, it said, would promote efficiency in production, resource allocation and investment. This would reduce costs and align tariffs and prices with costs. It cited the Industry Commission's (1995) calculation that this would increase national income by 1.4 per cent, the largest single benefit associated with the Hilmer reforms (ACCC 1997, ix).

The ACCC noted that some of this benefit had already been realised through corporatisation, industry restructuring, privatisation and the development of state-based trading arrangements. But it said that an interconnected national market would generate further significant benefits and affect whether the benefits of reform accrue to consumers or investors.

Those further benefits, the ACCC said, would arise in two ways:

- first by reducing the margin of reserve of generating plant in each region "by sharing between jurisdictions better management of non-coincident peaks"
- secondly, noting that electricity is difficult to store, it suggested that "interconnection between systems based on different technologies can make better use of existing generating capabilities and therefore increase flexibility and reduce costs" (ACCC 1997, x).

The ACCC did however anticipate that factors intrinsic and extrinsic to the NEM could offset "perhaps to a significant extent" (1997, xi) the anticipated benefits, including insufficient competition or weak regulation of the infrastructure (network) elements.

Has the NEM succeeded? Policy successes, like policy failures, are in the eye of the beholder (Leutjens, Mintrom and Herron 2019). Mindful of this, we examine outcomes in electricity generation, transmission and distribution. Other than in electricity distribution (which draws on the author's prior work), this chapter presents evidence of outcomes and discusses the evolution of institutions, rather than arguing causal explanations.

Generation

Prices

The chart in Figure 10.1 shows the mean quarterly wholesale (spot) prices from 2006 (when Tasmania joined the NEM) to the end of 2023. In the eight years between 1998 and 2006, average prices moved in a reasonably narrow range. In money of the day, the lowest average annual price in the NEM was in its first year.

From 2006 to July 2012 (when a carbon price was introduced) median prices were stable. They rose for the two years in which carbon prices applied, followed by stable prices – Tasmania's prices in the period were affected by the failure of the cable connected to the NEM – until the closure of the Hazelwood power station in Victoria in April 2017. After Hazelwood's closure, other coal-generation capacity withdrew from the market, thereby allowing coal generators to shadow-price much more expensive gas generators (Mountain and

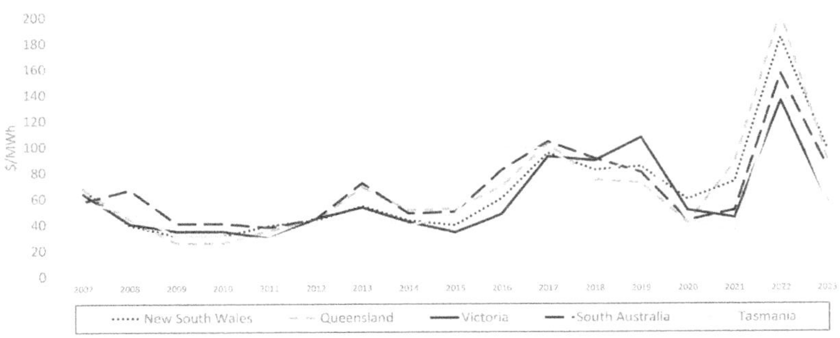

Figure 10.1 Mean annual spot market nominal prices ($/MWh) 2006 to December 2023. Source: *Victoria Energy Policy Centre* (VEPC) (2023).

Percy 2019). Increasing renewable generation limited the scope to exercise market power so that by the second quarter of 2020, median prices were around the levels before Hazelwood closed. The surge in prices in 2022 reflects (mainly) the increase in gas and coal prices associated with Russia's invasion of Ukraine.

Figure 10.2 shows the mean (Figure 10.2a) and maximum (Figure 10.2b) operating demand in the NEM from 2006 to June 2022. Other than in Queensland (where the growth of the liquefied natural gas industry has increased demand), mean (average) demand has declined. Distributed (behind-the-meter) solar electricity generation explains this in part, but consumption efficiency is likely to be more important, particularly in New South Wales and Victoria where behind-the-meter production is not yet a large part of aggregate supply.

Investment

Simshauser and Gilmore (2022) counted 229 utility-scale new-entrant generators that have together added 31,487 megawatts of coal, gas and renewables with aggregate value of $56.3 billion (2021$) in the NEM from 1998 to 2021. More than half of this – 15,939 megawatts ($27.2 billion) – occurred from 2016 to 2021.

Generation expansion was first mainly in coal, then gas and then renewables.

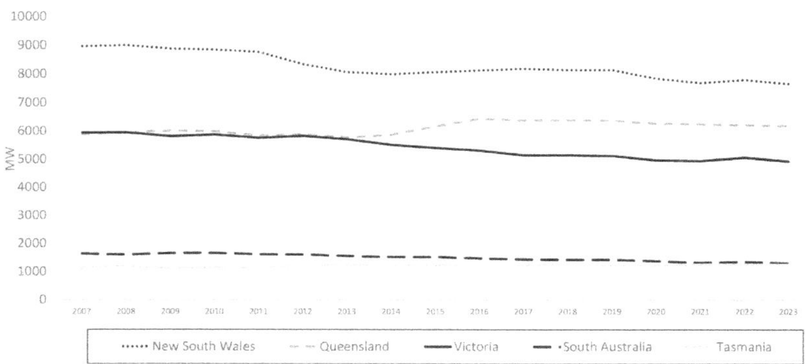

Figure 10.2a Mean operating demand 2007–2022. Source: VEPC (2023).

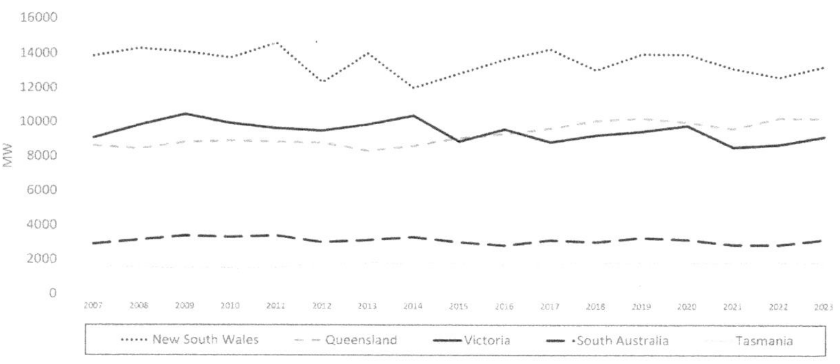

Figure 10.2b Maximum operating demand 2007–2022. Source: VEPC (2023).

- Around 2,750 megawatts of coal generation was commissioned; most of it planned or under construction (in Queensland) before the NEM started.
- Around 9,100 megawatts of gas generation was built, about half of which was in the period from 1998 to 2006 and the remainder from 2007 to 2010. In 2006 the Queensland government boasted that, when its scheme was announced in 2005, Queensland's gas-fired generating capacity was about 900 megawatts but that by mid-2006 Queensland's gas-fired power station capacity had risen to over 2,000

megawatts and "there is at least as much gas-fired generating capacity under development or under consideration in Queensland" (Wilson 2007).

- The remaining 21,500 megawatts of new generation has been in variable renewable generation, and, as noted, about half of this in the five years from 2016 to 2021. The expansion of renewable generation has been affected by policies, starting with an obligation on retailers to source 2 per cent of their sales from renewable sources by 2010. In 2009 this was increased to 41 terrawatt-hours by 2020 (then estimated to be 20 per cent of 2020 demand; a terrawatt-hour is 1 million megawatt-hours). In 2011 the scheme was then split into a small-scale and large-scale scheme. In 2017 a revised large-scale target of 33 terrawatt-hours by 2020 was established.

In addition, by mid-2023 there was 23.3 gigawatts (1 gigawatt is 1,000 megawatts) of rooftop solar systems smaller than 15 kilowatts and another 3,800 megawatts of rooftop solar and ground-mounted solar that is behind-the-meter or not large enough to be counted as grid-scale investment.[1] In 2022, 18.7 terrawatt-hours were produced from these small-scale, mainly rooftop, solar photovoltaics. This was equivalent to 9.4 per cent of the 200 terrawatt-hours of electricity produced in the NEM in 2022 (VEPC 2023). This rapid growth has been supported through a small-scale renewable certificate scheme for systems of 100 kilowatts or smaller, which became an unlimited volume fixed-price capital subsidy scheme.

Institutional developments

We distinguish developments from 1998 to 2017 and then from 2018 to the present. The segmentation reflects the re-entry of state governments that had previously privatised their generation.

1 https://www.cleanenergyregulator.gov.au/

From 1998 to 2017

In the first 10 years of the NEM, the Snowy region was subsumed into the New South Wales region in 2005 and Tasmania joined the NEM in 2006 after the Basslink Interconnector was commissioned. The first review of the market concluded that "Australia is respected internationally for its past reforms in energy with these reforms producing one of the most competitive and efficient energy sectors in the world" (Scales et al. 2007). The main problem it saw was inconsistencies in state and federal emission reduction policy; the review suggested that governments that still owned generation assets should be encouraged to privatise them, and that more effort should be made to centrally plan transmission development. The privatisation recommendation was heeded in New South Wales, but not in other states that still owned their generators.

Since 2018

From 2017 state governments contracted or invested directly (or both), starting in the states that had led on privatisation – South Australia and Victoria – and then New South Wales and then Queensland.

- In 2017 the South Australian government contracted the Hornsdale Power Reserve, the world's biggest battery when it was commissioned (Arena 2019). Around the same time, it leased and then subsequently purchased sufficient diesel generation capacity to meet 10 per cent of its peak demand.
- In 2018, the Victorian government purchased electricity for 15 years from six new wind and solar generators with a combined capacity of 928 megawatts (Parkinson 2018).
- In 2019 the Australian government announced it would build the Snowy 2.0 pumped hydro generator (one of the world's largest: Department of Climate Change, Energy, the Environment and Water n.d.).
- In 2020 the Victorian government announced the Victorian Big Battery, the world's biggest battery when it was commissioned in 2021 (Neoen n.d.).

- At the end of 2020 the New South Wales legislature passed the *Electricity Infrastructure Investment Act*, which committed the government to purchase the output of 2 gigawatts of long duration and 12 gigawatts of renewable generation by 2030.
- In 2021, the New South Wales government announced it would contribute to the funding of the 150-megawatt Tallawarra gas generator (Reneweconomy 2023) and shortly after the Australian government announced it would build the 660-megawatt Kurri Kurri gas generator (Gooley 2021).
- Also in 2021, the government of Victoria announced that it intended to contract for the output of 9 gigawatts of offshore wind generation by 2040.[2]

In 2022, announcements include the following:

- The Victorian government contracted six solar farms (623 megawatts) and 365 megawatts/600 megawatt-hours of battery energy storage (Victorian Government 2022a).
- The Victorian government committed to legislate energy storage targets of at least 2.6 gigawatts of energy storage capacity by 2030 and at least 6.3 gigawatts by 2035. (Victorian Government 2022b)
- The Queensland government published its Queensland Energy and Jobs Plan, setting a target of 70 per cent of electricity supply from renewables by 2030 in a scheme that the government expects will entail outlays of $65 billion, funded largely through government borrowing (Department of Energy and Public Works n.d.).
- The New South Wales government opened the first tender for generation and long duration energy storage, under its *Electricity Infrastructure Investment Act* (Vorath 2022).
- In the lead-up to the state election (Andrews 2022), the recently re-elected government of Victoria promised a power corporation (majority owned by the state) to develop 4.5 gigawatts of renewable electricity generation. At the same time, the government increased renewable energy and emission-reduction targets.
- The Australian Capital Territory (ACT) government conducted five reverse auctions between 2012 and 2016. This provided feed-in tariff

2 https://tinyurl.com/5ahmr3b4.

> support for 640 megawatts of large-scale wind or solar generation capacity that the ACT government calculated was needed to meet the government's target of 100 per cent renewable electricity supply to consumers in the ACT by 2020.

In 2023, shortly before the finalisation of this chapter, the Australian Government announced a Capacity Investment Scheme to contract for 23 gigawatts of variable renewable generation and 9 gigawatts of storage.

Discussion

Did prices decline following the creation of the NEM? Wholesale prices did not exist before the NEM and so the question cannot be answered. Certainly, over the life of the NEM prices have not declined. It might be suggested that this reflected the effect of capacity surpluses when the NEM started. But generation has expanded greatly and over the life of the NEM aggregate demand is hardly higher now than when it started. And much of the investment has been compensated outside the NEM (and driven by policies). How then have market prices not declined in response?

A lay observer might suggest the NEM seems to be a vigorous market. There is a highly organised five-minute auction ("spot market") and all generators bigger than 30 megawatts are required to offer their production into that spot market. There is an active market for financial contracts to hedge spot prices. There is an animated rule-making process. Energy regulators ("energy market institutions" in policy circles) administer the system, issue fines, undertake market investigations and so on. It is possible to report on prices and investment and identify when and how the market operator has intervened in the market (or suspended it, as it did for eight days in June 2022: Australian Energy Market Operator 2022a). Although state governments in Queensland and Tasmania and the Australian government (through Snowy Hydro) still own large amounts of generation, the vast bulk of new renewable generation (including in Tasmania and Queensland) has been privately financed by households, businesses, independent producers and large utilities.

Closer inspection suggests a different understanding. As noted, investment has been driven by policy, in coal, then gas and renewable certificate schemes and then reverse auctions first conducted in 2012 by the government of the ACT, then adopted in Victoria for its VRET 1 and VRET 2 auctions. The New South Wales government's *Electricity Infrastructure Investment Act* followed and is so far the biggest legislated program of generation (and storage) procurement in which the government will be the contracting entity. The Electricity Council (the association representing the large, mainly private, producers) declared that the New South Wales arrangement seemed to be designed "to take the industry back to the era that the Industry Commission and Hilmer Report had sought to escape" i.e., forgone efficiencies from national trade; using electricity as a lever of industry policy; wasteful overinvestment in generation resources; financial risks borne by captive customers rather than competing generators (MacKinnon and Skinner 2020).

Throughout the history of the NEM, there has of course also been much investment that, while influenced by policy, has been committed by private investors often after the negotiation of long-term contracts with customers directly, or with one of the major privately- or government-owned utilities.

The Commonwealth government's main contribution has been the Renewable Electricity Target, which has provided around $2 billion per year of subsidy for the development of large scale renewable electricity production and around $1 billion per year as capital subsidy of small scale renewable generation. A large part of the capacity expansion can be attributed to this policy.

Taking together the ACT's reverse auctions in 2012 (Herbert Smith Freehills 2019), the VRET, the New South Wales "Roadmap", Victoria's Offshore Wind Target and Electricity Storage Target and Queensland's Energy and Jobs Plan, state government demand has played a major role in large-scale generation investment.

On the supply side, most new capacity development even in Tasmania and Queensland is privately funded. In the last decade the Australian government alone (through Snowy Hydro) has been the only large government-financed generation development. The Queensland policy and Victoria's proposal to re-establish a government generator will increase government-owned production.

Government is also dominating the development of electricity storage. The largest batteries developed so far (Hornsdale in South Australia and the Victorian Big Battery) are mostly contracted to governments in their states. Government corporations are also dominant on the supply-side for hydro and pumped hydro storage (Snowy Hydro and Hydro Tasmania) – and are seeking support for expansion.

Evidently the NEM has evolved far from its origin. While investors, not governments, are taking most of the asset development and operation risks, it is the state and federal governments that dominate the selection of generators. Some volume but much price risk for new generation is now being borne by taxpayers rather than, as hoped, investors. How might this be explained? We suggest four possibilities.

First, Coalition federal governments from 2013 until their replacement by a Labor government in May 2022 did not agree with state governments (both Labor and Liberal) on emission reduction and renewable energy policies. The Coalition governments withdrew emissions taxes, watered down renewable energy targets, defunded renewable energy agencies, vigorously opposed the closure of private coal generators and funded the construction of a gas generator. In this context, state–federal consensus on energy policy became impossible and state governments progressively took matters into their own hands. Simshauser and Gilmore (2022) drew attention to divergent climate change and energy policy in explaining their observations of market outcomes. Rosewarne (2022) described a "coal-industrial complex".

Second, reliability became important after storms caused a blackout in South Australia in 2016, and after electricity prices soared after the closure of the Hazelwood power station in 2017. In 2017 the national Turnbull government appointed the Finkel Review to propose arrangements that ensured security of supply, but the government rejected its main recommendation – a clean energy target. In 2018 the Australian government then instructed its Energy Security Board (ESB) to recommend a new policy – the National Energy Guarantee – that the government first supported but then rejected after the Coalition Party room's rejection of it. The ESB then proposed a capacity mechanism in 2020, which was supported by the last energy minister of the Coalition government but rejected by state energy ministers. Whereas a regional agreement on reliability remained elusive, state governments found that they could make effective progress on their own. The South Australian government found proponents eager to demonstrate that they could develop what was then the world's biggest battery in less than 100 days

(*Financial Times* 2023). Victoria had similar success in quickly developing a battery five times bigger and then in agreeing to bring forward the closure of a coal generator (Premier of Victoria 2021). Queensland contracted for big batteries after one of its newest coal-fired turbines exploded (Nothling and staff 2021). In New South Wales, the government justified its Roadmap on the basis that it would bring forward replacement generation and support transmission to avoid price shocks that may result from the retirement of existing generation assets.

Third, coordination of investment in generation, transmission and storage is increasingly valued. Despite moderate levels of large-scale variable renewable investment, there are already non-trivial levels of curtailment as a result of transmission congestion: AEMO has reported average curtailed energy of around 125 megawatts in the 2022 (AEMO 2022b, Figure 59). Reducing the coordination difficulties attributable to vertical separation of generation and transmission, and the rise of storage as a substitute or complement to both is becoming more important. Such coordination is much easier to achieve regionally than multi-regionally.

Fourth, the decline in the capital cost of renewable electricity generation, combined with technology improvement, means the average costs of wind generation in the best areas in the NEM is not much higher than the worst. At the same time, transmission expansion is already expensive and becoming more so in the context of the appreciation of land values. Factors of production such as the availability of skilled workers and regional development and employment policy are now also significant determinants of generation development. This combination is motivating ever greater regionalisation of power system development.

Electricity transmission

Electricity transmission is the activity of transporting electricity on high-voltage transmission networks (typically higher than 132 kilovolts) from typically remote electricity generators to load centres. It is not a significant part of the bill for residential consumers (it costs about four times as much to distribute electricity on the low voltage networks as it

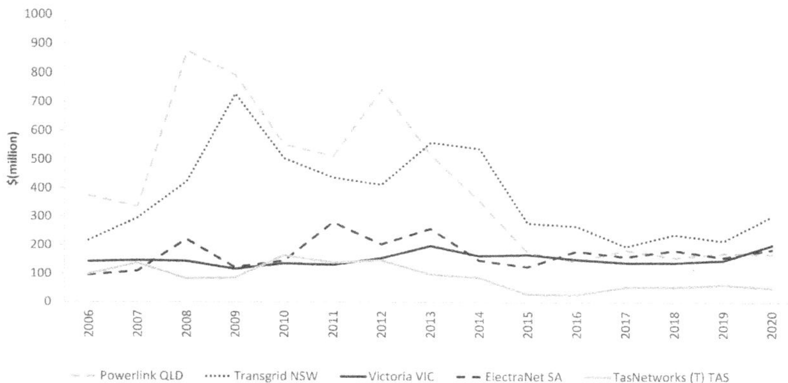

Figure 10.3 Transmission network service provider capital expenditure 2006–2020 ($m). Source: 2006 to 2020: Operational performance data spreadsheets produced by Australian Energy Regulator (2021).

costs to transmit it on the high voltage networks). But transmission is very important since it affects generation connection and reliable supply.

The centralisation or regionalisation of transmission expansion planning has been and remains contentious. This section starts with evidence on transmission expenditure outcomes and then discusses this evidence and the evolution of the debate over whether transmission expansion planning should be centralised or regionalised.

Expenditure outcomes

The main outcome in transmission expenditure has been large increases in capitalised expenditure (expenditure to operate transmission networks tended to remain roughly constant in real terms).

Figure 10.3 shows the transmission network service providers' annual capital expenditures from 2006 to 2020. The large increases from 2006 to 2014 are evident in New South Wales and Queensland. In states except Tasmania, which is affected by measurement issues as discussed, gradual increases are visible.

Figure 10.4 shows the transmission network service providers' regulated asset base, normalised by the operational demand (demand

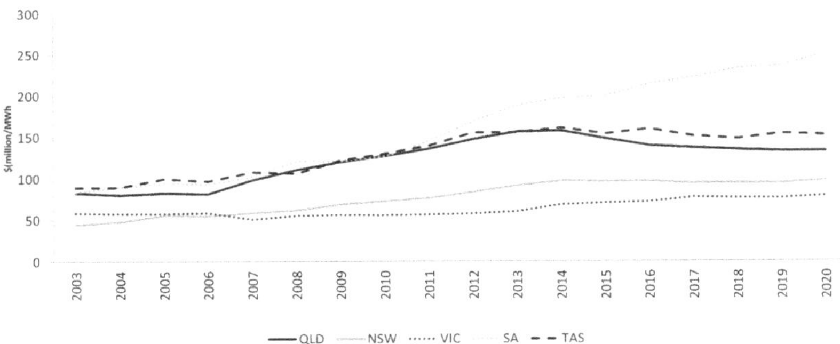

Figure 10.4 Transmission network service provider regulated asset base per megawatt-hour of operating demand 2006 to 2020 ($m). Source: 2006 to 2020: Operational performance data spreadsheets produced by Australian Energy Regulator (2021). Data for 2003 to 2005 obtained from network providers' regulatory submissions and regulatory decisions. Operating demand is sourced from VEPC (2023).

that is met by local scheduled generating units, semi-scheduled generating units, and non-scheduled intermittent generating units of aggregate capacity greater than or equal to 30 megawatts, and by generation imports to the region and by wholesale demand response). We can see that for all transmission network service providers, this ratio increased, mildly in the case of Victoria, but significantly for New South Wales, Tasmania and Queensland and by about 250 per cent for South Australia.

Other than in Victoria, all transmission companies increased their expenditure in real terms, after normalising for the volume of electricity they shipped (proxied by the operating demand). In all cases, operating expenditure increased but not by a large amount. Capital expenditures surged in the period from 2006 to 2015, particularly in New South Wales and Queensland. In all states, the regulated asset base per megawatt-hour of operating demand grew, particularly in Queensland, New South Wales and Tasmania.

Institutional developments

This subsection presents information on the main institutional developments in transmission. The next subsection discusses these developments.

The Council of Australian Governments' Independent Energy Market Review (the Parer Review) published a little under five years after the NEM began, was the first formal review of the NEM. It was critical of the arrangements for the provision of transmission, which it described as "the largest NEM problem" (Breslin, Sims and Agostini 2002, 22).

Its main criticisms were that transmission planning was fragmented and the calculation of the benefits of transmission interconnection failed to reflect the effect of the exercise of market power by the generators and so "fail[ed] to facilitate sufficient inter-regional trade and competition" (Breslin, Sims and Agostini 2002, 125). Its main recommendation was to strengthen the position of the National Electricity Market Management Company (NEMMCO, AEMO's predecessor) by making NEMMCO, rather than the regional transmission network service providers, responsible for transmission planning.

Evidently ministers were not satisfied with changes in response to the Parer Review and so four years later commissioned another report: *Energy Reform: The Way Forward for Australia* (also known as the Energy Reform Implementation Group or ERIG Review). The first point in the terms of reference of the report required it to make recommendations for achieving a "fully national transmission grid" (Scales et al. 2007, 4).

The ERIG Review came to quite a different view from the Parer Review. It started by asking what is meant by a fully national transmission grid and what characteristics such a grid would display. It noted that "the character and performance of a transmission grid cannot be assessed in isolation of the location and capacity of generators and of the loads they seek to serve" (Scales et al. 2007, 158) and concluded that "the current level of transmission and interconnection investment is reasonably appropriate for the installed generation capacity and peak demand" (Scales et al. 2007, 152). Nonetheless ERIG concluded that "whilst the general level of investment is reasonably appropriate and no new major interconnectors appear economical at present, the mechanisms are not in place to ensure the efficient ongoing development of the national transmission system" (Scales et al. 2007, 152). Accordingly it recommended "a more coordinated strategic approach to the development of the energy sector" (and like the earlier Parer Review, it too recommended "the establishment of a strategic national planner under a reformed NEMMCO" (Scales et al. 2007, iii). Specifically, ERIG recommended a National Transmission Network Development Plan to deliver an integrated, national plan for the efficient development of the overall power system, which would "inform the setting of the revenue allowance provided for TNSPs for a regulatory period" (Scales et al. 2007, 144) as a replacement for the cost-benefit analysis – the "Regulatory Test".

The inaugural National Transmission Network Development Plan was published in 2010. It followed after NEMMCO's Annual National Transmission Statement, which was first published in 2004 and itself took over from the Annual Interconnector Review. The inaugural network development plan described itself very much as information provision whose main purpose was to provide potential investors with information on "where and when electricity transmission expansion will be needed" (AEMO 2010, 3). It was described as based on information provided by transmission network service providers, and AEMO said that it did not itself question that information.

The National Transmission Network Development Plan was published for the next eight years. The third (2012 version) set out AEMO's vision for a national transmission system and the final version of the plan in 2018 then became the inaugural "integrated system plan". Over this period, the "plan" had evolved from information for investors of where transmission expansion was likely to be needed to outlining "targeted investment portfolios that can minimise total resource costs, support consumer value, and provide system access to the least-cost supply resources over the next 20 years to facilitate the smooth transition of Australia's evolving power system" (AEMO 2018, 3).

The inaugural 2018 integrated system plan was followed by new national electricity rules, designed to ensure that AEMO's recommendations were "actionable" by "transferring responsibility for the coordinated identification and assessment of options to address needs for investment across the integrated system, from TNSPs [transmission network service providers] to AEMO" (Department of Climate Change, Energy, the Environment and Water 2020).

This means that any transmission project that AEMO determines is "actionable" is very likely to be developed. The next steps for such projects are for the relevant transmission network service providers to apply the regulatory test to the project to demonstrate – to their own satisfaction – that the benefits of the project exceed its costs. The Australian Energy Regulator (AER) then wrote "guidelines", which means that any project that AEMO determines is "actionable" is assumed to occur and so its costs are excluded in any cost–benefit analyses. Specifically, the regulatory investment test for transmission (RIT-T) guideline issued by the Australian Energy Regulator (2020) says that the RIT-T proponent (in this case AEMO) is to include "actionable ISP [integrated system plan] projects" in all states of the world as if the "actionable project" is a committed project.

Finally, with respect to the Australian government's Rewiring the Nation Corporation, the commitments it has made so far – principally concessional loans and equity investment for interconnectors, intra-regional transmission, hydro generation (Prime Minister of Australia 2022a, b) – have been driven by AEMO's advice, although evidently also with the support of the recipient state governments.

Evidently the arc of the evolution of the transmission planning debate, at least as it was conducted by the energy market institutions, has been towards ever greater centralisation under the AEMO.

New South Wales developments since 2020

As discussed, the New South Wales *Energy Infrastructure Investment Act 2020* substantially altered the arrangements for the development of generation in that state. The object of the Act is, inter alia, "to co-ordinate investment in new generation, storage, network and related infrastructure" (Clause 3). The arrangements involve two new institutions: the "Consumer Trustee" and the "Infrastructure Planner" (now known as the Energy Corporation of New South Wales). The Consumer Trustee develops 20-year plans for generation, storage and transmission expansion, and then arranges and executes tenders for contracts that offer a floor price for the sale of electricity to the government.

The Infrastructure Planner works out the detail of the transmission development and recommends to the Consumer Trustee whether a monopoly should be awarded for the development of transmission projects it recommends or whether it should be contestably procured. The minister can override decisions by the Consumer Trustee or direct the Trustee. A new state-based regulator determines the compensation for new transmission projects, subject to a maximum capital outlay determined by the Consumer Trustee (and confidentially communicated to the regulator).

Victorian developments since 2020

The Victorian transmission arrangements developed when the industry was privatised entail an independent planner (for major augmentation projects). In 2020 the Victorian government was also the first state government to take back the authority (through the *National Electricity (Victoria) Amendment Act 2020*) to itself direct the construction of transmission (Hartmann 2020).

The first exercise of this authority was to tender for the development of the 300-megawatt Victorian Big Battery, which was commissioned in late 2021 (Department of Energy, Environment and Climate Action 2023). This battery was justified on the basis of the increase in interconnector capacity to New South Wales that it offered (by providing a source of rapid back-up supply in the case that one of the existing interconnectors tripped).

After these legislative changes, the government has now created VicGrid, currently a division of the Department of Energy, Environment and Climate Action. VicGrid will be responsible for planning the transmission grid in Victoria and establishing transmission access arrangements. It may also obtain new more expanded roles akin to those of the New South Wales Infrastructure Planner. As with the new arrangements in New South Wales, VicGrid will also apply its own investment tests: it has proposed (Engage Victoria n.d.) its own least-cost test to decide transmission expansion projects. There is a very significant difference between a least-cost test and a net-benefit test, the latter is a welfare economics calculation, the former an "engineering" calculation that takes a broader perspective on costs than is contemplated in the regulated investment test. It also follows more directly from a policy direction: for example, to find the least-cost way to expand renewable generation.

Discussion

The description of institutional developments in the previous subsection traced the path of progressively greater centralisation of transmission planning. This process might be argued to be consistent with a gradual realisation of the underlying objective for the creation of the NEM. Clause 1.2.1 of the first version of the National Electricity Code, which defined the NEM, pointed out that "The Code had its genesis in the Special Premiers' Conferences of October 1991 and July 1991, which led to the formation of the National Grid Management council, and in the Prime Minister's One Nation Statement of February 1992" (National Electricity Code 1996, 1.1). In that statement, Prime Minister Keating lauded "reforms now under way (that) have seen the States and the Commonwealth more willing to adopt a national outlook to the supply of electricity" (Keating 1992, 66). But the statement then lamented that what was really needed to drive the nail home was a national grid corporation, whereby the states would cede their state transmission monopolies to a "national" monopoly. In the One Nation Statement, the Commonwealth committed to spending $100 million to improve interconnection between states and to contribute equity into the national grid corporation, as long as the states set a timetable to transfer their transmission assets to the corporation for shares in it.

The Australian government's $20 billion Rewiring the Nation Corporation might be considered to be a realisation, 30 years later, of Prime Minister Keating's ambitions. But the case for stronger interconnection – and national coordination – gets ever weaker as renewable energy displaces coal-fired generation. AEMO's integrated system plan analysis shows that the major new interconnectors it promotes (between Victoria and New South Wales, and between Tasmania and Victoria) will defer renewable generation expansion and extend the life of existing fossil fuel generators relative to what would happen if they were not built (Mountain 2022b). It is this deferral that is the main source of the benefit that AEMO counts in justifying these interconnectors. The results of AEMO's analysis suggest that interconnection becomes relatively less valuable as renewable electricity expands, though it does not draw that conclusion from it. Indeed, this observation is evident by comparing AEMO's estimates of the levelised cost of electricity from wind or solar generation. AEMO's analysis finds inconsequentially small differences in this cost for large-scale solar on the mainland. For wind generation, the biggest difference between the wind cost in neighbouring regions (compared to the cost in the best renewable zone in each neighbouring region) is $12 per megawatt-hour (between New South Wales and Queensland). In other neighbouring regions the differences are $1 per megawatt-hour (South Australia–Victoria); $3 (South Australia–New South Wales); $5 (Queensland–South Australia); $8 (Victoria–New South Wales); and $10 (Tasmania–Victoria). These differences are obviously too small to justify significant transmission expansion (derived from AEMO 2020, 46, 47).

The proposal for a Rewiring the Nation Corporation 30 years after the proposal for a national grid corporation might suggest that despite the Annual National Transmission Statement, National Transmission Network Development Plan, the Integrated System Plan and finally the "Actionable Integrated System Plan", the "nationalisation" of transmission planning remains very much a policy priority, at least at the federal level and apparently also with broad state government support. Yet the legislation in both Victoria and New South Wales to take back for themselves decision making on the development of their power systems and for transmission expansion suggests that in reality "national" electricity transmission planning is even further away than when the NEM started.

Electricity distribution

Distributors transport electricity from high-voltage substations to customers' meters, and increasingly from distributed power sources situated behind the customers' meters to other customers. In Australia, electricity distribution accounts for around 80 per cent of the total regulated asset value of networks, with the higher voltage transmission companies accounting for the remaining 20 per cent.

From the late 1980s, the distribution sector was rationalised. In New South Wales, 25 local government distributors were merged into four and finally three. In Queensland, seven were merged into three and then two. In Victoria, 11 municipal and one regional distributor were merged to form five distributors.

There are now 13 distributors in the NEM, of which the five in Victoria were privatised in 1994 and the single distributor in South Australia in 2000. In other jurisdictions, until 2016, all distributors remained government owned. Two of the three in New South Wales have since been partially (51 per cent) privatised. The remaining 12 distributors vary considerably. One of the three government-owned distributors in New South Wales (Essential Energy), one of the Queensland distributors (Ergon), two of the investor-owned distributors in Victoria (PowerCor and AusNet Services) and the investor-owned South Australian distributor (SA Power Networks) and the Tasmanian distributor serve a combination of cities, small towns, villages and sparsely populated rural areas. The remaining five distributors (of which two are government-owned and three are investor-owned) serve mainly populated metropolitan areas that are relatively dense. The distributors in Victoria and South Australia were privatised in the mid-1990s and 2001 respectively. The others have remained government-owned until 2016 when New South Wales sold a 51 per cent share in two of its three distributors to private investors.

Outcomes

The main expenditure outcomes in electricity distribution networks are presented in Figure 10.5, which shows that the distributors' operating expenditure increased in all NEM regions, with a particular bulge in the period from 2006 to 2015.

Figure 10.6 shows distributors' capital expenditure, grouped by state. It shows increases in all states except Tasmania, and again a particular bulge is visible in the period from 2006 to 2015.

Figure 10.7 shows the value of the regulated asset base of all the distributors in each state, normalised by the volume of electricity (megawatt-hours) that they distributed. In all states an increase can be seen from 2006 onwards. This corresponds, except in Victoria (which

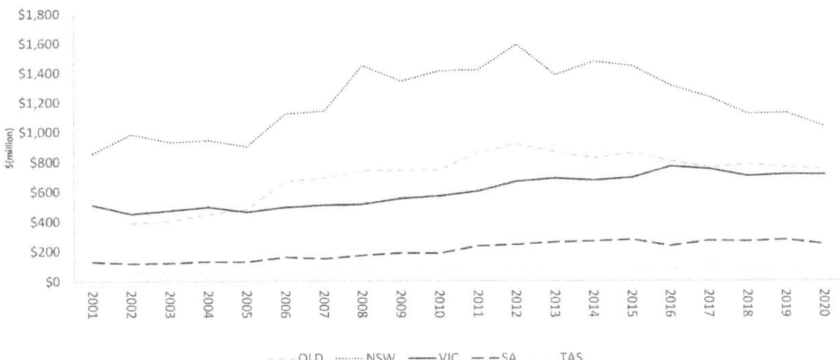

Figure 10.5 Distributor operating expenditure in each state ($m). Source: 2006 to 2020: operational performance data spreadsheets in Australian Energy Regulator (2021). Data for 2001 to 2005 obtained from network providers' regulatory submissions and regulatory decisions.

Figure 10.6 Distributor capital expenditure by state ($m). Source: 2006 to 2020: operational performance data spreadsheets in Australian Energy Regulator (2021). Data for 2001 to 2005 obtained from network providers' regulatory submissions and regulatory decisions.

did not show this increase until 2011) to determinations by the Australian Energy Regulator (before 2006 the decisions were made by state regulators).

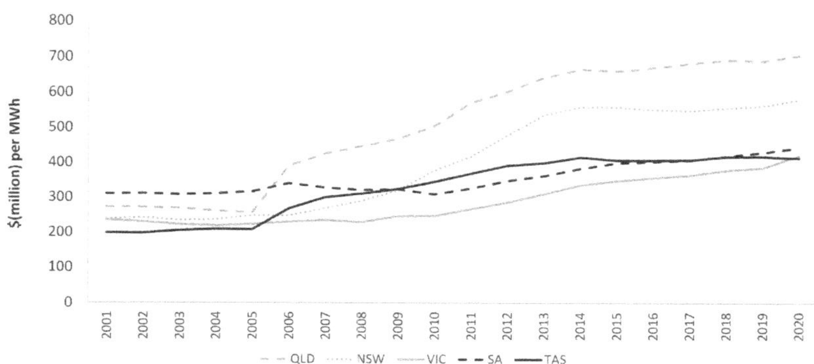

Figure 10.7 Regulated asset base ($m) per megawatt-hour distributed. Source: 2006 to 2020: Operational performance data spreadsheets produced by Australian Energy Regulator (2021). Data for 2001 to 2005 obtained from network providers' regulatory submissions and regulatory decisions.

Figure 10.8 narrows the focus to the period from 2006 to 2013 and compares the change in substation capacity (which accounts for the bulk of the capital expenditure) with the change in peak demand per connection over this period. The chart shows that, for the distributors that expanded substation capacity the most, peak demand in fact declined. Even those that expanded substation capacity the least (the Victorian distributors) had barely any increase in peak demand. The significance of this is outlined below.

Institutions

This descriptive section focuses on the relationship between ownership and regulation. This issue was anticipated by the ACCC at the time of the creation of the NEM when it authorised the Electricity Code. In particular, the ACCC expressed concerns over conflicts of interest that may arise when a government is both the regulator and owner of electricity assets. It suggested: "These potential conflicts of interest will be most acute in circumstances where the regulator is not at arms' length from government and where government budgets have come to rely on the dividend stream from publicly owned utilities" (ACCC

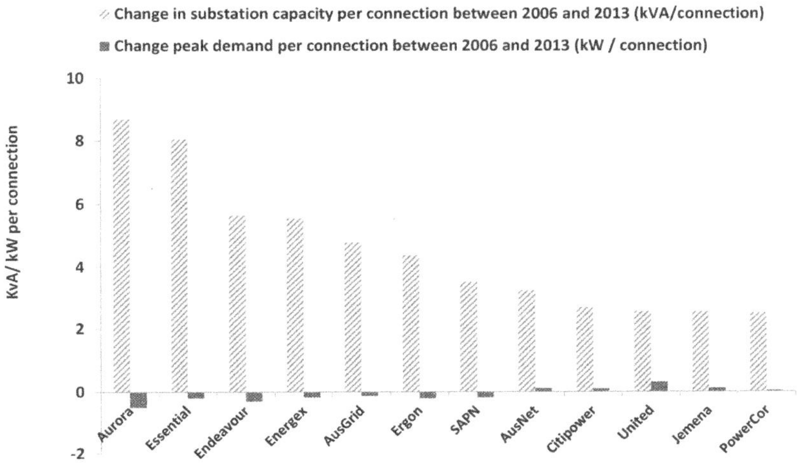

Figure 10.8 Change in substation capacity and peak demand, per connection from 2006 to 2013. Source: Regulatory Information Notices available from Australian Energy Regulator (n.d), author's analysis.

1997, xvii). It noted that, at the time of making its authorisation determination, the majority of the participating jurisdictions had established or were considering establishing, independent regulators for electricity network pricing and that while "the issue of independence of jurisdictional regulators has yet to be fully resolved", this should not stop the AER from authorising the code since "the Commission considers that the jurisdictional regulators should be statutorily independent of executive government by the time of the commencement of the NEM's network pricing regimes in 1999" (ACCC 1997, xvii).

The ACCC's wishes were granted when statutorily independent state-based regulators set the first price controls (also the second in Victoria) before regulatory implementation was surrendered by the states to the newly created AER in 2004 (initially branded as a "constituent part of the ACCC"). But at the same time the Australian Energy Market Commission (AEMC), a body appointed by the states and territories and answerable to them, was established to design the regulations that the AER was tasked with implementing.

Such institutional arrangements might be considered to have satisfied the ACCC's desire for statutory independence. Indeed, it was enthusiastic about the creation of the AER as a subdivision of the ACCC, albeit that powers for the design of regulation rested with a superior body, the AEMC, that the AER had no control over.

While the ACCC may possibly have been satisfied that its concern about conflicts of interest could have been resolved through statutory independence, state governments could still profit from the distribution of electricity by distributors they owned. The regulatory arrangements designed by the AEMC in 2005 strengthened the conflict of interest by insisting that regulation must not discriminate on the basis of the ownership of the regulated entity. Or, to be more precise, the AER was instructed to assume that government-owned distributors were investor-owned and hence awarded a rate of return that not only assumes they are privately financed but ignores that state governments also collect the income tax on the profits of the distributors they own. Formally the government-owned distributors have been set up under companies law and so are liable to income tax on their profits. But, under the Australian Constitution, the Commonwealth is prohibited from taxing the jurisdictions. Therefore the income tax collected on the profits of the government-owned distributors is passed back to the relevant jurisdictional governments. The ancestry of the "ownership-invariant" regulatory approach can be traced back to the Competition Principles Agreement agreed by the state, territory and Commonwealth governments in 1994. While the agreement was specifically about competitive neutrality in contestable markets – and was intended to protect against an unfair competitive advantage by increasing the price of government-supplied capital – all the state governments chose to also apply the agreement to the network monopolies they owned, and the AEMC developed regulatory arrangements that determined regulated prices accordingly.

Australia's regulators have defended the approach of assuming government distributors should be compensated for debt cost at the same rate as their privately owned peers. For example the AEMC argued that to have regard to the government's actual borrowing costs would underestimate the distributor's actual cost of capital and hence misallocate resources and that the governments' receipt of the income tax on their distributors' profits would not distort their investment decisions since the income tax was received by a different branch of the government than that of their distributors' shareholding ministers (AEMC 2012). (For an interesting critique of the application of capital asset pricing to regulated utilities in Australia, see Johnstone and Havyatt 2021.)

The AER and state governments that owned their distributors supported the AEMC's rejection. By contrast, in line with the arguments in Laffont and Tirole (1993), the Productivity Commission, an independent adviser to the Commonwealth government, recognised that distortions arose by awarding government distributors private funding rates. While the Productivity Commission continued to support an approach that allowed government distributors to charge customers private financing costs, it did nonetheless suggest that further thought be given to an adjustment to returns to account for the fact that state governments would not collect income tax on the distributors within their jurisdiction if those distributors were privately owned (Productivity Commission 2013, 351, 352).

Discussion

The Industry Commission's (1991) report justified its proposals for the national electricity market, in part, on the argument that it would improve the distributors' capital productivity. The evidence of expenditure outcomes summarised earlier suggest that this has not been achieved. In a 2018 review, the ACCC blamed increases in network charges for the largest part of the increase in electricity prices after 2006 (ACCC 2018). Total factor productivity (a measurement of productivity that accounts for labour and capital inputs) has declined over the period that the industry has been regulated by the AER (Cunningham, Lawrence and Coelli 2021). This is consistent with measures by Australian Bureau of Statistics researchers of multi-factor productivity, which showed this grew rapidly in the decade before the creation of the NEM, followed by almost as rapid a decline after the NEM was created (Topp and Kulys 2012, 31).

On closer inspection, the distribution expenditure data show a disparity in the outcomes delivered by government and private distributors. Having started from a similar position for prices and asset values when the NEM was created, over the course of successive regulatory controls the regulated asset value and hence prices of the government distributors grew more quickly than those of the privatised distributors.

Econometric analysis of a data panel that included distributors in Norway, New Zealand, Great Britain and the Canadian province of Ontario established the relationship between network ownership and regulated revenues and between network ownership and regulated asset values. This found that government ownership of distributors in the NEM is associated with regulated assets and regulated revenues that are 46 per cent and 26 per cent respectively, higher than investor-owned distributors. Network characteristics, size and density do not explain the difference in the regulated revenues or regulated assets of the government and private distributors (Mountain 2017, 2019).

Distributors, regulators, government departments and industry associations attributed distributors' higher spending and consequential increases in regulated revenues and asset values to various factors. These included rising peak demand, a need to catch up for previous underinvestment, a changing investment environment, flawed regulatory rules, excessively strict network planning standards and flaws in the arrangements for the review of the merits of the regulator's decisions. But none of these can explain the disparity between government- and investor-owned utilities (Mountain 2017). Instead, making customers compensate government distributors' borrowing costs at a rate substantially above their actual borrowing costs, motivated those distributors to wastefully add to their regulated assets in order to drive higher profits.

Consistent with this explanation, extraordinary profits encouraged government owners to attempt to limit the extent of regulatory power, such as through the bifurcation of regulation between the AEMC and the AER.

Evidently the ACCC, in considering whether to authorise the National Electricity Code, was quite right to have worried about the conflict of interest between regulation and ownership. But it also suggests that it was too optimistic in its assumption that statutorily independent regulators would resolve the conflict appropriately.

Conclusions

The proponents of the NEM suggested that competition and statutorily independent regulation of monopoly networks would lower costs and hence prices. The evidence of network charges for transmission and distribution, and of prices in wholesale markets suggests that the hopes have not been realised. Network prices (and costs) are much higher now than before the NEM was created, and wholesale prices have not declined over time.

With respect to wholesale markets, many complex internal and external factors might explain outcomes, and the observation that prices have not declined does not eliminate the possibility that they are lower than they otherwise would be if the NEM did not exist. We avoid causal judgement on wholesale market outcomes in favour of describing and interpreting the actions of policy makers, to understand their judgement of the NEM.

On this, the picture seems to be clear. Starting with Victoria (in 2018) and then New South Wales (in 2020) and Queensland (in 2022), the three large eastern and southern states – the first two of which had privatised their generation – have (again) become explicitly involved in directing the development of their electricity sector. This means various combinations of government procurement of generation and storage, or government power provision. Most recently the new government in Victoria was elected on a promise to revive the State Electricity Commission, though the details of what this means have yet to be worked out.

With respect to transmission, an enduring tension that has persisted since the start of the NEM is the extent to which transmission expansion should be centrally coordinated. In 1992 Prime Minister Paul Keating's One Nation Statement proposed the creation of the National Grid Company. This idea was rejected and, when the NEM began, the authority to plan and develop transmission remained with each state.

Over time, successive reviews have sought to strengthen "national" planning to the point that the AEMO now produces an "actionable integrated system plan" that ostensibly provides it with the authority to plan the development of the transmission system. The current

Australian government's Rewiring the Nation Corporation is perhaps a 30-year echo of Keating's National Grid Company and intended to support the implementation of AEMO's plans.

Yet despite apparent support for an integrated system plan (after all, who would not wish to have such a plan?) the big eastern and southern states have all legislated to take back their power to plan transmission and they have developed authorities to execute those plans. It is not at all clear that the much-vaunted integrated system plan will be implemented.

With respect to electricity distribution, in its authorisation of the rules the ACCC expressed its concern about conflicts of interest where governments also owned regulated networks but said that statutorily independent regulation would resolve this. The evidence in electricity distribution suggests that the ACCC's concern was well founded but that its solution – statutory independence – was not. Independent regulation of government-owned monopolies has proved to be an oxymoron.

In summary, what is now called the NEM seems to bear little resemblance to the designs of its founders. State governments' recent resumption of the direction of the development of the electricity sector within their boundaries has been likened by some to winding the clock back. But in important respects things are quite different from what they were when the NEM began: consumers can now choose their suppliers and there are many private developers offering a variety of generation and storage technologies for connection to the grid, or directly to customers' premises. It is in this context that state governments' new roles are to be contemplated. Much is be discovered and rediscovered.

References

Andrews, D. (2022). Putting power back in the hands of Victorians. Media release. https://tinyurl.com/3w3zudxm.

Arena (2019). World's biggest battery grows and gains new powers. *Arena*, 29 November. https://tinyurl.com/2crbncd9.

Australian Competition and Consumer Commission (2018). Restoring electricity affordability and Australia's competitive advantage. June. https://tinyurl.com/3nsefmy9.

Australian Competition and Consumer Commission (1997). *Applications for Authorisation: National Electricity Code*. https://tinyurl.com/264y2eur.
Australian Energy Market Commission (2012). Final Position Paper, National Electricity Amendment (Economic Regulation of Network Service Providers) Rule 2012. https://tinyurl.com/54ar92tf.
Australian Energy Market Operator (2010). National Transmission Network Development Plan 2013. https://tinyurl.com/yckfpu8s.
Australian Energy Market Operator (2018). Integrated System Plan for the National Electricity Market. https://tinyurl.com/26f7rkdc.
Australian Energy Market Operator (2020). Final 2020 Integrated System Plan. https://tinyurl.com/8jdp5b6v.
Australian Energy Market Operator (2022a). *NEM Market Suspension and Operational Challenges in June 2022: A Market Event and Reviewable Operating Incident Report for the National Electricity Market*. https://tinyurl.com/mwfzkfsy.
Australian Energy Market Operator (2022b). *Quarterly Energy Dynamics Q1 2022*. https://tinyurl.com/ysmwhn94.
Australian Energy Regulator (2020). *Application Guidelines: Regulatory Investment Test for Transmission*. https://tinyurl.com/msp7h5mc.
Australian Energy Regulator (2021). *Electricity Network Performance Report 2021*. https://tinyurl.com/mrfaa7md.
Australian Energy Regulator (n.d.). *Performance Reports*. https://tinyurl.com/webt4zw8.
Breslin, P., R. Sims and D. Agostini (2002). *Towards a Truly National and Efficient Energy Market*. Canberra: Department of Industry, Tourism and Resources. https://catalogue.nla.gov.au/catalog/687314.
Cunningham, M., D. Lawrence and T. Coelli (2021). *Economic Benchmarking Results for the Australian Energy Regulator's 2021 DNSP Annual Benchmarking Report*. https://tinyurl.com/2cpt8v3a.
Department of Climate Change, Energy, the Environment and Water (2020). Actionable ISP final rule recommendation, 27 March. https://tinyurl.com/mpdp2yvu.
Department of Climate Change, Energy, the Environment and Water (n.d.). Pumped hydro. https://tinyurl.com/2w8py9pv.
Department of Energy and Public Works (Queensland) (n.d.). About the plan. https://www.epw.qld.gov.au/energyandjobsplan/about.
Department of Energy, Environment and Climate Action (Victoria) (2023). Victorian Big Battery. https://tinyurl.com/2mvhjkc8.
Engage Victoria (n.d.). Victorian Transmission Investment Framework Final Design. https://tinyurl.com/32czex6n.

Gooley, C. (2021). Federal government will spend $600 million on new Kurri Kurri gas plant in the NSW Hunter Valley. *ABC News*, 18 May. https://tinyurl.com/599hwwj9.

Financial Times (2023). Tesla set to make world's biggest battery even bigger. https://tinyurl.com/4rd9hpp7.

Hartmann, I. (2020). Victoria side-steps NEM with new Amendment Act. *Energy*, 20 March. https://tinyurl.com/mexrjxr6.

Herbert Smith Freehills (2019). ACT renewable energy reverse auction. *Lexology*, 24 October. https://tinyurl.com/2p9en67x.

Industry Commission (1991). *Energy Generation and Distribution*. Volume 1. https://www.pc.gov.au/inquiries/completed/energy-generation.

Industry Commission (1995). *The Growth and Revenue Implications of Hilmer and Related Reforms: A Report by the Industry Commission to the Council of Australian Governments (Final Report)*. https://tinyurl.com/d78yz2y9.

Johnstone, D., and D. Havyatt (2021). Sophistry and high electricity prices in Australia. *Critical Perspectives on Accounting* 88: 102298. https://doi.org/10.1016/j.cpa.2021.102298.

Keating, P.J. (1992). One Nation Statement. https://tinyurl.com/y6shckza.

Laffont, J.-J., and J. Tirole (1993). *A Theory of Incentives in Procurement and Regulation*. Cambridge, MA: MIT Press.

Leutjens, J., M. Mintrom and L. Herron (2019). Successful public policy: Lessons from Australia and New Zealand. In J. Luetjens, M. Mintrom and P. 't Hart, eds. *Successful Public Policy: Lessons from Australia and New Zealand*. Canberra: ANU Press. https://doi.org/10.22459/SPP.2019.

MacKinnon, D., and B. Skinner (2020). NSW Electricity Infrastructure Roadmap: a highway to hell? *Australian Energy Council*, 19 November. https://tinyurl.com/37ya8nvb.

Mountain, B.R. (2017). Ownership-invariant regulation of electricity distributors in Australia: a failed experiment. PhD thesis. Victoria University, Melbourne.

Mountain, B.R. (2019). Ownership, regulation, and financial disparity: the case of electricity distribution in Australia. *Utilities Policy* 60. https://doi.org/10.1016/j.jup.2019.100938.

Mountain, B.R. (2022a). Commercial rooftop solar in Australia: state of play, innovations and future prospects. In F. Sioshansi, ed. *The Future of Decentralized Electricity Distribution Networks*. Amsterdam: Elsevier.

Mountain, B.R. (2022b). *Submission on VNI-West Project Assessment Draft Report*. https://tinyurl.com/5xzbskre.

Mountain, B.R., and S. Percy (2019). The exercise of market power in Australia's National Electricity Market following the closure of the Hazelwood Power

Station. Victoria Energy Policy Centre Working Paper No. 1903. https://www.vepc.org.au/research-and-insights-2019.

National Electricity Code (1996). Mark I. https://tinyurl.com/2hk99932.

Neoen (n.d.). Victorian big battery. https://victorianbigbattery.com.au/.

Nothling, L., and staff (2021). Large-scale battery to be added to Queensland power network after experts call for more renewables after Callide fire. *ABC News*, 27 May. https://tinyurl.com/2nxj6k7r.

Parkinson, G. (2018). Victoria to support six wind and solar farms after overwhelming response to auction. *Renew Economy*, 10 September. https://tinyurl.com/4464nzw6.

Premier of Victoria (2021). Statement from the Minister for Energy. 10 March. https://www.premier.vic.gov.au/statement-minister-energy.

Prime Minister of Australia (2022a). Rewiring the nation plugs in Marinus Link and Tasmanian jobs. Media release, 19 October. https://tinyurl.com/ncjhxrxd.

Prime Minister of Australia (2022b). Rewiring the nation to supercharge Victorian renewables. Media release, 19 October. https://tinyurl.com/yuk9w67r.

Productivity Commission (2013). Electricity Network Regulatory Frameworks. https://www.pc.gov.au/inquiries/completed/electricity/report.

Rosewarne, S. (2022). *Contested Energy Futures: Capturing the Renewable Energy Surge in Australia*. Singapore: Palgrave Macmillan. https://doi.org/10.1007/978-981-19-0224-6.

Reneweconomy (2023). EnergyAustralia gets government money for first "green hydrogen" gas generator. https://tinyurl.com/bdhtmtft.

Scales, B., G. Carmody, D. Swift and A. Rattray (2007). *Energy Reform, the Way Forward for Australia*. Report. https://tinyurl.com/dk29mmz7. [Energy Reform Implementation Group – ERIG – Review]

Simshauser, P., and J. Gilmore (2022). Climate change policy discontinuity and Australia's 2016–2021 renewable investment supercycle. *Energy Policy* 160(October 2021): 112648. https://doi.org/10.1016/j.enpol.2021.112648.

Topp, V., and T. Kulys (2012). *Productivity in Electricity, Gas and Water: Measurement and Interpretation*. Productivity Commission staff working paper. https://www.pc.gov.au/research/supporting/electricity-gas-water.

VEPC [2023]. Data sourced from the Australian Energy Market Operator, processed and accessed through the Victoria Energy Policy Centre V-NEM data dashboard. www.vepc.org.au. Accessed 13 December 2023.

Victorian Government (2022a). Victorian Renewable Energy Target auction (VRET2). 22 November. https://tinyurl.com/4c8ah85n.

Victorian Government (2022b). Australia's Biggest Renewable Energy Storage Targets. https://tinyurl.com/yawdv4jw.

Vorath, Sophie (2022). NSW hits go on Australia's biggest shift from coal to renewables. *Renew Economy*, 4 October. https://tinyurl.com/bdcm8hve.
Wilson, Geoff (2007). Queensland gas scheme proves a winner. Media statement. *Queensland Government*, 3 April. https://statements.qld.gov.au/statements/46171.

11
Superannuation and neoliberalism

David Richardson

Today superannuation involves funds worth some $3.3 trillion, which includes $865 billion in self-managed super funds (SMSFs) (Australian Prudential Regulation Authority 2022) as well as the giant industry funds and other retail super funds. SMSFs are small, self-managed funds with up to four members and tend to be family based. Some of those funds are large and are more likely engaged in tax avoidance and estate planning than genuine retirement provision. The other funds control around $2.5 trillion in investable funds on behalf of millions of fund members. How this all came about, what it means and where it is going raise a host of important issues for Australian economic management.

Background

An Australian Bureau of Statistics (ABS) survey in February 1974 showed that only 28.7 per cent of workers were covered by super in their present job while a further 7.8 per cent had some coverage from a previous employer. Those figures are reproduced in Table 11.1 along with a gender breakdown.

While a minority of employees were covered by super, there was nonetheless a severe gender gap with 35.6 per cent of male employees covered by super but only 15.1 per cent of women so covered. There was

Table 11.1 Workers with and without super coverage (%).

	Males	Females	Total
Employed	100.0	100.0	100.0
Covered in present job	35.6	15.1	28.7
Benefits from previous job	7.6	8.1	7.8
No coverage	56.8	76.8	63.5

Source: ABS (1974).

also a strong class bias in the coverage. The figures in Table 11.1 apply to all paid workers, but there are further biases in the system. That is evident in Table 11.2, which breaks down the super coverage by sex and blue- versus white-collar workers (or manual and non-manual workers as the ABS classified them).

The figures in Table 11.2 show that superannuation coverage was much higher in the government sector than in the private sector at 57.5 per cent and 23.9 per cent respectively. Within each there remained a strong bias against women's coverage with men's coverage at 66.0 per cent in the government compared with 37.4 per cent for women. In the private sector the ratio was worse at 31.5 and 11.1 per cent for men and women respectively. The ABS also provides a breakdown for manual and non-manual workers. As might be expected, coverage was biased against manual workers with 21.4 per cent coverage compared with 38.0 per cent for non-manual workers. Again, the gender bias was marked. Females covered by super were only 6.1 per cent of female manual workers compared with 25.5 per cent for their male counterparts. That compared with 20.1 per cent of non-manual female workers and 55.0 per cent of non-manual male workers.

Treasury described this period as one in which "superannuation was an employment fringe benefit which although more generally available, was still concentrated among professionals, managers and administrators; public sector employees; and the financial sector" (Treasury 2001).

Table 11.2 Workers with and without super by sector, and manual/ non-manual distinction (%).

	Males	Females	Total
Private sector			
Covered	31.5	11.1	23.9
Not covered	68.5	88.9	76.1
Total	100	100	100
Government sector			
Covered	66.0	37.4	57.5
Not covered	34.0	62.6	42.5
Total	100	100	100
Manual workers			
Covered	25.5	6.1	21.4
Not covered	74.5	93.9	78.6
Total	100	100	100
Non-manual workers			
Covered	55.0	20.1	38.0
Not covered	45.0	79.9	62.0
Total	100	100	100

Source: ABS (1974).

Plans for change

All up, in 1974 a male government worker was 11 times more likely to be covered by super than a female manual worker. These biases in the system caused the Australian Labor Party government under Gough Whitlam (1973–75) to initiate the National Superannuation Committee of Inquiry (1976) chaired by Keith Hancock. The inquiry recommended a partial contributory scheme that would comprise an earnings-related component on top of a universal pension. This proposal perhaps remains the ideal to which we should aspire. Developments since suggest that the ideal has to be somehow fashioned out of the present hybrid means-tested pension and mostly private superannuation based on accumulation funds.

The Hancock model was rejected by the Fraser Coalition government (1975–83), which succeeded the Whitlam government. The next main attempt to broaden access to superannuation awaited the following Hawke and Keating Labor governments (1983–96). The government set about tackling deficiencies in the old system and the basic model converted from a defined-benefit scheme to a contribution scheme.

These Labor governments thought that the generous retirement benefits enjoyed by managerial and upper white-collar workers should be extended to all workers. An important impetus for more comprehensive super cover came from the labour movement, seeking similar retirement benefits to the white-collar workforce. Industrial action succeeded in winning some super coverage initially in the building industry (Australian Council of Trade Unions 2021). The Building Workers Industrial Union was the first to win award-based super in 1984, with the Building Union Superannuation Scheme. Later the Hawke and Keating governments adopted the scheme, and super was extended to the whole workforce. The model chosen was a contributory one that was portable between employers in the industry and later between all employers. But we will argue that the establishment of a contributory system with individual entitlement based on contributions raised an additional set of problems.

The original industry super funds were managed by a board of equal employer and union representatives. Most of these remain although there have been some mergers and new entrants among the super funds.

Originally the government did not seem to seek budgetary savings. One of the Hawke government social security ministers, Brian Howe, said "the age pension system is primarily designed as social security, whereas compulsory superannuation is about encouraging savings over and above the pension system . . . It was never imagined that one would replace the other" (*ABC News* 2016). But a later social security minister, Neal Blewett, said, "our objective in widening superannuation cover is to moderate pressures on the budget from age pensions as the population ages" (*ABC News* 2016). Later governments also justified tax deductions for super because they would reduce outlays on the age pension. The ABC reported that in 2015 Assistant Treasurer Kelly O'Dwyer suggested that the "whole objective behind the superannuation system" is for people to be able to live on their superannuation savings without recourse to the age pension and emphasised the budgetary savings (*ABC News* 2016).

Superannuation would reduce age pension outlays if the individual's super had the effect of reducing the pension payable as a result of either the assets test or the income test. But the age pension means testing is quite lenient for people drawing down their super. The income test allows a couple to receive a combined income of $336 per fortnight before their pension is reduced. A part-pension is payable until their private income is $3,431.20 a fortnight (Services Australia 2023). If that couple draws a superannuation pension, then a large fraction of the amount is treated as a return of capital. Just as the age pension entitlement is not affected if you take some money out of a bank account, much of the super pension is treated as just a return of capital that does not affect the age pension. Super accounts are also treated concessionally in the assets test (Services Australia 2023). Rich individuals can also avail themselves of lawyers and accountants that can further disguise income and alienate the assets in trusts and the like.

The upshot of all that is that there is little scope for super to seriously reduce payments to those who claim the age pension. The government hence concurrently runs the two expensive schemes that barely interact with each other and, under present arrangements, present few options for redistributing from the high-wealth to low-wealth age groups.

Fixing deficiencies in the pre-1980s model

The old scheme had a host of deficiencies. As we have just seen, there was no entitlement at all for the majority of workers and especially women in the paid workforce. Often the employee had no entitlement at all until they had served a certain number of years with the one employer. The author remembers newspaper reports of people being sacked on the eve of their tenth year of service with an employer so that the employer could avoid their contractual obligations for retirement benefits. In a similar way, entitlements were not portable. On transferring to another employer, the worker was often not able to take any accrued entitlements. Either that or, if they received a payout, they had to manage their own fund. Against that, the system that dominated before the mid-1980s comprised mainly defined-benefits schemes. Treasury (2001) reported that in the early 1980s, 82 per cent of fund members were in defined-benefits schemes.

Risk

As the name suggests, a defined-benefit scheme is one in which eligibility for a retirement payment is based on a formula that reflects working history and salaries prior to retirement. Given certain assumptions about these variables, a worker can plan their working life, knowing the amount they will have in retirement. Of course, it behoves the employer to ensure that the funds will be available when the employee claims their benefits. For the employer, there is always the risk that any investments put aside to cover future super entitlements may not be sufficient. Retirement entitlements were something that had to be carefully managed. Private employers had to keep sufficient funds in reserve to ensure they could meet their obligations to their workers on retirement. Depending on the vagaries of the market, those funds could be in surplus or, more concerning, in deficit. The risk in meeting the obligations to retiring workers was borne by the employer, although, if the employer went out of business, the employees risked losing their entitlements.

From this account, it can be appreciated that the old defined-benefits schemes posed a risk to the employer who would have to make good if the amounts put aside for their workers' retirements fell short of their entitlements. By contrast, modern super arrangements transfer the risk of insufficient funds in retirement to the worker concerned. This topic will be considered again below.

Contribution model

The contribution model is fundamentally different from the pre-1980s system in that payments are made by workers and employers upfront, paid into a fund and earmarked for particular employees; under defined-benefit schemes prudent employers would maintain a fund sufficient to pay entitlements as they fell due based on actuarial advice. The ultimate value of the fund at retirement depends on how successful the fund's investments have been in the interim. This model was pushed by the union movement for two main reasons. First, the push for a national system had failed with the demise of the Whitlam government. Second, in the building industry where there had been early successes, workers frequently changed jobs and employers, and so needed a system that would be easily taken from one employer to the next and the final entitlement would be unrelated to who had contributed.

A later motivation for contributory super with individual accounts may have been the fostering of a pro-capital mindset in the same way as Margaret Thatcher tried to use housing as a way of giving the working classes a vested interest in property and, in doing so, become more sympathetic to the needs of business. Nevertheless, the model stuck, and it was therefore easy for the Labor government to later extend the model to all employees, which was the case in the 1992 legislation, the *Superannuation Guarantee (Administration) Act 1992.*

The scheme ushered in by the Building Workers Industrial Union remains much the same today except that the contribution rate has increased from the initial 3 per cent to 10.5 per cent today and increasing to 12 per cent ultimately (ACTU n.d.). The Coalition has from time to time attempted to undermine the industry funds, as we show below. Hence, rather than being allocated to an industry fund, workers are now given a choice. On taking a job, workers are asked to nominate a fund into which the employer pays the compulsory super contribution.

We mentioned that the risk has moved from business to worker as we moved from defined benefit to accumulation schemes. The risk is exacerbated if an individual is allocated to (or nominates) a "bad" super fund. The top 10 balanced super funds all earned an average 8.0 per cent or better over a 10-year period. That means every hundred dollars invested 10 years ago is worth $216 today. Productivity Commission figures show that, using reasonable assumptions, two workers otherwise identical might retire on $1.1 million or $610,000 depending on whether their super fund was in the top quarter of funds or the bottom quarter (SuperGuide n.d.).

Tax concessions

Super had always been a creature of the tax system. Without tax concessions, there may have been little or no super in years gone by. Tax concessions remain, despite the compulsory nature of the present system.

Of course, if the super concessions in the accumulation phase are to have any integrity, then they should be targeted at arrangements that genuinely meet people's needs in retirement. We mentioned earlier that superannuation is now a popular vehicle for tax planning and also avoidance, especially for those approaching the age of 55 or who are older and who will soon have access to their money again. (Super is generally not accessible until the retiree reaches 60 years if they were born after June 1964 and slightly earlier if they were born before 1964: Australian Taxation Office 2021.) For policy purposes it would be preferable if super were directed into products that provide a continuing income rather than lump-sum payments that can be accessed all at once. This would better meet the policy objective of providing for retirement incomes while reducing the use of super concessions as a tax-avoidance device.

When the Hawke government introduced compulsory occupational superannuation, the tax arrangements were essentially a tax on super payouts. Most super schemes at the time were defined-benefits schemes, which meant that there was nothing to tax until the worker retired and received a payment. When that happened, the payments were taxed lightly with the intention of encouraging superannuation. Had those arrangements remained, then future governments would have received the benefits in terms of huge increases in revenue. But the super scheme introduced by the Hawke government was an accumulation scheme, which meant contributions were collected and paid into a fund that was able to earn an income on its investment. Both of these streams could be taxed.

The Treasurer and architect of the super scheme, Paul Keating, changed the tax arrangements so that super fund earnings were taxed. Both streams of income into the super funds were taxed at 15 per cent, irrespective of the circumstances of the ultimate beneficiary of the fund. A tax of 15 per cent, if it is received in a super fund, is much lower than if the same income had been taxed at, say, 47 per cent (presently the top income tax rate in Australia; it had ranged up to 75 per cent under the

Liberal and Coalition Menzies governments in the 1950s and 1960s). In this case, 15 per cent is a variation from the 47 per cent that would otherwise apply and that difference gives rise to the "tax expenditure" estimate of the value of the super tax concession. We diverge for a moment to explain tax expenditures.

Tax expenditures and fiscal impacts

"Tax expenditures", as their name suggests, are concessions given through the tax system but in principle are equivalent to cash expenditures that the government could use for the same purpose. The attraction for governments is that using tax expenditures reduces total tax collections and so gives the appearance of a lower-taxing government. When the Howard Coalition governments of the late 1990s–early 2000s were running surpluses and not knowing what to do with them, they did things like abolish tax for super funds in the pension phase. These concessions were open-ended and meant the rich could exploit the super system. There was no requirement that concessionally treated super amounts had to be used to fund retirement.

Superannuation is subject to two main tax concessions:

- the concessional tax treatment for earnings on superannuation funds; this tax expenditure is expected to be worth $26.4 billion in 2022–23
- the concessional tax treatment of income paid into super funds; this tax expenditure is expected to be worth $21.8 billion for the same year.

For the first, income produced by super funds is generally taxed at 15 per cent rather than the taxpayer's normal tax rate. A taxpayer with an income of more than $180,000 would normally pay 47 cents in the dollar (including the Medicare levy) on any investment income. But income received by that taxpayer's super fund is taxed at only 15 cents in the dollar (using the 2022–23 tax scales). Likewise, that part of the taxpayer's income paid into a super fund is also taxed at only 15 cents in the dollar. That is a substantial 32 cents in the dollar tax concession for those high-income taxpayers. But a taxpayer on less than $18,200 per annum, maybe someone working only a day or so a week, normally pays no tax but they still pay the 15 per cent. So, the present system is regressive in that it heavily punishes the poor but gives generously to the rich.

Super tax concessions and age pensions compared

In the 2022–23 budget papers, super tax concessions for the estimates of large tax expenditures were estimated at $52.6 billion, which was just under the value of the age pension at $55.3 billion (Australian Government 2022). This would put tax concessions for super in the top three expenditure programs by cost, and above that of the National Disability Insurance Scheme. Tax concessions for super surpass expenditure on medical benefits at $31.3 billion and assistance to the states for hospitals at $26.6 billion. In this section, we present a graphical analysis that compares the super tax concessions and the age pension.

The Australian Institute of Health and Welfare (2021) estimated that, in March 2021, 2.6 million people received the age pension – 62 per cent of the population aged 65 and over. The age pension is the core retirement income for the bulk of that demographic. It is instructive to compare the amount the government spends on the age pension to the amount it spends on superannuation tax concessions for the wealthy.

Data from the federal budget allow us to examine the tax benefits going to people with superannuation and compare them with the amount paid out as income support for people who claim the age pension. Every year the government publishes the value of the tax concessions going towards superannuation. The government's budget papers also provide figures for government income-support payments for the age pension under the heading "support for seniors".

The data in Figure 11.1 are for the completed financial years to 2021–22 as well as the forward estimates and projections for the years to 2025–26.

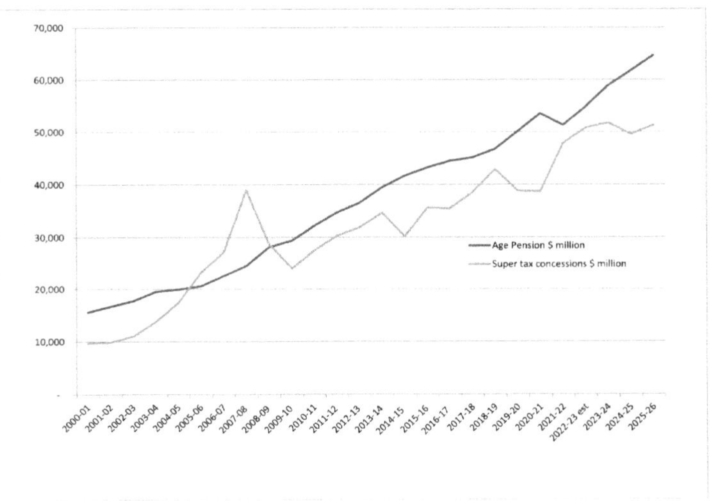

Figure 11.1 Tax concessions for superannuation and outlays on the age pension compared ($m). Sources: Treasury (2001 to 2022) and Australian Government (2001–02 to 2021–22).

As evident in Figure 11.1, super tax concessions tend to be volatile, especially the concession for the income earned in super funds. Those vary with the fortunes of the share market; as the returns to funds fluctuate, so does the value of the concessional tax on those returns. Nevertheless, it seems that the value of super tax concessions continues to fluctuate around or just below the value of the age pension payments. The fortunes of the share market seem to be reflected in the most recent data as they were in the period leading up to the Global Financial Crisis. That might be clearer if the figures are expressed as a share of gross domestic product (GDP) as is done in Figure 11.2.

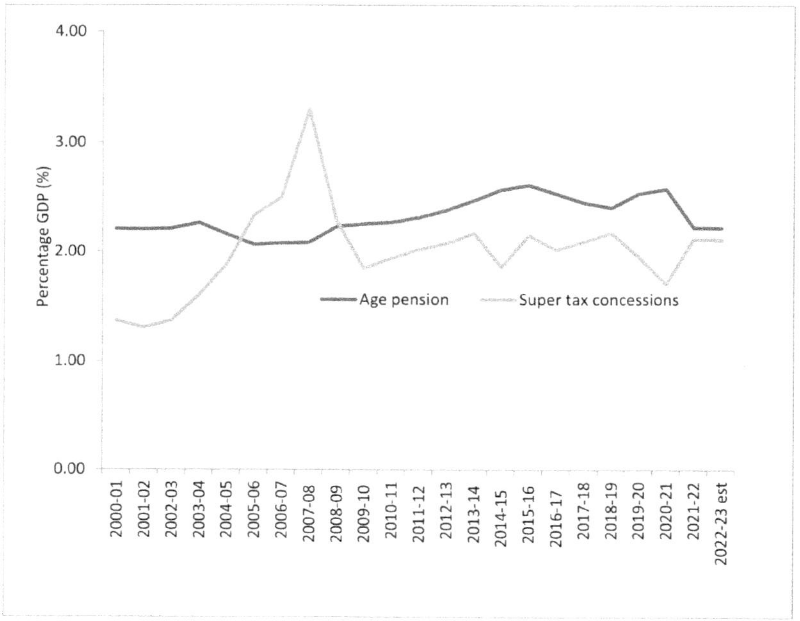

Figure 11.2 Tax concessions for superannuation and outlays on the age pension compared (% of GDP). Source: ABS (2022), Treasury (2001–2022) and Australian Government (2001–02 to 2021–22).

Figure 11.2 shows that both the super tax concessions and age pension payments tend to be reasonably stable shares of GDP in recent years. Attempts to slice bits from the salami stick of super concessions seem to have had no effect on the remaining salami. Indeed, on the most recent trends, super tax concessions are again likely to overtake payments for the age pension as they did just before the Global Financial Crisis (in 2007–08 the tax on fund earnings jumped to $22.1 billion, up $9.2 billion on the previous year).

From time to time governments have been concerned about the cost of super tax concessions and attempts have been made to limit the value of the concessions, especially the concessions going to high-income earners. For example, major changes were made in the

2016 budget that included caps on amounts that could be transferred to tax-free retirement accounts, limiting the concession on contributions for people earning $250,000 and above and various other initiatives (Treasury 2017). There is nothing in the data to suggest those measures have had a material impact on the use of super by the rich.

There is another way of thinking about the data summarised in Figure 11.2. Most people continue to receive the age pension in retirement, although there has been a fall in the actual proportion of the population aged 65 and over who receive the age pension (Australian Institute of Health and Welfare 2021). This model is financed by the taxpayer. But, in the 1980s and 1990s, we introduced a new model based on occupational super with employer and employee funding. We would expect that there would be an expensive transition phase during the time when taxpayers are paying for pensions on a pay-as-you-go model and employers are paying for the contributory system with, again, heavy taxpayer contributions via the tax concessions for super. But, as the super system matures, the pension system should have been phased out somewhat and the transition to the contributory system completed. But the data in Figure 11.2 suggests this is not happening and, if anything, funding seems to be trapped in the transition phase.

Distributional impacts

The age pension is best thought of as a fairly austere safety net, but it coexists with a rather generous constellation of tax concessions that favour the rich. One press report suggested that at least 11,000 people had more than $5 million in super, which would cost the government about $1.5 billion a year (Read 2023). The tax benefit is around $70,000 annually for a person with a super balance of $5 million. That is 2.6 times the age pension for singles (based on the single age pension rate – including the pension supplement and the energy supplement – applying from September 2022). It is not clear from the report but these figures probably come from both industry funds and other APRA-regulated funds as well as SMSFs (APRA regulates industry and other funds while the tax office regulates SMSFs).

A quick inspection of the Australian tax statistics for SMSFs is also revealing. There were 505,571 such funds in 2019–20 (ATO

2022). Of these, 897 produced taxable income in the range of $1 million dollars or more. A total of 45,560 funds produced taxable income of at least $100,000. For that group, the funds' gross income was $14.9 billion and tax paid was $1.61 billion or 10.8 per cent of the income. Had that income been imputed to the main trust beneficiary, the tax payable would have been at least $5.8 billion, around $4.2 billion higher on our calculations. These figures show the incentives in the system for the self-employed to establish SMSFs as a means of avoiding tax. We also note that assuming SMSFs are producing incomes of around 5 per cent implies there are 45,560 SMSF funds that are likely to have assets of $2 million or more (because a 5 per cent return implies the value of the assets are some 20 times the income). On this basis, the 897 funds mentioned above are likely to have assets worth around $20 million or so.

The data suggest tax concessions are being used for more than just providing a comfortable retirement and instead are being used to rort the system by tax minimisers and estate planners. It is now timely to revisit the question of subsidies to the super industry and how they have fared in the decade or so before and after that report.

It should have been relatively easy for governments to fix up the bias in the tax concessions for the rich. So long as the super tax rate was less than the top individual tax rate there was going to be a greater concession for the rich both in absolute terms and proportionately. But if the concession is tailored to the taxpayers' circumstances, then it would be possible to give the same proportionate or absolute benefit to all super contributors.

Poverty rates

We mentioned above that 62 per cent of people over 65 rely on the age pension. The rich are doing well out of the superannuation system whether they need it or not. The same cannot be said about the lower income groups relying on the age pension. In Figure 11.3, the poverty rates for those people aged 66 and over are plotted for various member countries of the Organisation for Economic Co-operation and Development (OECD) using OECD data and definitions. The countries

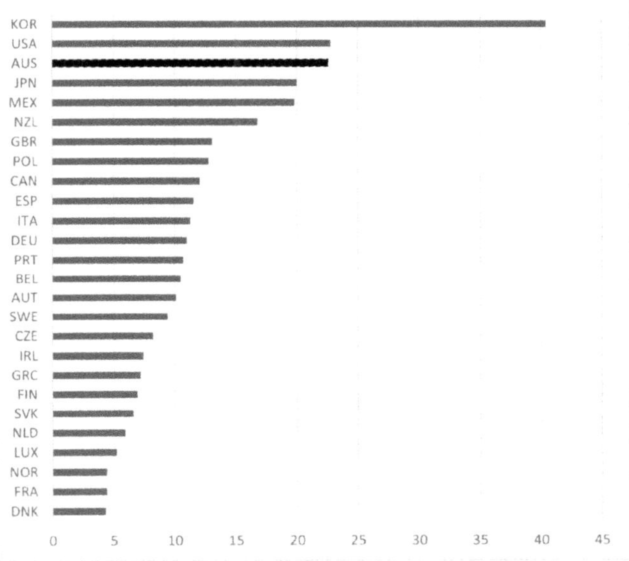

Figure 11.3 Poverty rates in selected OECD countries (% of those 66 years and above). Source: OECD (n.d.).

omitted are chiefly the smaller East European states formed after the breakup of the former Soviet Union.

Figure 11.3 shows that in Australia, 22.6 per cent of people 66 and over were in poverty and most countries that we like to compare ourselves to had substantially lower poverty rates. This graph would seem to suggest that the social security systems common in European countries perform better on distributional grounds. Of course, Figure 11.3 is only one bit of evidence and more evidence would be needed to be definitive. But it suggests Australia might have been better off adopting the recommendations of the Hancock Report mentioned above.

Distribution of super balances

For all households, it is interesting to look at the distributional impacts of superannuation by considering the value of super balances as a proportion of household wealth. Those figures have been calculated and are presented in Figure 11.4. These are based on the ABS household distribution tables by equivalised net worth quintiles.

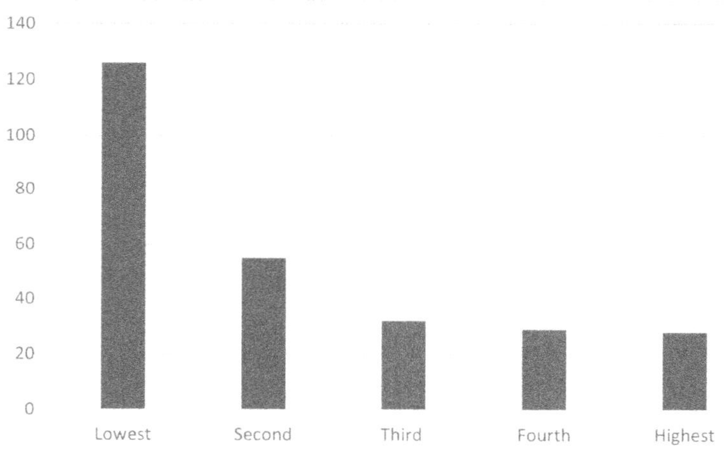

Figure 11.4 Super as a share of household wealth by quintile, 2019–20 (%). Source: Author's calculations based on ABS (2022).

Figure 11.4 clearly shows that super greatly increases the wealth of lower and middle groups. The data reported here suggests super has a powerful impact on the bottom income groups but, for the third and higher income groups, super is a flat share of total wealth. For the lowest quintile households super offsets a good deal of their debt which accounts for super being over 100 per cent of their net wealth. The top income groups are likely to hold their wealth in SMSFs that, in turn, hold shares, property and other assets that these groups would have held in their own right if they did not have access to superannuation tax concessions.

Note that while Figure 11.4 suggests super has a progressive impact on wealth distribution, gaps in coverage and other factors still imply poverty rates as shown in Figure 11.3.

Purpose of superannuation

From time to time there are suggestions that the government should legislate the purpose of superannuation. Most recently the Assistant Treasurer and Minister for Financial Services, Stephen Jones, is reported as saying that legislating an objective for superannuation would facilitate a crackdown on excessively high superannuation balances (Read 2023).

To see the point more clearly, we contrast the views of the SMSF lobby, which suggests such a narrow objective for superannuation would "discourage" people from creating successful businesses and building up their wealth. Obviously, the SMSF lobby would like the system to be rather open-ended, as it has been in the past, and would like to see it remain very generous. Of course, nobody wants to own up to supporting a system that encourages tax avoidance and boosts inheritance for the next generation – so the lobby group invents new purposes such as wealth creation.

This debate is reminiscent of the assets test debate in the early 1980s. To be eligible for the age pension there was an income test but no assets test. Relatively wealthy people were able to arrange their affairs so that they appeared to have little income and so were eligible for the pension or a higher pension (Treasury 2001).

Control of super funds

Before the present system, funds management, retirement incomes, life assurance and other aspects of the financial system were dominated by the private sector. But the super industry has been dominated by industry funds, as we saw above. The Coalition when in government has attempted to undermine the present structure of the industry. One of its first targets was the compulsory nature of super and the specification of the funds to which a particular industry should pay the contributions. Hence the Coalition emphasised the need for workers to have a choice as to which fund they might contribute. Of course, the fund members did not want a choice and had no idea about what they might choose if given the option. A report by the Australia Institute and Industry Super Network in 2008 found:

> the Coalition Government represented the Choice of Fund policy as a major victory for consumers. In reality, the majority of Australians have derived little benefit from greater choice and competition in the superannuation sector. In fact, the recent changes have benefited some sections of the community – the financial services industry and highly engaged consumers – but have failed to adequately protect those who choose not to choose (Fear and Pace 2008, vii).

By appealing to choice, Coalition governments were able to give others, such as the banks, an opportunity to compete for customers by, for example, bribing an employer to put their new employees in a retirement account with that bank. The bank super accounts have consistently underperformed compared with the industry funds (Industry Super Funds 2017). In 2020 the Coalition government tried to prevent industry super funds from advertising. New legislation in 2021 introduced a new Best Financial Interests Duty to ensure all super fund expenditure is in the interests of members apparently "motivated by the Coalition's desire to shut down what it considers to be overly political advertising by industry super funds" (Black 2021).

At risk in all this is the $3.3 trillion in assets controlled by super funds in Australia. The Coalition seems to dislike the union/employer control of such a large segment of the Australian capital stock. There was a strong push under the Abbott government to provide for independent directors and end the 50:50 representation of union and employer representatives on super boards (Main 2013). An employee of the Business Council of Australia has accused industry super funds of bankrolling unions (Long 2018). This is significant; industry super funds have grown from 14 per cent of all super funds in 2004 to reach 32 per cent by 2022 (APRA 2023).

We mentioned in the introduction that super funds have assets worth $3.3 trillion as of September 2022, but they had been even higher

– at \$3.5 trillion in December 2021. On the latest figures, we can calculate the proportions of those assets held in different forms. That data is presented in Table 11.3.

Table 11.3 Superannuation funds – allocation of assets.

	\$ billion	**% share**
Equities (Australian)	1,725	52
Overseas	654	20
Other	559	17
Bank and other deposits	263	8
Government and other bonds	81	2
Short-term securities	58	2
Total	3,340	101

Source: ABS (2022), in final column numbers do not sum to 100 because of rounding.

The \$3.3 trillion in assets held by super funds is a large number; greater than GDP at \$2.4 trillion in the four quarters to September 2022. Of that, \$1.73 trillion is held in Australian equities. By comparison, the total value of all companies listed on the Australian stock exchange was \$2.29 trillion in the same month (Statistica 2023). Of course, those two should not be directly compared because a lot of the equity held by super funds would be unlisted. Nevertheless, it indicates the magnitude of what is at stake and why the business interests would be keen to see the system controlled by the for-profit private sector.

It was not that long ago that the Australian financial system included a lot of mutually owned institutions such as credit unions, building societies and life assurance companies before they converted to for-profit institutions or were bought by existing for-profit entities. That experience points to a possible future for the super industry if Australia allows for-profit companies to buy out the funds. The inevitable consequence would be a reduction in workers' accounts matched by profits accruing to private owners.

Drawing this together

Superannuation in Australia raises a host of issues. We saw that the push for a national and universal scheme floundered with the dismissal of the Whitlam government. With the Whitlam government went the opportunity to create a national, publicly owned scheme based on contributions but biased towards low-income earners. It was then left to unions to win their own retirement benefits from employers and there were successful initiatives on the part of individual unions aimed at getting super for their members in particular industries. This was achieved through award-based decisions at the industry level and, as an industrial entitlement, the system was necessarily based around the male, full-time permanent individual worker and inevitably went down the contributory model. So when the Keating government legislated for universal super in 1992, it formalised that model for all workers. The compulsory super guarantee created an opportunity for private for-profit companies to pick up the workers not covered by industry funds. A lot of the subsequent changes brought about by the Coalition governments attempted to make it easier for the private sector to take business away from the industry funds.

The contributions model meant that workers faced the risk that their super fund may not perform and their retirement nest egg would be smaller than might be anticipated. While industry funds have performed well, others have shown poor returns. Among the poor performers were the bank-controlled funds that entered the industry after Coalition measures designed to give workers (or employers who offer default funds to new workers) more options for the fund they choose.

Despite the compulsory aspect of superannuation, tax concessions remain a major feature of the system. These tax concessions are an expensive drain on the federal budget and are directed to people motivated to avoid tax and maximise the wealth they might bequeath their children. Despite some recent attempts to fix these rorts, these concessions still massively benefit the rich and offset the transfer of wealth to lower-income retirees, which should be the major function of the retirement system. Hence the present system of tax concessions is very regressive as it boosts the incomes of the rich.

The present system involves massive tax expenditures, which used to exceed pension outlays and are again approaching the latter. Figure 11.2 suggests that any savings in the age pension have probably been modest as Australia transitioned from the pension-based retirement system to one based on an occupational super system. It is as if Australia became stuck in the transition period. One consequence is that, despite the massive funds involved, poverty among Australians 66 years and over is among the highest of the OECD countries with which we like to compare ourselves.

Australia now has massive super funds that own a good portion of Australian industry. At the moment, the large funds are mainly controlled by boards with 50 per cent union membership. A lot of the debates and legislative changes in the federal Parliament have reflected the aims of the private finance sector to share in this large pie and leave a smaller slice for the Australian workforce. The private finance sector in Australia is very profitable. Elsewhere it extracts super profits from people and businesses that have mortgages, transactions accounts, credit cards and so on. There is no doubt Australian finance would like to get its hands on the billions in workers' super funds it does not yet control.

References

ABC News (2016). Fact check: Was superannuation designed to get people off the pension? *ABC News*, 3 March. https://tinyurl.com/2nn3v28d.

Australian Bureau of Statistics (1974). *Yearbook 1974.* https://tinyurl.com/3zb4h633.

Australian Bureau of Statistics (2022). *Managed Funds, Australia*, 1 December. https://tinyurl.com/6y4pysdu.

Australian Council of Trade Unions (n.d.). Superannuation. ACTU. https://www.actu.org.au/our-work/superannuation.

Australian Council of Trade Unions (2021). How unions helped build superannuation. *Union History Blog*, 18 June. https://tinyurl.com/tbkaftkz.

Australian Institute of Health and Welfare (2021). Age pension snapshot, 16 September. https://www.aihw.gov.au/reports/australias-welfare/age-pension.

Australian Government (2002–2022). Budget Papers. https://archive.budget.gov.au/index.htm.

Australian Prudential Regulation Authority (2022). *Statistics: Quarterly superannuation performance.* https://www.apra.gov.au/statistics-0.

Australian Prudential Regulation Authority (2023). *Statistics: Annual superannuation bulletin – Superannuation entities*, 31 January. https://tinyurl.com/mv2aec3n.

Australian Taxation Office (2021). *When can you access your super.* https://tinyurl.com/yyv5w7xx.

Australian Taxation Office (2022). *Taxation Statistics.* https://tinyurl.com/4pnu6sad.

Black, E. (2021). The government has passed its Your Future, Your Super bill. Here's what that means. *New Daily*, 17 June. https://tinyurl.com/4f3v96kw.

Fear, J., and G. Pace (2008). *Choosing Not to Choose: Making Superannuation Work by Default.* Discussion Paper Number 103, Australia Institute. https://tinyurl.com/4kxby526.

Industry Super Funds (2017). Bank-owned super funds failing to meet their social license. Media release, 20 July. https://tinyurl.com/2t528hau.

Long, S. (2018). Industry Super Australia accuses BCA staff of "propaganda" against industry funds. *ABC News*, 9 July. https://tinyurl.com/bdz8n7yw.

Main, A. (2013). Coalition tackles union influence in super funds. *The Australian*, 8 October. https://tinyurl.com/4x4dyx4r.

Organisation for Economic Co-operation and Development (n.d.). Poverty rate. *OECD Data.* https://data.oecd.org/inequality/poverty-rate.htm.

Read, M. (2023). Labor aims at super hoards, sets up clash with industry, *Australian Financial Review*, 19 January. https://tinyurl.com/mr27jkfd.

Services Australia (2023). *Age Pension.* https://tinyurl.com/42kj47de.

Statistica (2023). Monthly domestic market capitalization of the Australian Securities Exchange (ASX) from January 2010 to December 2022. http://tinyurl.com/cjkyre5m.

SuperGuide (n.d.). Best performing super funds. https://tinyurl.com/mt8ufnee.

Treasury (2001). Towards higher retirement incomes for Australians: a history of the Australian retirement income system since Federation. *Economic Roundup Centenary Edition 2001.* http://tinyurl.com/mj7f2zrp.

Treasury (2002–2022). Tax expenditures statement, later called *Tax Benchmarks and Variations Statement.*

12

Regulation, deregulation and re-regulation: the apartment quality crisis in Sydney

Bill Randolph, Martin Loosemore, Laura Crommelin and Hazel Easthope

On 24 December 2018, news broke of cracks appearing in a new high-rise tower block in Sydney Olympic Park. For the unfortunate 3,000-odd residents of Opal Tower, the beginning of the holiday season had turned into the start of a nightmare. They were evacuated that night, and within days the New South Wales state government had launched an official inquiry. Some two-and-a-half years later, a multi-million dollar settlement had been reached with residents, and the structural defects had been repaired. But the legal fight over who was responsible – developer, builder, contractors, certifiers, engineers, planners – was still rumbling through the courts (Bartsch 2022).

With the Opal Tower evacuation following the tragic Grenfell Tower fire in London in 2017 (BBC 2019) and the 2014 Lacrosse cladding fire in Melbourne (Dunstan 2019), the risks of defective apartment construction were becoming harder to ignore. But for those paying attention, the evidence had long been accumulating that the New South Wales apartment building industry was in crisis. Fifteen years prior, a final report of the New South Wales Parliamentary Joint Select Committee on the Quality of Buildings (the Campbell Inquiry) recognised the lower level of consumer protection afforded to home buyers compared to other consumer items, especially with regards to defect rectification (Joint Select Committee on the Quality of Buildings 2002). It noted the failures of the deregulated building certification system and "the general lack of professional rigour" (Joint Select Committee on the Quality of Buildings 2002, ii) in the industry, which provided buyers with little visibility and assurance that apartments were free of defects. The report also dedicated a whole chapter to the issues around quality in residential strata schemes (i.e. apartment complexes).

Since 2002 there have been multiple government inquiries, committees and reports on a range of building quality issues, including a major report by Lambert (2015) on the New South Wales system and a high-profile national review by Shergold and Weir (2018). Researchers also raised the alarm long before the Opal Tower evacuation. Research published in 2012 by two of the authors reported that 72 per cent of strata owners in New South Wales were aware of defects in their buildings, rising to 85 per cent in buildings built since 2000 (Easthope, Randolph and Judd 2012). And owners' advocacy groups and industry participants had also been highlighting the issues (Owners Corporation Network 2017), to little avail.

Despite this history, the furore that erupted after the Opal Tower incident seemed to come as a sharp wake-up call to the New South Wales government and the development industry. Suddenly, defective apartment complexes were featuring on front pages (Saulwick, Gorrey and Visentin 2019), alongside reports of recalcitrant developers not fixing defects or creating shell companies to carry out apartment projects then shutting them down before they can be pursued over defects costs – a practice known as "phoenixing" (Gladstone and Fellner 2019). Further research also emerged to emphasise the extent of the problem. A report by the Construction, Forestry, Maritime, Mining and Energy Union (2019) estimated that more than 3,400 residential buildings across Australia had combustible cladding. Our own research examined documentation for a random sample of strata-titled properties completed between 2008 and 2017 across three Sydney local government areas, and estimated that at least 51 per cent had defects (Crommelin et al. 2021). Common defects included internal water leaks and external water ingress, structural cracking and fire safety defects – the same "big three" areas of concern identified by Johnston and Reid (2019). These findings made clear that many defects were not simply cosmetic issues, but problems that could threaten health and safety. Research also demonstrated that the costs of defective work are significant, both financially (with rectification expenses estimated at between $5.2 billion and $7.2 billion nationwide: Equity Economics & Development Partners 2020) and emotionally (with measurable mental health impacts on owners: Foster, Hooper and Easthope 2022).

With media and public attention now firmly focused on the issue, the resulting threat to "consumer confidence" (New South Wales Government 2019) in purchasing apartments prompted a rapid regulatory response. Most notably, this involved the appointment of a Building Commissioner dedicated to improving building quality, who drove the introduction of major legislative reforms in 2020. But why did it come to this? In many ways, the story of apartment defects in New South Wales is one of a confusion of regulation, deregulation and re-regulation, compounded by government and industry insouciance about enforcing quality compliance despite mounting evidence of the market's failure to police itself. This chapter draws on findings from our recent research (Crommelin et al. 2021), including interviews with 66 industry experts, to illustrate how the regulatory framework failed to offer sufficient protection to apartment buyers for decades. The result was a need for rapid government re-engagement with quality oversight, after the Opal Tower fiasco made the prevailing deregulatory approach politically untenable.

Where did it all start?

The start of the apartment defects crisis in New South Wales can be traced back to intersecting processes that came together during the latter part of the 20th century, in a climate of increasing market liberalisation.

Firstly, the introduction of strata titling in 1961 radically rebalanced the risks and responsibilities of apartment development. Previously, apartment buildings were owned either outright or through company title (where individual owners held shares in a company that owned the building). Company title exposed lenders to risk, as they could not gain access to a separate title in the event of a borrower default. Strata titling removed this risk by creating separate titles for individual apartments, thus greatly expanding the finance available for apartment buyers and freeing developers to sell to anyone who could secure a mortgage (Easthope 2019). This simple but fundamental change launched the strata revolution.

The second factor was the sugar hit of financial deregulation after the 1980s, which allowed funding to be funnelled into both the supply and demand side of the housing market. The deregulated financial market gradually built the pressure under a ballooning asset bubble, of which residential property became a major beneficiary. This "financialisation" of housing (Aalbers 2016) radically reshaped the supply and demand of housing as a financial asset generating capital gains. This was further boosted by the rise of the mum-and-dad investor landlord, supported by favourable tax changes in 1999 when the pre-existing negative gearing benefits for landlords making losses were compounded by the 50 per cent reduction in capital gains tax liability on sales. At the same time that governments were significantly reducing investment in public housing, these neoliberal policies drove the market provision of rental housing as a substitute and laid the foundations for a dramatic expansion of the private apartment landlord market (Pawson, Milligan and Yates 2020). When high immigration levels, the low interest rate regime of the 2010s and monetary easing were added to the mix, this further inflated property values and added to the attractions of apartment development (Wood and Viforj 2015).

Thirdly, the strata revolution gave rise to an asymmetric development model that allowed unscrupulous developers to take advantage of the "client" being an uncoordinated group of individual consumers who are likely to be relatively unsavvy (compared to commercial or institutional clients). This development model is characterised by fragmented responsibilities and split incentives for decision-making across the design, construction, marketing and operational phases of a building's life cycle, thus encouraging risk shifting to end users (Easthope, Randolph and Judd 2012; Easthope and Randolph 2016). This has been compounded by the increasingly common off-the-plan sales model that puts buyers in a weak market position by selling homes before they are fully specified and built, with limited opportunities to back out if the final product does not meet expectations (Reid et al. 2021).

Adding density into this heady mix was the final component. The growing aversion to urban sprawl among city planners by the 1990s, motivated by concerns around future sustainability (Haaland and van Den Bosch 2015), justified and spurred the new "compact city" planning orthodoxy favouring urban density and renewal (Randolph 2006; Bunker et al. 2017). Developers were now encouraged to build at much higher densities than ever before, inevitably adding complexity to the construction process.

Together, these elements – the strata revolution, the financialisation of housing, the favourable investment environment and compact city planning – set the scene for a 21st-century apartment boom across Australia. And boom it did! In the 10 years to the end of 2021, some 870,000 new multi-unit dwellings were approved nationally (ABS 2022, Table 6). By 2017, apartments accounted for around half of all dwelling output compared to just over a quarter in 2009 (Troy et al. 2020). Ninety per cent of this growth was in major urban areas (Rosewall and Shoory 2017) and, by 2020, around 20 per cent of the population lived in strata properties, with a shared insured value of over $1 trillion (Easthope, Thompson and Sisson 2020). In the process, apartment buildings also got taller. In the 15 years to 2018–19, the number of building commencements in medium-rise (4- to 8-storey) apartment buildings increased by 95 per cent, in high-rise (9- to 19-storey) buildings increased by 153 per cent, and in super-high-rise buildings (more than 20 storeys) by 361 per cent. In contrast, building commencements in walk-up buildings (up to three storeys) declined by 46 per cent (ABS 2020).

Motivated by the prospect of enormous profits in an undersupplied market, new developers entered the fray and began building increasingly tall and complex buildings. Tradespeople were now faced with new building techniques for which traditional methods were inadequate. But in the rush to maximise boom-time profits, developers often put contractors under extreme pressure to complete jobs quickly to meet tight financial deadlines. This market climate made strong regulatory oversight more important than ever, to counteract the strong financial incentives to finish things cheaply and quickly. Instead, the apartment boom coincided with a steady trend towards deregulation and industry self-regulation, as the next section will explain. The result was an ongoing decline in standards leading to the eventual "shock" of the Opal Tower evacuation.

Deregulating building quality governance

One of the biggest contributors to the apartment quality crisis has been the sequence of changes to the regulatory framework for ensuring quality in the building industry. Building regulation and certification are complex regulatory spaces with responsibilities spread across federal, state and local levels (Lambert 2015). In New South Wales, the Department of Planning and Environment has oversight of the building approvals process, while New South Wales Fair Trading sits under a different minister within the Department of Consumer Services, and is responsible for strata and for consumer protection as well as construction industry licensing. In addition, the Minister for Emergency Services oversees fire safety standards through Fire and Rescue NSW. Meanwhile, local government approves some development applications, undertakes some certifications and has some responsibility for compliance with building standards on completion. And last but not least, the federal government has responsibility for developing building standards, fulfilled through the creation of the National Construction Code, which incorporates the Building Code of Australia. It is hardly surprising that this fractured approach to responsibility has led to governance problems on the ground.

While this complexity would create challenges on its own, the system has also been subject to deregulatory pressures since the 1980s, as the neoliberal push towards "streamlining" regulation took hold across government. This was promoted by the Council of Australian Governments with the view that it would drive up productivity and efficiency (Ruming et al. 2014). State and federal governments shifted towards a light-touch approach to building regulation, which increasingly relied on industry self-regulation rather than government oversight. As one interviewee described it, the guiding ethos became "let's cut down, we don't need to see documentation of this, it doesn't need to happen, let's just get it done fast" (Architect).

This approach was justified by claims that deregulation would produce more housing more quickly and more affordably, thus responding to growing housing pressures as metropolitan populations grew rapidly (Gurran and Ruming 2016).

Prior to this deregulatory push, the oversight of building quality in New South Wales had been relatively strong, with clerks of works providing onsite oversight (City of Sydney 2019) and close monitoring of building professionals' licences. As one of our interviewees explained:

> The move has been, starting in the '80s, to move away from big government and move towards self-regulation and so forth ... I think 20 years ago you certainly saw a lot more people, for example, in [New South Wales] Fair Trading, who had been there in the '90s and were part of a very strong, highly resourced, highly budgeted regulatory and compliance machine. (Strata lawyer)

However, the landscape changed dramatically in the intervening three decades, as another participant confirmed:

> There's been no regulatory oversight. Just none, zero ... It's just a complete failure of regulation. There's a cultural issue, there's economic issues, but it's a regulatory issue where ... the neoliberalism movement towards self-regulation, which happened to coincide with globalisation so that we had more product being shifted around the world and imported, and then intersect that with urbanisation, so we had a rush on building. Each of those three things have happened simultaneously and the result is, we have bad product, bad buildings. (Academic)

This pared-back approach was supported by the development industry, which has regularly lobbied authorities to reduce the red tape of planning controls and building regulations (Forrest 2020). As a participant put it:

> [the] New South Wales government particularly is tied to, and its agenda has always been tied to, developer interests, which is why the strata laws have been so backward for so long. It's because every time that they try or the strata owners lobby tries to do something, the developers come in and say it's going to be the end of the world, and everyone backflips. (Supplier)

These dovetailing pressures of a booming market, a deregulatory agenda and political pressure from the development industry led to a multitude of shifts in how the apartment market operated and was overseen. Here we point to two key examples of how this deregulated landscape has contributed to poor-quality apartment construction over the past three decades – private certification and the downgrading of consumer protections – before turning to look at how the government has sought to fill these gaps through re-regulation in the past four years.

Privatising and deregulating the building certification system

In New South Wales, a neoliberal reform that has proved critical to the reduction of apartment quality was deregulation of the certification process. In the past, ensuring a dwelling was fit for habitation and built as permitted were primarily the concerns of local government, by way of the local council's building officer. But in 1997, the New South Wales government deregulated the certification system to allow accredited private certifiers to issue occupation certificates (Park 2010). Without an occupation certificate, the developer is unable to finalise the sale of apartments, as the building cannot be legally occupied. Ostensibly, the introduction of private certifiers was undertaken to inject a degree of competition into what was previously an entirely public authority activity. It was hoped that this would take the strain off under-resourced local governments and speed up the certification process where local governments were not providing certifications at the rate the booming market demanded.

Under this semi-privatised certification system, a principal certifying authority, which can now be either a local council certifier or a private certifier, is appointed by the developer before construction starts. This system creates an inherent conflict of interest for the private certifier who is paid by the developers, but whose building projects they are meant to monitor (Jewell 2016). Furthermore, the system is designed to be self-policing, with the certifier relying on tradespeople to confirm that their work has met the required standards. And while private certifiers can withhold an occupation certificate if they believe work is substandard, there are strong disincentives to do so, as it may mean the loss of future work with that developer.

In addition to the inherent flaws in the privatised certification model, the deregulatory push also led to a reduction in government monitoring of certifier professionalism. From 2005 onwards this had been the role of the Building Professionals Board (BPB), with responsibilities to investigate compliance and discipline certifiers. While creation of the BPB was meant to improve the oversight of certifiers, resource constraints and the light touch regulatory agenda meant the BPB "lacked teeth" (Local Government NSW – LGNSW 2014). While egregious malpractice could lead to the certifier being struck off, in practice this rarely happened; a 2013 inquiry noted that only seven certifiers had lost their accreditation in the preceding five years (Maltabarow 2013). The fact that BPB audits were primarily desktop reviews rather than onsite inspections compounded this issue (Maltabarow 2013; LGNSW 2014).

Furthermore, the light touch approach also informed Fair Trading's approach to the licensing of other building professionals, on whom certifiers relied to confirm works were up to standard. The lack of oversight here meant there was little risk if the work proved to be sub-par. As one participant explained:

> The early '90s [Fair Trading] had a group of 100-plus inspectors running all over the subcontractors, and the licensing of subcontractors. They disbanded that licensing regime and auditing regime. [It] used to run with an iron fist, so contractors were afraid. They valued their licence, they understood what it actually meant to lose their licence. The problem now is, we're not doing licence checks ... You have to make a licence worth something. (Private certifier)

Meanwhile, although local councils remain involved in certification of some projects and are responsible for collecting and managing records of private certification in their local government area, their ability to perform these roles has also been undermined. Councils have not been immune to the ascendant small-government ideology, and have come under increasing financial pressure in particular due to stringent rate capping. The internal functions of local planning departments were also reorganised in the name of greater efficiency, with responsibility for a particular development broken down into specific components of the process between different staff. This led to a loss of holistic oversight, as a council certifier explained:

> There is a disconnect even within a council between all the different roles, whereas in the old days ... I had a multidisciplinary team of engineers, planners, building surveyors, admin staff and all the rest of it. So whatever went on in [my local government area], you couldn't fart in [my local government area] unless I knew about it ... But now what's happened is everyone's gone away from area-based responsibility into application responsibility ... so that people don't tend to get that sense of overview, or care or responsibility. (Public certifier)

These changes have affected the certifiers' capacity to undertake certification in a comprehensive way. In addition, these insights speak to the wider structural issues that have resulted from the deregulation agenda reducing accountability across the industry. Private certifiers have often been made the scapegoat in recent years (Hair 2018), and it is clear that the self-regulation model of certification has proven inadequate. But private certification alone did not lead the industry to where it was by the time Opal Tower began cracking; the deregulation agenda has run much deeper, with impacts across all levels of government.

The reduction of consumer protections

One may argue that the deregulation agenda had a laudable aim in seeking to facilitate a faster and cheaper housing supply, and a small number of unlucky consumers buying a lemon was a reasonable price to pay for maintaining a property-induced economic boom that kept much of the New South Wales population feeling wealthy. But this perspective is hard to align with other regulatory changes that downgraded the rights of affected consumers to seek redress, even as deregulation meant the risks to consumers were growing.

Most notable here were changes to insurance requirements and statutory warranties that occurred in the 2000s. Before this, in New South Wales, the Home Builders Warranty insurance scheme required all builders to insure their buildings for future defects. After the collapse of the HIH Insurance Group in 2001, which had insured approximately a third of the market, the government found itself "carrying all significant risks from volatility and essentially subsidising the private market" (*icare*: Insurance and Care NSW 2020). A subsequent inquiry recommended an end to compulsory insurance coverage for builders of high-rise developments, with justifications including the expectation that members of a large development consortium would monitor other participants (*icare*: Insurance and Care NSW 2020). The government accepted this recommendation and, since 2003, Home Builders Warranty insurance is no longer required for the construction of new multistorey buildings of four or more storeys in New South Wales.

So while the government insurer *icare* still provides last-resort builders' insurance via the (renamed) Home Building Compensation Fund (HBCF) scheme for residential construction up to three storeys, builders in the high-rise market do not need to meet *icare*'s oversight requirements. This means owners in larger buildings have no last-resort recourse if their builder collapses or disappears, and may also attract less diligent developers towards larger developments, as one participant explained:

> Because there's no insurance product, all the dodgy builders, all the ones that are going to cut corners, they all go to the [high-rise] multi-unit apartments because there's no requirement for them to meet the criteria for them being allowed to offer [HBCF] insurance. (Developer)

Adding insult to injury, in 2012 the government shifted more risk onto consumers by reducing the statutory warranties under the *Home Building Act 1989* (New South Wales) from seven years for all defects, to six years for major defects and two years for other defects. Our research shows that these timeframes create major challenges for consumers. Defects often are not apparent immediately, meaning that owners may not know they have a problem until well into – or after – the warranty period. The fragmented nature of strata ownership also complicates bringing a claim within these timeframes, as it requires coordinating multiple owners. The net effect has prompted strata lawyers to conclude that "the worth of the [minor defects warranty] is doubtful" (Bannerman 2014).

Even before the Opal Tower evacuation, concerns about the effect of these cuts to consumer protections had gathered enough pace to prompt the New South Wales government to act, leading to the introduction of the Strata Building Bond and Inspections Scheme in 2018. The scheme applies to new strata buildings of more than three storeys, and works by requiring developers to lodge a building bond (2 per cent of the contract price) with Fair Trading, which can be drawn upon to pay for rectifying defective building work. If the bond is not needed to fix defects within two years of completion, the money is returned to the developer, thus creating an incentive to produce quality work, while also ensuring owners with defects are not left high and dry by phoenixing.

Yet even before the scheme was finalised, its shortcomings were apparent. Of particular concern was the inadequacy of a 2 per cent bond to cover the cost of rectifying serious defects, especially given past research on defects in houses has found that they cost on average 4 per cent of the contract price to rectify (Mills, Love and Williams 2009). An interviewee confirmed that these concerns were well founded: "Two per cent's a lot of money if you haven't got problems, and it's bugger-all if you really do have problems" (Developer).

Another problem is that the scheme's two-year window does not allow for many serious defects to become apparent. This is compounded by the requirement that inspections only be visual (rather than invasive), meaning that serious defects like faulty waterproofing membranes or fire dampers may remain undetected, and be excluded from cover.

Overall, our participants concluded that the scheme is largely ineffective. As one put it:

> I think it was a knee-jerk policy that, on paper looked like it was going to hold some level of accountability to the developer, but ... the system was so distorted initially and manipulated, to the extent where I have seen ... a fair amount of new developments – [but] I have not seen a building defect bond [paid out] personally

> ... So the system has already learnt how to divert around that level of culpability or liability or responsibility. (Strata manager)

In many ways, the story of the Strata Building Bond and Inspections Scheme perfectly reflects the regulatory landscape in New South Wales over the past three decades, where there was little appetite for stronger regulations, and the few attempts to improve consumer protection were inevitably watered down or stymied by poor implementation. But that all changed after Christmas Eve in 2018, when the government finally saw the writing on the wall and entered a new re-regulatory phase.

Enter the New South Wales Building Commissioner

Under intense political, media and community pressure following the Opal Tower evacuation, the New South Wales Premier, Gladys Berejiklian acknowledged that the deregulatory approach wasn't working (Saulwick, Gorrey and Visentin 2019) and announced the creation of a new role – the New South Wales Building Commissioner – to lead a suite of building industry reforms. The commissioner is responsible for investigation and disciplinary action for misconduct, overseeing end-to-end licensing and auditing, and driving legislative change. David Chandler OAM was appointed in August 2019 and has developed a strategy and implementation plan called Construct NSW, which aims to rebuild public confidence in the apartment market with reforms to be undertaken through to 2025.

The reforms are underpinned by two new pieces of legislation: the *Residential Apartment Buildings (Compliance and Enforcement Powers) Act 2020* (New South Wales) (RAB Act) and the *Design and Building Practitioners Act 2020* (New South Wales) (DBP Act). The RAB Act grants new powers to the Office of the Building Commissioner (OBC) to investigate building work and require rectification of defects in buildings under construction as well as existing buildings, for up to six years after occupation. These are the powers underpinning the OBC's highly publicised audit regime, under which selected new buildings are being inspected by government inspectors before completion. The Act authorises the issuance of a building work rectification order if the

Secretary of the Department of Customer Services "has a reasonable belief that building work was or is being carried out in a manner that could result in a serious defect in relation to a residential apartment building" (s.33). The secretary can also issue stop work orders (s.29) and prohibition orders (s.9), which prevent an occupation certificate being issued until quality issues are resolved.

Complementing these new inspection powers, the DBP Act has three main functions:

- to introduce new registration requirements for designers, engineers, specialists and builders, to provide greater oversight and ensure they are adequately qualified
- to require that designers lodge building designs before construction starts, and that builders lodge "as-built" plans upon completion. Builders must also declare that the completed building complies with the lodged designs and the National Construction Code.
- to introduce a statutory duty of care for practitioners, to make it easier for owners to sue if a person carrying out construction work fails to exercise reasonable care to avoid economic loss caused by defects (New South Wales Government 2020).

As part of the OBC's reforms, owners are also now being encouraged to report building defects to a newly reinvigorated New South Wales Fair Trading (NSW Fair Trading 2020). While responding to defects complaints is not a new function for Fair Trading, the light-touch approach had previously resulted in limited support for owners, with a focus on dispute management rather than investigation or enforcement. As one interviewee explained:

> At the moment you go to Fair Trading and you say "I've got a problem with my building, what can I do?" They'll say "well let's get people in and we'll have a chat, and we can see if we can resolve it". [Then] they say "well they're not going to talk to you" ... [so] do I have a good case to go to the Tribunal? Fair Trading will say, "well there's the law, you decide. We're not going to tell you. That's not our job". There's a big disconnect right there. (Strata journalist)

Due to these limitations, reporting defects to Fair Trading has not been common practice; the Building Commissioner recently found that only 17 per cent of buildings with major defects had reported (Chandler 2021). Time will tell whether reporting defects to the revitalised Fair Trading proves a more fruitful experience.

While these reforms give the OBC significant new legal powers, the government is also looking to market-led solutions to help improve building quality. Of particular note is the OBC's support for industry-led efforts to develop rating tools to assess the risk associated with developers (New South Wales Government n.d.). In response, the credit ratings agency Equifax has developed a tool called iCirt, which assigns ratings based on a range of data including creditworthiness, insurance data, regulatory breaches and legal claims. While the government may use tools like this to identify risky players and focus resources, it is also hoping these tools will enable consumers and industry players to better assess risk in the market. In this way the government is once again advocating a hands-off solution to regulatory oversight, with a poor rating meaning a poor performer is put out of business, rather than having to be disciplined by government.

Our participants generally expressed cautious support for these reforms. As one explained:

> So I think the Building Commissioner's on the right path and I really do think that he's tackling [the problem] from multiple directions that will eventually change the industry. But it's an industry that's – we may be looking at 50 years' deterioration in standards and crafts that needs to be addressed. (Rectification specialist)

While it is too early to assess the long-term impact of the re-regulation process on building quality in New South Wales, the scope of the reforms suggests that the New South Wales government is taking building quality issues more seriously than it has in years.

Conclusion

The history of the apartment defects crisis in New South Wales is a complex picture of regulation, deregulation and re-regulation, with time still to tell whether the new regime will right past wrongs. A large part of the story has been a failure of neoliberal public policy, which facilitated the steady erosion of checks and balances that previously protected apartment owners and residents.

The broader lesson from New South Wales' experience is that when markets involve power imbalances like those that exist between large developers and individual consumers, governments must be actively involved in maintaining a level playing field. Both the carrot and the stick must be in the regulatory toolkit, along with the resourcing for both to be wielded effectively. Otherwise, in the memorable words of one research participant, all you've got is "a tin-star sheriff": "He's sitting on the verandah of the sheriff's office with his empty shotgun on a rocking chair and the cowboys ride past. Everyone knows they've got no budget and [are] not going to do anything, [so] they'll keep playing" (Strata lawyer).

It is clear from the New South Wales experience that the "tin-star sheriff" approach to managing the construction industry is not good enough. Simply deregulating and relying on industry to police itself has not worked, as there are far too many misaligned incentives and power asymmetries at play. Without proactive government intervention, asymmetric markets like these will inevitably fail. And whether it be in a collapsing building or a market collapsing through loss of confidence, one way or the other it will be consumers who end up bearing the brunt of this failure.

References

Aalbers, M. (2016). *The Financialization of Housing: A Political Economy Approach*. Abingdon, UK: Routledge.

Australian Bureau of Statistics (2020). Telling storeys – apartment building heights. https://tinyurl.com/uhehpb3e.

Australian Bureau of Statistics (2022). Building approvals, Australia. https://tinyurl.com/3uzc6hyv.

Bannerman, D. (2014). NSW: Home Building Act statutory warranties – what is the two year warranty for non structural defects worth? *Look Up Strata*, 17 June (updated 25 August 2023). https://tinyurl.com/yc5p6ytv.

Bartsch, P. (2022). Out-of-court settlement reached over opal tower. *The Urban Developer*, 20 May. https://tinyurl.com/436yzhhe.

BBC (2019). Grenfell Tower: what happened. *BBC News*, 29 October. https://tinyurl.com/47hk7sp6.

Bunker, R., L. Crommelin, L. Troy, H. Easthope, S. Pinnegar and B. Randolph (2017). Managing the transition to a more compact city in Australia. *International Planning Studies* 22: 384–99.

Chandler, D. (2021). OC audits are now evidencing construction's fault lines. *LinkedIn*. http://tinyurl.com/2u2z7ytp.

City of Sydney (2019). Submission to the inquiry into regulation of building standards, building quality and building disputes (Submission No. 143). Sydney: New South Wales Parliament.

Construction, Maritime, Mining and Energy Union (2019). Shaky Foundations: the National Crisis in Construction. Sydney, NSW: Construction, Maritime, Mining and Energy Union.

Crommelin, L., S. Thompson, H. Easthope, M. Loosemore, H. Yang, C. Buckle and B. Randolph (2021). *Cracks in the Compact City: Tackling Defects in Multi-Unit Strata Housing*. Sydney: City Futures Research Centre, University of New South Wales.

Dunstan, J. (2019). Lacrosse apartment owners awarded $5.7 million in damages after flammable cladding blaze. *ABC News*, 28 February. https://tinyurl.com/43xjz8rj.

Easthope, H. (2019). *The Politics and Practices of Apartment Living*. Cheltenham, UK: Edward Elgar Publishing.

Easthope, H., and B. Randolph (2016). Principal–agent problems in multi-unit developments: the impact of developer actions on the ongoing management of strata titled properties. *Environment and Planning A: Economy and Space* 48: 1829–47.

Easthope, H., B. Randolph and S. Judd (2012). *Governing the Compact City: The Role and Effectiveness of Strata Management*. Sydney: City Futures Research Centre, University of New South Wales.

Easthope, H., S. Thompson and A. Sisson (2020). 2020 Australasian strata insights. *City Futures Research Centre*. https://tinyurl.com/adzt4a7f.

Equity Economics & Development Partners (2020). *The Cost of Apartment Building Defects*. https://tinyurl.com/mwepjwt5.

Forrest, T. (2020). Urban Taskforce responds ... to a host of issues on planning and fast tracking. *The Fifth Estate*, 28 April. https://tinyurl.com/4aype6yw.

Foster, S., P. Hooper and H. Easthope (2022). Cracking up? Associations between building defects and mental health in new Australian apartment buildings. *Cities and Health* 6(6): 1152–63.

Gladstone, N., and C. Fellner (2019). Small business flattened by "dodgy" builders in phoenixing epidemic. *Sydney Morning Herald*, 17 December. http://tinyurl.com/2s4m5szw.

Gurran, N., and K. Ruming (2016). Less planning, more development? Housing and urban reform discourses in Australia. *Journal of Economic Policy Reform* 19: 262–80.

Haaland, C., and C.K. van Den Bosch (2015). Challenges and strategies for urban green-space planning in cities undergoing densification: a review. *Urban Forestry and Urban Greening* 14: 760–71.

Hair, J. (2018). NSW government to crack down on dodgy building certifiers following Opal Tower saga. *ABC News*, 30 December. https://tinyurl.com/huns336k.

icare: Insurance and Care NSW (2020). NSW Home Building Compensation Scheme. https://tinyurl.com/3rrcfms6.

Jewell, C. (2016). NSW to take action on building certification failure. *The Fifth Estate*, 27 September. https://tinyurl.com/4h2jj8ph.

Johnston, N., and S. Reid (2019). *An Examination of Building Defects in Multi-owned Properties*. Melbourne: Deakin and Griffith universities.

Joint Select Committee on the Quality of Buildings (2002). *Report upon the Quality of Buildings*. https://tinyurl.com/3sk6efmn. [Campbell inquiry]

Lambert, M. (2015). *Independent Review of the Building Professionals Act 2005: Final Report*. https://tinyurl.com/mrxywysj.

LGNSW (2014). Submission to the Building Professionals Board Report on "Building Certification and Regulation – Serving a New Planning System for NSW". Local Government NSW, Sydney, Australia. https://tinyurl.com/5x5tufem.

Maltabarow, G. (2013). *Building Certification and Regulation – Serving a New Planning System for NSW*. https://tinyurl.com/3byz2euf.

Mills, A., P.E. Love and P. Williams (2009). Defect costs in residential construction. *Journal of Construction Engineering and Management* 135: 12–16.

New South Wales Government (2019). NSW Building Commissioner appointed. *NSW Government News*, 7 August. https://www.nsw.gov.au/news/nsw-building-commissioner-appointed.

New South Wales Government (2020). *Design and Building Practitioners Act*. 2020. https://legislation.nsw.gov.au/view/pdf/asmade/act-2020-7.

New South Wales Government (n.d.) Restoring confidence in the construction industry using iCIRT to rate building professionals. http://tinyurl.com/2s36zzsm.

NSW Fair Trading (2020). Strata. https://tinyurl.com/ynffc5va.

Owners Corporation Network (2017). Submission to the inquiry into the effects of non-conforming building products on the Australian building and construction industry (Supplementary Submission no. 88). Canberra: Senate Economic References Committee.

Park, H. (2010). *NSW Planning Framework: History of Reforms*. Sydney: NSW Parliamentary Library Research Service.

Pawson, H., V. Milligan and J. Yates (2020). *Housing Policy in Australia*. New York, NY: Springer.

Randolph, B. (2006). Delivering the compact city in Australia: current trends and future implications. *Urban Policy and Research* 24: 473–90.

Reid, S., M. Pocock, S. Caldera and T. Wilson (2021). Considering buying property off the plan? Here are 6 crucial steps to protect yourself. *The Conversation*, 13 October. http://tinyurl.com/pkt68deb.

Rosewall, T., and M. Shoory (2017). Houses and apartments in Australia. *Bulletin* (June). https://www.rba.gov.au/publications/bulletin/2017/jun/1.html.

Ruming, K.J., N. Gurran, P.J. Maginn and R. Goodman (2014). A national planning agenda? Unpacking the influence of federal urban policy on state planning reform. *Australian Planner* 51: 108–21.

Saulwick, J., M. Gorrey and L. Visentin (2019). "It hasn't worked": premier admits Sydney's building industry is failing. *Sydney Morning Herald*, 10 July. http://tinyurl.com/56zuasxh.

Shergold, P., and B. Weir (2018). *Building confidence: improving the effectiveness of compliance and enforcement systems for the building and construction industry across Australia.*, Canberra: Department of Industry, Science, Energy and Resources.

Troy, L., B. Randolph, S. Pinnegar, L. Crommelin and H. Easthope (2020). Vertical sprawl in the Australian city: Sydney's high-rise residential development boom. *Urban Policy and Research* 38: 18–36.

Wood, G., and R.O. Viforj (2015). The facts on Australian housing affordability. *The Conversation*, 12 June. https://tinyurl.com/3ds74za8.

13 The neoliberal reconstruction of curriculum and teaching in Australian vocational education

Steven Hodge

The Australian vocational education system as we know it arguably took shape as a sector with the Whitlam government, which commissioned a major study of provision with a view to determining a new national position. The study, led by personnel management expert Myer Kangan, was reported in 1974. The review called for Commonwealth investment to establish a national sector with a distinct identity and rationale. This new sector, labelled "Technical and Further Education" (TAFE), would sit alongside other recognised forms of provision: schools, Colleges of Advanced Education, universities. The Kangan Report (Australian Committee on Technical and Further Education 1974) furnished a philosophical rationale for TAFE, arguing that the sector should promote personal and community development with the satisfaction of employers' skill needs acknowledged as an important feature. This vision reflects the inherent complexity of vocational education and notably views economic benefit as an element in a larger concern for human flourishing that includes personal and community dimensions. The newly endowed TAFE sector was established through Commonwealth funding with states, each of which hitherto had led policy development, continuing to provide the bulk of resourcing. TAFE colleges around Australia offered programs that developed human potential, including basic skills in adult literacy and numeracy, along with trades and other specifically occupational forms of training such as nursing, software, business, building and engineering (Goozee 2001). TAFE colleges were important to communities and regions, providing a range of educational opportunities, including many that were not afforded by other educational sectors. In contemporary language, TAFE colleges were concerned with lifelong learning, a blend of adult and vocational education meeting multiple needs.

Training reform

Within 15 years the Kangan vision was challenged by a new Labor government. At a stroke, the systems, institutions and practices of the TAFE sector were set on a path to transformation. A widely accepted account has it that social and economic difficulties besetting the nation in the 1980s called for an urgent, wide-ranging national response and that vocational education, naturally, would be part of that (Smith and Keating 2003). These "reforms" were comprehensive, reaching to the very core of vocational education. In particular, the changes effectively transferred control of matters of curriculum, pedagogy and assessment from vocational education teachers and institutions to other parties, penetrating to the level of what, how and why educators practised.

Neoliberal principles informed policy making across government at that time. While a contentious and even vague term, "neoliberal" is useful for thinking about a shared ethos and theory of reform efforts in different spheres of government influence (Cahill and Toner 2018). A central tenet of this movement is the role and value of markets in serving the public. This doctrine goes back at least to Adam Smith (1981[1776]): the idea that markets moderate and coordinate a plethora of self-interested parties toward an overall good (of lower prices, innovation and higher quality). The neoliberal part here is the introduction of markets where there were none before, seeking the emergence of the goods conveyed by the hand of the market in new domains of application. According to Toner (2018), it was Milton Friedman who first made the case that governments should be responsible for education as a funder rather than provider, and that opening public funding to private concerns would be a way to remedy an assortment of problems thought to be compromising education as a public sector monopoly. Other theories in the neoliberal family, such as human capital theory (Marginson 1989), new public management theory (Zoellner 2017) and public choice theory (Buchanan 1984), were galvanised in support of reforms. But it is not only a complex, technical bureaucratic exercise in question here, but efforts tinged with moral purpose and weight (an aspect appreciated by Buchanan, who explicitly advanced a normative purpose to public choice theory). We see the moral side of neoliberal theory in the visionary fervour of leading neoliberal thinkers. Public choice theory is explicit about the evils that plague public sector activity in the absence of market mechanisms. Buchanan (1984) sought to dispel the prevailing "romance" that public servants act in the public interest. As Adam Smith made clear, self-interest is the ubiquitous mode of human action. Public choice theory elaborated that reasoning in the light of Friedman's theory of government. Public servants (and they include educators on the public payroll) are bound to engage in rent-seeking behaviour, placing their own interests above those of the publics they ostensibly serve. With doctrines like these behind them, it is not surprising that policymakers would be ready to sweep aside existing vocational education practices and norms in their quest for an efficient, responsive vocational education sector.

The training minister, John Dawkins, set out the vision for reform in this sector in a series of papers released in the late 1980s. In the first, titled *Skills for Australia* (c. 1987), a strong case was made for training reform as part of coordinated government action in the face of global and domestic pressures. The paper opens with a clear vision:

> The Government is determined that our education and training systems should play an active role in responding to the major economic challenges now facing Australia.
>
> The adjustments required in the structure of the economy, and improvements in Australia's international competitiveness, will make heavy demands on our human resources and labour force skills. Our skills formation and training arrangements are not yet adequate to meet those demands (Dawkins and Holding 1987, iii).

The necessary changes included increasing the total level of participation in training, enlarging capacity to meet the anticipated demand, boosting the productivity of the system and bringing in private investment. Improving the "distribution and balance" of the system is mentioned while tackling unemployment and disadvantage were identified as social goals. Creating a training market would be a high-level move that could underwrite these shifts. But how to do that? The *Skills for Australia* policy reveals:

> [that] the Government considers that there is scope for an approach to the use of Commonwealth funds for education and training which is more closely linked to performance, to labour market demands, and to national economic and industry development objectives (Dawkins and Holding 1987, 13).

The idea was that the focus of funding would need to change as a condition for wider reform including a training market. As luck would have it, a curriculum model called "competency-based training" was at hand that would prove a malleable device for effecting a whole set of reforms.

The paradox of competency-based training

Australian vocational education reform offers a case study of sheer good fortune coming to the aid of policymakers. For the competency-based training model, fashioned in other times and tried (and, to be sure, frequently dismissed) in other settings (Hyland 1993), was close to being the perfect solution for the problem of how to refocus funding for training in an educationally defensible way. What makes competency-based training a lucky break for neoliberal reformers is how, with a little tinkering, the model not only allows a cogent shift in the basis for funding as a way to facilitate introduction of a training market, but is permeable to other interests, including a widely intelligible approach to education such that stakeholders like bureaucrats, employers and unions could "see" what was going on in the sector, "balancing" educator and employer priorities, and a desire among unions to link skill acquisition to wage rises. The model appears elastic enough to apply without modification to diverse occupational areas, an extremely useful characteristic when a very large number of existing and emerging industry areas were to be encompassed. While accommodating goals like these, policymakers could proclaim the educational benefits of competency-based training by linking it with progressivist educational principles. Progressivism embraces student-centrism (as opposed to didactic, teacher-focused methods), self-paced learning (replacing a rigid, time-served routine of formal education), values informal and non-formal learning as much as formal provision, and seeks explicit, practical outcomes. Educators confronted with the competency-based training model could not deny the promise of such an approach to vocational education just as they could not refuse to help their students become "competent". But, while on the surface competency-based training satisfies an impressive range of needs, in its neoliberal incarnation educational quality is compromised. The problem here is that market forces interact with the reform-era competency-based training model to deprive in practice what it offered in theory. To understand how the model can have this paradoxical effect it is helpful to consider some of its intricacies.

Competency-based training is an eclectic skills development model, drawing on a range of influences. It owes much to the principles of behavioural objectives theory pioneered by psychologists working for the US military in the 1950s and 1960s (Reiser 2001). This theory was a revolutionary method for systematising educational delivery. It called for detailed specification of the end point or "terminal objectives" of learning and then working backward, articulating the "enabling objectives" that would build sequentially towards the terminus as a guide to development of curriculum or "instructional resources" (Yelon 1991). It should be stressed here that the designers of this approach considered terminal objectives as a component in a whole *system* of instruction, in which considerable weight is given to analysis of terminal objectives using learning taxonomies to determine instructional "strategies" or learning activities (Smith and Ragan 2005). In practice, thoroughgoing instructional systems design was resource-intensive and slow, requiring special expertise (Werner and DeSimone 2011).

Subsequently, the idea of basing educational efforts on highly specific terminal objectives became detached from the principles and practice of instructional systems design. This possibility of the model was used to great effect later. We see it in the wake of the Sputnik crisis, when political interest focused on the supposed failure of American education to form a scientifically advanced generation capable of overtaking Soviet technology (Tuxworth 1989). "Performance-Based Teacher Education" (later renamed "Competence-based Teacher Education") was among the measures introduced to remedy the issue in the 1960s (Norton, Harrington and Gill 1978). Noteworthy is the fact that this model was created to reform the US teaching profession, and it does so by making modular "competences" (conceptually identical with terminal objectives) a focus of specialist and political attention (even something of a public spectacle) and leaving the educational or developmental side to the colleges of teacher education.

Later again, in the early 1970s, Canadian bureaucrats devised a means of specifying outcomes for labour market programs intended for the unemployed (Joyner 1995). This method involved gathering skilled workers in a target occupation who, under the guidance of a trained facilitator, would identify the tasks and roles associated with a job. Rules surrounding the method were few but one of interest is the imperative to exclude teachers from the job analysis process (since, if they were to be involved, the occupational purity of the work description could well be sullied). A list of tasks and roles would be agreed among the expert workers and these would become the blueprint for training. This process was called DACUM (from "design – or develop – a curriculum"), and the educational model incorporating its outcomes was referred to as "competency-based education". A benefit of the DACUM process was that it was relatively rapid and inexpensive (compared with the instructional systems design approach), and it has evolved to become a mainstream approach to competency setting, informing, among other systems, the practice of Australian competency-based training (Department of Education, Science and Training 2007).

A division of labour between the work of specifying competencies and developing learner competency was institutionalised in Australian vocational education reform, too. In this case, bureaucrats, employer representatives and unions would oversee specification of the competencies, expressed using some of the ideas of behavioural objectives theory and drawing on the expertise of expert workers as per the evolving DACUM method (Norton 2004). In some cases this process would take a surprising turn toward consultants and futurists with a view to reforming whole occupations (a disciplinary interest witnessed in the performance-based teacher education movement in the United States). This turn was observed in the case of supervisors and frontline managers whose existing occupational practice was argued to be one of the factors contributing to the poor performance of Australian industry (Karpin 1995). The early Certificate IV in Frontline Management was in part created to reflect real industry behaviour but also to instil new practices (Ellerington 1998). The Certificate IV in Assessment and Workplace Training was another example. This qualification also mixed the real and ideal: in this instance, the ideal being that of educators whose role is narrowed to faithful implementation of competency-based training, with assessment taking priority over teaching, and the workplace rather than the college proclaimed the legitimate site of learning (Down, De Luca and Galloway 2010).

The competency-based training model could be educationally robust if the progressive potential of the model were to be unleashed. Research by Roger Harris and colleagues in the early 1980s that involved trialling competency-based training in panel-beating apprenticeship training at Croydon Park TAFE in South Australia offers a glimpse of what was possible (Harris et al. 1985). Units of competency were drawn up by the TAFE teachers in consultation with the employers of their trades' students, but also reflecting on their own sense of how the trade ought to be practised. These competencies were very specific and embedded ideal standards of the occupation (as opposed to the compromised practices the teachers knew of in some panel-beating workshops). At considerable expense, interactive learning resources (video demonstrations, mock-up exercises, workbooks) were developed that allowed students to study the unit(s) of competency that were most useful to pursue at a given time for the employer. The TAFE teachers, who were instrumental in developing the resources as well as standards, subsequently served as "facilitators" of learning rather than fulfilling a more traditional didactic role. They were on hand to guide individual students as they engaged with the learning resources. A given cohort of students would be studying different units of competency in the same workshops. The traditional lock-step approach (all students study the same thing at the same time) gave way to a self-paced mode. The facilitators would assess students' work when the latter were ready. Some students might complete their studies in less time; some would require more.

But the introduction of market principles with competency-based training set up a tension that significantly affected the day-to-day practice of the model. As cited above, one of the advantages of a competency-based system was that it facilitated a new way of allocating public funds to training – by paying providers for delivering training and passing students in individual competencies – that would allow private and public providers to occupy the same market, setting the stage for the expected benefits of a market (competition, innovation, lower prices, higher quality). At the same time, as just explained, an outcomes-focused system like competency-based training problematises traditional time-served approaches to learning, or the idea that people need a fixed period of time to learn. Terms and semesters, or practices like the three-year apprenticeship, came under question. A progressivist take on competency-based training dictates that what counts is not time in learning but rather demonstration of outcomes. Indeed, implementations like the trials by Harris and colleagues (1985) saw high-quality learning resources developed, facilitators deployed, and as much time devoted as a given learner needed to master a task or role as specified in a competency. This practice would lead to variable program length. Competitive pressures in the new system worked in a number of ways, including testing the time limits of learning. The question of the time it takes to learn came up against the business principle of "time is money". Some of the new market entrants acted exactly as the created market allowed. In some cases, innovation involved cutting back on the time required to learn to lower costs, with educators employed who were not equipped or paid to develop quality resources, nor authorised to challenge reductions in the amount of time allowed for learners to become competent. The problem came to a head in 2016 when the national vocational education and training (VET) regulator had to step in to curb the behaviour of providers offering excessively short courses (Australian Skills Quality Authority 2017).

At one level, what can be observed in this shift is a conflation of competencies and curriculum. Earlier versions of competency-based training, going back to the behavioural objectives movement, viewed statements of outcomes (competencies) as just one part of a quality educational system. "Curriculum" was where the bulk of the work of educators, resource developers and students themselves took place, with a view to developing learners to the point where they could confidently demonstrate competency once learning was complete. A relatively early textbook – written by Harris and colleagues in 1995 to inform and guide implementation of the new approach to vocational education and training in Australia – maintained a firm distinction between competency standards and curriculum, and advanced the idea that the former need to be actively "translated" into the latter. At the time of writing, these authors discerned an emerging problem: "One of the important but often not well-understood principles behind the translation of the development standards [e.g., processes like DACUM] and their translation into learning programs [curriculum] is that standards, themselves, are *not* curricular documents" (Harris et al. 1995, 131; italics in original). They go on to explain: "Curriculum development must, therefore, be concerned with *getting at and challenging* the underlying meaning of competency standards and organising learning experiences and activities in such a way as to develop and attribute competency as efficiently as possible" (Harris et al. 1995, 131; italics added). Unfortunately, market pressures conspired to undermine a focus on curriculum, with the new model of the vocational educator ill equipped to "get at" let alone "challenge" the underlying meaning of competencies. Rather, the problem called out by Harris and colleagues persisted and worsened, with the tendency to base teaching on units of competency rather than curriculum encouraged by funding mechanisms that paid per taught and passed unit, and regulatory practices that supposedly made quality curriculum development difficult because the latter relies on "clustering" units, whereas auditors from the national regulator had been reported to focus attention on the integrity of assessment and resources on individual units (Hodge 2014).

Researchers and other commentators have drawn attention to what might be termed a curriculum crisis in Australian vocational education. In a series of studies, Wheelahan (2019) detailed the fragmenting effect on learning of the conflation of competency standards and curriculum. Citing the knowledge requirements of selected occupations – such as community service work and electrical trades – when the competencies become the basis of curriculum, knowledge structures that apply over multiple tasks or roles may be simplified, or presented in a partial way, or lost altogether from the learning experiences of students. For instance, the mathematical knowledge necessary for some electrical work is internally organised in a way that units of competency cannot map – given that the latter describe the observable tasks and roles taken to constitute an occupation. A related critical analysis was offered by Robertson (2008) who compared the content of the units of competency making up the base qualification for vocational teachers and assessors. Benchmarking these competencies against international research on teachers' work, Robertson found that a much-reduced understanding of teaching was reflected in the units. Considering Wheelahan's and Robertson's analyses, it is imperative that the call from Harris and colleagues (1995) for educators and providers to get at and challenge competency standards was heeded. Robust curriculum making is the only way that the inherent limitations of units of competency could be overcome, shifting the focus of learning to those occupationally appropriate bodies of knowledge and skills. But as Wheelahan (2019), Harris and Hodge (2009), and Hodge (2014) found, there is a persistent tendency to centre courses and learning resources on units of competency. Certainly, some training providers do make the effort to generate rich curriculum, often involving clustering units, but funding and regulatory mechanisms tend to make this an optional measure.

Teaching in Australian competency-based vocational education

Neoliberal training reforms introduced competency-based training as a new curriculum model. At the same time, the teachers and trainers who do the work of the system day-to-day were repositioned as competency delivery and assessment workers. They were moved to the periphery of educational innovation, from a role with professional responsibilities to something more akin to service delivery. This shift has a few elements. At one level, the moral authority to reconceptualise the practice of vocational educators descended from neoliberal doctrine. As indicated earlier, theories like public choice theory were intended, among other things, to dispel the notion that public servants can be trusted to act in the public interest. Educators in public systems were tarred with the same brush. Informed by this ideology, policymakers were emboldened to reallocate educational labour in the vocational education sector to compel educators to do the bidding of those whose interests the system was now supposed to serve: the employers. Educators were negatively framed in other settings influenced by neoliberal thought. For instance, under the Thatcher government in the United Kingdom, teacher control of curriculum was first questioned then removed altogether (Timmins 1996). A public administration reformer at the time complained:

> There is little room for interference of the leadership with the work of the professionals [in this case, teachers], nor is work-related interaction among the professionals common; they operate autonomously and resist rationalisation of their skills. Consequently it is hard for educational administrators to control the work of the professionals even when cases of dysfunction are clear. Professionals oppose strict planning and external evaluation of their work (Scheerens 1992, 22).

It should be noted that any explicit negative messaging of public choice theory and public management theory was avoided in the context of Australian vocational education reform, although in numerous, indirect ways vocational educators were linked with the purported failure of the TAFE sector. Materials designed to induct educators into their new function in the system would often contrast the Kangan era and later reform visions of vocational education. For example, a manual prepared to develop a vanguard of practitioners exaggerated the contrasts as shown in Table 13.1.

As can be seen in Table 13.1, a number of disadvantages were attributed to the previous approach, and teachers and their institutions were positioned as contributing to the problem. But there was never

Table 13.1 Contrasting pre-reform and reform approaches to curriculum. Source: Department of Employment, Education and Training 1992, Unit 1.1–24.

Old	New
1. Different credentials for different states	Single nationally recognised credential
2. Credential = successful completion of course	Credential = specific competencies
3. Accreditation processes vary with states	Accreditation recognised nationally
4. Curriculum based on time served	Curriculum based on competencies derived from industry
5. Courses and outcomes influenced by teachers	Courses and outcomes consistent with required competency
6. TAFE only recognised providers with status	More providers registered and monitored
7. Recognition of prior learning (RPL) processes *ad hoc*	RPL processes formalised
8. Credit transfer *ad hoc*	Credit processes structured
9. Assessment processes variable	Assessment related to competencies

a rigorous test of these insinuations. It was not that problems of the system stimulated reforms but rather, from a neoliberal perspective, the absence of markets is undesirable in principle, which may explain why there is a dearth of clear-cut examples of failure of the existing vocational education system to illustrate the arguments of competency-based training advocates.

The Australian version of competency-based training is set up in a way that significantly curtails the professionalism of educators. This erosion occurs in three main ways. First, the occupational expertise brought by educators to their work is in tension with the system of competencies on which learning is based. Second, the press to reduce training time and get students passed produces ethical dilemmas that bedevil the work. Third, policymakers have determined that the credential required to deliver learning in the vocational education and training system is at a significantly lower level than what is accepted in the schooling sector, a move that has had a pernicious effect on the ability of educators to identify and help rectify the problems created by reform.

The competency standards upon which all learning in vocational and educational training is based constitute a kind of lowest common denominator for expressing learning outcomes, a form that can in principle be read and understood by employers, students and educators alike. But when occupational experts are compelled to use them for educational purposes a special problem emerges. That vocational educators need to bring a high level of vocational skills to their work is an expectation enforced to this day (Australian Government 2015). Occupational experts have a more sophisticated understanding of the work in question than is reflected in the competency standards. Further, once in educational roles, these experts articulate their understanding in ways that are more nuanced than dictated by the standards. The tension was most visible during the introduction of competency-based training. A poignant example is that of the chef who was a master at creating bechamel sauce (Robinson 1993a). When this teacher was required to structure student learning in terms of relevant competency standards, they found that the techniques, sensitivities and attitudes essential to bechamel sauce-making could not be foregrounded, but rather the work of making the sauce was considered as a task and broken into elements and performance criteria that bore little resemblance to the way the work was understood by the expert. Reflecting on the experiences of participants in her study, Robinson wrote:

> All the teachers in the study were experienced and were considered by their supervisors to be capable and professional. It would be expected that they would have highly developed tacit judgement about the competence of students and that they would feel comfortable in the exercise of that judgement. The observation of the researcher however was that the introduction

> of competency-based training has resulted in considerable anxiety on the part of the teachers regarding the exercise of tacit judgement (1993b, 24).

The case of the chef and the other educators studied by Robinson is typical of the experience of countless vocational educators, who have had to downplay their occupational expertise to suit the demands of competency-based training.

The tension between occupational expertise and the representation of occupations in units of competency was explored further in research by Hodge (2014). In this study, vocational educators were questioned about their reading, interpretation and implementation of units of competency for curriculum making, teaching and assessment. The majority of the 30 study participants described a range of challenges associated with using the competencies. Criticisms were expressed regarding the language of the units, with terms like "fuzzy" and "vague" frequently used. Educators were not always clear about the significance of the different parts of competency documents and how they were supposed to be reassembled for learning, with the result that in many cases educators would be selective about what parts of competencies they drew on for teaching. In a few cases, educators disclosed that they introduced material that they felt was missing from competencies, although this was an isolated practice undertaken by individual educators who were motivated by concern for the integrity of their students' grasp of the trade. By this time, the call of Harris and colleagues (1995) to get at and challenge units of competency was all but silenced, with any such robust curriculum practice undertaken furtively. The competency-based training model has continued to alienate vocational educators. A participant in Hodge's (2014) research said the units of competency were written for "insiders", but she was not referring to herself or other vocational educators:

> By the insiders, I don't mean teachers, I mean they're policy people. I think they seem to be political documents, written to satisfy too many masters. They don't seem to me to be written with the student or the teacher in mind. Because I, as a conscientious and intelligent person, should be able to read

> through one and have it make sense. Perhaps not immediately, but on the second reading, go, "Yeah, I get where this is going, I see what I need to do, what I need". They're written for auditing requirements I think (2014, 19).

The despair evident in the words of this educator illustrates the difficult position in which neoliberal competency-based training leaves occupational experts.

The pedagogies employed by vocational educators – how they teach – were also affected by the introduction of competency-based training. It was mentioned earlier that this approach to education could be promoted as innovative, embodying progressivist, student-centred practices as demonstrated in the Croydon Park competency-based training trials by Harris and colleagues (1985). In a later study, Harris and Hodge (2009) interviewed a handful of surviving teachers who had been involved in the trials and visited a private college specialising in automotive trades to compare contemporary competency-based training with that which was practised during the trials. By this time, competency-based training was again employing the old lock-step method, since the resources required for student- and employer-initiated study plans were too expensive to develop and maintain, and the business model demanded students in a given cohort start and finish at the same time. The surviving teachers – who had witnessed the sector-wide introduction of competency-based training – were scathing in their evaluation of the new practice for its loose standards and reversion to traditional didactic techniques. Interestingly, these teachers habitually referred to the competency-based training of the early 1980s trial as "self-paced" rather than competency-based learning. The competency standards had been a component in a sophisticated curricular practice that provided nuanced support for the learning journey.

Assessment issues have emerged over time. Assessment is the linchpin in a competency-based system, because the outcomes rather than the process of learning are stressed and assessment therefore becomes a more critical concern than one might find in a traditional setting (Harris et al. 1995; Smith and Keating 2003). While the neglect of curriculum and simplification of pedagogy might be comprehensible in a competency-based system, one might suppose assessment would be a different matter given the availability of agreed, clearly expressed statements of learning outcomes and the conspicuous place assessment practice holds in the Certificate IV teaching qualification. Two problems can be identified in this connection. One is made visible in the light of the behavioural philosophy underlying competency-based training. Behaviours or performances are observable, and, according to behavioural objectives theory, are that on which assessors should base judgements of competence. But occupational experts who assess occupational performances are attuned to something more holistic, for a given expression of competence is only a surface phenomenon. Yes, performances are observable and, in a sense, "objective" but they are never a sufficient basis for a confident appraisal of underlying competence. Teachers, who are generally also the assessors in Australian vocational education, are aware of the tension between expressed and unexpressed competence. Observing multiple demonstrations of competent performance, and those observations undertaken by multiple assessors, are the ways to arrive at more confident judgements of competency. But market forces intervene here, too, to make an optimal assessment practice difficult to attain in practice. It is uneconomical to employ multiple assessors, and mandating multiple demonstrations of competence is costly, too, for both training providers and in terms of time commitments by students and employers (as the case may be). A more troubling influence of the market can also be felt in assessment practice when providers place pressure on employee-assessors to pass students even when doubts exist as to the competence of the candidate (Nakar, Bagnall and Hodge 2018). This pressure derives from the funding mechanism that generally relies on the formal granting of competency to trigger payment to providers. Research has reported ethical dilemmas exercising vocational educators who feel students should not be passed but provider management, who hold the educators in thrall through precarious working arrangements, demand judgements of competency.

While these impacts on the practice of vocational educators can be viewed as outcomes of encroachments by a curriculum model riven by market forces, reform of educator preparation has undermined professionalism and the skill base as such, ultimately reducing the scope for educators to identify, call out and resist quality problems produced by competency-based training. Teacher preparation has already been touched on in this chapter. To review, it was mentioned that a new qualification, the Certificate IV in Assessment and Workplace Training, was devised to equip teachers to operate in the reconstructed sector. But it was a qualification that did not follow the path dictated by a DACUM-style occupational analysis. Rather, like the qualifications for supervisors and managers stemming from the "frontline management initiative" (Ellerington 1998), the qualification had the effect of disciplining and reforming the teaching occupation. The moral authority to do so has been noted. It was also pointed out that analysis of the content of the vocational educator qualification against international research into the bases of educator expertise reveals that only a limited selection of knowledge and skills has been retained (Robertson 2008). An important feature of the design of the credential that is consistent with Robertson's analysis is its level on the Australian Qualifications Framework (Australian Qualifications Framework Council 2013). Whereas schoolteachers are required to hold at least a bachelor's degree – a Level 7 qualification – vocational educators only require one at Level 4. To put that in perspective, an apprentice graduates with a Level 3 qualification. In the most recent version of the Australian Qualifications Framework, the "Application of skills and knowledge" for a Level 4 qualification states: "Graduates at this level will apply knowledge and skills to demonstrate autonomy, judgement and limited responsibility in known or changing contexts and within established parameters" (Australian Qualifications Framework Council 2013, 12).

In contrast, Level 7 graduates (such as schoolteachers), "will apply knowledge and skills to demonstrate autonomy, well developed judgement and responsibility: in contexts that require self-directed work and learning; within broad parameters to provide specialist advice and functions" (Australian Qualifications Framework Council 2013, 13).

The limited knowledge and skill base of the initial teacher qualification for vocational educators have prompted significant criticism from researchers (for example, Clayton 2009; Down, De Luca and Galloway 2010; Allen 2011; Harris 2019; Francisco 2020). At the very best, if well delivered, the Certificate IV can serve as an entry-level credential that should be built upon through continuing professional development (Productivity Commission 2011). Despite multiple reviews of the basis of vocational educator preparation, there has been no shift from the original position. Indeed, there have been recent calls to further dilute the initial preparation requirements (Department of Education, Skills and Employment 2021). To the credit of the profession, many vocational educators opt to build on the Level 4 qualification either through study at higher Australian Qualification Framework levels or via professional development opportunities, including structured capability development often seen in public providers.

Conclusion

At the start of the chapter something of the complexity of vocational education was indicated: it has individual and community development dimensions, it demands a sophisticated educational practice and, considered historically, is increasingly an object of social and economic policy. Neoliberal economic theory has been the source of direction for training reform since the late 1980s with that orthodoxy being still very much in place. The analyses and arguments presented above were intended to illustrate the ways the effectiveness and quality of vocational education in Australia have been undermined by these reforms. Two main aspects of this type of education were foregrounded: curriculum and teaching. These are inextricably linked – curriculum is intended for enactment, and teaching is always an enactment of curriculum – but are analytically separated in educational theory. On the side of curriculum, training reform in Australia is striking for its adoption of a single sector-wide curriculum model, so-called competency-based training. Paradoxically, the model is seen as an alternative to curriculum although it is clearly concerned with specifying what a learner in the system should learn (the very essence of curriculum). In a further twist, when market forces interact with competency-based training, the full system of curriculum – that is, the unity of statements of outcomes with the staged learning resources that lead to them – is broken apart. The outcomes are prioritised, expressed in units of competency that have become the basis of funding, while it is left to training providers and teachers to take care of the rest. But market pressures, activated through reform, intervene to compromise curriculum quality.

On the side of teaching, neoliberal reform carries a moral message. Educators were, at least indirectly, identified as contributing to an inefficient system that served their interests at the expense of those the system should serve. But as explained, the reformed educator role creates a series of problems for the system. Employing occupational experts as vocational educators is a widely condoned practice that is enshrined in legislation for the Australian system. Yet these same specialists are expected to focus their efforts on delivering units of competency that are simplified and partial representations of an occupation. Considering that curriculum compromise or neglect (or both) is an endemic temptation for providers in a competitive market, vocational teachers may not be empowered to develop robust curriculum to make up for what is glossed over in units of competency. While these challenges to teaching practice can be regarded as deriving from neoliberal competency-based training implementation, the entry-level qualification for teachers, trainers and assessors, currently the Certificate IV in Training and Assessment, fosters development of a relatively narrow set of skills. Vocational educators are thus caught in a situation where the competency-based training system creates a set of obstacles to quality professional practice, while their base of professional knowledge and skills may be inadequate to equip them to identify and help overcome problems springing from market-based competency-based training. The neoliberal reconstruction of Australian vocational curriculum and teaching, briefly described in this chapter, has arguably created a densely woven tangle of quality problems that may be, at least under the prevailing neoliberal regime, beyond resolution.

References

Allen, R. (2011). *National Strategic Industry Audit TAA40104 Certificate IV in Training and Assessment: 2011 Stage 2 Report*. Canberra: TVET Australia/ National Quality Council.

Australian Committee on Technical and Further Education (1974). *TAFE in Australia: Report on needs in technical and further education*. Canberra: Australian Government Publishing Service. [Kangan report]

Australian Government (2015). *Standards for Registered Training Organisations (RTOs) 2015*. Federal Register of Legislation. https://www.legislation.gov.au/Details/F2019C00503.

Australian Qualifications Framework Council (2013). *Australian Qualifications Framework, Second Edition*. Canberra: Australian Qualifications Framework Council.

Australian Skills Quality Authority (2017). *A Review of Issues Relating to unduly Short Training*. Brisbane: Australian Skills Quality Authority.

Buchanan, J.M. (1984). Politics with romance: a sketch of positive public choice theory and its normative implications. In J.M. Buchanan and R.D. Tollison, eds. *The Theory of Public Choice II*, 11–22. Ann Arbor, MI: University of Michigan Press.

Cahill, D., and P. Toner (2018). Introduction: situating economic reform. In D. Cahill and P. Toner, eds. *Wrong Way: How Privatisation & Economic Reform Backfired*, 1–18. Melbourne: La Trobe University Press and Black Inc.

Clayton, B. (2009). *Practitioner Experiences and Expectations with the Certificate IV in Training and Assessment (TAA40104): A Discussion of the Issues*. Adelaide: National Centre for Vocational Education Research.

Dawkins, J., and A. Holding (1987). *Skills for Australia*. Canberra: Australian Government Publishing Service.

Department of Education, Science and Training (2007). *Training Package Development Handbook*. Canberra: Commonwealth of Australia.

Department of Education, Skills and Employment (2021). *VET Workforce Quality Consultation Feedback*. https://tinyurl.com/2v5kf8x4.

Department of Employment, Education and Training (1992). *Implementing Competency-Based Training*. Adelaide: National Centre for Vocational Education Research.

Down, C., W. De Luca and P. Galloway (2010). The Certificate IV in TAA: how is it valued by early career VET practitioners. *VET Research: Leading and Responding in Turbulent Times, AVETRA 2010, 13th Annual Conference*.

Ellerington, K. (1998). The frontline management initiative. In F. Ferrier and D. Anderson, eds. *Different Drums One Beat?* 177–81. Adelaide: National Centre for Vocational Education Research.

Francisco, S. (2020). What novice vocational education and training teachers learn in the teaching workplace. *International Journal of Training Research* 18(1): 37–54.

Goozee, G. (2001). *The Development of TAFE in Australia*. Adelaide: National Centre for Vocational Education Research.

Harris, R. (2019). Reflections on VET teacher education in Australia, against the backdrop of VET teacher education in Germany. In M. Pilz, K. Breuing and S. Schumann, eds. *Berufsbildung zwischen Tradition und Moderne*, 347–63. Wiesbaden, Germany: Springer.

Harris, R., G. Barnes, B. Haines and R.B. Hobart (1985). *CBVE or Not To Be? The Design, Implementation and Evaluation of a Competency Based Vocational Education Program in Panel Beating at Croydon Park College of TAFE.* Adelaide: TAFE National Centre for Research and Development.

Harris, R., H. Guthrie, R.B. Hobart and D. Lundberg (1995). *Competency-based Education and Training: Between a Rock and a Whirlpool.* Melbourne: Macmillan Education Australia.

Harris, R., and S. Hodge (2009). A quarter of a century of CBT: the vicissitudes of an idea. *International Journal of Training Research* 7(2): 122–33.

Hodge, S. (2014). *Interpreting Competencies in Australian Vocational Education and Training: Practices and Issues.* Adelaide: National Centre for Vocational Education Research.

Hyland, T. (1993). Competence, knowledge and education. *Journal of Philosophy of Education* 27(1): 57–68.

Joyner, C. (1995). The DACUM technique and competency-based education. In J. Dennison, ed. *Challenge and Opportunity: Canada's Community Colleges at the Crossroads.* Vancouver, Canada: University of British Columbia Press.

Karpin, D. (1995). *Enterprising Nation.* 2 vols. Canberra: Australian Government Printing Service.

Marginson, S. (1989). *Human Capital Theory and Education Policy.* Discussion Paper No. 3, November. Sydney: University of New South Wales.

Nakar, S., R.G. Bagnall and S. Hodge (2018). A reflective account of the VET FEE-HELP initiative as a driver of ethical dilemmas for vocational education teachers in Australia. *Australian Educational Researcher* 45(3): 383–400.

Norton, R.E. (2004). The DACUM curriculum development process. *International Vocational Education NS Training Association 14th IIVETA International TVET Conference.*

Norton, R.E., L.G. Harrington and J. Gill (1978). *Performance-based Teacher Education: The State of the Art.* Athens, GA: American Association for Vocational Instructional Materials.

Productivity Commission (2011). *Vocational Education and Training Workforce. Productivity Commission Research Report.* Canberra: Commonwealth of Australia.

Reiser, R.A. (2001). A history of instructional design and technology: Part II: A history of instructional design. *Educational Technology Research and Development* 49(2): 57–67.

Robertson, I. (2008). VET teachers' knowledge and expertise. *International Journal of Training Research* 6(1): 1–22.

Robinson, P. (1993a). The strange case of the béchamel sauce. *Proceedings of the 1st International Conference on Post-compulsory Education and Training, Griffith University.*

Robinson, P. (1993b). *Teachers Facing Change: A Small-scale Study of Teachers Working with Competency-based Training.* Adelaide: National Centre for Vocational Education Research.

Scheerens, J. (1992). *Effective Schooling: Research, Theory and Practice.* London: Cassell.

Smith, A. (1981 [1776]). *An Inquiry into the Nature and Causes of the Wealth of Nations.* Vol. I. Indianapolis, IN: Liberty Classics.

Smith, E., and J. Keating (2003). *From Training Reform to Training Packages.* Melbourne: Cengage Learning.

Smith, P., and T. Ragan (2005). *Instructional Design*, 3rd edn. Hoboken, NJ: John Wiley & Sons.

Timmins, N. (1996). *The Five Giants: A Biography of the Welfare State.* London: Fontana Press.

Toner, P. (2018). A tale of mandarins and lemons: creating the market for vocational education and training. In D. Cahill and P. Toner, eds. *Wrong Way: How Privatisation & Economic Reform Backfired*, 58–83. Melbourne: La Trobe University Press and Black Inc.

Tuxworth, E. (1989). Competence based education and training: background and origins. In J. W. Burke, ed. *Competency Based Education and Training.* Abingdon: Routledge Falmer.

Werner, J., and R. DeSimone (2011). *Human Resource Development*, 4th edn. Melbourne: Cengage Learning

Wheelahan, L. (2019). Knowledge, competence, and vocational education. In D. Guile and L. Unwin, eds. *The Wiley Handbook of Vocational Education and Training*, 97–112. Hoboken, NJ: Wiley.

Yelon, S.L. (1991). Writing and using instructional objectives. In L.J. Briggs, K.L. Gustafso and M.H. Tillman, eds. *Instructional Design. Principles and Applications*, 2nd edn, 75–121. Englewood Cliff, NJ: Educational Technology Publications, Inc.

Zoellner, D. (2017). *Vocational Education and Training: The Northern Territory's History of Public Philanthropy.* Canberra: Australian National University Press.

14

The extraordinary case of Transurban, the Australian toll roads company

Phillip O'Neill

The delivery and operation of public infrastructure in cities around the world has changed profoundly since the late 1970s. Modes of ownership and management of utilities and their regulatory settings have been reformed with the twin goals of enhancing the quality of infrastructure services and shoring up public infrastructure budgets. But success has been limited. One issue is the difficulty in aligning urban infrastructure as a public good with infrastructure assets as quality investment products. In other words, the shift to the private ownership and operation of infrastructure (privatisation) and the elevation of the pursuit of financial returns over other outcomes (financialisation) have not proven to be successful public policy initiatives. By the 2020s, it is not possible to nominate a template or model or pathway for urban infrastructure provisioning, be it in public or private hands, that might be transferred from city to city as a way forward. Rather, public policy settings for urban infrastructure provision seem everywhere to be in crisis, in richer and poorer nations alike. The problem of maintaining or replacing older assets persists from one municipality to another. Management behaviours that tackle operational inefficiencies and supply inequities are difficult to find. User pricing schemes seem successful only in a limited number of cases. Ways to embed environmental sustainability and climate resilience into new-build infrastructure are elusive.

This chapter interrogates the unusual case of the Australian toll roads operator, Transurban Ltd, for ideas about the ownership, financing and management of urban infrastructure that might tackle this urban infrastructure problem. Transurban is arguably the world's most efficient toll road operator, yet it is a most peculiar thing. It is the monopoly controller of toll roads, bridges and tunnels in Australia's east-coast cities. Its corporate structure is unusual and innovative. It carries high debt ratios on a balance sheet absent of tangible assets. It is a for-profit entity dealing almost exclusively in the supply of public goods, dependent almost exclusively on government contracts and regulated road use. Yet Transurban has grown to become a common presence among the top dozen Australian-listed companies, just outside the nation's mining and banking oligopolies, and has recently become the target of global private-wealth investors. Transurban's credit ratings are consistently of medium to high–medium investment grade with an ownership register dominated by long-term investors, like pension funds, attracted by stable returns. What can we learn about infrastructure financing and delivery from this corporate success story? Can strategies be copied and behaviours transferred to other settings? Of course, such questions are confronting to many from the political left, especially those yearning for that golden age of public ownership and control of infrastructure, back in the day. Yet identifying that time when infrastructure delivery under public ownership and operation was successful, fair and sustainable is not easy. Rather, should we be open to modes of financing and management that deliver on our urban infrastructure aspirations, even if the consequence is a creation of a hybrid format of private and public sector roles and responsibilities?

Six sections follow this introduction. The next section outlines a method for exploring the questions raised above. Then follow sections on Transurban in general, on the company's organisational and financial structures, and on the regulatory environment it confronts. The final section discusses the consequences and implications of these characteristics for urban transformation, and makes some conclusions.

A framework for analysing the private financing of urban infrastructure

A major challenge for contemporary political economy is the formulation of progressive public policy that intersects in constructive ways with prevailing financial, organisational and regulatory structures. Such intersection means that public policy solutions can be enacted in a timely manner, in the places where intervention is required. Dealing with the world in hand is surely more productive than futile calls for resurrection of the circumstances of past periods or invocations of imagined worlds that are never attainable. In which case, what are the lessons of the here and now – the logics and practices of actual investment in toll roads, in devising a progressive agenda capable of delivering just, sustainable urban transport? Elsewhere (O'Neill 2019) I propose a threefold framework for guiding such analysis using the categories of organisation, capital, and regulation (Table 14.1).

The framework recognises that the privatisation of infrastructure and its financialisation are inextricably linked. Selling a public utility involves formally reassigning its assets, including intangibles, as private property. This enables them to be quantified and valued on a commercial balance sheet, meaning they become capital, available to be deployed into commercial production, be the subject of legal exchange and be offered as surety in raising credit. These are significant roles, and their performance depends on three dimensions (as shown in Table 14.1): the entity's organisational structure; its financial or capital structure; and the regulatory environment in which it operates. Organisational structure is the format of ownership and management within which, in this case, infrastructure assets are possessed and operated. Capital structure is the mix of fractions of capital, chiefly identifiable as equity – or debt-based claimants over assets and revenues. Regulatory structure is the set of rules, decisions and practices that circumscribe how infrastructure services are delivered.

In the next section I commence the application of this framework to the analysis of Transurban. Data cited come largely from Transurban's publicly released reports and investor briefings. Additional data and information come from media reports and analyst briefings. Further

Table 14.1 The dimensions of infrastructure financialisation. Source: derived from O'Neill (2019).

Dimension	Role
1. Organisational structure	• To enhance market power • To secure returns to investors over very long time periods • To consolidate supply of advanced producer services
2. Capital structure	• To control the asset • To satisfy credit needs • To control revenue streams • To satisfy yield expectations
3. Regulatory environment	• To generate and legitimate a regulatory setting for operation in complex urban situations • To script long-term capital–state relations

insights come from interviews conducted in an Australian Research Council project related to infrastructure privatisation and investment.

The case of Transurban

Transurban – a term referring to the entire group – was formed in 1995 as a special-purpose vehicle to construct and operate the CityLink toll road in Melbourne. A special-purpose vehicle is an entity created for the purpose of isolating a commercial asset from its parent body. This enables ring fencing of unusual financial risk and the separate treatment of returns that don't sit readily within a firm's ongoing financial management and accounting practices (see Sainati et al. 2020). Transurban listed on the Australian stock exchange in 1996 using the controversial stapled security structure as its base investment instrument. Its primary financial adviser was investment banker Macquarie Group, a pioneer in the conversion of public utilities into private investment assets. Important too in the Australian scene was the growth of retirement savings in Australian superannuation funds, creating an appetite for long-term, steady-yield assets (Clark and O'Neill 2023). In 2020, Transurban operated 20 toll roads across Australia and North America, with road users growing from an average of 200,000 users per day in FY2000 to 2.2 million in FY2019 (Transurban 2020, 5).

For Transurban, growth and monopolisation proceed hand in hand, based on rolling renewals of government concessions to operate toll roads. Heavy levels of debt drive Transurban's pursuit of concession extensions, its acquisition of concessions from failed ventures, and its new concessions, including via unsolicited proposals to governments. Transurban's operations, therefore, necessarily involve close partnership with government. Transurban's organisational structure and its financial structure are designed for winning and managing concessions, and for alignment – a contested one it should be said – with the distinctive regulatory environment that each concession generates.

Transurban's toll road assets in Sydney, Melbourne and Brisbane are shown in Figure 14.1. The maps reveal the steps that drive Transurban's growth and monopolisation strategies: maximising control over the tolled roads presently operating, securing rights to extend existing roads on this network and positioning to take control of the toll roads of the future. Holding its monopoly position and maintaining barriers to the entry of competitors into the future are core concerns of Transurban. They require a lot of attention. Monopolisation of toll road concessions needs a corporate structure capable of robust transactional and regulatory outcomes through time. Second, there is the need for a capital structure capable of maintaining investor confidence despite high debt and a revenue base dependent on a sheaf of time-limited concession contracts. And, third, there is the need for positive relations with governments and a toll-paying public across state and national jurisdictions (see also Searle and Legacy 2020). I now explore these issues.

Transurban's organisational structure

In comparison with other listed corporations, Transurban has a peculiar asset and earnings profile. First, as a utility operator, Transurban makes large up-front investments, meaning there are substantial delays to the time when distributions can be made genuinely from earnings, however long and stable the concession profile might be. Second, Transurban's asset register is dominated by

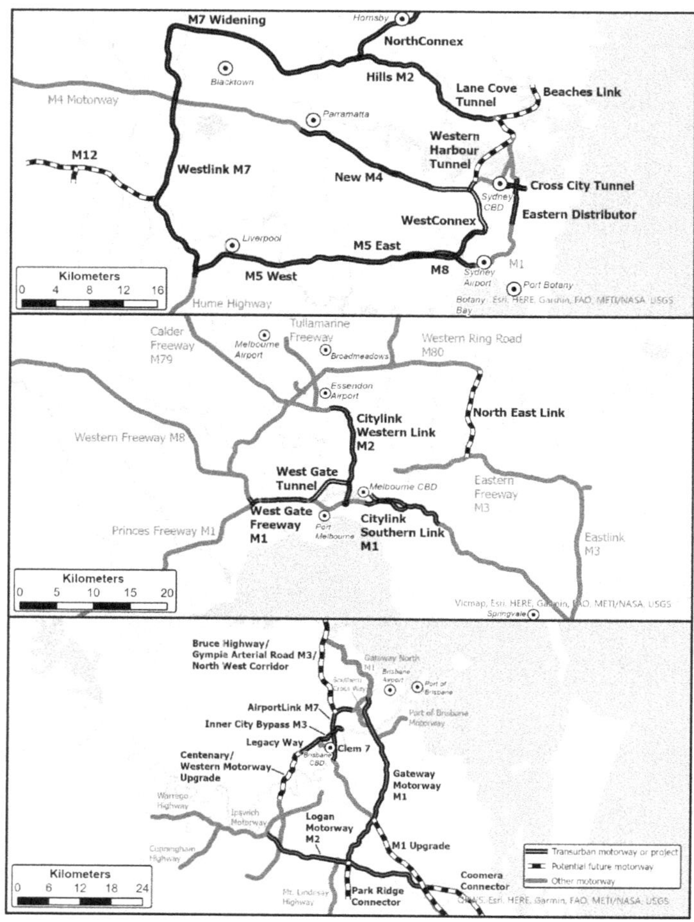

Figure 14.1 Transurban toll roads in Sydney, Melbourne and Brisbane, 2020. Source: Compiled from Transurban 2020, 13–15.

intangibles: the thick sets of contractual relations, rights and obligations contained in the concessions awarded to Transurban by governments. This complexity makes it difficult for individual toll road assets to be sold or transferred. So, toll road concessions are relatively illiquid. Third, and as a consequence of these asset characteristics, Transurban is attractive to long-term investors such as superannuation (or pension) funds and private wealth funds. These entities have an appetite for low-risk, guaranteed returns, which align with the divesting obligations of funds well into the future.

A toll road company needs an organisational structure that addresses these concerns. At stake is control over the assets by core (equity) investors, and assurance of the asset's monopoly position. The capacity of Transurban to grow while holding seemingly elevated levels of debt depends on this control and market position, as we see below. Not surprisingly, then, Transurban adopted a novel organisational structure in anticipation.

The Transurban organisational structure is designed to maximise asset control, earnings longevity, market domination and growth opportunities. It pursues these objectives with a threefold assembly: via a domestic corporation, a trust and an offshore entity (Figure 14.2). When an investor buys a basic unit, or share, in Transurban, a stapled security is issued, indicating ownership of one share in the Transurban corporation registered in Australia, one security in the Transurban Holding Trust, and one share in Transurban International. Transurban International was registered in the Bahamas in 2006 and shifted its domicile to Australia in 2012 (Transurban 2006, 2012). These ownership segments are inseparable, or stapled, a device that is uncommon outside Australia (see Davis 2017).

Crucial to the structure is the Transurban Holding Trust. A trust structure has become common in privatised infrastructure operations in Australia. The trust is a vehicle enshrined in common law to protect the rights of designated beneficiaries over assets and earnings for long periods of time, typically with suspended tax treatment. The Transurban trust and its subsidiary trusts hold Transurban's assets and maintain credit facilities. Transurban Holdings Ltd, the registered corporation and its subsidiary companies, then operate and maintain the toll roads.

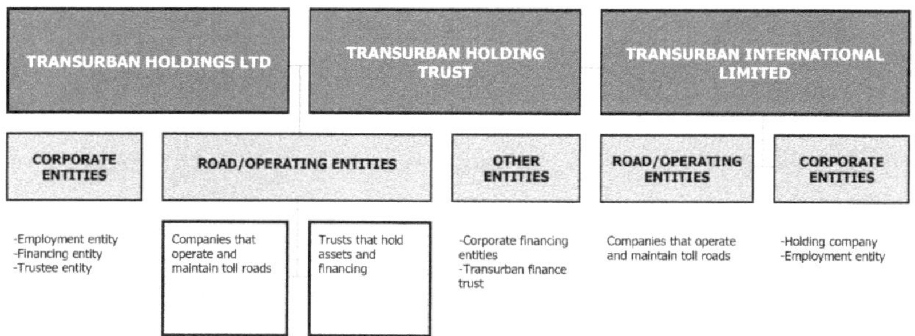

Figure 14.2 Transurban's organisational structure, 2020. Source: Compiled from Transurban 2020, 26.

Outside Australia, assets are owned and operated by Transurban International, which also maintains a separate credit profile.

A specific issue affecting Transurban's organisational structure is the nature of its assets: the toll roads. In essence, a toll road concession is the monopoly right over a fixed period to tax the passage of a vehicle along a road. Importantly, there is no residual value to Transurban, the concession holder, at the end of the contract. Of course, the concession is a legal property right held by the concession holder with clear ownership and use rights defined and protected by the state. The intangible status of the asset in accounting terms comes from it being a right to tax the use of the road rather than a right to ownership of the tangible thing, the road itself. The point of this otherwise pedantic distinction is that it defines Transurban's primary business as the acquisition and operation of exclusive rights to levy fees on public road use. Transurban's organisational structure, therefore, needs to house capacity to acquire these rights, manage them over long periods and make distributions with favourable tax treatments.

Transurban's financial structure

Not surprisingly, Transurban's organisational structure plays an enabling role in the structuring of Transurban's finances. Of primary concern for Transurban is the nature and timing of revenues. Like large real estate projects, the toll roads sector requires substantial project finance upfront in order to purchase a concession – a large cash return is a key motivation for government in privatising an asset. A financing requirement can also be enlarged if there is an obligation to construct the road. A construction obligation further delays revenue generation and would typically involve an extended concession/earnings profile.

Since the 1980s, public–private partnership (PPP) entities in Australia have used a trust structure to manage the irregular revenue patterns in toll road concessions (Transurban 2017). Rather than wait for an operating surplus, a trust structure allows distributions to security holders early on in a project life cycle from uncommitted equity funds or from credit, actions that are constrained by law in conventional corporate operations (Davis 2017). A trust structure also provides taxation benefits. A trust is a pass-through vehicle for taxation purposes, meaning tax liability falls to the end recipient of the earnings flow, with tax rates assessed on the basis of the recipient's obligations rather than the earnings level of the operating enterprise, as is customary. This tax treatment is attractive for pension funds and overseas entities (especially those registered in tax havens) for which tax rates are lower than the Australian corporate rate. This means for an Australian superannuation fund investor – with higher education industry fund UniSuper the largest security holder with 12 per cent of stock at the end of 2020 – a tax rate of 15 per cent, being the legislated rate for pension funds, rather than at a 30 per cent rate payable by listed corporations. For an overseas investor, say with a listing in a tax shelter, the stapled security structure bypasses the legislated 10 per cent withholding tax.

The capacity to detach the level and timing of distributions from the flow of corporate earnings is important in meeting the expectations of institutional investors for smooth distributions through time. This detachment also frees up Transurban in its management of earnings across the many projects and concessions under its control, with wide variations in earnings cycles. Yet the power to smooth distributions depends heavily on maintaining market power through time. Transurban's market power is cemented by the nature of its concession rights. These give Transurban highly predictable toll revenues, drawn from the lock-in of motorways in the rhythms of passenger and freight movements in large cities. This lock-in ensures Transurban's position as a monopoly supplier of a public good. Curiously, Transurban's monopoly, and its monopoly pricing power (Fourie 2006), do not flow solely from the inherent logic of public good provision whereby, in general, there is no point in having competing suppliers (Oakland 1987). Transurban's monopoly positions also depend on government actions to restrain motorists' access to viable untolled routes, and the failure of governments to provide public transport alternatives.

This means Transurban revenues depend heavily on contract negotiation with governments, rather than on the success of supplying an attractive product to a competitive market. A concession negotiation is relatively straightforward and transparent when a single-asset public–private partnership is involved. In such a case, tolls are nominated, revenue levels readily predicted and the auction value of the contract easily calculated using industry comparators. Yet, as we have seen, Transurban's credit-driven growth strategy involves multiple concessions across many cities. Revenue is not just assigned to interest cover on borrowings for an existing concession but also for cash *accumulation* to fund new projects and acquisitions. Thus, Transurban needs to be aggressive in negotiations over revenue rights. It bargains forcefully, seeking not only annual inflation adjustments but also additional increments (see Transurban 2020, 36). Transurban also pursues hefty toll multipliers for large vehicles, a user group stripped of route alternatives by traffic regulators in Australia's toll road–dense cities and holding little political sway in the politics of urban management. (The development of toll roads in Australian cities has been accompanied by the development of sites easily accessed from toll roads for transport and logistics activity. Trucks are regulated onto toll roads as cargo is moved from ports to warehouses, and on to retailing centres or direct to households.) Finally, Transurban pushes for concession extensions when it negotiates road upgrades (such as adding lanes to ease traffic congestion) to ensure enriched revenue flows into the future. It is a neat way to quietly enhance the net present value of an asset (Transurban 2020, 20) and so enhance borrowing capacity, while avoiding the cost and uncertainty of a concession auction.

Then, there is the need to maintain credit access. Transurban's operating companies typically access credit by a combination of loans sourced externally and loans from assigned trusts (Morgan Stanley

2016). This two-tiered debt structure, by reason of leverage, significantly improves returns to equity investors without lessening equity investors' control over assets. Carefully engineered tax arrangements further enhance the desirability of gearing. Details of Transurban's two levels of debt are found in Morgan Stanley (2016). The first is asset- or project-level debt, which can be assigned non-recourse status. While such status gives project-level debt holders senior rights to project-level cash flows, it removes claims by debt holders on assets held by Transurban outside the project concerned. The second tier of debt is group-level debt, which are monies borrowed by the corporate entity, Transurban Holdings. Repayment of this tier of debt comes from distributions paid to Transurban Holdings from individual toll road projects. Morgan Stanley (2016) cited three reasons for the two-tier debt structure. First, project-level financing is a common requirement of concession deeds, especially as a way of isolating the integrity of a project from claims arising from other corporate ventures. Second, the non-recourse lender demands a project-level structure, for similar reasons. Third, there are cost and tenor (repayment period) advantages for credit initiation at the level of the project perhaps unattainable at a corporate level. One might add that the two-tier borrowing strategy generates competitive advantage over concession bidders, especially through opportunities for raised levels of leverage.

Heavy up-front outlays at the commencement of a new concession mean that revenue streams in the earlier period of a concession, unencumbered by tax payments, provide higher levels of debt cover than would be possible in a conventional corporation. On top, distributions to security holders are assured by access to a deeper pool of credit-enriched cash. Moreover, when concession periods are lengthened as toll road upgrades are negotiated, tax liabilities are pushed further into the future, providing comfort for senior debt holders.

All this said, the presence within the Transurban Group of multiple borrowing and lending entities with obligations to multiple concession contracts generates a ceaseless agenda of debt renegotiation, forcing Transurban to be an active manager of its future obligations. Transurban (2020, 27) reported an average weighted maturity period of 8.4 years across all debt, which reflects the relatively short-term nature of Transurban concessions, even after renegotiated concessions are factored in. Yet, as we have seen, at the final moment of a concession, a motorway needs to be passed back to the state unencumbered and in good condition, meaning there is no exit cash available for paying down debt or meeting outstanding tax obligations. This commercial brick wall elevates renegotiation as a desirable option for Transurban since an extended concession period not only pushes out debt and taxation settlement dates but extends the earnings horizon, strengthening Transurban's hand when refinancing debt positions. A revised concession with raised revenue expectations can also improve credit ratings (see Transurban 2020, 30). Thus, the question of aggregate leverage, of whether the combined debt of the overall Transurban entity is modest, as maintained by Transurban (2018a, 42), or excessive, as claimed by some commentators (for example, West 2020; Simply Wall St 2021), is less important than one of ongoing debt management (see Morgan Stanley 2016). Transurban has acute awareness of the interplay between its organisational structure and the structure of its finances, specifically of the way debt is lodged in every Transurban project, and that the format of every concession has been framed by assumptions of how debt is to be raised and repaid. Figure 14.3 illustrates the time sensitivity of this debt-management process as concession periods fall away and are renewed. Not surprisingly, there is close monitoring by all parties of the performance of Transurban's concession-dependent revenue flows: simply, the daily trafficking of cars and trucks along bitumen lanes.

In summary, Transurban's capital structure is motivated by magnifying returns through leverage, shoring up the control and earnings of long-term equity holders, and minimising the taxation obligations of investors. I now turn to the management of Transurban's portfolio of concession holdings and the company's deep immersion in government regulatory processes.

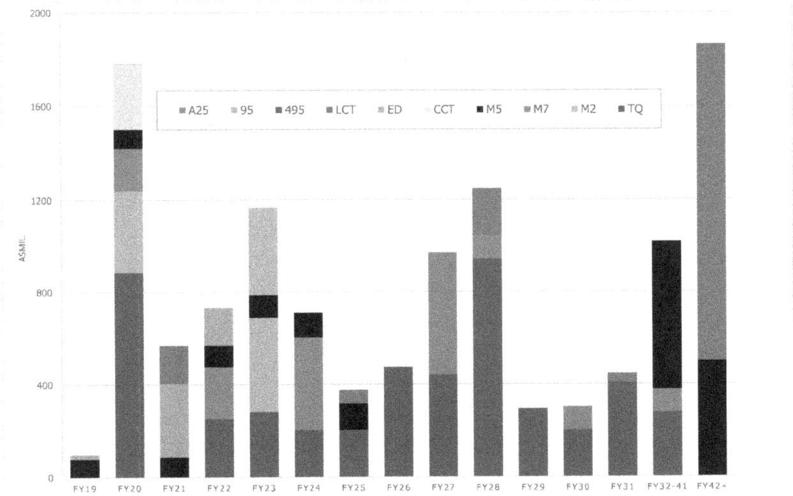

Figure 14.3 Maturity profile of Transurban, non-recourse debt at asset level.
Source: Compiled from Transurban (2018b, 14).

Transurban's regulatory environment

In its shareholder briefing in 2020, Transurban explained its regulatory strategy with remarkable frankness (Transurban 2020), highlighting partnership as a driver of corporate success (see, for example, page 4). As we have seen, the acquisition and management of concessions, including their configuration as monopoly rights to levy tolls, are critical to Transurban's existence. We have also seen how the timing of revenue flows across Transurban concessions is central to Transurban's management of an elaborate set of debt obligations. As a consequence of these complexities, Transurban's engagement with government and regulators is essential daily business. Table 14.2 shows Transurban's asset portfolio for Australia and North America, highlighting the variety of concession periods for its toll roads, many of which have been renegotiated after upgrades. The Melbourne concession, CityLink, for example, was initially contracted to end in 2034 but has been extended to 2045 in conjunction with road upgrades and extensions. The search for new concessions is also critical. In its June 2020 briefing to investors, Transurban identified six concessions with significant extension opportunities (NorthConnex, M8, M5 East, M4–M5 Link and the Rozelle Interchange in Sydney; the West Gate Tunnel in Melbourne), with further possibilities in Sydney, Melbourne and Brisbane into the future (Transurban 2020, especially 13–15, 35).

Transurban's successful acquisition of the WestConnex concession in Sydney is a telling example of the company's dance with government and regulators (see also McManus and Haughton 2021). The WestConnex sale packaged a brownfield state-owned motorway, newly widened lane sections and a new set of linking tunnels into a 33-kilometre-long toll road through high-volume traffic zones in Sydney's sprawling western suburbs. The concession was won by Transurban and its investment partners (Australian Super, Canadian Pension Plan Investment Board, Abu Dhabi Investment Authority and Caisse de dépôt et placement du Québec) in a two-stage auction process between 2018 and 2021 for a final total payment of $20.4 billion (New South Wales Treasury 2021). Analyses of media reports relating to the acquisition (chiefly in the *Australian Financial Review*) plus Transurban's investor briefing (Transurban 2018a) give insight into the vast regulatory field that Transurban navigated to make the WestConnex concession a commercial success. In respect to the bidding and initiation process, there was the need for intensive contractual negotiation and documentation covering ownership structure, operating conditions, toll rates, and so on; and the formation of an interim governance arrangement, a dual-trust structure based on an independent corporation, Sydney Road Partners. Pre-approval was required from Australian Consumer and Competition Commission, the market regulator (Wiggins 2018a, b). In respect to finance – and details here relate only to stage one of the auction – there was the need for new equity totalling $4.2 billion, debt refinancing totalling $4.1 billion, new debt issue totalling $1.5 billion, migration of new equity and debt into Transurban's complex trust-linked structures, and resolution of tax treatments for the acquisition. Transactions costs relating to finance matters for stage one were estimated by S&P Global Ratings to total $100 million (Thompson and Macdonald 2018), an indication of the extent of the professional services required. In respect to material and engineering

Table 14.2 Transurban asset portfolio, 30 June 2020. Source: Compiled from Transurban (2020, 33–5).

Asset	Opening date	Remaining concession period	Concession end date	Length	Ownership
CITYLINK Melbourne	Dec 2000	25 years	Jan 2045	22 km	100%
M5 WEST Sydney	Aug 1992	6 years	Dec 2026	22 km	100%
M2 Sydney	May 1997	28 years	Jun 2048	21 km	100%
M4 Sydney	May 1992	41 years	Dec 2060	14 km	25.5%
ED Sydney	Dec 1999	28 years	Jul 2048	6 km	75.1%
M7 Sydney	Dec 2005	28 years	Jun 2048	40 km	50%
LCT Sydney	Mar 2007	28 years	Jun 2048	3.8 km	100%
CCT Sydney	Aug 2005	15 years	Dec 2035	2.1 km	100%
GATEWAY MOTORWAY Brisbane	Dec 1986	32 years	Dec 2051	23.1 km	62.5%
LOGAN MOTORWAY Brisbane	Dec 1988	32 years	Dec 2051	39.5 km	62.5%
CLEM7 Brisbane	Mar 2010	31 years	Aug 2051	6.8 km	62.5%
GO BETWEEN BRIDGE Brisbane	Jul 2010	43 years	Dec 2063	0.3 km	62.5%
LEGACY WAY Brisbane	Jun 2015	45 years	Jun 2065	5.7 km	62.5%
AIRPORT LINK M7 Brisbane	Jul 2012	33 years	Jul 2053	6.7 km	62.5%
495 EXPRESS LANES North America	Nov 2012	67 years	Dec 2087	22 km	100%
95 EXPRESS LANES North America	Dec 2014	67 years	Dec 2087	63 km	100%
A25 North America	May 2011	22 years	Sept 2042	7.2 km	100%

matters, there was the need for due diligence and risk assessment on road and tunnel linkages and identification of relationships with road construction contractors and contracts for further extensions to the WestConnex road portfolio. Finally, there was the need to merge Transurban's toll collection vehicle (Linkt) with those WestConnex users tagged by other toll collection agencies. The list represents a vast, detailed, regulatory agenda; yet the prize – the concession – is celebrated because it is the company's lifeline.

As is the pattern, the WestConnex acquisition was a major play in the Transurban strategy of raising the net present value of its revenue streams by extending concession periods and raising toll rates so as to maintain distributions to security holders while managing debt repayment and tax obligations into the future. Yet the acquisition further embeds Transurban into the decision-making and regulation-making orbit of, in this case, the New South Wales government and its agencies. The WestConnex acquisition shows the need for Transurban to manage its regulatory environment with a level of intensity as least equal to the level needed for the management of its organisational and capital structures. The three are not only inseparable, they also play out in concert.

Discussion and conclusion

The case study has opened Transurban for examination as a private infrastructure entity created by, and encased in, state-led property and organisational rights, a melee of state–capital and urban relations with an infinite range of actor involvement and outcome possibilities. We have seen how Transurban negotiates this field in three ways. First, it operates inside an organisational structure that gives Transurban legitimacy in exploiting and growing its monopoly positions. Second, it maintains a financial structure that maximises returns from a largely intangible asset base using a range of potentially precarious revenue, taxation and distributional vehicles. Third, Transurban manages its state relations with an intensity rarely seen in commerce. Ultimately, the reproduction of Transurban's worth depends on what the state authorises – Transurban's concession rights, its revenue streams, its privileged participation in rounds of state-led privatisation and financialisation processes. That is what has to happen when you are a quasi-utility, when you deal in the delivery of monopoly public goods (see also Hossain and Fuller 2021).

My argument, then, is that we should not overlook the benefits from the privatisation and financialisation of major road use in eastern Australia, at least so far. Very classy roads have been built, with more efficient road use than would have been possible without them. The projects have been fully funded – meaning, the cost of capital has been paid for by the user, not the taxpayer. This cost shift would have been unlikely at the state level in Australia, given the inflammatory politics it would create, even after consideration of state access to cheaper borrowing. The state has been able to extract considerable free externalities from the large amount of private investment involved, including the removal of non-local traffic from suburban streets, especially in inner-urban areas, improved fuel efficiency, and enhanced jobs access for workers in outer suburbs not served by public transport and denied local work opportunities. Finally, there has been the successful introduction of a road-user pricing scheme, a difficult political and technological undertaking.

Yet these benefits are fixed in time, arguably appropriate only for the early decades of the 21st century. The presence of toll roads is increasingly questioned on social, environmental and economic grounds, such that there is a strong argument that the roads operated by Transurban need to be repurposed. Two mutually supporting conversions are argued for. First, as publicly owned passageways stretching through our large, congested cities, the toll roads need to be repurposed for public transport, for the operation, say, of collective-use, low-emission vehicles. Second, the passageways need to be pivotal to a transformation of transport flows in our large cities. Increasingly, urban planners – say, as part of smart city initiatives – seek ways to instil in a city a hierarchy of movements that are logical and coherent to both transport providers and users (see Kitchin 2019). The luxuriously equipped passageways operated by Transurban could be powerful tools in such a reshaping of transport flows in Australia's east-coast cities. After all, in the end these are state-owned assets, funded by road-user fees.

But unleashing the potential of the Transurban passageways means retiring them from their revenue-raising role, as each of the concessions expires. A problem, though, as has been explained, is that Transurban's financial security depends singularly on the rolling acquisition and renewal of concessions. A disassembly and retirement of concessions cannot be done without regard to Transurban's substantial creditor and shareholder obligations, which suggests a long timeframe will be needed. Yet, unwinding the dependence of Sydney, Melbourne and Brisbane on private vehicular travel will not be an easy or quick task either. Importantly, the politics of a transformation need to be novel, and generous – beyond the angry, oppositional politics that has accompanied toll road development and operation in Australia. A real opportunity for the development of a regenerative policy position has arisen, yet it needs to acknowledge the need for unwinding a complex corporation with significant financial liabilities.

That said, the recovery of the Transurban passageways through our cities will also be an intellectual process. As we have seen, Transurban's participation in toll roads development has been an experiment in hybridism involving the state, new forms of private finance and a new regulatory terrain. The transformation of the passageways needs to advance this experimentation in hybridism. The future use of Transurban's vast urban passageways will involve autonomous vehicles, new travel formats and strategies to distribute services efficiently and fairly. All these directions require the participation of innovative, entrepreneurial actors, sparked by the presence of private finance. Indeed, it seems possible that parts of the Transurban enterprise, a company well advanced in the techniques of urban travel management, could re-emerge as major players in repurposed east-coast transport systems. There is, for example, an arguable case for major changes to the way travellers pay for their journeys, whatever the mode. In Sydney, users of public transport contribute little more than a quarter (26.8 per cent) of total public transport costs through payment of fares (Centre for International Economics 2020). Yet, across the duration of a Transurban concession, road users pay the entire capital and operating costs of travelling on a toll road. Shifting to sustainable, more effective transport modes and patterns will inevitably involve a revamp in transport charges, including for the use of both public transport and roads. Transurban expertise and technology might be important in this redesign.

There is a further knowledge task. Knowing how to get the right mix of hybridism, in financing and management, requires that we revisit the concepts of public goods and the public interest so they realign with new realities of infrastructure ownership and operation. In economic theory, the delivery of a public good does not necessarily require a publicly owned vehicle (Fourie 2016). Shining a powerful light to steer ships safely through a tricky passageway is the delivery of a public good, but the lighthouse operation can still be privately owned and fee-charging (see Coase 1974). The transformation of toll roads requires that we can identify the public good outcomes that we seek, including the maximisation of positive externalities, which will enable us to speak in an informed way about how private finance and management can be involved. In short, the regulatory dance of the state with Transurban opens new choreographies to press for the conversion of Australia's east-coast toll roads.

Acknowledgements

Parts of this chapter, including some text, figures and data, can also be found in an article written by the author that appears in the journal *Geographical Research* (see O'Neill 2022). The use of this material in this chapter accords with the copyright agreement with the journal's publisher.

I am grateful to the Australian Research Council for funding the research (DP130104319) that underpins this work and to key informants for their generous participation. Many thanks to Dr Elissa Sutherland for research assistance and Ms Susanna Rouillard for the cartography. Finally, my sincere thanks to editors of this book for their invaluable advice and insights.

References

Centre for International Economics (2020). *Measuring Cost Recovery of NSW Public Transport Services*. Prepared for IPART, 19 February. https://www.thecie.com.au.

Clark, G. L., and O'Neill, P. (2023). An economic and financial geography of the Australian superannuation industry. *Geographical Research* 61(4): 443–457. https://doi.org/10.1111/1745-5871.12611.

Coase, R.H. (1974). The lighthouse in economics. *Journal of Law and Economics* 17: 357–76.

Davis, K. (2017). *The Case against Stapled Securities*. University of Melbourne and Australian Centre for Financial Studies, Monash University. Prepared for the Australian Taxation System, The 2017 Great Debate, 16 August, Sydney. Organised by The Tax Institute. Mimeo available at https://www.kevindavis.com.au.

Fourie, J. (2006). Economic infrastructure: a review of definitions, theory and empirics. *South African Journal of Economics* 74(3): 530–55. https://doi.org/10.1111/j.1813-6982.2006.00086.x.

Hossain, S.R., and S. Fuller (2021). Understanding conflict in transport mega-projects: social impacts and power dynamics in the WestConnex project, Sydney. *Australian Geographer* 52(3): 293–313. https://doi.org/10.1080/00049182.2021.1964162.

Kitchin, R. (2019). The timescape of smart cities. *Annals of the American Association of Geographers* 109(3): 775–90. https://doi.org/10.1080/24694452.2018.1497475.

McManus, P., and G. Haughton (2021). Fighting to undo a deal: identifying and resisting the financialization of the WestConnex motorway, Sydney, Australia. *Environment and Planning A: Economy and Space* 53(1): 131–49. https://doi.org/10.1177/0308518X20933279.

Morgan Stanley (2016). *Transurban Group: Analyst Report*. Morgan Stanley Research, February 12. Supplied.

New South Wales Treasury (2021). Completes Sale of WestConnex. Media release, 29 October. https://tinyurl.com/mw8xbjc8.

Oakland, W.H. (1987). Theory of public goods. In A.J. Auerbach and M. Feldstein, eds. *Handbook of Public Economics* 2: 485–535. London: Elsevier. https://doi.org/10.1016/S1573-4420(87)80004-6.

O'Neill, P.M. (2019). The financialisation of urban infrastructure: a framework of analysis, *Urban Studies* 56(7): 1304–25. https://doi.org/10.1177/0042098017751983.

O'Neill, P. (2022). Privatising and financialising roads: the peculiar case of Transurban. *Geographical Research* 60(2): 328–41. https://doi.org/10.1111/1745-5871.12528.

Sainati T., G. Locatelli, N. Smith, N. Brookes and G. Olver (2020). Types and functions of special purpose vehicles in infrastructure megaprojects. *International Journal of Project Management* 38(5): 243–55. https://doi.org/10.1016/j.ijproman.2020.05.002.

Searle, G., and C. Legacy (2020). Locating the public interest in mega infrastructure planning: the case of Sydney's WestConnex. *Urban Studies* 58(4): 826–44. https://doi.org/10.1177/0042098020927835.

Simply Wall St (2021). Does Transurban Group have a healthy balance sheet? *Simply Wall St*, 7 November. https://tinyurl.com/3k5rupvy.

Thompson, S., and A. Macdonald (2018). Transurban and friends ready to sign WestConnex deal. *Australian Financial Review*, 31 August. https://tinyurl.com/ychhs24x.

Transurban (2006) *Financial Statements 2006*. https://tinyurl.com/yshmxru8.

Transurban (2012) *Annual Report 2012*. https://tinyurl.com/2y739vjt.

Transurban (2017). *Stapled Structures. Treasury Consultation Paper. Transurban Submission*, April. https://tinyurl.com/3nv5fdm9.

Transurban (2018a). *WestConnex Acquisition: Transurban Equity Raising*. Investor Presentation, August. https://tinyurl.com/4yfm3bpa.

Transurban (2018b). *Transurban Annual Report 2018*. https://tinyurl.com/3rw2bf36.

Transurban (2020). *Transurban Overview*. https://tinyurl.com/yc4vrem3.

West, M. (2020). For whom the tolls bell: traversing Transurban's $20 billion debt and tricky tax lurks. *Michael West Media*, 8 April. https://tinyurl.com/th54pebz.

Wiggins, J. (2018a). Transurban's WestConnex bid gets green light from ACCC. *Australian Financial Review*, 30 August. https://tinyurl.com/bdhtt4fu.

Wiggins, J. (2018b). Transurban secures control of Sydney's WestConnex with $9.3 billion bid. *Australian Financial Review*, 30 August. https://tinyurl.com/5xjzt8j5.

15 Friedman, HECS and income-contingent loans

Mike Rafferty, Phillip Toner and Scott MacWilliam

Introduced to Australia in 1989 by the Australian Labor Party government led by then Prime Minister Bob Hawke, the Higher Education Contribution Scheme (HECS), now called the Higher Education Loan Program or HELP (hereafter for brevity both here referred to as HECS) is the student fee and loans system for university tuition in Australia. HECS is often framed as a uniquely Australian social democratic innovation that opened up university tuition to a new and larger cohort of students in an equitable and affordable way. Under HECS, loan repayment occurs when a graduate's income exceeds a specified level (conceptually at or more than the average wage – a premium on the "investment" in university education). The loan is therefore income *contingent* (Chapman 1988; Wran 1988). Income-contingent loans (or ICLs) to repay university tuition fees now operate in many countries and are endorsed by prominent left-of-centre economists internationally, including Joseph Stiglitz (2014, 2016) and Nicholas Barr (1998). They are also promoted by leading development policy institutions, including the World Bank (Salmi 1999). Advocates of income-contingent loans have proposed extending this funding mechanism to a broad range of government support, including unemployment, drought relief, maternity leave, solar panel installation, retirement benefits, childcare and pandemic relief.

However, student debt is also under growing critical glare in Australia and elsewhere. In Australia, HECS debt per student and repayment times have grown significantly. According to Warburton (2023), university students are currently graduating with HELP or HECS debts of between $50,000 and $60,000, which will typically take 12 years (about a quarter of a working life) to repay. Repayment of HECS debt now commences at $48,361, compared to average full-time earnings of $90,000. The legal full-time minimum wage is currently $42,000, so repayment of HECS debt begins at only $3.00 per hour above the minimum wage, meaning that virtually any graduate in full-time employment will be forced to repay some of their HECS debt. Yet the initial organising principle of HECS was that it was to be a charge on the wage premium earned after university education (Sharples 2021). The size of HECS fees and the debt repayment burden are increasingly onerous and contributing to university graduates delaying adult life choices, including home purchase and family formation (Brancatisano 2022; Ross 2023).

Student debt also has well-known adverse gender-equity effects. Female graduates have more outstanding HECS debt, will typically earn less than male counterparts and so take much longer to repay their HECS debt and be more affected by the indexation of HECS debt (Ross 2023; Warburton 2023). For instance, financial services company Futurity Investment reported the results of a survey of 1,000 university graduates that found that university-educated women had more outstanding HECS debt and earned lower salaries than their male contemporaries. The survey also found that more than half of respondents over 40 still had HECS debt (cited in Ross 2023).

HECS is also under pressure from changing labour market developments. Skill shortages are emerging in a growing range of professions, forcing governments to offer fee-free or highly subsidised degree and diploma programs, while there are signs that growing domestic university enrolments have peaked (Cassidy 2023) and many employers are no longer requiring degrees for jobs or promotion (Lobell 2023). Paralleling the US debate about college debt and the corporatisation of universities, one political party is now calling for HECS debt cancellation and an end to HECS (Cockburn 2022).

Given the emerging problems with HECS and student loans systems internationally, it is time to review the conceptual origins of HECS, and its current structure. It turns out that contrary to its depiction as an Australian social democratic innovation, HECS owes its origins to what was then a frontier development in mid-20th-century neoliberalism. In particular, the origins of HECS are to be found in the mid-1950s work of Milton Friedman, who made the case for an income-contingent student loan scheme for higher education in 1955, based on his political opposition to rising postwar US government expenditure on and delivery of higher education.

Friedman elided the fact that his proposed income contingent loan funding model for post-school education could not satisfy the neoclassical welfare economics conditions for a competitive and free market as it was framed, and which were critical to the proposal's claims to equity and efficiency. Nor could he construct sound empirical measures for key economic concepts underpinning the model. And the proposal depended on private banks and insurance companies to calculate the interest rates and administer the repayment of that debt, which he conceded would be impractical. Friedman's 1955 intervention was a strident anti-statist, normative and prescriptive proposal, and it was, unsurprisingly, largely unsuccessful at the time. But the income-contingent concept offered a prototype of what would become an alternative neoliberal vision and later provide the scope for shifting risks and costs to households and individuals, but requiring an activist state to implement. This project of mass individualisation administered by an activist state was not a contradiction of neoliberalism, but as HECS demonstrates, was a development within neoliberal practice. Indeed, Friedman's own neoliberalism evolved, and he later accepted an activist role for the state (Stedman Jones 2012).

It would take 30 years of increasing neoliberal proselytising and improvising state practice before the income-contingent loan proposal was implemented anywhere at a national level. Somewhat ironically perhaps, it was a social democratic government in Australia, using the rhetoric of equity and expanded access for working class cohorts, framing free higher education as regressive and inequitable middle-class welfare. Fees and income-contingent loans were said to be a way of expanding enrolments to include many more students. But HECS was itself a regressive project from its inception: imposing fees to fund a planned expansion in student numbers to more working-class students, while funding significant tax cuts for corporations and higher income earners. In fact, during the Hawke and subsequent Paul Keating-led Labor governments, the combination of wage restraint (LaCava 2019), user pays fees and charges and tax cuts (Tilley 2021), saw the largest redistribution of income from labour to capital in the postwar period (Whiteford 2013). Carson and Kerr (1988) noted that the redistribution from labour to capital achieved during the Hawke–Keating years was likely greater than that under the Margaret Thatcher Conservative government in the United Kingdom.

HECS is not just a project initiated by an activist state; the state remains central to fee-setting and debt collection. Neoliberalism as a state project of privatisation and creating markets is now familiar territory. So too is the disciplinary nature of the neoliberal welfare state. HECS represents a different neoliberal initiative, a form of state-planned and run commodification with clear coercive content (Dukelow and Kennett 2018).

In this sense HECS has been a pioneering international neoliberal innovation, establishing a template for later Third Way policy moves in the United States (by President Bill Clinton 1993–2001) and the United Kingdom (by Prime Minister Tony Blair 1997–2007) that were,

> derived from American post-war neoliberal market-based approaches to social policy … fused with a social democratic rhetorical appeal … [T]heir method was neoliberal and the "values" were supposed to be from the centre-left (Stedman Jones 2018, 168).

Having introduced the terms under which HECS was developed and implemented, the next section of the chapter outlines Friedman's arguments for the use of income-contingent loans in higher education. It shows that despite its influence on later thought and policy around college and university financing, especially HECS in Australia, Friedman's 1955 paper is infrequently referenced by advocates of income-contingent loans. Friedman's work was notably absent from the policy reviews that led to the development of HECS, primarily those by Wran (1988) and Chapman (1988). This was despite one of its key proponents having been to Yale which had its own income contingent loan program at the time (Nerlove 1975). Even in 2014, for example, an International Economic Association Symposium on income-contingent loans, mentioned Friedman's work in only five of the 22 chapters, and only as a passing reference in four of those five. The LSE economist Nicholas Barr has recently, and notably, been more candid conceding that income-contingent loans for university tuition "have a direct lineage from Friedman's writing 70 years ago" (Barr 2016, 5).

The second section of the chapter shows how the founding document of HECS in Australia, the Wran Report (Wran 1988), was both informed by and included some important differences from Friedman's neoliberal ideologically free market vision. The chapter concludes with some current proposals to extend the use of income-contingent loans to many other life contingencies and the contradictions of that vision.

Income-contingent loans for college tuition – conceptual origins

In 1955, Friedman wrote an essay on the role of the state in education, responding to the growth of the postwar liberal democratic state in the US economy and society. He opened the essay by calling these moves a dangerous "trend toward collectivism". One of the specific political purposes of that essay was to attack the rapid growth in publicly funded tertiary education, labelling it "an indiscriminate extension of governmental responsibility" (Friedman 1955, 123). Friedman's essay was published in a book that is now extremely difficult to access directly; but the text of the chapter is now available online and we have used that text here (although it was also published as a chapter in Friedman's 1962 book *Capitalism and Freedom*).

Against existing and emerging social democratic practice, Friedman's essay proposed to establish "a society that takes freedom of the individual ... [and] the family as its ultimate objective and seeks to further this objective by relying primarily on voluntary exchange among individuals for the organisation of economic activity" (Friedman 1955, 123–24). Individual autonomy was to be given priority except if private action caused "harm" to others. Friedman argued that the market was the primary generator and guarantor of such individual freedom. This highly normative ideological political philosophy framed Friedman's view of the legitimate role of government in the economy and society: "government's primary role is to preserve the rules of the game by enforcing contracts, preventing coercion and keeping markets free". He advanced this position irrespective of whether it contradicted the principles of liberal democracy (MacPherson 1968), the conditions of neo-classical welfare economics (Nerlove 1975), or the political will of postwar American society for better education, including school desegregation. In this sense the essay was a founding document in how neoliberal reason sought to remake the precepts and principles of the capitalist state (Brown 2015, Schwarz 2022).

One of the key proposals in Friedman's essay to give effect to his vision was an alternative funding arrangement, namely fees and an income-contingent loan scheme, to be managed by private financial institutions with the explicit goal to effect "a sizeable reduction in the direct activities of government".

Education for citizenship and for human capital accumulation

Friedman developed his anti-statist college fees and loans project by differentiating between two types or functions of education: "general education" for citizenship and leadership; and "specialised vocational education". Friedman considered the former type of education as accruing a social benefit, while the latter accrues an individual benefit. Friedman conceded that in practice it is "extremely difficult to draw a sharp line between the two types of education". The credibility of the fee proposal is predicated on the clarity of this distinction.

General education or education for citizenship was to establish a common set of values, encourage social integration and provide a minimum level of literacy and numeracy. In welfare economics terms, it is a public good. Friedman claimed this function is provided by primary and secondary schools. The education for values importantly produces economic externalities or "neighbourhood effects" or as Friedman argued, "The gain from the education of a child accrues not only to the child or to his parents but to other members of the society". Given these externalities "the imposition of a minimum required level of education and the financing of education by the state can be justified". Not surprisingly, Friedman argued that actual delivery of education by the state is unjustified, representing a "nationalisation" of the bulk of the "education industry". His solution is for the state to supply parents with "vouchers redeemable for a specified maximum sum per child per year if spent on 'approved' educational services". Vouchers would promote "choice", and "competition" between schools, stimulate the creation of for-profit schools and improve productive and allocative efficiency and innovation. This proposal to extend public funding to US private schools in the mid-1950s was quite radical as public funding was highly restricted (National Center for Education Statistics n.d.).

The other type of education in Friedman's schema is post-secondary "vocational" and "professional" education encompassing, for example, trades as well as college and university degrees, such as engineering, commerce and law. This type of education is not said to be generative of positive social externalities or neighbourhood effects; rather as Friedman opined,

> [i]t is a form of investment in human capital precisely analogous to investment in machinery. Its function is to raise the economic productivity of the human being ... there are no obvious unborne costs or unappropriable returns that tend to make private incentives diverge systematically from those that are socially appropriate (1955, 135).

Tertiary education is in this framing almost solely an investment good – in human capital – that generates individual higher productivity, reflected in higher lifetime earnings compared to those without such qualifications. According to Friedman, "investors" in their own human capital upgrading should be charged for the individual benefit that accrues. The 1955 essay is significant in being arguably one of the earliest articulations of human capital theory, predating his doctoral student, Gary Becker's works. Certain key ideas in the 1955 paper relating to human capital theory and income-contingent loans can be found in emergent form a decade earlier in his joint work with Simon Kuznets into the incomes of professional occupations published by the National Bureau of Economic Research. Interestingly, the director of the bureau, C. Reinold Noyes, attached a director's note to the volume that was both sceptical and critical of the arguments of Friedman and Kuznets, anticipating many of the standard criticisms of human capital theory advanced decades later.

The case for an income-contingent loan

Friedman argued that, because of a lack of wider externalities in higher education, state funding of tertiary education was unwarranted. Drawing on his work with Kuznets, Friedman noted the earnings of professionals greatly exceed the cost of their investment in education and even asserted that "the rate of return on investment in training is very much higher than the rate of return on investment in physical capital". Friedman then concluded that these "facts" are indicative of a "sizeable underinvestment in human beings", even though higher education was then undergoing a significant increase. Yet government funding and provision were ruled out by Friedman because the state could not judge the optimal level of post-school investment.

At this point in the argument, Friedman made a decisive rhetorical move and one central to the specific case for an income-contingent loan scheme. He located the explanation for the underinvestment in an "imperfection in the capital market: investment in human beings cannot be financed on the same terms or with the same ease as investment in physical capital".

For Friedman, underinvestment generates allocative and productive inefficiencies, as well as social losses, leading to an undersupply of vocationally trained labour and high occupational rents. This distortion of the "education industry" also means that education is oriented more to the needs of educators than students. Anticipating the later social democratic advocates of income-contingent loans, Friedman also claimed that this distortion affected social inequity, as access to higher education is then limited mostly to higher income groups. This proposition subsequently provided the basis for the Labor government

Finance Minister Peter Walsh's description of higher education as middle-class welfare.

Having explained why full private funding was not feasible, Friedman then argued that the existing limited government funding of US higher education was also undesirable, since it led to the "rationing" or undersupply of education places. One possible solution was simply to extend "government subsidy of vocational or professional education financed out of general revenues" to all students who met minimum entry conditions. But Friedman ruled this option out. Universal state funding combined with the assumption of little or no positive externalities from post-school education would, it was claimed, worsen the existing inequitable distribution of income and tax expenditures as "those fortunate enough to get their training subsidised would receive all the returns from the investment whereas the costs would be borne by the taxpayers in general. This seems an entirely … perverse redistribution of income". Friedman was not just critical of redistribution from poorer taxpayers to higher income groups who then participated disproportionately in higher education; he was also against any "subsidising" of "education … making it available free or at a low price" for low-income students. Instead, rectifying capital markets was Friedman's key policy solution to inequality, not "outright income redistribution".

This perceived capital market imperfection was attributed to certain unique properties of labour viewed not as individual citizens in a democracy, but as a factor of production. Firstly, unlike physical capital, and due to the prohibition on slavery, investors in human capital are unable to obtain collateral or gain security over an investment in labour. An "individual embodying … an investment [in human capital] cannot be bought and sold". Second, predicting the size and pattern of future earnings of individual graduates is highly uncertain due to inherent individual differences in graduate careers, family responsibilities, illness and luck. Third, enforcement and administration costs for private loans would be unreasonably high since humans are geographically mobile, contracts will have a long duration and some borrowers may seek to evade repayments. These features generate high risk and cost for private investors. Investors employing what Friedman called traditional "fixed money loans", with set interest and repayment terms, would have to impose such a high rate of interest as to "conflict with usury laws and make the loans unattractive to borrowers".

Friedman's first best solution – a human equity income scheme

The challenge Friedman set himself was thus to overcome the so-called capital market imperfections to make a private student-financing project viable. His stated goal was to "make capital available for investment in human beings on terms comparable to those on which it is available for physical investment". Having dismissed traditional loan financing, Friedman turned first to share ownership or "equity" as the most appropriate financial instrument. Unlike debt instruments, equity investing confers legal ownership to a "share" of an asset or future income it may generate. Equity ownership also spreads risk as it permits financing multiple students, in the manner of a joint stock company, so that returns from more financially successful graduates would help balance the lower returns from the less successful. An important benefit of equity financing for Friedman is that, like education vouchers, funding is directed to individuals (students) rather than institutions. This would, it is said, promote choice and competition between providers and so be conducive to innovation and efficiency in financing the "education industry". However, Friedman acknowledged that such an equity holding is "equivalent to the purchase of a share in an individual's earning capacity *and thus to partial slavery*" (emphasis added).

Despite being convinced of the merits of equity financing, Friedman noted that, for reasons such as "novelty" of the idea, the "likelihood of irrational public condemnation" (of the slavery-like implications) and high administrative costs, the private sector had not actively advanced the idea, resulting in market failure. Friedman paradoxically suggested governments *could* run the higher education equity scheme since it would have lower transaction costs compared to being operated by the private sector. This was due to government's "natural monopoly" on the type of information about citizens required to efficiently administer the scheme and have the capacity to enforce contractual obligations, such as equity repayments, notably for the later development of HECS, through the federal government income tax system. Government engagement may also be warranted here since an equity income scheme is consistent with "improving the operation of the market".

Under the equity scheme, a graduate would be required to repay an investor for an indefinite term after their income exceeds a "base sum" (termed "*y*"), such as the average wage of workers without a college degree with the rate of equity payment (termed "*x*") set "so as to make the whole project self-financing". Again, with implications for later advocates of HECS, Friedman claimed such a scheme was "equitable" because repayments only occur when the graduate has a capacity to pay and, secondly, it assures that "costs are borne by those who benefit most directly".

Friedman therefore recognised a (limited but necessary) role for the state in an income-contingent equity scheme, though he lamented, "[I]t would be preferable if similar arrangements could be developed on a private basis by financial institutions ... non-profit institutions ... or individual universities and colleges". The "financial intermediaries that would be best suited to engage in such investments ... [are] life insurance companies" given that risk management and actuarial calculation is their core activity. In addition, an optimal allocation of investment for education would entail each individual student being risk-rated with the values of *x* and *y* adjusted to reflect "any differences in expected earning capacity that can be predicted in advance – a problem similar to that of varying life insurance premia among groups that have different life expectancy". Friedman did not provide an example of individual risk rating but ironically considering the claims for equity, presumably students from a wealthier background would be a lower "risk" and receive more *x* and be subject to a lower proportional *y* than those from a poorer background.

Impossibility of meeting economic optimality conditions

The formal standard against which Friedman assessed the performance of existing markets for education, capital and labour is that of perfect competition. The explicit goal here is to shift the system to approximate perfect competition. Perfect competition thus serves as both an assessment tool and an end point of reform (Marginson 1997). The claim here is that redressing market failures in the post-school education "market" will result in a system in which "investment should be carried to the point at which the extra return repays the investment and yields the market rate of interest on it". In turn, this will raise allocative and productive efficiency and innovation in the "education industry" and enhance competition in vocational and professional labour markets. Once again, this assumes that all benefits of post-school education are privately generated and appropriated.

While Friedman's essay was couched in many standard neo-classical terms, it was done so in a loose and often contradictory way. For instance, he insisted that the proposed "program would eliminate existing imperfections in the capital market and so widen the opportunity of individuals to make productive investments in themselves" (1955). Equally, he conceded that the income-contingent loan and income-contingent equity schemes must fail to reach this end point. Friedman also conceded that the present and future "reformed" world would remain characterised by irreducible uncertainty, ensuring the price mechanism could not deliver an optimal and stable equilibrium. Introducing an equity scheme, even one run by a private insurance company, does not eliminate the problem that economic agents do not have perfect information. And for both investors and students, investment in education remains inherently risky as workers' productivity will continue to vary greatly between individuals. Pricing the pooled risks of investment in education is therefore not only inefficient on its own terms but also inequitable as low-risk students are required to overcompensate for future losses from students who fail courses or otherwise do not meet equity repayments. Also, "non-pecuniary advantages" differ across occupations; for example, some jobs are financially rewarding while some are more socially rewarding. Some are interesting but others boring, and these "advantages" are not fully reflected in wages: it follows that investment in education can never "be distributed in the optimum manner".

Not only did Friedman concede his economic ideal could not attained in practice, but contemporaneous with his article, Lipsey and Lancaster (1956) developed the general theory of the second best. That theorem demonstrated that the effect of "piecemeal policy" changes such as the reforms proposed by Friedman are fundamentally uncertain: "[I]n a situation in which there exist many constraints which prevent the fulfillment of the Paretian optimum conditions, the removal of any one constraint may affect welfare or efficiency either by raising it, by lowering it, or by leaving it unchanged" (Lipsey and Lancaster 1956, 12). Lipsey and Lancaster pointed out that it is logically impossible to promise to maximise both efficiency and equity where more than one market imperfection exists, a conclusion that simply formalised a problem that was widely known by orthodox economic theory at the time (Lipsey and Lancaster 1956, 11). And the problems of human capital theory, on which the income-contingent loan proposal was based, were significant. As early as 1976 Mark Blaug identified a conceptual and empirical crisis in human capital theory and warned that it was in danger of degenerating as a research paradigm, due in large part to its inability to empirically test core hypotheses: ignoring confounding and contradictory data on the link between education and earnings and it being monocausal – excluding plausible alternative explanations for this link.

Friedman's education essay was essentially a highly normative prescriptive political provocation to attack the postwar growth of publicly-funded and provided higher education. His typology of education was vague and instrumental, the income-contingent equity proposal was effectively an advocacy of partial slavery, and a private income-contingent loan system would require high interest rates and intensive risk management and intrusive supervision. The essay began with an explicit ambition to reverse the postwar "trend toward collectivism" and ended with the expectation that implementing his proposal for "denationalising education" would result in "a sizeable reduction in the direct activities of government". Friedman's essay then needs to be read as an attack on the postwar liberal democratic state in which government was expanding education, as well as health and social welfare. Friedman's income-contingent loan was not picked up at the time, except by one or two universities, notably Yale University. But it did contain the seeds of a later state project to restructure higher education on neoliberal terms.

HECS in Australia – the realisation of Friedman's ICL vision

Two broad cycles in Australian postwar government policy towards tertiary education can be discerned. The first was a period of rapid expansion in enrolments and public funding. From 1949 to 1973 the Australian population increased by 69 per cent but university enrolments increased by 600 per cent with an attendant increase in government funding (Department of Education 2014, Table 1; Australian Bureau of Statistics 2019). Moreover, government scholarship support for students widened, so that by 1973 only 20–26 per cent of full-time university students paid tuition fees (Wran 1988, 3). Just over half (54 per cent) of all students also received some form of income support (Wran 1988, 7). This cycle reached its peak in 1974 when the Whitlam Labor government (1973–75) abolished all university tuition fees and introduced a generous means-tested student income support scheme.

The second cycle began with the election of the Liberal–National Country Party Coalition government led by Malcolm Fraser (1975–83). In 1981, an attempt was made to introduce fees for second and higher degrees (excluding recognised double degrees) and establish a Tertiary Fees Loans Scheme for affected students. Universities would be required to collect this fee and federal government grants would be reduced by the level of fee income raised (Harman 1981, 36). Based on historical practice in Australian universities before 1974, student tuition fees were to be charged on a sliding scale, reflecting differences in course recurrent costs. In 1982, a Bill for the scheme was defeated in the Senate. Importantly, this loan scheme was explicitly intended to have private sector involvement, with the Education Minister stating in Parliament: "Commonwealth officers have had useful discussions with representatives of the Australian Bankers' Association and the Commonwealth Bank on the details of the proposed loan scheme for tertiary students" (Commonwealth of Australia 1981).

The final challenge to the postwar publicly funded expansion legacy prior to the introduction of HECS was the proposal for the introduction of a flat fee for all university students in 1986 under the Hawke Labor government (1983–91). Championed by the Finance Minister, Peter Walsh, the higher education administration charge "was the first chink in the armour of free tuition that had been ALP ideology since Whitlam and provided impetus for the reforms to come" (Higgins 2019, 66).

Simon Marginson (1989) provided a persuasive case to explain these two large cycles in Australian education policy, giving prominence to changing political economic and social conditions, and ideologically to the rise of human capital theory as a policy rationale for government funding. From the early 1960s, human capital theory had started to become increasingly influential among Australian economists and policymakers, with particular weight given to the claimed high social returns to tertiary education that served to justify rising state expenditures. During the long postwar economic boom (1949–74) a positive association between rising incomes, technological advancement and improved educational attainment appeared self-evident. But by the late 1970s this association was being subject to growing critique.

Second, and here the story becomes more complex, with the end of the economic boom in 1974, and subsequent low growth in gross domestic product (GDP), high unemployment and inflation, confidence weakened in the notion that there were public benefits of rising investment in education and a more "credentialled" workforce. Unemployed graduates and declining returns to university qualifications seemed to support such scepticism. "The logic was clear – if education had been instrumental in achieving the high rates of growth, could deficiencies in education not also be held part-responsible for the recession?" (Marginson 1989, 16). Moreover, from the late 1970s onwards, a group of prominent economists, such as George Fane at the Australian National University and Richard Blandy at Flinders University, using Friedman's perspective, began emphasising the private returns to education and advocated radically reducing government funding of higher education (Marginson 1989, 20–1).

Finally, in the second half of the 1970s, increasing doubt about both the wider public benefits of higher education and postwar Keynesian orthodoxy found a powerful ally in the economic doctrine of monetarism that academia, Treasury, the Reserve Bank and the major political parties increasingly adopted. Milton Friedman was by then also the chief advocate for monetarism. In 1975, following his visit to Chile after the bloody military coup by General Pinochet, he made a well-publicised visit to Australia. The visit focused on challenging the existing Keynesian "hegemony" over macro-economic policy. Courvisanos and Millmow (2006) noted that Friedman's Australian tour had a major impact on economic policy making, including on both main political parties. In 1976, Chicago school colleague, and Mont Pelerin Society member, Friedrich Hayek, also toured Australia where he spoke of the importance of markets not just as bastions of freedom but also as disciplinary processes on individuals (Champion 2015). An educational economist writing in 1981 reflected the change in mood, observing that education generally "no longer commands the same degree of support that it appeared to enjoy during the late 1960s" (Harman 1981, 29). From 1977 to 1992, real government expenditure per equivalent full-time student fell by more than 50 per cent (Abbott and Doucouliagos 2003, Table 4).

Just as Friedman's 1955 essay was a response to growing government involvement in higher education in the United States, so too the decade and a half before HECS is defined by a reaction against macro-economic instability and the rising postwar tide of public funding of tertiary education. By the early 1980s, economic and education policy in Australia was in the midst of a major neoliberal turn and significant policy changes were being mooted.

Friedman's neoliberal vision realised: HECS

Thanks to Friedman's 1955 essay, a comprehensive rationale and detailed plans for implementing HECS were readily available before its introduction in 1989. Indeed, Yale University had in the 1970s implemented a commercial student loan scheme, the Tuition Postponement Option, from 1971 to 1978. While it was subject to a substantial orthodox critique (Nerlove 1975), one of the key architects of HECS, Bruce Chapman, was an alumnus of Yale, attending on a Yale University Graduate School Fellowship.

The decisive policy shift toward HECS occurred in the late 1980s, when Susan Ryan, the Minister for Education, was ousted in a cabinet reshuffle and John Dawkins appointed to a super ministry of education and training. Minister Dawkins immediately commissioned a

Discussion Paper (Dawkins 1987) and later a Higher Education Green Paper (Dawkins 1988). Both emphasised the need to greatly expand university student intakes, given technological and economic change, but in a context of other fiscal options (notably a desire to deliver tax cuts), the review raised the question about who would pay for that student expansion.

After the discussion paper, Minister Dawkins commissioned a review into higher education financing, which appeared in May 1988, chaired by former New South Wales Labor premier and then merchant banker, Neville Wran, who engaged Australian National University economist Chapman as an adviser (Chapman and Nicholls 2013, 111). Chapman later recounted that Dawkins and Finance Minister Walsh were committed to reintroducing fees even before the Wran Committee was established (Bessant 2002). Indeed, the terms of reference for the review required it to identify "sources of funding involving the direct beneficiaries of higher education", but also to "have regard to the social and educational consequences of the schemes under consideration" (Wran 1988, ix). In a phrase repeated many times in the Wran Report, the stated objective was "growth and equity".

Crucially, the Wran Report was couched in social democratic rhetoric, but was also heavily indebted to Friedman for the human capital theory and ICL conceptual underpinnings to justify the introduction of HECS. Despite these obvious influences, neither Friedman nor the term "human capital theory" are referred to in the Wran Report, or the other key documents of Dawkins (1987, 1988) and Chapman (1988) arguing for "reform" of higher education. Holliday and Gide (2015) provided a useful comparison of the key economic ideas in Friedman and Wran. They note that HECS differs from Friedman's proposal in three distinct ways. First, with an income-contingent equity scheme, the returns to investors and repayment term are not fixed but, under Wran's proposals, repayment would finish when 20 per cent of course costs were repaid. Second, Friedman assumed no externalities from higher education, but Wran assumed an 80:20 split of public and private benefits. Third, unlike Friedman, HECS formally imposed no interest, but it did index the debt to inflation, and offered a significant discount for early payment.

The Wran Report laid out the key design parameters for HECS and successfully framed subsequent debate in Australia regarding the reintroduction of a user-pays fees scheme, and implementation of an income-contingent loan scheme to pay for them. The basis of HECS was a user-pays model to fund a planned large increase in higher education enrolments, with the budget needing to make way for tax cuts to corporations and higher income earners.

Second, Wran employed human capital theory (without naming it) to characterise university education as an individual "investment", imparting mostly private benefits to individuals through higher lifetime earnings. This proposition and the notion of higher education as a province of middle-class privilege underpinned the application of a user-pays principle to higher education funding. As the Report argued "the advantaged who use and directly benefit from higher education ought to contribute more directly to [its] cost" (Wran 1988, x). Wran sought to balance Friedman's rejection of any positive externalities from higher education by arguing that public investment in universities is justified in part due to the diverse positive social benefits it generates (Wran 1988, 10). This justified the report's planned 80:20 split of public and private funding under HECS. Wran also rejected the neoliberalism of Friedman's anti-statism, by making fee setting and debt collection central state activities.

Finally, Wran used the same neoclassical economic efficiency arguments that Friedman advocated – also absent the cautions of welfare economics – to support HECS. For example, allocative efficiency is said to be improved by imposing a price on the "direct beneficiaries of higher education" for their use of scarce resources (Wran 1988, x).

The Wran Report was therefore innovative in at least two ways. First, it cast its appeal in social-democratic terms, consistent with a Labor government pursuing "equity" to justify the "user-pays" principle, it argued that:

> The fundamental inequity in our present system of financing higher education is that the small and privileged section of the community who benefit directly from access to higher education make no direct contributions to their tuition costs. The bulk of the

> funding burden falls on PAYE taxpayers, the majority of whom are middle to low-income earners (Wran 1988, 15).

Equity was also said to be achieved since student debt payment would not be triggered until the graduate achieved a level of post-study income at which, it was argued, repayments would not be excessively burdensome. This deferred repayment would facilitate university access by disadvantaged groups since it avoided "up-front payments". Setting a moderately high income repayment threshold would also satisfy the "capacity to pay" principle (Wran 1988, 64). Wran (1988) argued the pre-Whitlam system of up-front student fees created a barrier to the participation of smart but poorer students. Finance Minister Walsh, along with Dawkins, a strong supporter for introducing HECS, framed pre-HECS university funding as regressive in its effects, notably dubbing it as a form of "middle-class welfare" (Chapman and Nicholls 2013, 112).

But HECS was not just an agenda to introduce a user-pays scheme, to individualise the costs of university funding, it was also designed to create space for fiscal redistribution to corporations and the wealthy. As the Wran Report itself noted, the context of the introduction of HECS had some important political features, responding to:

> strong pressures to cut both corporate and personal taxation, to reduce the levels of public sector debt and to maintain or increase Commonwealth outlays in areas such as social welfare and health … [and] to reduce the public sector's total share of GDP (Wran 1988, 12).

The Wran Report made two key recommendations: to impose a substantial rise in student tuition fees to better reflect the cost of producing university qualifications; and to introduce an income-contingent loan scheme for those who did not pay their fees up-front (repayments to be delayed until the graduate's income reached average weekly earnings). Both the administration of fee setting and repayment through the income tax system would be a state-run project. Students would at the outset only bear a portion of the total tuition costs, limiting the financial barrier to participation (Wran 1988, 67).

HECS repayments were set at 2 per cent of course costs per annum and designed to recoup 20 per cent of recurrent course costs, giving an expected repayment term of 10 years with a significant discount for up-front or early repayment (Wran 1988, xi).

Wran thus attempted to pragmatically accommodate both neoliberal fiscal rationality and the demand for a significant growth in university enrolments. This was packaged in both formal-sounding economic analysis blended with a social democratic narrative. But rather than an extension of postwar social democracy, HECS should be seen as a response to a fast changing economic and political context, with priority given to a restoration of corporate profits and constraining state expenditures. Wran (1988, xvii) concluded that over time "the net revenue raised from the Committee's proposals represents a significant real addition to the funds available for higher education in ... the order of 22 per cent over current levels".

Reflecting the monetarist and neoliberal intellectual milieu in which HECS was founded, Wran adopted an asymmetric attitude to public and private debt. The fiscal restraint argument, a key rationale for HECS (and indeed for all subsequent income-contingent loans) assumed that shifting financial liabilities from government to private households represented a better form of debt burden with less systemic risk. The Global Financial Crisis in 2007–08 proved this assumption was flawed.

HECS: contradictions and criticisms

Even within its own formal logic, the case for HECS was flawed and contradictory. The first problem was the conflicting and idiosyncratic definition of "equity". The terms of reference required Wran to develop recommendations consistent with the government's commitment "to expanding the capacity and effectiveness of the higher education sector and to improving access to higher education for groups that are currently under-represented" (Wran 1998, vii). This objective was capable of opening an expansive policy agenda, the most obvious relating to overcoming educational disadvantage in early school or even preschool years. In fact, Wran (1988, 53) narrowed this to mean "minimise financial barriers to access at the point of entry" to university via no up-front fees and expanding financial support for low-income students. Even here the Wran Report was quite sceptical that finance was the most significant barrier. It cited studies on the effect of Whitlam's free higher education policy from 1974 to the mid-1980s that found that "fee abolition had a marginal effect at best, on the accessibility of higher education for socially and economically disadvantaged groups" (Wran 1988, 5). More recently Chapman and Nicholls (2013, 122) reported: "An important finding from disparate case studies … is that the socio-economic mix of higher education students seems fairly insensitive to funding regimes". If fee abolition had a marginal effect on class structure of higher education participation, a much stronger case surely needed to be marshalled for the claim that simply delaying fee payment until capacity to pay was attained would promote socio-economic equity. This, after all, along with the user-pays principle, was the main argument of the Wran Report that HECS would be equitable. At best, even its chief advocate conceded that after more than a decade HECS had not significantly improved access for poorer cohorts: "The evidence concerning the effects of HECS on the access of the poor to higher education seems fairly clear … HECS has had a negligible impact overall" (Chapman 1996, 45).

What could explain this narrow interpretation of equity? Here it is worth recalling Friedman, for whom meaningful remedial action in equity terms to lift the participation of disadvantaged groups in higher education is precluded by his "desideratum" that disallows "income redistribution". For some economists, equity equates to redressing (capital) market imperfections simply to enable all to participate in market exchange. For the proponents of income-contingent loans, a precondition was government spending restraint.

Second, the distinction between public and private benefits to education is central to the Wran Report. But the report conceded that this distinction is empirically unverifiable:

> it is not possible to ascertain the exact proportion of higher education benefits which accrue either directly to students or to society. Consequently, it is also difficult to determine the exact level of the appropriate contribution from the individual beneficiaries of higher education (Wran 1988, 53).

Chapman later quantified the scale of uncertainty (or ignorance) around the allocation of private and public returns to higher education:

> Sadly for labour economists and the Wran Committee, even if ... externalities are real, there are no indicators as to their size ... The externalities argument could be interpreted to require a charge to students of 99 per cent of direct costs, zero, or even a government subsidy exceeding direct outlays (Chapman 1988, 175).

The Wran Report discussed several funding options aside from income-contingent loans, but notably did not include for instance in higher education participants paying for their education through progressive income tax over their life course. Indeed, delivering tax cuts explicitly framed the move to a user-pays university financing model, when all the while proponents were claiming that free tuition was regressive! Despite accepting the human capital theory proposition that degrees confer a lifetime earnings benefit, the student contribution to public investment is restricted to the partial cost of the degree. But human capital theory requires higher education be viewed as an investment yielding a return to both the student and taxpayer. Under HECS, after they have paid the costs, graduates do not share the ongoing direct and indirect pecuniary returns with the original investors: that is, the taxpayers. To permit this Wran (1988, 15) also assumed that the investment "return" to taxpayers takes the form of a non-pecuniary externality; that is, "the valuable but amorphous benefit of living in a well-educated society". Orthodox economics also recognises pecuniary externalities, most importantly in this example, a level of GDP higher than the private return to investment in education. Friedman's income-contingent equity scheme presumes an indefinite return to the investor from the student and his income-contingent loan applies an interest charge to the loan to capture these returns.

To arrive at the recommended initial 20 per cent private student fee contribution, Wran relied not on economic theory or rigorous data, but on university course student costs in other nations and pre-1974 Australian student fees; that is, "historical and overseas precedents" (Wran 1988, 53–4). As Chapman (1988, 175) observed, the 80 per cent externality "can't be defended on the basis of empirical evidence". Similar objections apply to deriving the income threshold for HECS and its rate of repayment (*x* and *y* respectively in Friedman's terminology). In 1973 student fees comprised 15 per cent of total course costs, implying a ratio of private to public return of 1:6.6 (Wran 1988, 3). HECS implied a ratio of to 1:5, based on a 20 per cent student fee. In 2022 Universities Australia (2022, 17) suggested the aggregate private:public "split" at 1:1.04. For worthy subjects, such as agriculture, the ratio is 1:7.7. But for unworthy subjects, like economics, the private benefit exceeds the public benefit by a ratio of 14.3:1. (Mysteriously, the calculus of public utility for some courses, such as economics may be correct!)

Finally, like Friedman, Wran used economic terms like allocative and productive efficiency to argue for the benefits of altering university funding and the disposition of funds within universities, yet used these terms instrumentally and selectively, and in deeply contradictory ways.

HECS debt is increasingly regressive and oppressive

The essay has demonstrated that HECS was regressive from its inception. But it has become even more so over time. HECS was premised on the logic of human capital theory that university education confers a substantial wage premium, allowing new graduates to earn higher lifetime incomes. Initially HECS debt repayment would begin only at average weekly earnings (Chapman 1988, 173). Since HECS was implemented, the user-pays principle has expanded, with fees rising and the income threshold at which HECS repayments commence declining substantially in real terms. HECS repayments rates expressed as a percentage of total after-tax income are in effect added to an individual's marginal tax rate until the debt is repaid. In 1989, the first year of HECS, repayments commenced when graduates earned the equivalent of 84 per cent of adult average weekly ordinary full-time earnings. Repayment rates ranged from 1 per cent of post-tax earnings for those on this income threshold; 2 per cent commencing for those on 96 per cent and up to 3 per cent when a graduate's pay exceeded 134 per cent of adult average weekly ordinary full-time earnings (Parliamentary Library 2021, Appendix B). By 2023, the income threshold started at just 52 per cent of adult average weekly ordinary full-time earnings

(Australian Bureau of Statistics 2023, Table 1 November 2022; Australian Taxation Office 2023). Repayment rates now range from 1 per cent of after-tax income for those on this lowest income threshold up to 10 per cent for those on 151 per cent of the average weekly earnings. A 6 per cent rate currently applies to those on average full-time earnings, a tripling of the repayment rate since 1989.

Combined with an increase in the real price of university courses the effect is that "HELP [HECS] loans as a share of total [government] higher education outlays increased from less than 16 per cent in 1989 to 34 per cent in 2020–21" (Universities Australia 2022, 13). The inability to quantify the public–private benefit split from higher education has resulted in "the shifting rationales for student contributions" and generally rising HECS debt (Norton 2022, 30).

There are currently around 3 million Australians with HECS liabilities. In 2021–22, the average time it took to repay student loans was 9.5 years compared to 7.3 years in 2005–06, an increase of 30 per cent (Australian Taxation Office 2022, Table 3). But for current cohorts, the average debt is now about $50,000–60,000 and repayment times likely to be around 12 years, about a quarter of a working life. While no interest is applied to HECS debt, it is indexed to the rate of inflation. With inflation rising faster than wages for some decades, this has pushed up the repayment burden. Notably in 2022, inflation was in excess of 7 per cent; when combined with rising tuition fees for some courses, the increasing rate of inflation has contributed to both previous graduates' existing HECS debts increasing, and new graduates facing larger debt burdens. Indeed, under the current HECS repayment schedule, if the forecast 7.5 per cent CPI indexing is implemented in 2023, only those earning above $120,000 would not find their HECS debt increasing, despite making scheduled repayments (Australian Taxation Office 2022).

Inherent in an income-contingent loan is that those students from wealthier families can pay up-front and receive a discount, and that graduates with higher incomes can repay more quickly. This means that the temporal burden of HECS is much greater for graduates with lower incomes and broken employment. Australian Taxation Office data reveals that women hold the majority of all outstanding student debt, with teachers and nurses the professions carrying the biggest repayment burden. Combined with the changing nature of graduate labour markets and other costs and taxes faced by young workers, Warburton concluded that the long shadow of HECS debt is now helping to create a poverty trap for many young people (cited in Marchant and Young 2023). A recent survey of 1,000 graduates found that not only did women in the survey have higher HECS debt but that they also earned less than their male contemporaries (cited in Ross 2023).

The individualisation of education costs has not helped to make professional labour markets function more efficiently. There have been well known surpluses in professional labour markets such as law, and there are now well-known skill shortages in several key professional labour markets. Some Australian governments are now directly tackling the "debt problem" by offering fee-free tuition scholarships in certain fields to remedy those skill shortages.

HECS and neoliberalism

Neoliberalism is practised through a variety of mechanisms. Some of the dominant mechanisms include opening up state activities to the private sector that are, or can be made, profitable. Privatisation of state assets, public–private partnerships and the contracting out of government services are the archetype of such neoliberal "reforms". A second common mechanism is deregulating markets, especially those for capital and labour. In both cases, it needs to be emphasised, the state has not withdrawn and left the field to market forces. Rather, for a broad range of reasons, the state remains central to the design and operation of these activities; only its management tools have changed. Misreading neoliberalism as a pure free-market agenda is common, but an activist state is now understood as central to the neoliberal project (Block 2008; Stahl 2019; Berry 2022). For example, regulation of former monopoly state assets is needed for some degree of price control and quality, as well as the geographic spread of service provision. Other forms of state control include enacting new labour laws to facilitate "flexibility" in wages, working hours and conditions, or inventing radically new monetary policies to manage the collapse of asset bubbles caused by financial deregulation.

HECS, and income-contingent loans more broadly, represents a different mechanism of neoliberal practice. During the neoliberal era from the 1970s, governments have been seeking to unbundle the rights inherent in the idea of liberal and social democratic citizenship, instead requiring people to manage these essential activities as risks in financial markets. If mass consumers were, to paraphrase Godden (1990), the most important product of mid-20th-century capitalism, then the mass individualisation of households as risk managers is an equally important product of late 20th- and early 21st-century capitalism. Income-contingent loans are a frontier form in this historical process of transforming the relationship between the state and citizen (Clarke et al. 2007; Trentmann and Soper 2008). In the language of neoliberal economics, income-contingent loans substitute for the core risk-management functions of the welfare state. Specifically, income-contingent loans can provide individualised "insurance" against life course needs and contingencies that may have been provided by the state and threaten household survival without formal state entitlement. The sorts of ICL-type schemes that the state could refashion include public healthcare for illness, and "consumption smoothing", such as unemployment benefits and subsidised childcare (Chapman 2006, 1).

Policy initiatives like HECS (along with compulsory superannuation and private health insurance) have developed an individualistic risk-management paradigm where risks and costs are shifted from capital to labour and from the state to households and individuals (Bryan and Rafferty 2018). HECS is one way that labour's financial exposures have been expanded and financial risk products such as income-contingent loans have been created to compel individuals to manage them. Cost shifting and risk shifting are not only means to individualise and financialise life risks but also subject people to the logic and disciplines of finance capital (Crouch 2011; Bryan and Rafferty 2018). Seen in this light, HECS is significant not just in itself but also because it institutes financial contracting for younger people as a condition of entry to adult labour markets. HECS and other policy initiatives are best understood as an (ongoing) state project to decompose and individualise risk and to deny a central (formal) premise of the liberal democratic order: the expansion of the realm of public life and goods. Risk shifting sees a derivative financial logic moving inside the state, transforming the terms of state relations with labour towards a model of "debt-fare" or more broadly "risk-fare" (Soederberg 2014a, 2014b; Bryan, Rafferty and Tinel 2024).

Extending income-contingent loans?

Up to 10 nations are now funding university attendance with user-pays fees and HECS-comparable income-contingent loan schemes (Botterill et al. 2020). There are now also many suggestions to extend the application of income-contingent loans to other areas of state activity. Two important extensions can be identified. First, as above, there is the use of income-contingent loan-type financing to replace a range of government transfers or services currently funded from general government revenue. Second, financial market innovation allows income-contingent loans and equity-contingent loans to be provided directly by private capital markets.

Income-contingent loans have since been proposed to replace – in whole or in part – state expenditure on drought relief, unemployment benefits, grants for small business facing insolvency during COVID, maternity and parental leave, subsidies for solar panel installation for poor people and state-funded economic development of poor regions (Chapman 2006, 2020; Botterill et al. 2020). Important innovations in some proposals are that the income-contingent loans charge interest (unlike HECS) and operate as a public–private partnership. In one example of "joint bank and government lending", the state underwrites bank risk by funding early repayment of commercial loans that, as the proponents note without apparent irony, is "beneficial for the banks" (Botterill et al. 2020). Some proposals argue that there is an underlying market failure justifying the income-contingent loan that is rarely clearly articulated, aside from claims to a generalised financing constraint. Most new income-contingent loan proposals entail picking winners by risk-rating prospective debtors to minimise government liabilities and avoid moral hazard.

Innovations in finance over the last decade in the United States have also permitted the realisation of Friedman's vision of income-contingent *equity* schemes, where instead of a debt, individuals promise a share of their post-study incomes for a certain period. These new financing structures are touted to "enable investors to provide funding to individuals in exchange for a percentage of that individual's future earnings over a specified time period" (Oei and Ring 2014, 266). Equity-contingent loans have been applied to education, business costs and even to budding college athletes. As noted, Friedman recognised the element of "partial slavery" inherent in such human-equity loan contracts; an "analogy" current proponents even accept with some qualifications (Lleras 2002, 2004; Schwartz 2015).

Remarkably, in an inversion of the debt-versus-partial-slavery dichotomy, many advocates of income-contingent equity suggest that the now well-established onerous debt burdens of millions of American graduates reinforces one of the main reasons for income-contingent equity financing as more attractive and "progressive". Income-contingent equity investors currently manage risk by either rationing equity contracts to potential high-performing students in top universities or impose very high rates of return, long income share periods and/or high administrative fees (Schwartz 2015, 1134).

Despite being neither an income-contingent loan nor an income-contingent equity scheme, the system of public and private student-debt funding for college education in the United States provides an insight into a possible future of what one author has called the "debt-fare" state (Soederberg 2014a, b). The stock of US student debt now exceeds $1.6 trillion among 45 million debtors, 16 per cent of whom are in default. Significantly, one-third of all debtors did not complete their studies so receive either no or limited return on their educational "investment". Student debt is also exacerbating class and racial divides. For example, as of 2022 "the typical Black borrower who started college in the 1995–96 school year still owed 95 per cent of their original student debt" (White House 2022). Such is the scale of the problem President Biden recently moved to cancel the outstanding debt of up to 20 million of the current 45 million student debtors, among other measures. What is clear is that student debt in Australia and other countries is now in crisis, and in Australia HECS has blighted more than a generation of university attendees. While also of critical importance, the effects of HECS and fee-based education on the corporatisation of universities is beyond the scope of this chapter.

Conclusion

HECS owes its conceptual origins to an ideologically anti-statist intervention by Milton Friedman in the 1950s, responding to the postwar growth of government funded and provided higher education. But it required an evolution in neoliberal state practice in Australia to realise Friedman's vision, albeit through a neoliberal state rather than a faux free market. HECS, in effect, combined Friedman's ideologically driven project of mass individualisation through imposing fees and income-contingent loans for access to higher education but delivered by the neoliberal state in Australia. HECS has made debt a condition of access to professional labour markets and subjects graduates to the disciplinary effects of debt repayment now typically stretching for over a decade or more. The state's role here combines fee setting, writing debt contracts and debt collection. Through HECS, higher education has been commodified and financialised, not as a free market but more closely as a form of state-imposed coercive commodification (Dukelow and Kennett 2018).

HECS was introduced in Australia in the late 1980s by a social democratic government in advance of a large and planned expansion in higher education enrolments. The arguments used to motivate HECS were framed in broadly social democratic terms such as equity and access, and as a way of correcting a purportedly regressive free education said to amount to middle-class welfare. Income-contingent loans mean that costs are individualised, and that people earning lower incomes and with broken employment patterns will take longer to repay their loans. Thanks to the compounding effects of inflation indexation, they are likely to also pay more than those graduates with higher incomes. And contrary to the claims that HECS was an equitable and progressive policy, it was introduced as an explicit part of a fiscal strategy to lower the top marginal rate of income tax and the corporate tax rate, the two most progressive forms of taxation. HECS is therefore not just conceptually a child of Friedman's neoliberal vision, but its design and implementation were a crucial innovation in neoliberal practice. The fact that this neoliberal innovation was introduced by the Australian Labor Party shows the bipartisanship that has characterised the neoliberal epoch in Australia and elsewhere.

One line of criticism of social democratic (Third Way) governments has been that they did not go far enough in *rolling back* the neoliberalism of previous conservative administrations in countries like the United States, United Kingdom and Australia. But as Stedman Jones recently observed, "[that] would be a misreading of the intentions of the policies of the Third Way 'modernisation'. In fact, what was being attempted was an application of certain crucial neoliberal insights" (2018, 169). With HECS, an Australian social democratic party took the formative moves toward fees and loans from the previous Fraser Coalition government and advanced it to implementation. HECS was and remains a neoliberal project that draws on market ideology, combined with welfare state discipline, debt collection and supervision, but is touted as equitable and fair.

The former Australian National University-based neoliberal economist Max Corden criticised the Dawkins reforms, including HECS, as an inconsistent mixture of free market and state planning reforms that "moved the system both towards Moscow *and* towards the market" (Corden 2005, 7). As with Friedman's proposals, HECS was an unacknowledged application of neoliberal human capital theory. Marginson (1989, 35) noted that human capital theory is a universalising agenda, an expression of an illiberal turn reframing humans not as citizens with complex subjectivity and social rights, but as analogous to a capital good, with education as an augmenting "investment" in the value of a human capital subject. Marginson made the critical point that human capital theory seeks not just to offer a theory of education, labour markets and income distribution, but more importantly a highly normative and prescriptive model to recast the world in its own image:

> [human capital theory] reaches conclusions that produce its own model, its own free market assumptions, which are its own conditions of possibility. Producing the human capital model in

> real life therefore becomes the object of educational policies informed by human capital theory (Marginson 1989, 35).

What for Corden was a contradiction between markets and the state in higher education through HECS is better understood as a reflection of an important feature of contemporary neoliberal practice. For neoliberalism to gain hegemony it had to not tear down the state and free up markets, but to become part of the organising logic of the state. It turns out that the state has been integral in neoliberalism's broader political and cultural project of mass individualisation and securitisation. In this, the role of the state is not diminished in the fashion of ideological versions of market liberalism, but rather its role shifts from funding and administering activities to establishing the conditions for citizens to be financial subjects responsible for managing their life-course risks, with the state both shifting risks and costs, as well as supervising those who may not be "self-managing". In this sense, HECS and other income-contingent loans can be seen for what they really are: a foundational neoliberal innovation with a direct lineage to Milton Friedman's earliest policy proposals. The current contradictions and flaws of HECS are also reflective of the divisive and unequal, as well as crisis and conflict-ridden, nature of neoliberalism. Confronting the crisis in HECS and student debt more generally will require confronting the logic of neoliberalism, because one of the strengths of that logic is to exclude all other possible alternatives, not just in funding but in the organising logic of higher education. The purpose of this chapter has been to provide a historicising critique of HECS and the flawed and socially destructive logic that underpins it in the hope of developing those much-needed alternatives.

References

Abbott, M. and Doucouliagos, C. (2003). *The Changing Structure of Higher Education in Australia, 1949–2003*. School Working Paper 2003/07. School of Accounting, Economics and Finance, Deakin University. https://tinyurl.com/2wc87w25.

Australian Bureau of Statistics (2019). *Australian Historical Population Statistics, 2019*, Cat. no. 3105.0.65.001.

Australian Bureau of Statistics (2023). *Average Weekly Earnings, November 2022, Australia*. Cat. no. 6302.0.
Australian Taxation Office (2022). *Higher Education Loan Program HELP Statistics, 2005–06 to 2021–22 Financial Years*.
Australian Taxation Office (2023). HECS-HELP debt. https://tinyurl.com/38hvuw38.
Barr, N. (1998). Higher education in Australia and Britain: what lessons? *Australian Economic Review* 31(2): 179–88. https://eprints.lse.ac.uk/archive/00000285.
Barr, N. (2016). Milton Friedman and the finance of higher education. In R. Cord and J. Daniel Hammond, eds. *Milton Friedman: Contributions to Economics and Public Policy*, 436–63. Oxford: Oxford University Press.
Berry, C. (2022). The substitutive state? Neoliberal state interventionism across industrial, housing and private pensions policy in the UK. *Competition and Change* 26(2): 242–65.
Bessant, J. (2002). Dawkins' Higher Education Reforms and How Metaphors Work in Policy Making. *Journal of Higher Education Policy and Management* 24(1): 87–99.
Blaug, M. (1976). The empirical status of human capital theory: a slightly jaundiced survey. *Journal of Economic Literature* 14(3): 827–55.
Block, F. (2008). Polanyi's double movement and the reconstruction of critical theory. *Papers in Political Economy* 38. https://doi.org/10.4000/interventionseconomiques.274.
Botterill, L., B. Chapman, G. Withers and W.J. McKibben (2020). Give people and businesses money now they can pay back later (if and when they can). *The Conversation*, 29 March. https://tinyurl.com/2vedrmvv.
Brancatisano, E. (2022). 'It's depressing': Millions of Australians face growing HECS debts as indexation rate hits 10-year high. *SBS News*, 23 July. https://tinyurl.com/58xaawnd.
Brown, W. (2015). *Undoing the Demos - Neoliberalism's Stealth Revolution*. Princeton: Princeton University Press.
Bryan, D., R. Martin and M. Rafferty (2009). Financialisaton and Marx: giving labor and capital a financial makeover. *Review of Radical Political Economy* 41(4): 458–72.
Bryan, D. and M. Rafferty (2018). *Risking Together – How Finance Is Dominating Everyday Life in Australia*, Sydney: Sydney University Press.
Bryan, D., M. Rafferty and B. Tinel (2024). Financialisation and the Riskfare State mimeo.
Carson, E. and H. Kerr (1988). Social welfare downunder *Critical Social Policy* 23(Autumn): 70–82.

Cassidy, C. (2023). Number of Australian enrolled in bachelor degrees falls by 12% in less than a decade. *The Guardian*, 16 November.

Cockburn, G. (2022). Greens' Mehreen Faruqi makes election promise to scrap student debt if the party holds balance of power. *Canberra Times*, 24 March. https://tinyurl.com/5ey7kn6k.

Chapman, B. (1988). An economic analysis of the Higher Education Contribution Scheme of the Wran Report. *Economic Analysis and Policy* 1(2): 171–88.

Chapman, B. (1996). The rationale for the Higher Education Contribution Scheme. *Australian Universities Review* 1: 43–50.

Chapman, B. (2006). *Government Managing Risk: Income Contingent Loans for Social and Economic Progress*. London: Routledge.

Chapman, B. (2020). Income-contingent loans: the fair(er) financing system. *EOS*, 2 May. https://tinyurl.com/vh6f998t.

Chapman, B. and J. Nicholls (2013). HECS. In G. Croucher, S. Marginson, A. Norton and J. Wells, eds. *The Dawkins Revolution: 25 years on*, 108–125. Melbourne: Melbourne University Publishing.

Champion, R. (2015). Hayek in Australia, 1976. In R. Leeson, ed. *Hayek: A Collaborative Biography. Archival Insights into the Evolution of Economics*. London: Palgrave Macmillan.

Clarke, J., J. Newman, N. Smith, E. Vidler and L. Westmarland (2007). *Creating Citizen-consumers: Changing Publics and Changing Public Services*. London: Sage Publications.

Commonwealth of Australia (1981). *Parliamentary Debates*, House of Representatives. 18 November: 3138 (Wal Fife, Minister for Education). https://tinyurl.com/yc6a6jpr.

Corden, M. (2005). Australian universities: Moscow on the Molonglo. *Quadrant Magazine* 49(November): 7–20.

Courvisanos, J. and A. Millmow (2006). How Milton Friedman came to Australia: a case study of class-based political business cycles. *Journal of Australian Political Economy* 57(June): 112–36.

Crouch, C. (2011). *The Strange Non-Death Of Neoliberalism*. Cambridge: Polity Press.

Department of Education (2014). *Higher Education Students Time Series Tables*, https://tinyurl.com/ytuk8524

Dukelow, F. and P. Kennett (2018). Discipline, debt and coercive commodification: post-crisis neoliberalism and the welfare state in Ireland, the UK and the USA. *Critical Social Policy* 38(3): 482–504.

Friedman, M. (1955). The role of government in education. In R. Solow, ed. *Economics and the Public Interest*, 123–44. New Brunswick, NJ: Rutgers University Press. https://tinyurl.com/y9mbj642.

Friedman, M., and S. Kuznets (1945). *Income from Independent Professional Practice*. Cambridge, MA: National Bureau of Economic Research. https://www.nber.org/books/frie54-1.

Godden, R. (1990). *Fictions of Capital: The American Novel from James to Mailer*. Cambridge, UK: Cambridge University Press.

Harman, G. (1981). The "razor gang" decisions, the guidelines to the commissions, and Commonwealth education policy. *Vestes* 24(2): 28–40. https://files.eric.ed.gov/fulltext/EJ253967.pdf

Higgins, T. (2019). The Higher Education Contribution Scheme: keeping tertiary education affordable and accessible. In J. Luetjens, M. Mintrom and P. Hart, eds. *Successful Public Policy: Lessons from Australia and New Zealand*. Canberra: ANU Press.

Holliday, S. and E. Gide (2015). Moving towards market driven higher education in Australia: is it time to look at economist Milton Friedman? *International Journal of Arts and Sciences* 08(05): 303–20.

Lobell, K. (2023). Why Fewer Employers Are Requiring College Degrees. *Society for Human Resource Management*, 11 September.

LaCava, G. (2019). The Labour and Capital Shares of Income in Australia, *Reserve Bank of Australia Bulletin*, March.

Lleras, M.P. (2002). Human Capital Contracts: "Equity-Like" Instruments for Financing Higher Education, *Policy Analysis*, 16 December.

Lleras, M.P. (2004). *Investing in Human Capital: A Capital Markets Approach to Student Funding*. Cambridge: Cambridge University Press.

Lipsey, R., and K. Lancaster (1956). The general theory of second best. *Review of Economic Studies* 24: 11–32.

Marchant, G., and E. Young (2023). How HECS and HELP debt have helped entrench women's economic disadvantage. *ABC News*, 4 March. https://tinyurl.com/yc4v8xr3.

Marginson, S. (1989). Human Capital Theory and Education Policy, Discussion Paper No. 3. Social Policy Research Centre, UNSW, November.

Marginson, S. (1997). *Markets in Education*. Sydney: Allen & Unwin.

MacPherson, C.B. (1968). Elegant tombstones: a note on Friedman's freedom. *Canadian Journal of Political Science/Revue canadienne de science politique* 1(1)(March): 95–106. https://www.jstor.org/stable/i362111.

National Center for Education Statistics (n.d.). Indicator 45: Source of Funds for Education. https://nces.ed.gov/pubs/eiip/eiip45s1.asp.

Nerlove, M. (1975). Some problems in the use of income-contingent loans for the financing of higher education. *Journal of Political Economy* 83(1): 157–84.

Norton, A. (2022). *From Public to Private Benefit: The Shifting Rationales for Setting Student Contributions*. Melbourne Centre for the Study of Higher Education Occasional Paper. https://tinyurl.com/3t6sp3t7.

Oei, S.-Y. and Ring, D.M. (2014). The New 'Human Equity' Transactions (June 2014). 5 *California Law Review Circuit*, Boston College Law School Legal Studies Research Paper No. 315, Tulane Public Law Research Paper No. 13-20. https://doi.org/10.2139/ssrn.2353673.

Parliamentary Library (2021). *The Higher Education Loan Program (HELP) and Related Loans: A Chronology*. https://tinyurl.com/4975ddts.

Ross, J. (2023). Australian student loan debt getting higher, lasting longer. *Times Higher Education*, 7 March.

Salmi, J. (1999). Student loans in an international perspective: The World Bank experience. The World Bank. LCSHD paper series no. 44: Washington: World Bank Group. https://tinyurl.com/2yr8a6y2.

Schultz, T. (1961). Investment in human capital. *The American Economic Review* 51(1): 1–17.

Schwartz, J. (2015). The corporatization of personhood. *University of Illinois Law Review*, 1119–76.

Schwarz, J. (2022). The Origin Of Student Debt: Reagan Adviser Warned Free College Would Create A Dangerous "Educated Proletariat", *The Intercept*, 6 August. https://tinyurl.com/wupk7nn6.

Sharples, S. (2021). Australia's average full-time salary now above $90,000. *News.com.au*, 20 August. https://tinyurl.com/cbat9wy8.

Soederberg, S. (2014a). *Debtfare States and the Poverty Industry: Money, Discipline, and the Surplus Population*. London: Routledge.

Soederberg, S. (2014b). Student loans, debtfare and the commodification of debt: the politics of securitization and the displacement of risk. *Critical Sociology* 40(5): 689–709.

Stahl, R. (2019). Economic liberalism and the state: dismantling the myth of the naïve laissez-faire state. *New Political Economy* 24(19): 473–86.

Stedman Jones, D. (2012) *Masters of The Universe – Hayek, Friedman and the Birth of Neoliberal Politics*. Princeton, NJ: Princeton University Press.

Stedman Jones, D. (2018). The neoliberal origins of the Third Way: How Chicago, Virginia and Bloomington shaped Clinton and Blair. In D. Cahill, M. Konings, M. Cooper and D. Primrose, eds. *The SAGE Handbook of Neoliberalism*, 167–78. London: Sage Publications.

Stiglitz, J. (2014). Remarks on income contingent loans: how effective can they be at mitigating risk? In B. Chapman, T. Higgins and J.E. Stiglitz, eds. *Income Contingent Loans: Theory, Practice and Prospects*, 39–48. Basingstoke, UK, and New York, NY: Palgrave Macmillan.

Stiglitz, J.E. (2016). Income-contingent loans: some general theoretical considerations, with applications. In J.E. Stiglitz and M. Guzman, eds. *Contemporary Issues in Microeconomics*, 129–36. International Economic Association Series. Basingstoke, UK and New York: Palgrave Macmillan.

Tilley, P. (2021). 1985 reform of the Australian tax system, TTPI - Working Paper 7/2021 April 2021, Tax and Transfer Policy Institute, Crawford School of Public Policy, Australian National University, Canberra.

Trentmann, F., and K. Soper, eds (2008). *Citizenship and Consumption.* Basingstoke, UK: Palgrave Macmillan.

Universities Australia (2022). *Higher Education Facts and Figures.* https://tinyurl.com/2p8fm24r.

Warburton, M. (2023). *Gender, Equity and Policy Neglect in Student Financing of Tertiary Education.* Occasional paper, Melbourne Centre for the Study of Higher Education. https://tinyurl.com/32k4axwt.

White House (2022). President Biden announces student loan relief for borrowers who need it most. Fact Sheet, 24 August. https://tinyurl.com/yr2fjt4w.

Whiteford, P. (2013). *Australia: Inequality and prosperity and their impacts in a radical welfare state*, HC Coombs Policy Forum, Australian National University, Canberra, March.

Wran, N. (1988) *Report of the Committee on Higher Education Funding*. Canberra: Australian Government Publishing Service. [Wran Report]

16

Port privatisation in Australia: Justifications and outcomes

Darryn Snell and Victor Gekara

Privatisation is typically at the forefront of neoliberal political policies. But transferring public assets to private hands is often controversial and unpopular with a cross-section of society. While public ownership, particularly in relation to strategic infrastructure, has long been considered a public good, neoliberal advocates seek to present the business case for, and market virtues of, privatisation. By presenting privatisation as a smart business decision that will benefit consumers, the neoliberal aim is to distract from the political decision to allow the appropriation of public assets by capital (Graham and Silke 2017). The neoliberal business case for privatisation also often seeks to identify, blame and discipline labour all at the same time. Public sector workers are identified as overly entitled, costly and the source of inefficiencies. Privatisation is therefore often presented as the way to discipline labour and improve competitiveness (forgetting that public sector organisations had not been held to the same competitive forces, standards and expectations as private ones).

This chapter considers the privatisation of ports and the neoliberal narratives surrounding it, with a focus on port privatisation in Australia. Port privatisation in Australia took a particular form as a result of problems that emerged with earlier port privatisation abroad. We begin by presenting the history of port privatisation followed by a discussion of Australia's approach to port privatisation and the neoliberal narratives surrounding it. Central to our assessment of port privatisation in Australia are government efforts to reduce the level of worker control and union influence on the nation's ports to make them more attractive and lucrative for international port operators.

Port privatisation

The history of port privatisation, internationally, goes back to the early 1980s when British Prime Minister Margaret Thatcher introduced some of the earliest and most aggressive neoliberal policies of the late 20th century. The mass sell-off of public assets was at the core of Thatcher's policies and this included a wholesale offloading of port ownership and operations to the private sector. In the history of port reform, it was not until the middle of the 20th century that ports became central in the organisation of global supply chains. Their role until then, albeit significant, was simply as points of trade transfer as opposed to central facilitators of trade, as happened in the late 20th century. From this point on, two critical developments started, leading to a series of reforms that eventuated in privatisation. First, as commercial significance of ports became apparent, the opportunity for making private profit from operating ports became apparent to private investors. Second, the increasing importance of ports meant that large amounts of capital investment were required to develop and upgrade port infrastructure, which governments, under the influence of finding market solutions, were either unable or less inclined to provide.

A variety of reforms between the 1960s and 1990s saw increasing involvement of the private sector in port development and management and, by extension, increasing intra-port (that is, between terminal operators), and in some cases inter-port, competition, even at the local level. With increasing global competition and heightened demand for rapid processing of global products through port facilities, resulting from accelerated global integration, a key focus for governments became port efficiency and productivity as a way of improving overall global economic performance. The prominent neoliberal narrative that bureaucratic structures of the governments that owned and operated ports had contributed to port inefficiencies and productivity problems became increasingly common, as did the notion that governments no longer had access to the resources required to invest in port infrastructure.

Like many other sectors of the economy, privatisation in ports was, therefore, commonly promoted on the basis of claimed positive economic outcomes: improved efficiency and higher productivity. As many also observed, it was underpinned by the political motivations to reduce long-term financial and administrative responsibility for governments (Andic 1990; Roman 1993; Ferdousi 1996; Kelly 1996; Cullinane and Song 2002). The prevailing neoliberal economic policies of the time, under the Reagan and Thatcher regimes in the United States and United Kingdom respectively, created an environment in which deregulation was long seen as the way to harness the wealth-creating efficiencies of private enterprise for public good. Following Adam Smith, proponents believed that limiting government control and promoting the profit motivations of business would enhance the competitiveness necessary for wealth creation and overall socio-economic prosperity (Smith 1776). In this argument, port privatisation was motivated by several factors, as highlighted in Brittan (1986):

- the economic benefit promise of enhanced productive performance
- the political objective of reducing government financial and administrative responsibility
- the need to resolve the tension between government and nationalised industries
- the raising of revenue
- the reduction in the power of public sector unions, and
- the promotion of the neoliberal capitalism agenda.

In the mid-1980s when the Thatcher government was in the midst of a privatisation frenzy, British economists began vigorously debating the virtues and long-term legacies of these decisions. The privatisation of natural monopolies was by far the most controversial. George Yarrow and his colleagues made this noteworthy observation:

> There is no necessary presumption for the superiority of the private over the public sector. Indeed, one can make quite a good case for saying that in many contexts public management would

> do better than selfish private management wishing to exploit a natural monopoly (1986, 366).

These criticisms certainly applied to Thatcher's sale of 19 ports in 1983, which comprised the former state-owned Associated British Ports. Other countries soon followed the United Kingdom in port privatisation. But many countries came to perceive the British approach to port privatisation as too extreme, both in scale (selling all off in one go) and the approach (complete sale as opposed to short-term or long-term leases) to be replicated at home. Furthermore, many academic studies of such radical approaches, against the promised economic benefits, concluded that the transfer of ports into private hands never translated into the anticipated enhancements in productive efficiency. Kay and Thompson (1986), for example, found no evidence of superior port performance under private ownership. Similar conclusions were reached by Brittan (1986) and Vickers and Yarrow (1988) in the United Kingdom, and Jörgensen (1990) in Canada. But governments did achieve the political goal of relinquishing financial and administrative responsibility for port assets. Many of these researchers concluded that boosting productive efficiency of ports never required privatisation; rather, as Vickers and Yarrow (1988) argued, it is competitive pressure that primarily drives performance and most national ports were natural monopolies. Because port competition is mostly at the level of terminal operators, there was never any need for the wholesale approach that was adopted. The general consensus of this research was that no real efficiency gains arose from the mass privatisation exercise.

What were the other available options?

Port ownership and administration, internationally, follow one of three broad models, which are defined based on the extent of private-sector involvement. At one extreme end is the public service port in which ownership and operations are solely controlled by government, while at the other is the private service port, where private entities own and manage all aspects of the port, including the land. In the middle are tool and landlord ports, where ownership and administration of port assets and operations are shared by public and private entities to varying degrees (see Table 16.1).

The tool and landlord port models, where ownership and administration are shared between public and private, tend to be more popular currently. Although some governments, particularly in developing countries, own and operate their ports under the public service port model, elsewhere the majority have found the associated financial burden too heavy. But in their approach to privatisation, many, unlike the United Kingdom, choose to maintain title to port land, and a degree of regulatory oversight, because of strategic importance attached to ports. Like public service ports, therefore, private service ports are also rare.

Table 16.1 Port ownership and administration models.

Models	Infrastructure	Superstructure	Operations	Other services
Public service port	Public	Public	Public	Majority public
Tool port	Public	Public	Private	Public/ private
Landlord port	Public	Private	Private	Public/ private
Private service port	Private	Private	Private	Majority private

Source: *Port Reform Toolkit* (n.d.), Module 3.

As indicated earlier, and perhaps due to lessons learned from the United Kingdom, privatisation in Australia adopted a landlord approach (Chen, Pateman and Sakalayen 2017). Rather than a complete sale of port assets and transfer of all rights and liabilities, including port land title to the private sector, a long-term lease approach was chosen. In this case, the state governments retained title to port land and leased out all assets and operations rights to private business – often 98- or 99-year terms. As Chen, Pateman and Sakalayen explained:

> Australian governments retain the port land title but grant a century long-term lease of port land and operation to the

> established state-owned transaction holding company, where other port assets and the liability and rights of port corporations are transferred, to be privatised through the sale of shares. It is a long-term leasehold sale, different from the full privatisation cases in the UK, in which the government relinquished the land property rights to the private sector (2017, 207).

The dominant justification for port privatisation in Australia was the promised enhancement of the productive efficiency of these critical institutions, which would translate into efficient international trade operations and lower associated costs. Yet many studies and neoliberal economic advocates argued that enhancing the productive efficiency and performance of such institutions primarily depends on competitive pressures. The general conclusion seems that it is only when such organisations operate in a competitive environment that their innovativeness, efficiency and productivity will increase (Aghion et al. 2018). In the UK case, misalignment between the motivations and approaches led to the conclusion that little, if any, gains accrued in the productive efficiency of the privatised ports and associated national economic benefits (Vickers and Yarrow 1988; Goss 1998; Baird 2000). But it is worth noting that, while efficiency, productivity and performance were the supposed key considerations in those earlier privatisation projects, other factors were at play including revenue generation through sale of public assets, reducing the power of unions and promoting the wider neoliberal capitalist agenda (Brittan 1986; Cullinane and Song 2002). Everett (1995) made a similar distinction between the explicitly stated government rationales for port privatisation in Australia and the real or implicit reasons associated with dealing with government budgetary problems and broader ideological agendas. It is similarly worth noting that, considering that the most efficient port in the world currently is the publicly owned port of Singapore, privatisation was never the only, or even the best, way to achieve productive efficiency.

We argue that promoting the neoliberal capitalist agenda and undermining the power of unions were core objectives, not simply other factors, and that the observed outcomes were neither unexpected nor unintended. The coincidence of Britain's privatisation with

Thatcher's famous crackdown on unions and the acceleration of Australia's port privatisation in the wake of the historic 1999 waterfront dispute (Dabscheck 1998; Griffin and Svensen 1998; McConville 2000; Davies 2019), for example, were not accidental. The important questions here include the following: how has the Australia port privatisation project differed from that of the United Kingdom, in terms of motivations and outcomes? And what are the implications for the future of ports and port work?

Australia's port privatisation approach

Australia's post-2000 port privatisation accelerated the transfer of control of public ports to private businesses, allowing extensive restructuring of work in ways that significantly undermined the power of the Maritime Union of Australia (MUA) and other transport workers' unions. This opened the window to the rapid implementation of labour-saving technologies and organisational changes with significant transformation of the industry and its workforce (Griffin and Svensen 1998; Shaw 1999). The privatisation journey in Australia has been more complex than that in many countries because of the complex structure of traditional port ownership. Traditionally, Australian ports had been owned and administered by states and territories. Only a few are purely private from the start and those are mostly operated by private mining companies for their exclusive transfer of export commodities, such as iron ore and coal. This meant that each state and territory followed different motivations and processes, and was guided by different regulatory frameworks, while at the same time operating under the overarching national economic interests and operating within the federal laws.

In its privatisation project, Australia has undertaken incremental port governance reforms since the mid-1990s, starting with commercialisation of port management followed by the corporatisation of port authorities. This, in most cases, paved the way to full privatisation. Although full privatisation, in the current form, started in 2001 with the 99-year lease of land and an operating licence for the ports under the South Australian Port Corporation to Flinders Ports

Pty Limited, it was not until a decade later, from 2010 onwards, that this model of privatisation took root and accelerated across the country (see Chen, Pateman and Sakalayen 2017 for a detailed discussion of this evolution of port governance in Australia).

Port privatisation and worker control

This chapter argues that privatisation in the 1980s was a key part of the neoliberal capitalist agenda, where private business stood to gain the most. And here unions' push for better wages and working conditions was largely viewed as a threat to this agenda, and reducing union influence became a focus of successive governments internationally. But the social democratic underpinnings of many of these states, and the widespread sympathies for unions on the left of politics, ensured that privatisation was not without contention.

Despite the growing international evidence that privatisation was not a panacea to port efficiency, governments in Australia continued to pursue port privatisation, suggesting that other agendas might have lain behind this public policy shift. The debates, as important as they were, failed to appreciate that the end was not solely about improving efficiencies and productivity through private means, but about the other factors driving privatisation decisions: advancing neoliberal capitalism and undermining workers' control and union influence. Dealing with efficiency and productivity concerns through privatisation of the public sector was, in many ways then, a smokescreen for advancing an anti-union neoliberal agenda aimed at reducing worker control. In Australia, this became most blatant in the 1999 waterfront dispute involving Patrick Stevedores and the MUA.

Up until the early 1990s, Patrick Stevedores was a government-controlled company that was "culturally close to the maritime union" (Trinca and Davies 2000, 17) and that competed with P&O Ports for port services on government-owned and government-controlled ports. In 1994, the Australian Labor Party government led by Paul Keating sold its share in Patrick Stevedores to the merchant banker Chris Corrigan who proceeded to take full control of the company and pursue aggressive workplace reforms (Griffin and

Svensen 1998; McConville, 2000; Davies, 2019). Segments of Australia's business community and farmers had long complained that Australia's waterfront was inefficient and a major threat to the country's international competitiveness. Wages and work practices related to staffing levels, recruitment and training, as well as the career progression maintained by the MUA, were commonly presented by business leaders, farmers and conservative governments as the major barrier to achieving improvements in port efficiency (Sheil 2017). The MUA's preparedness to use industrial action to protect the wages and conditions they had achieved through the bargaining process further confirmed, for these reactionary business and government interests, that minimising the MUA's influence on the ports must become a national priority. With the election of the conservative Howard Coalition government in 1996, workplace reform on the waterfront was given increased attention, with the government working closely with Patrick Stevedores on a plan to lock out port workers and employ a non-union workforce. Although the dispute was nominally between the MUA and Patrick Stevedores, it was widely seen as much bigger than that. Griffith and Svensen (1998, 194), for example, describe it as "the first real trial of strength between the then conservative [John Howard-led] government elected in 1996 and the union movement".

The core of the dispute involved a move by Patrick Stevedores to break the power of the union by replacing the entire workforce with non-unionised workers. This move, as long established in the literature, was actively orchestrated and coordinated by the government (Trinca and Davies 2000). The express objective, for both the Commonwealth government and Patrick, was to reduce waterfront labour costs and boost waterfront productivity and efficiency, improving the economy by reducing the cost of shipping. Post-dispute analyses have concluded that the strategy adopted, in its design and implementation, had little to do with this stated objective. Instead, many have concluded, as Griffin and Svensen (1998, 196–7) did, that "either the government choice of strategy for 'waterfront reform' was inept, or there were other, unstated objectives". We argue that the primary objective of the government was to debilitate the MUA, whose notoriety for its militancy in responding to employer exploitation at the waterfront and elsewhere, in collaboration with other unions, was seen as an obstacle in the way of Howard's neoliberal project. The thinking around the orchestrators of the dispute was that Patrick's success would pave the way for a large-scale replacement of worker-negotiated collective agreements with individual contract agreements. Apparently, this would make Australia a more business-friendly destination. Although there was no clear winner from this dispute, the general consensus was that the MUA was bruised but not defeated, with union collective agreements still a feature regulating work on the waterfront. The immediate implications – for Patrick and for the MUA – are easily understood: the MUA cemented its position on the waterfront and Patrick achieved concessions for voluntary redundancies and a reduced wage bill. The Howard government underwrote the redundancy bill under the condition that crane-lift efficiencies improved to 25 crane-lifts an hour. Trinca and Davies (2000, 281) noted that, by 2000, the crane rates had improved to around 21 lifts per hour, but savings had not been passed on to shipping companies, much to their disappointment.

The outsourcing of stevedoring to private operators like Patrick Stevedores and P&O Ports was, in many ways, the precursor to a more comprehensive port privatisation agenda. The resolve and single-mindedness with which the Commonwealth government pursued the MUA left little doubt that the war against the union was not over. The flurry of port privatisation in the two decades after the dispute was, therefore, not surprising (see Table 16.2). It is also not surprising that, at the time, the waterfront dispute was widely viewed as a contest between the unions and the conservative government actively promoting a neoliberal economic agenda and laying the grounds for an unfettered free market economy. By entering into long-term lease agreements with port operators for full responsibility for port operations and maintenance, government involvement in the ownership and management of ports was significantly reduced, allowing employers the powers to restructure waterfront work and labour on their terms, including introducing a wide range of worker-displacing technologies. Under the previous arrangements, port operators like Patrick were expected to consult more widely with government before introducing major changes to the port.

Table 16.2 Ownership and administration of privatised ports in Australia. Source: Adapted and revised from Chen, Pateman and Sakalayen (2017, 204, 206).

Port	Year of privatisation; duration	State/ Territory	Regulator	Landlord
South Australian Ports	2001; 99 year-lease	SA	SA state government	Flinders Ports
Port of Brisbane	2010; 99 year-lease	Qld	Qld Department of Transport and Main Roads	Port of Brisbane Pty Ltd
Port Botany	2013; 99 year-lease	NSW	Port Authority of NSW	NSW Ports
Port Kembla	2013; 99 year-lease	NSW	Port Authority of NSW	NSW Ports
Port of Newcastle	2014; 98 year-lease	NSW	Port Authority of NSW	Port of Newcastle Investments
Darwin Port	2015; 99 year-lease	NT	Public: Regional Harbourmaster; Minister. Independent Regulator: Northern Territory Utilities Commission (Access and pricing). Private: Darwin Port Operations Pty Ltd	Darwin Port Operations Pty Ltd
Port of Melbourne	2016; 50-year lease	Vic	Ports Victoria	Lonsdale consortium

Privatisation is not only about transferring publicly owned assets and operations to the private sector but also revising the terms and conditions of employment (Fairbrother 1994). Commonly associated with privatisation are attempts to terminate collective agreements, as part of public-to-private ownership transfers, allowing new private owners to put in place new agreement conditions and change staff as deemed necessary. In the case of the Australian waterfront, this has been a common battleground for the MUA and other port unions. Unions have sought to minimise the fallout from such action by negotiating provisions for the transfer of existing conditions and the entire workforces to new private owners in cases involving privatisation, with varying degrees of success (Workplace Express 2012).

With the ability to disrupt supply chains, waterfront workers are in a powerful position to resist these sorts of attacks on their members' wages and conditions (Gekara and Fairbrother 2013). Australia maintains highly restrictive industrial relations legislation which enables employers to apply to the industrial courts to have industrial action lifted in situations where they can demonstrate that such action is a threat to the national economy. Qube Holdings, current owners of Patrick Terminals, is one of the most recent private operators to pursue a wide range of challenges to working in their enterprise-bargaining negotiations with the MUA in 2021 (Workplace Express 2021c).

Negotiating agreements with private operators has not proven easy for Australia's waterfront unions. There are a number of areas where private owners have sought major concessions from the MUA including over rosters, staffing levels, influence on hiring and career progression practices, the use of contractors, redundancy and workplace reorganisation provisions. Private operators have also sought concessions that make it easier for them to introduce major technological changes. As noted by Snell and Gekara (2023), internationally, port operators are pursuing rapid technological change aimed at port automation. Employers have argued, and research has consistently highlighted, these technologies have delivered efficiency, productivity and cost benefits (e.g., Kia et al. 2000, xxvii; Choi et al. 2003; Gekara and Thanh-Nguyen 2018). But, as Gekara and Fairbrother (2013) observed, these private terminal operators also saw these technologies as a solution to the industrial power of port workers' unions.

While Patrick has automated all yard cargo movement at its Sydney and Brisbane terminals, Victoria International Container Terminal (VICT), operated by the Philippine-based International Container Terminal Services, Inc., has proven to be the most aggressive terminal operator in Australia in terms of introducing port automation and changes to employment conditions. VICT led in the redevelopment of its operations in Port of Melbourne to become Australia's first fully automated terminal. In doing so, VICT sought to introduce new work practices and employment conditions, which led to a protracted industrial battle between the company and the MUA that lasted four years and came to be dubbed "robodock" wars. Through automation, VICT replaced operators in cranes with remote control-tower–based operators who use joysticks, screens and robotics to move containers through the port, enabling them to reduce staffing levels to about a third of traditional container terminals (Workplace Express 2021a). VICT also sought to rely on a casual and contract workforce for remaining work (e.g., pinning and lashing of containers) and enforce a non-union agreement. After an extensive industrial campaign by the MUA, VICT finally signed a union agreement with the MUA in July 2021 that covered a substantially reduced workforce of 128 employees (Workplace Express 2021b).

In our view, the innovation and efficiency gains promised by privatisation of ports are proving elusive. Instead, as long argued in the empirical literature, firms involved in privatised natural monopolies are more likely to pursue rent-extraction strategies rather than innovation and productivity gain strategies (Myers 1972; Megginson and Mueller 2022). A recent report by the Australian Competition and Consumer Commission (ACCC) into port efficiency barriers makes this point very explicitly. The ACCC identified a number of port efficiencies emerging from how privatisation was handled and the fact that "privatised container ports in Australia were privatised without effective regulation being put in place" (ACCC 2021, 28). It raised particular concern about the rent-seeking behaviour of governments, as well as port operators, as a major contributing factor in the productivity challenges for the nation's ports: "Container ports in Australia are regional monopolies and, in the absence of appropriate regulatory oversight, can extract monopoly rents from port users who are unable to choose to go to an alternative port" (ACCC 2021, 28).

The Productivity Commission's *Lifting Productivity at Australia's Ports* report (2022) comes to similar conclusions, finding:

> lack of competition in some parts of the maritime logistics system means consumers pay too much ... Transport operators have no choice about which terminal they use when picking up or

> dropping off a container, so must pay whatever price a terminal operator sets (Productivity Commission 2022, 2).

These arrangements also help to ensure monopoly port operators are able to protect profits. The *Australian Financial Review*, for example, in its reporting of Qube Holdings' annual profits, noted:

> Patrick's volumes were about 2 per cent down on a year earlier in the 12 months to June. But the container port group still contributed some $40 million to Qube's profits, up from $27.7 million on a year earlier. Qube said increases in the infrastructure fees charged to users of ports had helped offset costs (Wiggins 2022).

That conclusion merely confirms the findings of earlier studies that pointed out that privatisation, on its own, without an appropriate competitive business environment, would achieve little in the ways of productive efficiency and overall performance (Vickers and Yarrow 1988). With regard to the underlying objective of reducing union influence and undermining workers' control, the effect can be seen in the MUA's declining membership, after the massive reduction in the waterfront workforce due to automation. The merger with the Construction, Forestry, Mining and Energy Union (CFMEU), concluded in 2018, is clear indication of this declining capacity. We argue this outcome follows from the core motivations underpinning government and company actions leading to the waterfront dispute, as well as the privatisation agenda.

Conclusion

The port industry across a number of countries has been a testing ground for neoliberal economic philosophy, which maintains that industries operate most efficiently and more competitively when the role of government is minimised, and key decisions regarding organisational structure, investment and technological uptake are left up to private, for-profit companies. This neoliberal experiment into port privatisation began in the United Kingdom under the Thatcher government and gradually spread internationally as neoliberalism expanded. In the case of Australia, port privatisation started in the 1990s and, given the extent of this market-driven policy experiment, and the lessons learned from earlier adopters like the United Kingdom, one would think Australia's port sector would today be one of the most efficient and competitive industries in the world. The reverse has been true, and governments, still captured by the neoliberal orthodoxy, continue to pursue inquiries through the Productivity Commission or ACCC as to the reasons. Unsurprisingly, these inquiries rarely question if privatisation was a wise decision but accept this as desirable and irreversible. But they do find it difficult to ignore increases in land rents by governments and concerning employer behaviour like the passing on of these rents by port operators to shipping companies and transport operators, which in turn pass them on to cargo owners as identified by the ACCC (2021) and Productivity Commission (2022). The tendency among conservative governments has been to cherrypick report findings and overlook the structural key efficiency barriers associated with natural monopolies and focus primarily on alleged restrictive industrial relations and workforce issues, thus continuing the well-rehearsed strategy of using workers and unions as the scapegoat for the failings of neoliberal policy approaches. The Albanese Labor government is less likely to pursue such an approach but whether it will take action to tackle the rent-seeking behaviour of port operators more seriously is an open question.

The one clear outcome from the decades of port privatisation is the declining strength and influence of the union movement and workers' control of the labour process. As the private operators went about introducing labour-displacing technologies, from process computerisation to operations automation, the size of the waterfront workforce gradually reduced, thus severely undermining MUA membership and, by extension, its bargaining capacity. As we have argued in this chapter, this was always the most important, though often unstated, objective of privatisation for government and business ever since the waterfront dispute in 1998.

References

Australian Competition and Consumer Commission (2021). *Container Stevedoring Monitoring Report 2020–21*. Canberra: Australian Competition and Consumer Commission.

Aghion, P., S. Bechtold, L. Cassar and H. Herz (2018). The causal effects of competition on innovation: experimental evidence. *Journal of Law, Economics, and Organization* 34(2): 162–95.

Andic, F.M. (1990). The case for privatisation: some methodological issues. In D.J. Gayle and J.N. Goodrich, eds. *Privatization and Deregulation in Global Perspective*, 35–47. New York: Quorum.

Baird, A.J. (2000). Port privatisation: objectives, extent, process, and the UK experience. *International Journal of Maritime Economics* 2(3): 177–94.

Brittan, S. (1986). Privatisation: a comment on Kay and Thompson. *Economic Journal* 96: 33–8.

Chen, P.S.L., H. Pateman and Q. Sakalayen (2017). The latest trend in Australian port privatisation: drivers, processes, and impacts. *Research in Transportation Business and Management* 22: 201–13.

Choi, H.R., H.S. Kim, B.J. Park, N-K. Park and S.W. Lee (2003). An ERP Approach for container terminal operating systems. *Maritime Policy & Management* 30(3): 197–210.

Cullinane, K., and D.W. Song (2002). Port privatization policy and practice. *Transport Reviews* 22(1): 55–75.

Dabscheck, B. (1998). The waterfront dispute: of vendetta and the Australian way. *Economic and Labour Relations Review* 9(2): 155–87.

Davies, A. (2019). How the Howard Government set up its bruising 1998 waterfront union showdown. *The Guardian*, 1 January. https://tinyurl.com/yc4jeb7r.

Everett, S. (1995). Privatisation of ports: the Victoria and New South Wales experience. *Australian Journal of Public Administration* 54(4): 556–63.

Fairbrother, P. (1994). Privatisation and local trade unionism. *Work, Employment and Society* 8(30): 339–56.

Ferdousi, S.A. (1996). Survey report: Bangladesh. In *Privatizing State-Owned Enterprises: Experiences of Asia Pacific Economies*, 3–71. Tokyo: Asian Productivity Organisation.

Gekara, V.O. and P. Fairbrother (2013). Managerial technologies and power relations: a study of the Australian waterfront. *New Technology, Work, and Employment* 28(1): 51–65.

Gekara, V.O. and V. Thanh Nguyen, (2018). New technologies and the transformation of work and skills: a study of computerisation and automation

of Australian container terminals. *New Technology, Work, and Employment* 33(3): 219–33.
Goss, R. (1998). British ports policies since 1945. *Journal of Transport Economics and Policy* 32(1): 51–71.
Graham, C., and H. Silke (2017). Framing privatisation: the dominance of neo-liberal discourse and the death of the public good. *Triple C* 15(2): 796–815.
Griffin, G., and S. Svensen (1998). Industrial relations implications of the Australian waterside dispute. *Australian Bulletin of Labour* 24(3): 194–206.
Jörgensen, J.J. (1990). Managing privatization and deregulation: the telecommunications sector in Canada. In D.J. Gayle and J.N. Goodrich, eds. *Privatization and Deregulation in Global Perspective*. New York, NY: Quorom.
Kay, J.A., and D.J. Thompson (1986). A policy in search of a rationale. *Economic Journal* 96: 18–32.
Kelly, J. (1996). One piece of a larger puzzle: the privatization of VIASA. In R. Ramamurti, ed. *Privatizing Monopolies: Lessons from the Telecommunications and Transport Sectors in Latin America*, 241–77. Baltimore, MD: Johns Hopkins University Press.
Kia, M., E. Shayan and F. Ghotb (2000). The importance of information technology in port terminal operations, *International Journal of Physical Distribution & Logistics Management* 30(3/4): 331–44.
McConville, C. (2000). The Australian waterfront dispute 1998. *Politics and Society* 28(3): 393–412.
Megginson, W., and P. Mueller (2022). Natural monopoly privatisation: minimising regulatory trade-offs between rent extraction and innovation. *Academy of Management Perspectives* 36(1): 11–124.
Myers, S.C. (1972). The application of finance theory to public utility rate cases. *Bell Journal of Economics and Management Science* 3: 58–97.
Port Reform Toolkit (n.d.). 2nd edn. https://tinyurl.com/4ay9dev4.
Productivity Commission (2022). *Lifting Productivity at Australia's Ports*. Draft report. Canberra: Productivity Commission.
Roman, Z. (1993). Privatization in Hungary: regulatory reform and public enterprise performance. In V.V. Ramanadham, ed. *Privatization: A Global Perspective*, 77–91. London: Routledge.
Shaw, J.W. (1999). The public and private politics of industrial relations – are we in or out? *Economic and Labour Relations Review* 10(1): 149–57.
Sheil, C. (2017). The Productivity Commission and the waterfront dispute: a cautionary tale. *Journal of Australian Political Economy* 79(1): 39–64.
Smith, A. 1993[1776]. *An Inquiry into the Nature and Causes of the Wealth of Nations*, ed. K. Sutherland. Oxford, UK: Oxford University Press.

Snell, D. and V. Gekara (2023). Re-examining technology's destruction of blue-collar work. *New Technology, Work, and Employment* 38(3): 415–33.
Trinca, H., and A. Davies (2000). *Waterfront: The Battle that Changed Australia*. Sydney: Doubleday.
Vickers, J., and G. Yarrow (1988). *Privatization: An Economic Analysis*. Cambridge, MA: MIT Press.
Wiggins, J. (2022). "We're not just a one-trick pony," says Qube CEO. *Australian Financial Review*, 25 August. https://tinyurl.com/4zek93pf.
Workplace Express (2012). Fremantle Ports and MUA agree to deferred arbitration, 18 December. https://www.workplaceexpress.com.au/.
Workplace Express (2021a). MUA members back protected action at robo-dock, 4 February. https://www.workplaceexpress.com.au/.
Workplace Express (2021b). Landmark union deal for Melbourne "robo-terminal", 1 July. https://www.workplaceexpress.com.au/.
Workplace Express (2021c). Patrick looks to guillotine wharf strike, 9 November. https://www.workplaceexpress.com.au/.
Yarrow, G., M. King, J. Mairesse and J. Melitz (1986). Privatisation in theory and practice. *Economic Policy* 1(2): 323–77.

Conclusion

The chapters assembled in *Captured* can be thought of as a response to the criticism our colleague, Evan Jones, made about the study of liberalism. Jones noted liberalism, conceived as a political philosophy and ideology, has generated extensive scholarship, but much less has been written on liberalism as a practice: "The philosophy of liberalism has been the subject of a vast but frustrating literature. Too much is oriented to the philosophy of liberalism, not enough to liberalism as it played out historically in politics and policy" (Jones 2020, 61). So too, we argue, with neoliberalism. A vast literature exists on neoliberalism as an ideological project and its intellectual progenitors. In contrast, much less has been written on the practice of neoliberalism.

Neoliberalism is a cosmopolitan idea that acquired political traction with the end of the long boom and the stagflation crisis from the mid-1970s, commencing in the UK and USA and then spreading worldwide, including to Australia. We have lived through almost 50 years of neoliberalism as a mode of governance, and research has turned to considering the different "modes" of neoliberalism across multiple nations (see Slobodian and Plehwe 2022). What we have learned from these studies is that neoliberalism has both general or common characteristics but also local particularities. The latter reflect differences across nations, for example in the: industrial structure and existing state–private ownership of assets prior to neoliberalism and thus the actual scope for privatisation and contracting-out; relative strength of working class and union organisation; divisions within the different "fractions of capital" (such as finance, manufacturing and agriculture) whose economic interests may not always align; level of development and per capita income (low per capita income too often implies excessive dependence on international institutions such as the IMF, which can impose neoliberal solutions to financial crises); and strength of democracy and legal/constitutional institutions that may serve to restrain neoliberal policy overreach.

This conclusion identifies some of the main findings of the chapters and engages them with international academic debates. We note here that as editors our reading of the key themes may not necessarily align with those of all individual contributors. Nevertheless, it is hoped opening this wider context stimulates further research, debate and action.

The major themes of the book

Four key themes emerged from the chapters assembled in *Captured* that are especially germane to current international research on neoliberalism:

- beyond the market–state dichotomy
- the (ongoing) crises and end of neoliberalism
- resistance to critique and alternatives
- after neoliberalism?

Beyond the market–state dichotomy

Neoliberalism is often presented and understood simply as an anti-statist pro-free market philosophy. For instance, Nobel laureate Joseph Stiglitz (2019) recently opined that neoliberalism can be defined as "the idea that markets, left alone, are efficient and the best way to achieve prosperity". But this depiction of neoliberalism as primarily a free-market dogma is overly simplistic and misleading. It is misleading because it fails to differentiate between what some high-profile and influential neoliberal intellectual advocates, such as Milton Friedman, and many politicians identify as the key problem; that is, "too much state" with the solution being "more markets", and actual neoliberal practice. In practice, neoliberals are indifferent to the form markets take, especially rising oligopoly and moreover, many – if not almost all – public activities subject to neoliberal "reform" such as privatisation and contracting-out, have substituted direct control for indirect but highly intrusive regulation.

Characterising neoliberalism as primarily a free-market dogma is unhelpful in examining the contemporary features of capitalism and the intellectual origins of neoliberalism. Partly because of this type of characterisation, the term "neoliberalism" is now often used in pejorative terms and criticised for being overused, vague and moralistic (Venugopal 2015; Rodgers 2018). This form of critique can end up being more consoling than revealing (Barnet 2005). Further, it suggests an equally simplistic response; a politics of partial reform with the state *per se* posed as a form of opposition to neoliberalism, almost as if more state activity represents less neoliberalism and a step towards the restoration of social democracy. Fortunately, the Stiglitz-type conceptualisation of neoliberalism is increasingly being challenged and transcended. Given that misunderstanding, it is perhaps no coincidence then that Stiglitz himself has been a vocal supporter of income-contingent loan schemes, which Chapter 15 has argued is a founding neoliberal policy idea.

One of the common findings from *Captured* is that the market versus state dichotomy is not a useful way to understand the practice of neoliberalism. The neoliberal project took the form of an insurgency in and through the state during a period of capitalist crises, expansion and re-composition to give it its dominant standing (Overbeek and van der Pijl 1993). Neoliberalism as a state project did promise to restore market competition and constrain the collectivist state, an idea informed and propagated by what Philip Mirowski has called a "neoliberal thought collective" (2009). But we now know that neoliberal restructuring did not seek to restore anything like laissez faire capitalism. Nor was that even its intention as a form of governmentality. The enduring character of neoliberalism has not been the growth of more competitive markets and greater freedom; on the contrary, the dominant trend has been to increased oligopoly in which fewer firms have significant control over prices and outputs. In *Captured,* neoliberal reform leading directly to private oligopoly is described (O'Neill on Transurban; Gekara and Snell on port privatisation; Slattery and Johnson on water markets and Mountain on electricity markets). Even former heads of Australian regulatory agencies set up during the neoliberal era along with senior policy advisers have conceded that competition has greatly diminished in many industries resulting in price gouging, lower productivity and intensified inequality (Sims 2021, 2022; Garnaut 2023; Fels 2024). Neoliberalism in Australia is increasingly not about the rule of textbook neoclassical "free" markets but more about what Dick Bryan (2000) observed two decades ago: the "rule of capital".

Nor has the neoliberal state withered away. Instead, neoliberalism has successfully established a hegemony by becoming part of the organising logic of the state, changing the scope of state regulation and activity, but not reducing its size and reach in any meaningful sense. The neoliberal state has not been laissez faire or free market-oriented, but rather has provided the rationale and techniques for new forms of interventionism. *Captured* provides several case studies of new forms of interventionism. The development of the university fees system and the Higher Education Contribution Scheme (HECS) to ensure students repay those debts through the tax system is just one case in point. Another key state initiative has been compulsory superannuation, which has used the political authority of the state to mandate workers pay a proportion of their wages to privately managed financial entities to be invested in the stock and other capital markets.

In this sense neoliberals have been able to capture and impose on the state a new form of governance, not in order to reduce its size and scope or create "free" competitive markets, but to change its organisational logic. In fact, neoliberalism as state policy has helped to blur more of the boundaries between the state and markets, and markets and society. A core project has been to attempt to ensure that politics and society conform to the logic of markets to make all spheres of life individualised, competitive and calculative. As Davies (2016) argues, markets are prioritised both as a benchmark for assessing and producing "value and knowledge" and a tool for generating efficiency, transparency and choice.

This blurring of state and markets brings us to another sense in which neoliberalism has captured the state. The Australian state has become what Abbey Innes (2021) has noted about Britain, a semipermeable membrane whereby corporate interests have gained access and often control of public authority and revenues. Neoliberalism increasingly functions politically as a justification not for libertarian individual enterprise, innovation and liberty but for dominant economic power relations.

But many of the chapters also point to an apparent paradox. On the one hand there has been a new and expanded role for the state, for example in divesting assets, contracting-out and administering remaining services, expanding regulation of these activities and prodigious legislative attempts to diminish unions and the scope of industrial relations institutions. But on the other hand, there is also significantly diminished internal capacity to formulate and implement policy, evaluate outcomes and learn. This paradox is evident in Chapter 2 by Quiggin on new public management, Chapter 3 by Rundle on the COVID-19 quarantine debacle, Chapter 4 by Jones on industry policy, Chapter 13 by Hodge on VET and Chapter 12 by Randolph and colleagues on building defects. Quiggin emphasises the role of new public management, a specific neoliberal form of public sector administration marked by, for example, excessive reliance on contracting out policy formulation, a preferment of generalist management skills over specific subject matter expertise and an increasingly constrained definition of "acceptable" policy advice that must conform to principles of deregulation and market incentives. One can also point to the creation under a former Labor government of the Senior Executive Service (SES) for head bureaucrats whose employment contract and preferment are now fully dependent on the pleasure of their Minister. Rundle attributes the loss of capacity to excessive confidence by politicians and bureaucrats in the ability of markets to substitute for good governance. This, in turn, reflects "neoliberalism as the animating political philosophy of contemporary Australian statecraft, and the consolidation of its institutional design prescriptions as the go-to tools for doing the work of government".

It is an open question whether reduced internal competence was the intention of the original implementers of neoliberalism in Australia who, as we identified in the Introduction, comprised enthusiastic Labor and Coalition governments, but reduced proficiency is widely regarded as the result.

Crises and the end of neoliberalism?

Neoliberalism had its origins in critiques of socialist and social democratic planning arising from the Great Depression, the necessity of an activist state during World War II to marshal resources for "total war" and growth of the postwar welfare state. It proffered an optimistic, indeed messianic, utopia of market capitalism and sought to develop a popular consensus about how prosperity, stability and freedom is best achieved through competitive practices. But after nearly five decades of dominance, neoliberalism as a ruling ideology is undergoing a serious crisis on a number of levels.

Most chapters in *Captured* and its companion, *Wrong Way* (2018), describe and explain dissatisfaction and disappointment with government policies, especially service delivery, institutions and economic performance that have been subjected to neoliberal reform. Certainly, within Australia neoliberal reforms are electorally unpopular and many governments are attempting to reverse previous policy by, for example, repudiating further privatisations; subjecting past actions to critical public inquiries (for example the inquiry into the outsourcing of private building certification outlined in Chapter 12); attempting to address problems with service quality and private oligopolies through tougher regulation; and enhancing internal public sector capacity by reducing reliance on external consultants. In sum, there is considerable support for Quiggin's claim that "the era of unchallenged neoliberal dominance is clearly over" (Quiggin 2022, 105).

Neoliberalism emerged as an alternative policy framework amid a series of crises in the 1970s. It is now a commonplace observation that neoliberal policy responses have themselves generated unresolved crises. These include extreme inequality, financial instability, low growth, pervasive corporate monopoly and state capture, and diminished legitimacy of the status quo (Gerstle 2023a; Stiglitz 2023). Historically, capitalism has relied on robust growth and innovation for profitability, conditions that neoliberalism has not delivered and is arguably incapable of providing (Streeck 2011, 2017). In response, populism and dissatisfaction of many with the present order of things has caused leading analysts to identify:

> two existential challenges to democracy and to capitalism . . . there's more and more people that are questioning capitalism as a system, and there are more and more people that are questioning democracy as it's been constructed in the West (Wolf 2023).

This sentiment of disappointment, of high expectations unfilled, is occurring even within the commanding heights of state policy making. As noted in the Introduction, in Australia the Productivity Commission and Treasury now concede that the promises that neoliberal policies would improve economic performance, competitiveness, innovation and common prosperity have been largely unmet. Most recently, the phenomenon of "profit-driven inflation" has emerged as a major policy dilemma in advanced economies. Increased industry concentration over the last 40 years has created a large wedge between production costs and producer margins, acting to further lower real living standards already squeezed by sustained low wage growth (Organisation for Economic Co-operation and Development – OECD 2023). As observed several times, neoliberal policy has also not reduced the state's call on national resources.

Growing inequality and associated problems, such as a large proportion of the population having low educational attainment, low-income growth and declining health, are undermining economic, social and political conditions. Even the International Monetary Fund has called into question some of the fundamental tenets of neoliberalism that it had both advocated for and enforced, including unrestricted capital flows and fiscal austerity (Ostry, Lougani and Furceri 2016; Sherman 2016). In response, a key emerging theme of leading global institutions, including the World Bank and OECD, is "inclusive growth" (Boarini, Murtin and Schreyer 2015).

Aside from these widely recognised crises in neoliberalism, it is worth briefly mentioning two other important and interrelated challenges that have recently emerged: geopolitical conflict and climate change. Strategic competition between the United States and China over military capability and economic dominance has driven a fundamental reassessment of the links between trade, technology development and industrial capacity. US supremacy in these fields is seen by many in the political establishment as being undermined by neoliberal policies. This view has been forcefully expressed by Jake Sullivan, National Security Advisor to President Biden, with precedence now given to promotion of "industrial policies" to shift the strategic and economic balance in favour of the United States.

> Today's national security experts need to move beyond the prevailing neoliberal economic philosophy of the past 40 years. This philosophy can be summarized as reflexive confidence in competitive markets . . . advocating industrial policy (broadly speaking, government actions aimed at reshaping the economy) was once considered embarrassing – now it should be considered something close to obvious . . . The US national security community is rightly beginning to insist on the investments in infrastructure, technology, innovation, and education that will determine the United States' long-term competitiveness vis-à-vis China . . . The foreign-policy community should actively reach for a new economic model. America's national security depends on it (Harris and Sullivan 2020).

This effectively amounts to a repudiation of many tenets of neoliberal economic orthodoxy as defined in Chapter 1. Public investment "crowds in" rather than "crowds out" private investment; the economic structure is too important from a strategic viewpoint to leave to the market's resource allocation. More broadly, experiments with quantitative monetary easing have challenged monetarist doctrine and empirical estimates of the non-accelerating inflation rate of unemployment (NAIRU) are proving as elusive as ever.

Similar concerns have emerged over who controls manufactured inputs such as batteries, photovoltaic cells, wind turbines and high-efficiency electrical generators and motors to transform energy, transport and production systems in response to climate change. These inputs are currently dominated by China (International Energy Agency 2022). The sheer gargantuan scale of investment required to "green" virtually all aspects of production and consumption is also argued to require not just extremely large public investment but is only achievable with the state playing a central role in design and coordination of private investment. Driven by these and related matters, nations have embarked on large-scale industrial policies, notably the *Inflation Reduction Act* (2022) in the United States, which has in turn stimulated other nations, including Australia, to respond in kind (Clean Energy Council 2022).

Resistance to critique and alternatives

This book and its companion volume assembled leading experts on public policy to provide detailed assessment of an extraordinarily wide range of neoliberal policies introduced over the last 40 years in Australia. The results are in general highly critical. In the Introduction we also noted former senior bureaucrats who have recanted their previously strong advocacy for neoliberal public policies.

Part of the durability of neoliberalism has not been the success of its policy outcomes in orthodox terms, but rather its ability to crowd out alternatives through its ideological and cultural dominance. To paraphrase former British Prime Minister Margaret Thatcher's aphorism, neoliberalism has actively worked to ensure there is no alternative: "the great victory of the neoliberals is precisely to have undermined the credibility of public institutions, both de facto (chronic under-funding) and in people's minds, per the principle according to which the market is necessarily better" (Larrouqué 2023).

Finally, as noted in the Introduction, Philip Mirowski (2013) advanced the important argument that, as neoliberal doctrine and practice were consolidated from the late 1970s, it became clear neoliberalism was resistant to the sort of empirical falsification applied by many critics. A critique of neoliberalism that simply points to internal inconsistencies (of which there are many) or failures to achieve explicit outcomes would, Mirowski claimed, miss the radical nature of neoliberalism, because neoliberalism does not actually seek to achieve the goals on which many critiques seek to judge it. Neoliberalism persists in Australia and elsewhere because it has largely succeeded in its own terms in having extended and created markets, largely vanquished organised labour and delivered an unprecedented shift of national income from labour to capital. Chapter 6 details the long-term changes in industrial relations legislation which facilitated these shifts in national income while Chapter 9 provides a specific case study of the industrial relations difficulties created by government policy for women in the care workforce.

After neoliberalism?

Despite deep-seated problems and resurgence of state economic activism we concur with Crouch (2011) that it is much too early to declare the "death of neoliberalism". Identifying a crisis of neoliberal hegemony has a considerable history. Especially in the wake of the Global Financial Crisis of 2007–8, there has been a growing chorus of calls about the imminent demise of neoliberalism, which has not eventuated (Birch and Mykhnenko 2010). Others argue that current neoliberalism has evolved and is different from that in the 1970s and 1980s with perhaps a new phase of neoliberalism emerging (Davies 2016; Davies and Gane 2021).

Several reasons are advanced for this assessment. From the 1980s, neoliberalism has been comprehensively embedded in existing and new institutions, which severely limits the degree of freedom governments can exercise to implement alternatives. For example, Australia's National Competition Policy constrains attempts by government to reinstate former social-democratic practice, such as re-establishing public enterprises, as it limits competition between public enterprises and private firms, even when the former have a natural advantage, such as lower borrowing costs, from which consumers may benefit. Under both federal Labor and Coalition governments, financial incentives continue to be provided to states to encourage asset privatisation under so-called "asset recycling" schemes. The task of recreating an efficient bureaucracy capable of emulating for example, state electricity commissions or the Commonwealth Employment Service, is a potential multigeneration endeavour. It is also the case, as demonstrated in chapter 1, that within key economic agencies neoclassical and indeed neoliberal ideas remain highly influential. An example of the latter is the Reserve Bank's continuing commitment to the concept of NAIRU, originally propounded by Milton Friedman (Beggs 2018). Others are more sceptical about the prospects of climate change effecting a significant shift in support for neoliberalism (Plehwe 2022). Finally, while there is growing recognition of the need for different forms of governance, no clear consensus has emerged on what the alternatives should or might be (Byrne 2023).

So, what are the emerging alternatives to neoliberal governance? There are several, though none so far either on its own or in combination with others can yet be said to have demonstrated itself to represent a decisive challenge to the existing order. But since historically neoliberalism did not, except in the case of military coups in countries like Chile, emerge instantly as a systemic regime, it is very unlikely that neoliberalism will end in a systemic one-off defeat at some point in time. It may continue to suffer a series of defeats over time. That makes it important to look at what some alternatives are seeking to do and how they are being advanced.

Gerstle (2023a, b) presents an optimistic post-neoliberal scenario, and posits three future possibilities: "disorder", as the system staggers on with diminished legitimacy due to absence of a consensus alternative; "authoritarianism" and populism such as a resurgence of Trump; or "a new progressive order", a recreation of social democracy but also incorporating contemporary concerns regarding gender and the environment.

Many other writers have also identified an increasingly paternalistic or authoritarian path constraining democratic processes and institutions as a possible and indeed likely "innovation" in the path of neoliberalism (Streeck 2011; Brown 2015; Cooper 2018; Mattei 2022).

One possible driver of a "progressive" outcome is the recent push of national governments to revive activist industry policies for geopolitical and green energy motives. The basic argument is that successful industrial policy requires governments to enact measures that are largely incompatible with past neoliberal policies. This is evidenced not just in terms of a much greater role for the state in directing and encouraging – through incentives or complementary government investments – the disposition of private capital but also altering private consumption patterns to support these private investments. An example of the latter is the use of financial incentives and regulation to lift demand for local renewable industries, such as the "made in America" provisions of the *Inflation Reduction Act*. Successful industrial policies also require a large skilled and engaged workforce as a pre-condition to expand these innovation-based industries. Historically this requires a "skill formation ecosystem" underpinned by strong organised labour (Toner 2011). In sum, influential advocates of "progressive" industrial policies such as Harris and Sullivan (2020) see the current geopolitical and climate crises as the key stimuli to, in effect, reinvent the foundations of social democracy.

Such claims have also been the subject of strong criticism (Wigger and Horn 2018). Bramble (2000) and Ewer and colleagues (1992) provide a cautionary assessment of Australia's experience with industrial policies as a tool to promote social democracy in the last decades of the 20th century. There are important lessons here for current advocates.

One of the problems with debates about the historical arc of neoliberalism is that, because it has been a governing mode for almost half a century, it is now inextricably tied up with capitalism itself. This raises the systemic question as to whether the crises are properly considered as crises of capitalism rather than just crisis in one historical mode of capitalist governance. When debates occur about the crises of neoliberalism, and about possible supersession of the neoliberal era, it should not be surprising that others are contemplating this in terms of challenging core elements of capitalism.

These "post-capitalist" thinkers are a diverse group though the common element is the necessity for transcending the neoliberal era and challenging capitalism itself by re-constituting the institutional foundations for social democracy (Mason 2015; Bastani 2020; Cruddas and Pitts 2020; Azmanova 2021; Bryan et al. 2023). Some of these thinkers identify the social, technological and economic potential in the present to make a transition away from capitalism a real possibility (Mason 2015). Innovations in information technology and money, such as blockchain, are allowing for new forms of sociality, valuation and cooperation, making it possible to build new social forms and making engagement with capitalism optional (Bryan et al. 2023).

Challenges are also posed by the "post-growth" movement, which is critical of capitalism's environmental rapacity and its promise to grow its way out of problems and crises. Pollin (2018), among others, argues that post-growth capitalism offers the prospect of creating a more equitable and environmentally caring society (Blühdorn 2017; Jackson 2017; Banajee et al. 2021).

For others, recent crises are better conceptualised as systemic and pose the question not just of transcending the neoliberal era, but challenging capitalism itself (Mason 2015; Bastani 2020; Cruddas and Pitts 2020; Bryan et al. 2023). Post-capitalism is an approach that takes the contradictions and crises as internal to capitalism in its neoliberal phase (Azmanova 2021).

A final word

Captured has presented a series of critical essays reporting on new research on neoliberal public policy in Australia. A key point is that these chapters provide a litany of crises, failure and contradiction. Yet, neoliberalism persists.

As one observer has noted about neoliberalism in England, there is a key challenge in moving from critique to political action, and therefore:

> [to develop] an alternative economic paradigm capable of constituting the present crisis as a crisis. And in the absence of a perceived alternative, it is neither in the government's nor the opposition's interest to draw attention to paradigmatic failure. This leaves us with something of an impasse (Hay 2009, 551).

The many failures of neoliberalism are now so mixed up with the wider problems of contemporary capitalism that breaking through the impasse that Hay has identified requires some radical thinking. *Captured* has provided a series of critiques of neoliberalism in Australia as a way of trying to find ways to think through that impasse. But challenging neoliberalism in practice will also require new ways of organising and mobilising that critique. Whether that will come from existing institutions like trade unions and political parties or different sorts of organisational forms, it is too early to tell. Whatever the organisational forms that challenge might take, the basis of such mobilisation will surely be the critiques of the concept and practice of neoliberalism assembled in publications like this.

References

Azmanova, A., S. Turner and G. Delanty (2021). Post-capitalism: the return of a radical critique. In G. Delanty and S. Turner (eds), *Routledge International Handbook of Contemporary Social and Political Theory*, 522–30. London: Routledge.

Banerjee, S., J. Jermier, A. Peredo, R. Perey and A. Reichel (2021). Theoretical perspectives on organizations and organizing in a post-growth era. *Organization* 28(3): 337–57.

Barnett, C. (2005). The consolations of "neoliberalism". *Geoforum* 36(1): 7–12.

Bastani, A. (2020). *Fully Automated Luxury Communism: A Manifesto*. London: Verso.

Beggs, M. (2018). Monetary policy and unemployment. In D. Cahill and P. Toner (eds). *Wrong Way: How Privatisation & Economic Reform Backfired*, 257–75. Melbourne: La Trobe University Press and Black Inc.

Birch, K. and V. Mykhnenko (2010). *The Rise and Fall of Neoliberalism: The Collapse of an Economic Order?* London: Zed Books.

Blühdorn, I. (2017). Post-capitalism, post-growth, post-consumerism? Eco-political hopes beyond sustainability. *Global Discourse* 7(1): 42–61.

Boarini, R., F. Murtin and P. Schreyer (2015*). Inclusive Growth: The OECD Measurement Framework*. OECD Statistics Working Papers, 2015/06. Paris: OECD Publishing.

Bramble, T. (2000). Social democracy and the "failure" of the Accord. In K. Wilson, J. Bradford, and M. Fitzpatrick (eds), *Australia in Accord: An Evaluation of the Prices and Incomes Accord in the Hawke-Keating Years*, 243–64. Melbourne: South Pacific Publishing.

Brown, W. (2015). *Undoing the Demos – Neoliberalism's Stealth Revolution*. New York: Zone Books.

Bryan, D. (2000). The rush to regulate: The shift in Australia from the rule of markets to the rule of capital. *Australian Journal of Social Issues* 35(4): 333–48.

Bryan, D., J. Lopez and A. Virtanen (2023). *Protocols for a Postcapitalist Future*. London: Minor Compositions.

Byrne, L. (2023). Social democracy's muted revival. *The Political Quarterly* 94: 175–84.

Clean Energy Council (2022). The *Inflation Reduction Act*. https://tinyurl.com/yv54umxw.

Cooper, M. (2018). *Family Values: Between Neoliberalism and the New Social Conservatism*. New York: Zone Books.

Crouch, C. (2011). *The Strange Non-Death of Neoliberalism*. Cambridge, UK: Wiley.

Cruddas, J., and F.H. Pitts (2020). The politics of post capitalism: labour and our digital futures. *Political Quarterly*, 91: 275–86.

Davies, W. (2016). The new neoliberalism. *New Left Review* September–October: 121–34.

Davies, W., and N. Gane (2021). Post-neoliberalism? An introduction. *Theory, Culture and Society* 38(6): 3–28.

Ewer, P., I. Hampson, C. Lloyd, J. Rainford, S. Rix and M. Smith (1992). *Politics and the Accord*. Leichhardt: Pluto Press.

Fels, A. (2024). Inquiry into price gouging and unfair pricing practices, report to the Australian Council of Trade Unions, February. https://tinyurl.com/5fsj3ydt.

Garnaut, R. (2023). The economic public interest in a world of oligopoly. *Economic Papers*, https://doi.org/10.1111/1759-3441.12403.

Gerstle, G. (2023a). *The Rise and Fall of the Neoliberal Order: America and the World in the Free Market Era*. Oxford: Oxford University Press.

Gerstle, G. (2023b). The neoliberal order is over. What comes next? Podcast. *Roosevelt Institute*, 4 May. https://tinyurl.com/2xxswejr.

Harris, K. and J. Sullivan (2020). America needs a new economic philosophy. foreign policy experts can help. *Foreign Policy*, 7 February. https://tinyurl.com/2xyr3u9x.

Hay, C. (2009). The winter of discontent thirty years on. *Political Quarterly* 80(4): 545–52.

Innes, A. (2021). Corporate state capture: the degree to which the British state is porous to business interests is exceptional among established democracies. *LSE British Politics and Policy*, https://tinyurl.com/y3s7eu68.

International Energy Agency (2022). *Solar PV Global Supply Chains*. IEA Special Report. https://tinyurl.com/ye4mbjk6.

Jackson, T. (2017). *Prosperity without Growth: Economics for a Finite Planet*. London: Routledge.

Jones, E. (2020). The underbelly of liberalism. *Journal of Australian Political Economy* 86: 61–84.

Larrouqué, D. (2023). *Damn neo-liberalism*. In P. Dardot, H. Guéguen, C. Laval and P. Sauvêtre, eds. *Le Choix de la Guerre Civile: Une Autre Histoire du Néolibéralisme*, translated by Tiam Goudarzi. *Books and Ideas*, 27 June, https://tinyurl.com/56d5amnr.

Mason, P. (2015). *Postcapitalism: A Guide to Our Future*. London: Allen Lane.

Mattei, C. (2022). *The Capital Order – How Economists Invented Austerity and Paved the Way to Fascism*. Chicago, IL: University of Chicago Press.

Mirowski, P. (2013). *Never Let a Serious Crisis Go to Waste: How Neoliberalism Survived the Financial Meltdown*. London: Verso Books.

Mirowski, P. and D. Plehwe (2009). *The Road from Mont Pelerin – The Making of the Neoliberal Thought Collective*. Cambridge, MA: Harvard University Press.

Organisation for Economic Co-operation and Development (2023). *OECD Economic Outlook*. https://tinyurl.com/42f96a5m.

Ostry, J., P. Lougani and D. Furceri (2016). Neoliberalism: oversold? *Finance and Development* 53(2): 38–41.

Plehwe, D. (2022). Reluctant transformers or reconsidering opposition to climate change mitigation? German think tanks between environmentalism and neoliberalism. *Globalizations* 20(8): 1277–95. https://doi.org/10.1080/14747731.2022.2038358.

Pollin, R. (2018). De-growth vs a green new deal? *New Left Review* 112: 5–25.

Quiggin, J. (2022). The evolution of neoliberalism. In S.J. Williams and R. Taylor (eds), *Sustainability and the New Economics Synthesising Ecological Economics and Modern Monetary Theory*, 89–106. Switzerland: Springer.

Rodgers, D. (2018). The uses and abuses of "neoliberalism". *Dissent*. https://tinyurl.com/2bf63xbf.

Sherman, E. (2016). Even the IMF sees 30 years of neoliberalism as a mistake. *Forbes*, 5 June. https://tinyurl.com/mubjcc84.

Sims, R. (2021). Protecting and promoting competition in Australia. Key note speech at Competition and Consumer Workshop 2021, Law Council of Australia, 27 August. https://tinyurl.com/y77ew36d.

Sims, R. (2022). From groceries to energy, there's not enough competition in Australia, *The Guardian*, 20 June. https://tinyurl.com/dst9v54s.

Stiglitz, J. (2019). After neoliberalism. *Project Syndicate*. https://tinyurl.com/mr26ju27.

Stiglitz, J. (2023). Inequality and democracy. *Project Syndicate.* https://tinyurl.com/ykfes26s.

Streeck, W. (2011). The crises of democratic capitalism. *New Left Review* 71: 5–29.

Streeck, W. (2017). The return of the repressed. *New Left Review* 104: 5–21.

Toner, P. (2011). *Workforce Skills and Innovation: An Overview of Major Themes in the Literature.* Directorate for Science, Technology and Industry Working Paper. Paris: OECD.

Wigger, A., and L. Horn (2018). The bed you made: social democracy and industrial policy in the EU. In C. Hay and D. Bailey (eds), *Diverging Capitalisms. Building a Sustainable Political Economy*: SPERI Research and Policy. Cham, Switzerland: Palgrave Macmillan. https://tinyurl.com/y66mr6yb.

Venugopal, R. (2015). Neoliberalism as concept. *Economy and Society* 44(2): 165–87.

Wolf, M. (2023). Martin Wolf on saving democratic capitalism: the "democratic recession". *Financial Times*, 3 June. https://tinyurl.com/yyw7j6tk.

Contributors

Laura Crommelin is a senior lecturer in the City Planning program at UNSW Sydney, teaching planning law and governance and working on research related to urban and housing policy. She is also a fellow at UNSW's City Futures Research Centre. Laura's research interests cover a range of trends and issues in post-industrial cities, including urban renewal, urban governance, digital disruptions (e.g., Airbnb), place branding, and DIY urban revitalisation practices.

Bob Davidson is an honorary research fellow at Macquarie University. He has extensive experience as a senior government official and private consultant. His research and consultancy work is largely centred on the intersection of economics, social policy, and organisational theory, with a particular focus on human service markets and the service providers in those markets.

Hazel Easthope is the deputy director of the City Futures Research Centre at UNSW. She leads the Centre's Compact Cities research program, focusing on the development, management, governance and planning implications of apartment buildings and estates and the experiences of their residents. She has qualifications in sociology and geography and more than 20 years' research experience.

Victor Gekara is a professor in the Department of Supply Chain and Logistics Management at RMIT University. He has extensively studied container port terminal work, among other things, and leads the Skills Training and Industry Research Network (STIRN) at RMIT.

Steven Hodge is deputy head of school (research) at the School of Education and Professional Studies, Griffith University.

Greg Jericho is the chief economist of the Australia Institute and the policy director: labour market and fiscal, at the Centre for Future Work. He also writes a weekly column for *Guardian Australia* and won the 2016 Walkley Award for Best Commentary, Analysis, Opinion and Critique.

Evan Jones lectured in economics and political economy at the University of Sydney from 1973 to 2006. He is currently an honorary associate in the Department of Political Economy at the University of Sydney.

Martin Loosemore's research focuses on construction industry reform. He has contributed significantly to numerous construction industry reform initiatives including being an advisor to the Australian federal government's 2003 Royal Commission into the Building and Construction Industry and being a founding member of the federal Built Environment Industry Innovation Council as well as the NSW Office of the Building Commissioner's "Construct NSW" Building Industry Reform Pillar 6 Working Group (using data and research to drive continuous improvement).

Fiona Macdonald is policy director: industrial and social, at the Centre for Future Work at the Australia Institute. She has published widely on gender and employment.

Scott MacWilliam has researched and written on the political economy of development internationally. His work focuses on corporate capitalism, imperialism, and poverty, particularly among rural populations. The importance of ruling ideas for state policy remains central to his research.

Bruce Mountain is the director of the Victoria Energy Policy Centre at Victoria University. He is a well-known Australian energy economist whose research and advisory work has focused on the economic regulation of network monopolies, the analysis of retail energy markets and the design of emission reduction and renewable energy policies. He has a bachelor's and master's degree in electrical engineering from the University of Cape Town and qualified as a chartered management accountant in England.

Phillip O'Neill is professor of economic geography at the School of Social Sciences, Western Sydney University.

John Quiggin is a professor of economics at the University of Queensland. He is a prominent research economist and commentator on Australian and international economic policy.

Mike Rafferty has been researching, writing and teaching about political economy for over three decades. His work has focused on the rise of finance as a form of capital accumulation and increasingly as a social logic of unbundling and shifting risk in more and more domains of life.

Bill Randolph FASSA, MPIA (Fellow), MHIA is professor at the City Futures Research Centre at UNSW. Bill was the foundation director of the Centre from 2005 to 2020, where he led research on housing policy and markets, urban policy, urban renewal and urban inequality. He has over 40 years' experience as a researcher in the academic, government, non-government and private sectors.

David Richardson is a senior research fellow at the Australia Institute.

Kristen Rundle is a professor of law at the University of Melbourne. She teaches and researches in the fields of legal theory and administrative law, with a particular interest in the design and exercise of administrative power in conditions of contemporary government.

Susan K. Schroeder is a senior lecturer in the Department of Political Economy at the University of Sydney. She specialises in frameworks of financial fragility, country and sovereign risk, economic policy and methodology. She is also a consultant for the United Nations and a lifetime member of Wolfson College, University of Cambridge, UK.

Maryanne Slattery and **Bill Johnson** are experts on water policy and management in the Murray–Darling Basin.

Darryn Snell is an associate professor in the School of Management and coordinator of the Work in Transition research group at the Business and Human Rights Centre at RMIT University.

Jim Stanford is economist and director of the Centre for Future Work. Jim has offices in Canberra and Vancouver, Canada and is author of *Economics for Everyone: A short guide to the economics of capitalism* (Pluto Press, 2015).

Phillip Toner is an honorary senior research fellow in the Department of Political Economy at the University of Sydney. His interests include industry policy, innovation studies, labour market analysis and international skill formation systems.

Index

www.ingramcontent.com/pod-product-compliance
Lightning Source LLC
LaVergne TN
LVHW051937100826
845154LV00002B/8
* 9 7 8 1 7 6 1 5 4 0 3 2 5 *